Africa: A Guide to Reference Material

Regional Reference Guides

General Editor:
John McIlwaine
School of Library, Archive and Information Studies

No.1: Africa: A Guide to Reference Material
JOHN MCILWAINE

No.2: South-East Asia: A Guide to Reference Material
ANDREW DALBY

Africa: A Guide to Reference Material

John McIlwaine

School of Library, Archive and Information Studies

University College London

HANS ZELL PUBLISHERS

London • Melbourne • Munich • New York • 1993

Hans Zell Publishers
is an imprint of Bowker-Saur Ltd, a division of Reed Reference Publishing.
60 Grosvenor Street, London W1X 9DA, United Kingdom.

British Library Cataloguing in Publication Data

McIlwaine, John.
   Africa : Guide to Reference Material -
   (Regional Reference Guides: Vol. 1)
   I. Title II. Series
   016.96

   ISBN 0-905450-43-4

Library of Congress Cataloging-in-Publication Data

McIlwaine, John.
   Africa : a guide to reference material / John McIlwaine.
   512p. 240cm. -- (Regional reference guides: no. 1)
   Includes bibliographical references and index.
   ISBN 0-905450-43-4
   1. Africa--Bibliography. I. Title. II. Series.
   Z3501.M3 1992
   [DT3]
   016.96--dc20   92-38578
                                                          CIP

Cover design by Robin Caira

Printed on acid-free paper.

Printed and bound in Great Britain
by Antony Rowe Ltd., Chippenham, Wiltshire.

CONTENTS

Contents

Contents

Contents

Contents

Contents

Contents

PREFACE

The intention behind the compilation of this work is to provide a guide to the major reference sources, other than bibliographies, which relate to Africa south of the Sahara.

Bibliographies of Africa are comparatively well covered. J.D. Pearson's **World bibliography of African bibliographies** (Oxford, Blackwell, 1975) provides a detailed listing to to its date, although without annotation, and the magisterial Yvette Scheven's **Bibliography of African bibliographies, 1970-1985** (Oxford, Hans Zell, 1988) is comprehensive and annotated. More specific regional coverage is available from L. Porgès, **Sources d'information sur l'Afrique noire Francophone** (Paris, ORSTOM, 1988). However, coverage of *other* categories of reference work is much less readily available. The most substantial work in existence is of course the **Guide to research and reference works on Sub-Saharan Africa**, comp. by Peter Duignan and Helen Conover and edited by Peter Duignan (Stanford, Hoover Institution, 1971) which in 1102pp. has over 3,000 numbered and annotated references. The greater part of the text of this work was also reproduced as P. Duignan & L.H. Gann, **Colonialism in Africa, 1870-1960: vol. 5. A bibliographic guide to colonialism in sub-Saharan Africa** (Cambridge, Cambridge University Press, 1973), with some small amendments, and an "Addenda", pp. 463-474. Duignan includes bibliographies, reference works of the quick-reference nature, and major secondary works in the shape of standard works (both monographs and journals) on history, geography, anthropology, politics and the like. The argument in the preface to the 1971 volume was that since works of a "quick-reference" nature were comparatively few for Africa, and those that existed left obvious gaps, it was necessary to supplement these by listing "standard" monographs as well. The resulting work remains extremely useful, but to attempt to provide an up-dated version with the same scope would now be trying to do much at once: indeed the title given to Duignan & Gann in its second manifestation in 1973 shows that it was then being offered simply as a general bibliography of significant works on Africa, rather than as a guide specifically to reference sources.

The present work covers only one of Duignan's three categories, namely "reference material", in the narrower sense of the term, leaving bibliographies to be covered by the sources noted above, and standard works on individual topics to be covered by appropriate subject or regional guides. The question that then needs to be asked is: what is meant by "reference material"? With bibliographies, the question is perhaps simpler: a bibliography is a bibliography (when it is not an index, a union list, a library catalogue, an on-line database etc.!). "Reference material", even when one has specifically excluded bibliographies, is a much vaguer term. Two main characteristics of the titles that will be found in this work are firstly that they are concerned primarily with providing **factual** data, rather than interpretation, and secondly, that their arrangement is intended to facilitate **rapid** consultation, rather than requiring the whole text to be scanned to locate facts. Such tidy guidelines are of course easy to draw and impossible to maintain. For example, perhaps the first "reference work" for Africa that would come into many minds would be Lord Hailey's **An African survey**, a volume that accompanies its extensive factual data by equally extensive comment and interpretation, and that is arranged as a straightforward monograph with chapters, rather than having a "quick-reference" structure. It is of course also wrong to suggest that collections of factual information imply no interpretation: the very process of selection of what data to include and what to exclude, and how it should be presented obviously involves interpretation. The decision on what to include and exclude in this guide is therefore ultimately a very personal one, and must inevitably reflect what Humpty-Dumpty might have said, "a reference book is what I have chosen to call a reference book".

Inevitably there have been certain emphases in selecting items for inclusion. The attempt is to cover material in any language, produced during the last hundred years or so (the cut-off date for inclusion is 1991, although one or two titles issued in 1992 have been added). The view taken is that older sources retain their value for their coverage of data contemporary with publication, and that older editions of a single source are potentially as valuable as later editions. Additionally, older sources may never have been succeeded by more modern titles covering the same field, and may remain the only convenient source of reference. "One has only to realize how often historians return to Hailey's 1938 **African survey**, to appreciate how rapidly information which appears to be common currency slips into an oblivion whence it is hard to retrieve" (David Birmingham, *Journal of African History*, 21, 1980, 139). To reinforce this point, and to provide a meaningful means of access to titles included, these are arranged by date of publication (first publication in the case of works with more than one edition) rather than alphabetically by author. This concern to give due emphasis to older published sources does mean that as the volume of publication increases in more recent years, so I have been more selective in choosing items to include. The selection process has also been modified by the varying degrees of availability of material for differing regions of Africa. I have for example been much more selective in listing sources for South Africa (although hopefully covering most significant titles) than for some of the less well recorded countries of west and central Africa.

It may be useful at this stage to provide a list of some categories of material which have been deliberately **excluded**:

Interlingual dictionaries. These are covered in detail by M.K. Hendrix, **An international bibliography of African lexicons** (Metuchen, NJ, Scarecrow Press, 1982) which records over 2,600 dictionaries and phrase books.

Collections of printed texts of laws, treaties and other documents, although of course some of the more general compendious sources that are included may contain sections which include such material.

Handbooks & guides whose focus is narrowed by the specific group for whom they were intended. Examples would include those for the immigrant, (a feature particularly of the earlier part of the 20th century with information emphasising regulations, health care, and financial help), for the businessman (a feature of the post-independence period with emphasis on trade and financial information, and hotels) and for the tourist. Exceptions have of course been made and materials included from all these categories, where the works concerned were significantly more detailed or up-to-date than their fellows or where there was a noticeable absence of any other reference source for the region and period covered (examples include the Hachette **Guides bleus**, and works produced by the Touring Club Italiano and the Office du Tourisme du Congo Belge). In general more exceptions have been made for older publications in this category. For contemporary travel guides, the reader is referred to Louis Taussig, **Sub-Saharan African travel resource guide** (Oxford, Hans Zell, forthcoming 1993).

Works relating to the biological sciences, for example guides to flora and fauna. These it is felt are better covered and indeed will be sought by users, in guides specific to the biological sciences. Coverage is therefore basically limited to works relating to the humanities, arts and social sciences although for example thematic atlases relating to topics such as agriculture and climate are included since they have value to researchers in other fields.

General reference sources, covering the whole world, or the Third or "Developing" world have been included only sparingly. Where a general source has a specific and readily identifiable section, usually a separate volume, devoted to Africa, this is of course included. Thus for example Gale's **Cities of the world, vol. 1 Africa** is included, but not the same publisher's **Countries of the world and their leaders yearbook** or **Handbook of the nations** where African countries are not covered in a discrete sequence. Again exceptions are made in cases where little or no specific African coverage is available, and general works on the European colonial empires, where African content often dominates, are usually included.

More specific categories of exclusion are noted below under "major categories included".

Reviewing of reference works

It is very noticeable that reference works of the sort listed in this volume comparatively rarely feature in detailed reviews in the specialist Africanist journals. If treated at all, they will often be only in the "shorter review" section with comments limited to little more than : "researchers will be glad to note the appearance of a new edition of ... ". No doubt such summary treatment also discourages publishers of reference works, often expensive titles in small editions, from a wide provision of review copies. The result is that there is often little real analysis of the merits, demerits and significance in relation to existing works of new publications, or re-assessments of continuing sources and new editions.

A notable exception to this lack of interest has been the attention awarded to the series of "African historical dictionaries" published since 1974 by Scarecrow Press. Even here, over a dozen volumes had been published before what was probably the first really detailed critical review appeared, that by Dennis Cordell of the volume for Chad (1977) in the *International journal of African historical studies*, 11, 1978, 376-379. This was followed rapidly by two major assessments, one by David Henige, 'African historical dictionaries: through the looking glass', *Africana journal*, 10, 1979, 120-128, where he considered the volumes for Burundi, Dahomey and Togo (all published in 1976), Lesotho, Sierra Leone and Mali (published in 1977) and Tanzania and the Sudan (published in 1978) and the second by David Tambo, 'African historical dictionaries in perspective', *ASA review of books*, 6 1980, 199-209 which also discussed the volumes for Tanzania and the Sudan, together with those for Chad (1977) and Guinea (1978). These two reviews are critical of the publisher's choice of authors for the series, of the chosen format and presentation, and of the inaccuracy and lack of balance of the contents (only the volume for the Sudan emerges comparatively unscathed from both).

They also make a number of interesting points about reference works in general. Henige is severe about the use of a monographic series as a publisher's device to increase sales by persuading libraries to place a standing order without waiting to assess each individual volume as it appears. Tambo is unhappy about what he sees as the largely uncritical acceptance of the series in reviews appearing in the professional library journals, for example *Choice* and *Library journal* as opposed to the specialist Africanist journals. He feels the volumes themselves are trying to be too many things at once: "encyclopedias, area handbooks, current biographies, handbooks of source materials". Henige justifies severe criticism of errors because "the compilers of reference tools cannot be satisfied merely to aspire to being reasonably accurate, or even almost accurate. Rather they must attempt perfection, knowing that most users will be unable to distinguish what happens to be correct from that which happens not to be".

Possibly stimulated by these detailed analyses, book review editors in the Africanist journals seem to have made a point of featuring later volumes in the Historical dictionaries series. Criticisms could be fierce: the volume for Tanzania, already considered by both Henige and Tambo, was "a volume to be avoided" (Norman Bennett, *IJAHS*, 12, 1979, 321) and "this type of book could bring African studies into disrepute" (Alison Redmayne, *Africa*, 50, 1980, 101). In the *Journal of African history* alone there have been interesting group reviews by Q.N. Parsons, *JAH* 20, 1979, 146-147, looking at the volumes for Botswana, Lesotho & Swaziland (all published 1975) who suggests that 'African political dictionaries' might be a better term; by Andrew Roberts, 'Good and bad guides', *JAH* 23, 1982, 139-140, reviewing volumes for Tanzania, Zambia and Zimbabwe/Rhodesia with praise reserved for the last as "a systematic and generally reliable work of reference"; and by S. Martin, 'West African references', *JAH* 30, 1989, 340-341 considering the volumes for Nigeria and the Ivory Coast.

Some of the criticisms may well have been noted by the publishers in commissioning later volumes in the series, or revised editions of existing works. As early as 1981, reviewing the volume for Niger, Anthony Kirk-Greene was wondering if some of his colleagues were not being unnecessarily harsh : "has not the series given many not-too-specialist users a lot of useful data on a lot of countries about which many Africanists know too little?" (*Africa*, 51, 1981, 788-789). The second edition of the volume for Botswana (1989), reviewed once again by Q.N.Parsons is praised for its choice of compilers and its content, and for being "one of the dozen or so essential works of reference" on the country (*JAH*, 32, 1991, 174-175). David Henige, one of the earliest and severest critics, was able to welcome the second edition of the dictionary for Zimbabwe "as the best reference on Zimbabwean history, as well as a challenge for most other volumes in the series" (*ARBA*, 23, 1992, 40). Adam Jones however, looking back over more than forty volumes in his review of the example for the Ivory Coast (*IJAHS*, 22, 1989, 347-348) feels that although "some volumes merit revision ... we would be better served by a completely fresh attempt undertaken by a team of recognized historians".

Returning to reviews in general, the two titles that I have myself found especially useful because they have been consistently interested throughout their publication history in providing critical analytical reviews of reference works, are two of those represented above : the *Journal of African history* (*JAH*) 1960-, and *African historical studies* (*AHS*) later *International journal of African historical studies* (*IJAHS*), 1968-. In the text below, I have provided references to all reviews of substance in these two journals, and to those in the short lived *ASA review of books* with more selective citation of reviews from the two more specialised titles *Africa* and the *Geographical journal* (*GJ*), and occasional references to reviews in other sources. This will I hope, for the comparatively small proportion of titles represented, provide access for the user to critical assessments. A scan of the standard guides to reviews in this field, D.L. Easterbrook, **Africana book reviews, 1885-1945** (Boston, MA, G.K. Hall, 1979) and D. Henige, **Works in African history: an index to reviews** (Waltham, MA/Los Angeles, African Studies Association, 1976-1984, 3 vols.) covering 1960-1982, will add other sources, but I think confirm the paucity of coverage of "reference material" in the Africanist journals.

GEOGRAPHICAL COVERAGE

Coverage is of Africa south of the Sahara - that is of all Africa other than the countries of the Mediterranean littoral: Morocco, Algeria, Tunisia, Libya and Egypt. The islands and island groups of Cape Verde, the Comoros, Madagascar, Mauritius, Réunion, St. Helena and the Seychelles are included. Christopher Fyfe has argued that Sub-Saharan Africa is a "sloppy, lazy-minded" division which "presents the Sahara as a barrier rather than the bridge it has always been" (*JAH*, 20, 1969, 311), but in the context of the present work the division does make sense, since many reference sources take the 'Middle East and North Africa' as their concern. It should be noted that titles of this nature, that is works whose major focus is on the Middle East, but which may include material relevant to the Islamic or Arabic-speaking world as a whole, and may therefore be of significance for the Sudan, Western Sahara, Mauritania and other regions, will not be found in the present work but in its forthcoming companion in the series of 'Regional reference guides', **The Middle East and North Africa**.

ARRANGEMENT

Following a general section on Africa as a whole, material is **arranged**

under the broad regions of North-East Africa, East Africa, Central Africa, West Africa and Southern Africa, and then by individual countries. Allocation of countries to regions is reasonably conventional, and can be traced from the table of contents. For Central, West and Southern Africa, countries are initially arranged in groups corresponding to their major European language and former colonial affiliation: for West Africa for example, there are sections for Anglophone, Francophone, Lusophone and former Spanish-speaking areas. This corresponds to the coverage of many of the sources listed, especially of the older literature. Reference works confined to smaller administrative divisions within countries: states, provinces, etc., are only included sparingly, and where there is strong historical warrant (e.g. Zanzibar, the major states of South Africa).

Under each geographical unit (whether West Africa, Anglophone West Africa or Ghana for example) material is arranged **according to six broad categories:** *Handbooks, Yearbooks, Statistics, Directories of organizations, Biographical sources* and *Atlases and Gazetteers.* This corresponds fairly closely to the presentation adopted by Raymond Nunn's **Asia: reference works** (London, Mansell, 1980) a guide which I have always found particularly helpful to use. There are notes below on the type of sources which one may expect to find under each of these headings. For regions or countries with a substantial number of references under any one heading, there will be further sub-divisions: full details are in the table of contents.

Under each heading, actual titles are arranged **chronologically by year of publication** (where there is more than one item for a year, further arrangement is alphabetically by author). This method has been chosen to be of potential value to those looking for example for a source contemporary with a particular period of a country's history. For those who want to find the entry for a known work by author or title, the index should provide. It should be noted that details of subsequent editions will all of course be provided within the entry at the date of the earliest edition.

MAJOR CATEGORIES INCLUDED

Handbooks

This is the section with the most diverse contents. The intention is to include compendious works (which may be entitled handbooks, dictionaries encyclopedias, companions, guides, surveys and similar terms) which are concerned with presenting information in a readily accessible format about a region, country, or subject. These include multi-volume encyclopedias, such as the **Encyclopédie coloniale et maritime** and the **Standard encyclopedia of**

Southern Africa; individual works which nevertheless conform to a pattern, such as the guides produced by colonial administrators with classic examples by W.N. Brelsford, **Handbook to the Federation of Rhodesia and Nyasaland**, and G.F. Sayers, **Handbook of Tanganyika**; official works produced for a particular event, such as the various volumes produced by the governments of Afrique équatoriale française and Afrique occidentale française for the 1931 Exposition coloniale internationale in Paris or by British territories for the 1924 British Empire Exhibition in London; official works produced by Ministries of Information and more commercially oriented titles produced by various local concerns such as newspapers, railway companies or airlines, and chambers of commerce. Also included are more general works such as Sir Harry Johnston's volumes on British Central Africa, Liberia and Uganda, Lord Hailey's **African survey**, and scholarly compilations like the International African Institute's **Ethnographic survey of Africa** and **Handbook of African languages**.

Many of the volumes listed in this section come from one of several extensive series each with a range of titles relevant to Africa. Rather than annotate each and every example, general comments on some of the major series follow.

British War Office series: précis, military reports, route books and handbooks. A large and varied collection with volumes covering African countries issued by the War Office Intelligence Department (later Intelligence Division) from the 1870s up to the 1930s with one or two examples in the 1940s. Most were initially confidential and for official use only, and although they later became publicly accessible, holdings in libraries are very patchy. Many volumes were issued in the 'A' papers series (applied from 1886 onwards) or in the 'B' papers series (applied from the early 1900s) which appears to have been used for what was considered less sensitive material.

For many regions of Africa these War Office volumes provide some of the earliest examples of structured compilations of data. Although matters of military concern may be emphasised, the volumes in general provide a very wide range of miscellaneous information. A fairly standard sequence of topics dealt with by a W.O. précis would be: geography and topography; harbours, roadsteads, landing places; communications; towns and settlements; forts, arsenals, dockyards; climate; trade, agriculture, natural resources; inhabitants and languages; history; administration; finance; currency, weights and measures; army and navy; books of reference. The information contained in "military reports" and "handbooks" may be different in arrangement from this but hardly in content and in most cases there is little about the contents to be inferred from the different titles. "Route books" (and the "routes" sections in précis and reports) comprise itineraries, often very detailed, and containing much information about the surrounding topography, peoples, crops, vegetation and wildlife.

British Admiralty series. Compiled and issued by the Naval Intelligence Department (later Intelligence Division) these were similar in nature and indeed in topics covered to the various War Office series described above. These too were initially issued confidentially, often in the 'I.D.' series, the 'C.B.' (Confidential Books) series from 1916, or the 'B.R.' (Books of Reference) series from 1942.

For both the War Office and Admiralty series, an attempt has been made to trace and include all the more substantial volumes of a general nature relating to Africa. Many other volumes of a much briefer nature, for example the "Short geographical reports" for individual countries produced by the Admiralty and a number of very brief collections of routes produced by the War Office have not been included. The major collections of these materials in the U.K. are in the Ministry of Defence Whitehall Library and in the Public Record Office (War Office 'A' series in WO 33, 'B' series in WO 287; Admiralty 'C.B.' series in ADM 239, 'B.R.' series in ADM 234)

British Foreign Office Handbooks. These were compiled by the Foreign Office to provide the British delegates to the Paris Peace Conference (1918-19) "with information in the most convenient form - geographical, economic, historical, social, religious and political respecting the different countries with which they might have to deal" (introduction to each volume). Originally issued in 1920 in a long series of individual volumes, with volumes 89 to 130 covering Africa, they were also republished as the Foreign Office "*Peace handbooks*" in 25 volumes (vols. 15 to 20 covering Africa). Initially confidential, they were later released for public consumption. Each volume had a consistent structure: 'Geography: physical and political' (including : frontiers, coasts, rivers, lakes; climate; health; race and language; population); 'Political history' (with chronological lists of major administrative developments and boundary changes); 'Social & political conditions'; Economic ocnditions' (including communications, industry, commerce, finance). Appendices provide trade statistics and details of significant treaties. The data overall basically relate to the situation in 1914 with a few later details.

Area handbooks/Country studies. A series originally designed to provide compilations of basic facts for use by United States military and diplomatic personnel in their relationships with the rest of the world. Compilation and editing is undertaken by the Foreign Area Studies Division of the American University in Washington, under contract for the U.S. Department of the

Army. A largely standardised format has a brief 'country profile' followed by 'historical setting', 'political system', 'physical and social setting', 'the economy' and 'national security'. Each section usually has an extensive bibliography, there are numerous statistical tables, a glossary of terms and an index. In 1978 the name of the series was changed to *Country studies*. This was applied to new volumes, to new editions of existing volumes, and in one or two cases to unchanged reprints of existing volumes. The basic intention of the change was to make the series have appeal to a wider audience, which often led to a significant reduction in the amount of detail. Earlier editions for some countries therefore remain valuable not just for their contemporary relevance but because they contain treatment of topics that are omitted from later editions.

"African historical dictionaries", a series from Scarecrow Press, commenced in 1974 with the intention of providing a separate volume for each country. This has been virtually achieved with over forty volumes published by 1992, and some dozen having gone into second editions. The basic layout of each volume comprises a note on place-names, and a chronology of major events followed by the dictionary proper, with entries for events, individuals, political parties, etc. There is usually a substantial bibliographical section without annotations. Criticisms of this series in the Africanist journals has been fierce (see above xxiv-xxv for details) noting in particular inaccuracies in detail and lack of overall editorial control so that for example some volumes are much more heavily weighted either to the colonial or to the independence period. The critical welcome accorded to certain volumes, for example Zimbabwe/Rhodesia (1979), Botswana, 2nd ed. (1989) only makes the contrast with the less satisfactory examples the sharper. Perhaps their most valuable contribution is in providing guidance for the English-speaking reader for some of the less well known countries of Francophone, Lusophone and former Spanish Africa.

"Terres lointaines" and "Pays africains". These two related series were issued by the Société d'éditions géographiques, maritimes et coloniales in Paris. Volumes in the "Terres lointaines" series give encyclopedic treatment to groups of countries, mostly French colonies (e.g. L'Ouest africain français) but also to other regions (L'Est africain Brittanique). The "Pays africains" series provides shorter handbooks, concentrating on the contemporary scene, for individual countries, all Francophone.

"Notes et études documentaires". Issued by the French government's Direction de la Documention. These provide brief (usually 40/60pp) background surveys for individual countries of Francophone Africa emphasising the administration, the economy, and statistics at the time of compilation. Most countries were covered by volumes issued in the late 1950s and early 1960s giving data contemporary with the coming of independence. Some were also later covered by revised editions in the late 1960s and early 1970s.

"Die Länder Afrikas" series published by the Deutsche Afrika-Gesellschaft during the late 1950s and 1960s provides individual volumes compiled by specialists for most African countries, with much factual data in compact form, and an emphasis on statistics. A number of volumes went into significantly expanded 2nd editions.

Yearbooks

A mixed category containing works variously entitled 'Yearbook', 'Annual/Annuaire/Anuário', 'Almanack', 'Directory'. In a sense, these are compendious sources, like many of those in the **Handbooks** category above, that are updated and re-issued on a regular basis and normally emphasize the recording of current information. Many yearbooks and annuals of course appear much more infrequently than annually, and indeed a number of the sources noted here never proceeded beyond their first issue. Two major categories will be found here. **Official sources** will usually emphasize the current structure of the administration and its activities during the preceding year, often with extensive statistics. The general "annual reports" issued by the colonial powers, and exemplified by the long series produced by the British Colonial Office and Foreign Office are listed here. The complexity of the British series in terms of where the individual reports may be located within Parliamentary and non-Parliamentary papers has led to the provision of further bibliographical details in a separate Appendix. A brief summary of the publishing history of each report is included in the main sequence, with fuller details including Command numbers provided in the Appendix. **Commercial sources** will often concentrate on providing economic, industrial and financial information and some will be largely confined to providing lists of organizations in these spheres. Works which are solely concerned with giving names and addresses of commercial firms, and which proliferate in South Africa for example, have been listed only sparingly, with the major examples for any country cited. Among categories **excluded** from this section are telephone directories, annual reports of individual ministries (as opposed to the national or colonial government as a whole) and annuals, often produced by local journals, which contain articles rather than structured factual data. It should be noted that some titles which call themselves "Handbooks" are nevertheless listed here, since their emphasis is on regular production of new issues with data such as civil lists and commercial directories (see for example **Gold Coast handbook** and **Nigeria handbook**).

Statistics

Coverage is of any substantial "one-off" statistical compilations, and of the principal **general** statistical series (bulletins and yearbooks) for each region or country as issued by the regional or national statistical agency, or by the appropriate colonial power or international agency. No attempt is made to cover more specialized statistical series, e.g. for trade or agricultural production, for which reference may be made to the bibliographies listed at the beginning of the section for **Statistics: Africa: general.** Similarly **population census reports** are not listed, but details are provided of the major sources which will give information on these.

Directories of organizations

This somewhat clumsy title is chosen to emphasize that these are not general "directories" in the sense of titles which are included with almanacks and annuals under **Yearbooks.** Rather these are guides which are confined to listing organizations: lists of societies, research institutions, libraries, museums, universities. Also included are directories of individual specialists (scientists, researchers) which offer an alternative guide to the names of the institutions to which they are attached. Government organization manuals as issued by national governments are not included. Many of the titles listed in the *Yearbooks* category above will also have sections devoted to listing organizations.

Biographical sources

Listed here are works of collective biography of the "who's who" or "dictionary of national biography" nature. Normally, only works which contain a minimum of fifty biographical entries are included. Coverage is usually limited to works covering a whole region or country, or substantial and significant groups within these (political leaders, members of a particular ethnic or social group) and does not include biographical works confined to a particular profession (e.g. lawyers). Lists of current government officials (civil lists) are not included. Many of the works in the two previous categories, *Handbooks* and *Yearbooks* will of course include biographical sections and the annotations endeavour to draw attention to this. Also included here, especially in the case of South Africa, are works on genealogy and family names.

Atlases & gazetteers

This section is subdivided according to these two categories of source.

Under **atlases**, in addition to specialist titles, some fairly popular works are included for certain countries, where little else in atlas form provides specific coverage. Historical atlases are included in this section rather than under handbooks. Collections of facsimiles of early maps are treated as atlases and entered here. In the annotations, indications are given where possible and appropriate of the major scales of the maps provided, providing some indication of the depth of coverage available. Under **gazetteers** are also entered guides to place-names, and a selection of works that discuss the characteristic features or problems of local place-names and can be useful in interpreting gazetteers; also a variety of works such as "Guides to post offices" all of which can be used to trace localities.

ENTRIES

As noted above, under each heading and sub-heading, items are arranged chronologically by date of publication. Where a work has a title in English and another language, the English form is chosen for entry. The English form of places of publication is used. Following the entry for the original work, translations into English are given precedence in listing before translations into other languages. Where an entry for a later edition of a title records only place of publication, this indicates that the author and publisher are unchanged since the previous edition cited. The principal intent of the annotations is to provide information on the scope of the work recorded, particularly in terms of matters such as the number of entries in a directory, gazetteer, or biographical source, the number and major scales of maps provided by an atlas, and the range of topics covered by a handbook or yearbook. The bibliographical relationship of the work to others is noted, as also (so far as possible) are changes in title and frequency in serially published titles. No attempt has been made to record all changes in name of issuing bodies for the latter. As noted above, selected reviews from a limited range of journals are cited.

SOURCES USED

The original basis for this compilation was the series of indexes to sources covering all countries of the Third World which I have accumulated over 25 years of teaching courses related to area studies bibliography. These were originally compiled from a very wide scan of bibliographies, journals, and library's holdings, and much the same range has been used to check references and gather further detail for the present work. For material produced in recent years, the compiler's task has been greatly aided by the important wide-ranging and continuing series compiled by members of the African Studies Association entitled "Africana reference works". This has appeared for: **1980 & 1981**, *ASA news*, 15, 1982, 41-46; **1982**, *ASA news*, 16, 1983, 19-24; **1983**, *ASA news*, 18, 1985, 36-42; **1984/85**, *ASA news*, 19, 1986, 18-28; **1984/85**, *ABPR*, 12, 1986, 81-92 (expanded version of the list already published in *ASA news* (above); **1986**, *ABPR*, 13, 1987, 93-98; **1987**, *ABPR*, 14, 1988, 87-93; **1988**, *ABPR*, 15, 1989, 79-87; **1989**, *ABPR*, 16, 1990, 87-96; and **1990**, *ABPR*, 17, 1991, 81-92. I have also been able to see the list for **1991** in proof (forthcoming in *ABPR* 18 (2) 1992). The compilers are Phyllis Bischof, *et al* (1980/81-1984/85 in *ASA news*); Joseph Lauer (1984/85-1987) and Yvette Scheven (1988 to date). Entries in the issues for 1980/81 and 1982 are alphabetical by author; 1983-1987 issues are arranged under broad categories: bibliographies (general, subject, regional), biographical sources, directories, handbooks and manuals, etc; 1988-1991 issues are arranged under specific headings, including individual countries. All entries since *ABPR* took over publication have been annotated.

The great majority of titles listed in the present work have been personally inspected. For material not seen, a note of the source of information is normally added (especially if secondary sources give conflicting data). A list of the sources most frequently cited is provided in the section for "Abbreviations". It has not been possible of course to see every volume in a series, for example of yearbooks or statistical bulletins, since few libraries hold complete collections, and this category has presented the most severe problems. Details of change of title, frequency, coverage, relationships with other titles, and dates of publication have been conflated from a number of sources including partial holdings in more than one library, and entries in bibliographies and catalogues. In many cases details of all copies, or of the latest copy actually traced are included. Information for several items remains lacking, and although hopefully some errors and "ghosts" present in existing lists have been exorcised, I have no doubt at all but that others have been perpetuated or perpetrated. This is one area in particular where I hope that publication will stimulate users to provide corrections and additional information for a future edition. As indeed I hope they will for a work as a whole.

ACKNOWLEDGEMENTS. Compilation of this work has relied principally on the resources of the British Library, the Bodleian Library (especially the collections at Rhodes House), and the libraries of the Royal Commonwealth Society, the Foreign and Commonwealth Office, the Institute of Commonwealth Studies and the School of Oriental & African Studies of the University of London in the U.K., and the library of the Afrika-Studiecentrum in Leiden. I am grateful to the staff of all these for their help. It is sad that during the final stages of editing, two of the above collections should have encountered particular problems. Special thanks are due to Terry Barringer of the Royal Commonwealth Society for allowing ready access to her stacks at a time when the Library was formally closed, and its whole future in doubt, and to Margaret Cousins for extracting numerous volumes from parts of the collection at the Foreign and Commonwealth Office that were scheduled for disposal in a programme of cutting stack space by 50 per cent. I am most grateful also to Michael Chambers of the Whitehall Library, Ministry of Defense for checking the Library's entire holdings of War Office reports on Africa, making them accessible to me and supplying information about the War Office and Admiralty series numbering systems. Among those who offered advice on specific points, I am especially grateful to Donald Simpson, and Harry Hannam. My daughter Anne proof-read with a keen eye. As always, my greatest debt is to my wife, Ia, who spent an enormous amount of time that she could ill afford with her other responsibilities, compiling both the entries for the British Colonial and Foreign Office annual reports, and the index, and patiently striving to improve my consistency in citation. Finally my thanks to Hans Zell for his patient encouragement and tolerance as completion dates slipped ever further away.

JHM

University College London
September 1992

ABBREVIATIONS

Countries, institutions, organizations

AEF	Afrique équatoriale française
AOF	Afrique occidentale française
ASA	African Studies Association (U.S.A.)
BL	British Library
CARDAN	Centre d'analyse et de recherche pour l'Afrique noire
CODESRIA	Council for the Development of Economic & Social Research in Africa
IAI	International African Institute
IFAN	Institut Français (*later* Fondamental) pour l'Afrique noire
OAU	Organization of African Unity
OECD	Organization for European Co-operation & Development
ORSTOM	Office de recherche scientifique et technique d'outre-mer
RCS	Royal Commonwealth Society
SCOLMA	Standing Conference on Library Materials on Africa
SOAS	School of Oriental & African Studies, University of London
UNECA	United Nations Economic Commission for Africa

Sources cited

Africa	*Africa: journal of the International African Institute*
ABPR	*African book publishing record*
AHS	*African historical studies* (later *International journal of African historical studies*)
ALEA	*Accessions list, Eastern Africa* (Washington, Library of Congress)
ARBA	*American reference books annual*
ARD	*African research & documentation*
Barry & Perkins	R.B. Barry & C.R. Perkins. **World mapping today.** London, Butterworths, 1987.
Darch	C. Darch. **Mozambique.** Oxford, Clio, 1980.
Duignan	P. Duignan, *ed.* **Guide to research & reference works on Sub-Saharan Africa,** comp. H.F. Conover & P. Duignan . Stanford, CA, Hoover Institution, 1971.
GJ	*Geographical journal*
Gregory	W. Gregory **List of the serial publications of foreign governments, 1815-1931.** New York, Wilson, 1932.

IJAHS	*International journal of African historical studies* (formerly *African historical studies*)
JAH	*Journal of African history*
Mendelssohn	S. Mendelssohn. **South African bibliography**. London, Kegan Paul, 1910.
Musiker	R. Musiker. **South African bibliography**. Oxford, Clio, 1979.
NUC	**National union catalog**
QBSAL	*Quarterly bulletin of the South African Library*
SAB	**A South African bibliography to the year 1925** comp.by the South African Library, Cape Town, Tansell, 1979.
Westfall	G. Westfall. **Bibliography of official statistical yearbooks and bulletins**. Cambridge, Chadwyck-Healey, 1986.
Willett & Ambrose	S. Willett & D.P. Ambrose. **A comprehensive bibliography of Botswana**. Oxford, Clio, 1980.

In bibliographical entries

col.	coloured (of illustrations and maps)
ed.	edition/editor/edited
fasc.	fascicle
ff.	following
illus.	illustrations
irreg.	irregular (in publication frequency)
n.p.	no place (of publication)/no publisher
n.s.	new series
pt.	part
pub.	publisher/published
rev.	revised
trans.	translation/translator/translated
vol.	volume

AFRICA IN GENERAL

HANDBOOKS

General

1
Johnston, A.K. **Africa**: Stanford's compendium of geography and travel for general reading, based on Hellwald's *Die Erde und ihre Völker*, trans. by A.H. Keane, ed. and extended by K. Johnston. London, Edward Stanford, 1878. xvi, 611pp.

- - 2nd ed. London, 1880. xvi, 611pp.

- - 3rd ed. London, 1884. xvi, 616pp.

- - 4th ed. London, 1884. xvi, 616pp.

Later extensively revised and re-issued in 1895 (*see* 3).

2
Heichen, P. **Afrika Hand-Lexikon: ein Nachschlagebuch für Jedermann.** Leipzig, Gressner & Schramm, 1885. 3 vols. (1344pp.) illus. maps.

Brief entries arranged alphabetically covering places, peoples, biographies, flora and fauna. Longer entries for countries (e.g. "Abessinien", 18 cols. including historical chronology).

3
Keane, A.H. **Africa**. London, Edward Stanford, 1895. (Stanford's compendium of geography and travel). 2 vols. illus. maps.

Vol. 1, North Africa (including Sudan, Ethiopia); vol. 2, South Africa (including west, central and east Africa). Extensively revised version ("of the original, nothing remains except a few passages") of the vols. ed. by A.K. Johnston (*see* 1). Includes data on topography, natural resources, peoples, administration and commerce. 169 illus. and 20 folding maps.

- - 2nd ed. London, 1904-1907. 2 vols.

4
Kinsky, K.R.F.A. *Graf.* **Vademecum für diplomatische Arbeit auf dem**

1

afrikanischen Continent. Vienna, Gerold, 1897. 104pp.

- - 3rd ed. Leipzig, Veit, 1900. x, 133pp.

- - English trans. **The diplomatist's handbook for Africa**. London, Kegan Paul, Trench, Trübner, 1897. viii, 121pp.

Arranged by region. For each country gives details of frontiers (with citations for agreements establishing them), administrative divisions, and political history, emphasising activities of European powers, in addition to general topographical and demographic information. Also pub. in French as **Le continent africain: manuel de diplomatie**. Paris, Challamel, 1897.

5
Martens, O. & Karstedt, O. **Afrika: ein Handbuch für Wirtschaft und Reisen**. Berlin, D. Reimer, 1930. xv, 940pp. illus. maps.

- - 2nd ed. Berlin, 1931. xv, 988pp.

- - 3rd ed. Berlin, 1936. 2 vols. (xii, 532pp; xvi, 642pp.)

- - 4th ed. Berlin, 1938. 2 vols. (xii, 525pp; xvi, 693pp.)

- - English trans. **The African handbook and traveller's guide**. London, Allen & Unwin, 1932. xvi, 948pp. illus. 23 maps.

"On the one hand ... a dependable guide to the geographical, climatic and economic conditions of ... African countries, and on the other, to be of assistance to persons travelling" (preface). An immensely detailed guide-book arranged by region. Includes 17 city plans.

- - 2nd ed. **The African handbook: a guide to West, South and East Africa**. London, Allen & Unwin, 1938. xv, 726pp. ilus. maps.

Includes considerably less factual data and statistics than the 1st ed. with more emphasis on information for tourism, and an additional 25 town plans.

6
Hailey, W.M. *1st baron Hailey*. **An African survey: a study of problems arising in Africa south of the Sahara**. London, Oxford University Press for Royal Institute of International Affairs, 1938. xxviii, 1837pp. illus. maps.

Following a plea for a continent-wide survey made by General Smuts in his Rhodes Memorial Lecture at Oxford in 1929, the Committee of the African Research Survey was set up by the Royal Institute of International Affairs in 1931. Preliminary collection of data began in 1933, and Hailey became involved in 1935. Chapter 1, Physical background; 2, Peoples; 3, Languages; 4, Population records; 5, Political and social objectives in government; 6, Systems of government; 7, Law and justice; 8, Non-European immigrant communities; 9, Native administration; 10, Taxation; 11, Labour; 12, The state and the land; 13, Agriculture; 14, Forests; 15, Water supply; 16, Soil erosion; 17, Health; 18, Education; 19 & 20, External and internal aspects of economic development; 21, Co-operatives; 22, Minerals; 23, Transport; 24, The future of African studies; 25, Conclusions. The classic compilation of data for its time. For contemporary discussion of the work see **Lord Hailey's African survey, surveyed for the Royal African Society by the Rt. Hon. Lord Harlech [etc.]**, ed. F.H. Melland. London, Macmillan, 1938. 70pp. (issued as a supplement to the *Journal* of the Society).

- - **revised 1956**. London, Oxford University Press for Royal Institute of International Affairs, 1957. xxvi, 1,676pp. maps.

"The present volume, though similar in its objectives and in the arrangement of its material ... is, in many respects, a new work" (preface). Compilation commenced in 1952, and the revision attempts to cover developments to the end of 1955. Contains an additional 5 maps. Reviews, *Africa*, 28, 1958, 168-170; *African affairs* 56, 1957, 325-327; *GJ* 124, 1958, 380-384.

7
Mendes Corrêa, A. **Ultramar Portugues I: Síntese da Africa**. Lisbon, Agência-Geral das Colonias, Divisão de Publicações e Biblioteca, 1949. 436pp. illus. maps.

Broad overview which emphasizes Portuguese territories but covers the whole continent with sections on geography, climate, vegetation, fauna, peoples, languages and education, health, politics and administration, economics. English and French abstracts of each section are included. Over 100 illus.

8
Migliorini, E. **L'Africa**. Turin, Unione Tipografico-Editrice Torinese, 1955. (Geografia universale illustrata, 5). 821pp. illus. maps.

Provides coverage of physical, social, economic and political geography, lavishly illustrated.

9
Legum, C. *ed*. **Africa: a handbook to the continent**. London, Anthony Blond, 1961/New York, Praeger, 1962. xiv, 553pp. maps.

"Something that lies between Lord Hailey's invaluable *African survey* (written by experts for experts) and John Gunther's *Inside Africa* (written by a non-expert for non-experts)" (preface). Pt. 1 covers Africa by region, pt. 2 is a series of essays on themes: economics, art, literature etc.

- - 2nd ed. rev. and enlarged. London, 1965/New York, Praeger, 1966. xii, 558pp.

Adds essay coverage of the press and trade unions. "Recommended to anyone ... requiring a well-informed understanding of African affairs" (*GJ* 134, 1968, 419-420).

- - rev. ed. Harmondsworth, Penguin, 1969. 682pp.

For the completely revised version, **Handbooks to the modern world: Africa** (1989) *see* 28.

10
Meyers Handbuch über Afrika. Mannheim, Bibliographisches Institut, [1962]. 779pp. illus. maps.

Pt. 1, thematic treatment of Africa as a whole with sections for natural resources, peoples, history, industry, communications etc. Pt. 2, country by country accounts in a standardized format. Includes biographies for 63 African leaders. A very detailed work.

11
Afrika: entsiklopedicheskii spravochnik, ed. I.I. Potekhin. Moscow, Sovetskaya entsiklopediia, 1963. 2 vols (474; 376pp). illus. maps.

- - rev. ed., ed. in chief A.A. Gromyko. Moscow, 1986-1987. 2 vols. illus. maps.

Published under the auspices of the Institut Afriki of the Akademiia nauk. General articles on natural resources, peoples, and the economy, followed by regional surveys. 2nd ed. contains numerous coloured illustrations.

12

Junod, V.I. *ed*. **The handbook of Africa**. New York, New York University Press, 1963. xiv, 472pp.

Arranged alphabetically by country in the form of summarised data (based on format of U.K. Colonial Office *Fact sheets*). Data up to December 1961. Notes on sources. Lengthy appendices on "Colonial policies in Africa", regional groupings of African countries, and foreign aid.

13

Worldmark encyclopedia of the nations. 2nd ed. **Vol. 2: Africa**, ed. L. Barron. New York, Worldmark Press, 1963. 5 vols.

- - 3rd ed. New York, 1967.

- - 4th ed. New York, 1971.

- - 5th ed. New York, 1976.

- - 6th ed. New York, 1984.

- - 7th ed. New York, 1988.

1st ed. of the encyclopedia, 1960, treated all countries of the world in a single alphabetical sequence. 2nd and subsequent eds. present the information by continent, covering "the geographical, historical, political, social and economic status of all nations" (preface).

14

Kitchen, H. *ed*. **A handbook of African affairs**. London, Pall Mall Press/New York, Praeger for African-American Institute, 1964. vii, 311pp. 9 maps.

Reprinted from material originally published in *Africa report*. Pt. 1, country by country surveys with basic data; pt. 2, armies of Africa; pt. 3, OAU; pt. 4, contemporary African poetry and prose.

15

Mveng, P.E. **Dossier culturel Pan-Africain**. Paris, "Présence africaine", 1965. 236pp.

Sees itself as complementing the largely political and economic emphasis of other contemporary reference works on Africa. Initial data on population distribution is followed by a series of 25 maps of "les foyers culturels" (e.g.

use of symbols in house decoration), and features on religion (with statistics and distribution maps), languages, writers, universities, research institutes, and relationships of African countries with Unesco.

16
Africa at a glance. Sandton, South African Freedom Foundation/Pretoria, Africa Institute of South Africa, 1967.

New eds. pub. every 2/3 years. 5th ed. Sandton, 1978. 65pp. Tables, statistics, diagrams, 8 thematic maps. Gives basic data on rulers, political parties, population, production, communications and recent political events for African countries.

17
Afrika-handbuch für Wirtschaft und Reise. Hamburg, Übersee Verlag for Afrika-Verein Hamburg-Bremen, 1967-1968. 2 vols. (430pp; 456pp.) illus. maps.

Ed. P. Colburg, *et al*. Describes itself as "Martens/Kardstedt" (*see* 5) for a new generation. Vol.1, North, west and central Africa; vol. 2, North-east, east and southern Africa. Introductory sections on geography, history, peoples and languages, then wide-ranging basic data for each country. Includes list of major African organizations and index to place-names. Maps include 25 street plans of sub-Saharan African cities.

- - 2nd ed. **Klett Handbuch für Reise und Wirtschaft in Afrika**. Stuttgart, Klett, 1967-1968. 2 vols. illus. maps.

- - 3rd ed. Stuttgart, 1971-1975. 3 vols. illus. maps.

Vol. 1, West & central Africa; vol. 2, North and north-east Africa; vol. 3, Southern Africa.

18
Balandier, G. & Maquet, J. **Dictionnaire des civilisations africaines**. Paris, F. Hazon, 1968. 448pp. illus.

- - English trans. **Dictionary of black African civilization**. New York, Leon Amiel, 1974. ix, 350pp. illus.

Note to English ed. "we have attempted to up-date the original French ed. on a limited basis", mostly by amending political articles to reflect recent events.

Numerous brief entries with many illus.

19

Meyers Kontinente und Meere; Daten, Bilder, Karten: Afrika. Mannheim, Bibliographisches Institut, Geographisch-Kartographisches Institut Meyer, 1968. (Meyers Kontinente und Meere, 1). 380pp. illus. maps.

Ed. W. Jopp. First section covers the continent as a whole: geology, topography, climate, vegetation, history, peoples (including a tribal map showing 985 groups), and then the major sub-regions. Second section gives coverage of each individual country with a wide range of data.

20

Sergiacomi de'Aicardi, S.L. **Africa internazionale.** Milan, Istituto Internazionale per l'Africa, 1971. 391pp. map.

Pt. 1, international organizations and Africa; pt. 2, country by country surveys with brief topographical and historical details, and population and economic statistics for 43 African states.

21

Morrison, D.G. *et al.* **Black Africa: a comparative handbook.** New York, Free Press, 1972. 483pp.

To present "in a clear and readily accessible form the latest comparable information available ... for 32 independent black African nations" (preface). Pt. 1 gives comparative profiles under topics such as demography, social & economic development, political development, and urban and ethnic patterns. Pt. 2 gives individual country profiles. Much of the information is in tabular form.

- - 2nd ed. New York, Irvington Publications/London, Macmillan, 1989. xxii, 716pp.

A very substantially revised compendium of data, retaining the same basic structure as the 1st ed. Country coverage is expanded to include Angola, Djibouti, Equatorial Guinea, Guinea-Bissau, Madagascar, Mozambique, Namibia, Swaziland and Zimbabwe. For the sections in Pt. 1 ("Demography, ecology & pluralism", "Economic development & social mobilization", "Political development", "International relations") an attempt is made to provide comparative data for each of the years 1955, 1961, 1966, 1972 and 1977. For the country surveys in pt. 2, data goes up to 1982. Contains 187 separate tables. For the companion vol. **Understanding black Africa**, *see* 29.

7

The text of the **Comparative handbook** forms one component in a "Black Africa database" marketed separately on disk by the publishers.

22

African encyclopedia. London, Oxford University Press, 1973. 544pp.

Ed. W. Senteza Kajubi, L.J. Lewis and C.O. Taino, with a range of British, African and American contributors. Over 1,800 short articles. African emphasis, but also general articles, e.g. on "space exploration". Some 500 photographs, 200 maps and diagrams. Review in *IJAHS* 8, 1975, 477-478.

23

Macdonald's encyclopedia of Africa. London, Macdonald Educational, 1976. 224pp.

U.S. ed. pub. as **The encyclopedia of Africa**. New York, F. Watts, 1976. Popular, multi-illustrated approach with thematic sections ("Economy", "The land", "The arts" etc.) and including useful "Gazetteer" with long entries for each country and major cities, and "Guide to peoples and languages" compiled by J.D. Pearson and based on the card index of the International African Institute.

24

Bourges, H. & Wauthier, C. **Les 50 Afriques**. Paris, Éditions du Seuil, 1979. 2 vols. (684pp; 682pp.)

Vol. 1. North, north-east, and west Africa; vol. 2, East, central and southern Africa. Individual entries for all 54 countries with map, basic factual details, and a narrative account of history, topography, resources, politics, culture.

25

Africa today. London, "Africa journal", 1981. (Know Africa series). xx, 1506pp.

- - 2nd ed. London, Africa Books, 1991. xx, 2056pp. illus. maps.

Ed. R. Uwechue. Based on the pattern of **Africa yearbook and who's who** (*see* 120). Sections on Africa in general (topography, languages etc.), and regional organizations, followed by country by country surveys, and an atlas of 24 col. thematic maps using Peters' projection. A major source of contemporary reference.

26

Cambridge encyclopedia of Africa. Cambridge, Cambridge University Press, 1981. 492pp. illus., maps.

Ed. by R. Oliver & M. Crowder, with over 90 contributors. Four sections : "Africa past" with treatment of pre-colonial history, European occupation and rule to 1939; "Struggle for independence"; "Contemporary Africa" with brief profiles of each country and general chapters on government, natural resources, politics, economics, society, religion, arts and recreation; "Africa and the world". Numerous illus. and 46 maps. Lacks an introduction explaining the policy of coverage. Favourable review in *JAH* 24, 1983, 545, although coverage of the pre-colonial era is seen as giving undue emphasis to North Africa and to activities by Europeans.

27

Burton, F. & Bhushan, K. **Africa factbook: basic data on and for the continent.** Nairobi, Newspread International & International Press Institute, 1989. 136pp.

Africa-wide data on population, agriculture, minerals, communications etc., with economic and population statistics for individual countries.

28

Moroney, S. *ed.* **Handbooks to the modern world: Africa.** New York & Oxford, Facts on File, 1989. 2 vols.

Extensively rev. version of Legum, **Africa: a handbook to the continent** (*see* 9) with over 30 contributors. Vol. 1 contains factual information alphabetically by country, covering topography, recent political and constitutional history, the economy, social services, education, and the mass media. Includes biographical sketches and comparative statistics (pp. 625-665). Vol. 2 contains thematic essays covering Africa as a whole.

29

Morrison, D.G. **Understanding Black Africa: data and analysis of social change and nation building.** New York, Paragon House & Irvington Publications, 1989. xvii, 237pp.

"[It was] apparent at the time we were preparing **Black Africa** [*see* 21] that there was also a need for a relatively inexpensive comparative handbook for students of Africa ... this book is the result" (preface). Forms part of a set of three with **Black Africa.** 2nd ed. (1989) and **Conflict and violence.** Basically an abbreviated version of **Black Africa** with some 85 tables. Pts. 1 to 4 (pp.

1-134) cover themes: population, languages, education, urbanization, communications, religion, politics, development, economics, and foreign relations in relation to Africa as a whole; pt. 5 (pp. 135-229) provides individual country profiles.

30

Grace, J. & Laffin, J. **Fontana dictionary of Africa since 1960: events, movements, personalities**. London, Fontana Press, 1991. xix, 395pp.

A work for the more popular market with entries for countries, individuals (principally in political life) and political groupings.

31

[**Encyclopaedia Africana**]. A project with editorial headquarters in Accra since 1963, but with origins going back to the concept of W.E. DuBois (1868-1963) for an "Encyclopaedia of the Negro" first voiced in 1909: "in celebration of the 50th anniversary of the emancipation of the American Negros, I am proposing to bring out an encyclopaedia covering the chief points in the history and condition of the Negro race" (Letter to Edward Blyden, *Correspondence of W.E. DuBois*, ed. H. Aptheker, vol. 1. Amherst, 1973). DuBois and various collaborators returned periodically to this proposal, and in 1945 the **Encyclopaedia of the Negro: preparatory volume with reference lists and reports** was published in New York by the Phelps-Stokes Fund. The larger part of this was occupied by a list of potential topics to be covered in the main work itself.

Failing to make further progress in the U.S.A., DuBois moved to Ghana in 1961, where the project, now named "Encyclopaedia Africana", was given support by Nkrumah. "I propose an encyclopaedia edited mainly by African scholars, but I am anxious to have this encyclopaedia a scientific production and not a matter of propaganda, and to have included among its writers the best students of Africa in the world. I want, however, to have the encyclopaedia written mainly from the African point of view, from people who know and understand the history and culture of Africans". (DuBois to Charles Julien, 17 April 1961, quoted by Julien in his **Les Africains**, vol. 1, 1977, *see* 300).

Following the death of DuBois in 1963, the Editorial Committee met for the first time in 1964 with representatives from 24 African countries and formally declared its aim to "compile and publish a scientific and authentically African compendium of the known facts of African life, history and culture". Work on planning the encyclopaedia can be followed through the pages of its own newsletter, *For co-operation towards an Encyclopaedia Africana*, Accra, issues 1-18, 1962-1979. Proposals included the production of

English, French and Arabic versions, and abridged one volume editions for use in schools. Lists of topics to be covered and proposed contributors provide an interesting insight into the attempt to construct the most ambitious reference work on Africa ever conceived.

To date no volume as originally devised by the Editorial Office has appeared. An agreement was reached with an American publisher, Scholarly Press of Algonac, Michigan, to publish the biographical content as a separate series: the **Encyclopaedia Africana dictionary of biography**, commencing in 1971. This series too has run into difficulties. Announced as 20 vols. with each covering 2 or 3 countries, only two vols. had appeared by 1991, with a third announced for 1992 (*see* 229, 459, 885, 979, 1079). For an account of the historical origins of the project *see*: C.G. Contee, 'The *Encyclopaedia Africana* project of W.E. Du Bois', *African historical studies* 4, 1971, 77-91; for some indication of the problems that the Editorial Board faced after its creation in 1964, see 'Interview with Professor L.H. Ofusu-Appiah, Director *Encyclopaedia Africana* project', *ABPR* 1, 1975, 289-291 and M. Afrani, 'An African dream come true', *African concord*, 9 July 1987, 12-14.

Anglophone Africa

32

Encyclopedia of the British Empire. London, Rankin Bros., 1924-1925. 3 vols. (1772pp.) illus. maps.

"The first encyclopedic record of the greatest empire in the history of the world" (sub-title). Ed. C.W. Domville-Fife, with numerous contributors "largely among those whose life is being spent in the regions described" (preface). Originally issued in 24 fortnightly parts. A combination of alphabetical entries for countries and topics. Regional coverage of Africa under "Africa" (pp. 1-124) also "Egypt and the British Sudan" (pp. 777-856); "Mandatory territories : Africa" (pp. 1232-1258); "Mauritius" (pp. 1288-1297); "Seychelles" (pp. 1474-1477); "Somaliland" (pp. 1478-1481); "St. Helena" (pp. 1482-1485). Over 2,000 photographs.

Francophone Africa

33

Petit, M. **Les colonies françaises: petite encyclopédie coloniale.** Paris, Larousse, 1902. 2 vols.

Vol. 1, xxviii, 772pp. 247 illus. 24 maps. Covers colonial organization in general, North Africa, and West Africa; vol. 2, 839pp. 213 illus. 25 maps. Pp. 1-276 cover Congo, Madagascar and its satellites, and French Somaliland. Each political division has a standard treatment: geography, ethnography, history of French conquest, the economy, principal settlements.

- - **Supplément**. Paris, 1912. 120pp. 5 illus. 12 maps.

Covers the most important changes in administration since the original vol. Africa, pp. 15-87.

34
Afrique française: Afrique occidentale française, Afrique équatoriale française, Togo et Cameroun. Paris, Société d'éditions géographiques, maritimes et coloniales, 1931. (Guide des colonies françaises). various paging. illus. maps.

"L'art negre", 13pp; "L'A.O.F.", 69pp; "L'A.E.F.", 76pp; "Togo et Cameroun", 31, 43pp. Each section has a topographic index. One of the numerous vols. prepared by the publishers for the Exposition coloniale internationale in Paris in 1931.

35
Encyclopédie coloniale et maritime [etc.]. Paris, Éditions de l'empire français, 1940-1951. 7 vols. in 10.

Compiled "sous la direction d'Eugène Guernier". A very detailed work with a complex publishing history on which none of the standard bibliographical sources agree. A preliminary ed. was issued in fascs. of 24 to 40 pp. each, 1936-?1940. The publishing plan as set out in each fasc. was for 150 (later amended to 132) fascs. to be issued, eventually comprising 9 vols. of c.400pp each; however fasc. 23 (1940) is the last traced. Published vols. in the 1940-51 ed. are: **Le Maroc** (1st ed. 1940; 2nd ed. 1948); **Tunisie** (1942); **Algérie-Sahara** (1946) 2 vols; **Madagascar-Réunion** (1947) 2 vols; **Afrique occidentale française** (1949) 2 vols.; **Afrique équatoriale française** (1950); **Cameroun-Togo** (1951). The last four titles are discussed below under the appropriate region (*see* 760, 1115, 1117, 1633). In all vols. published up to 1950, the introduction refers to the plan for a complete *Encyclopédie* of 15 vols., with individual vols. proposed for Indochina, French Pacific territories, French North American and Caribbean territories, and a general survey of the French empire. The whole work is referred to variously as the *Encyclopédie de l'empire français* and the *Encyclopédie de l'union française*. By the **Cameroun-Togo** vol. of 1951, the introduction refers to the whole work as the *Encyclopédie de l'Afrique française* in 10 vols. Early titles claimed that coverage of the "Côte française des Somalis" would be included in the vol. for "Afrique occidentale française".

This was not the case, and later titles promised inclusion of Somaliland with the vol. for Indochina which was never published.

- - **Encyclopédie coloniale et maritime: revue encyclopédique des pays d'outre-mer**, Paris, 1950-1958. Monthly.

Title varies : **Encyclopédie mensuelle d'outre-mer** (1951-58); **Encyclopédie mensuelle de l'Afrique** (1958). Early issues claimed this to be not only a review of current events but "en même temps compléter et développer les volumes de l'*Encyclopédie de l'Afrique française*". Every 24 issues were to form a complete volume of supplement. By 1953 it was claiming only to be a current affairs monthly.

36
États africains d'expression française et République malgache. Paris, René Julliard, 1962. 342pp.

- - 2nd ed. Paris, 1964. 344pp.

Individual surveys of 14 countries (omitting Comoros, Djibouti, Réunion), with sections on major regional organizations, French agencies for technical assistance, and international aid organizations.

37
Encyclopédie africaine et malgache. Paris, Larousse, 1964-1968. 19 vols.

The basic 463pp text with a 16pp atlas (originally issued in 7 fascs.) is common to each vol. in the series, and comprises "Le monde que nous habitons", "Histoire du monde", "Histoire de l'Afrique" (pp. 161-208), "Littérature et grammaire français", "Arithmétique et géométrie", "L'homme, anatomie et santé", "La vie quotidienne". For the last two sections, there is heavy emphasis in both text and illustration on Africa. Each regional vol. then has an additional separate section (some 30 to 80pp) covering the region concerned added to this basic text. Vols. for Burundi, Cameroon, Central African Republic, Chad, Congo (Brazzaville), Congo (Kinshasa), Ivory Coast, Dahomey, Gabon, Guinea, Madagascar and Somalia, Mali, Mauritania, Niger, Rwanda, Senegal, Togo, Upper Volta.

38
Guide pratique sur les républiques ... à l'usage des agents de la coopération. Paris, Ministère de la Coopération, Direction de la coopération culturelle et technique, 1964. 222pp. illus. maps.

Covers 15 Francophone countries, with geographical, economic, social, political and administrative information.

39

L'Afrique noire de A à Z. Paris, Ediafric-La documentation africaine, 1971. [317pp].

- - 2nd ed. Paris, 1975. [394pp].

Pub. as special numbers of *Bulletin de l'Afrique noire*. Covers Francophone countries of west and central Africa and for each contains assorted information arranged under alphabetical headings (from "Aerodromes", "Armée" to "Universités", "Villes").

40

Martin, J. **Lexique de la colonisation française**. Paris, Dalloz, 1988. xiii, 395pp.

Approximately 1,000 alphabetical entries for countries, cities, persons, organizations, treaties, wars, trading companies, concepts (e.g. "esclavage"). Very useful detailed coverage.

Former German Africa

41

Meyer, H.H.J. *ed*. **Das deutsche Kolonialreich: eine Länderkunde der deutschen Schutzgebiete**. Leipzig & Vienna, Bibliographisches Institut, 1909-1910. 5 parts in 2 vols. illus. maps.

Vol. 1, xviii, 635, xlv pp. 144 plates. maps; pt. 1; Ostafrika by H.H.J. Meyer; pt. 2; Kamerun by S. Passarge. Vol. 2, iv, 575pp. 91 plates. maps; pt. 1; Togo by S. Passarge; pt. 2; Südwestafrika by L. Schultze. Pt. 3 covers Germany's Pacific and Far Eastern colonies. Each part has its own index. Detailed information on all aspects of the countries covered, with lengthy bibliographies.

42

Deutsches Kolonial-Lexikon. Leipzig, Von Quelle & Meyer, 1920. 3 vols. illus. maps.

Ed. H. Schnee, Governor of German East Africa, 1912-18 and a leading advocate during the 1920s of the restoration of Germany's colonies. Text mostly completed by 1914. Scholarly signed articles with bibliographies from over 80 contributors arranged alphabetically with no general index. Major entries for individual territories (e.g. "Kamerun", 50pp.) and for themes ("Kolonialpolitik Deutschlands", "Presse, Koloniale") with short specific entries for ethnic groups, crops, flora and fauna and biographies. Over 400 photos and text figures.

43
Zahe, H. *ed.* **Das deutsche Kolonialbuch.** Berlin, Wilhelm Undermann, [1925]. 512pp. 275 illus. 7 maps.

Pp. 11-248, "Deutschland als Kolonialmacht": general chapters on trade, missions, etc.; pp. 249-350, "West Afrika"; pp. 350-466, "Ost Afrika". Regional chapters have sections on topography, history, peoples, and the economy.

44
Das Buch der deutschen Kolonien. Leipzig, Goldmann, 1933. 352pp. illus.

- - 2nd ed. Berlin, R. Gobbing, 1936, 327pp. illus.

- - 3rd ed. Leipzig, Goldmann, 1937. 367pp. illus.

- - 4th ed. Leipzig, 1938. 446pp. illus.

- - 5th ed. Leipzig, 1940. 446pp. illus.

- - 6th ed. Leipzig, 1942. 446pp. illus.

Ed. P.J. Vahl (1st to 4th eds.), A. Haenicke (5th & 6th eds); "under the direction of the former Governors of the German colonies". Heavily illustrated general overview of former German Africa.

Lusophone Africa

45
Meyer, H.H.J. **Das portugiesische Kolonialreich der Gegenwart.** Berlin, D. Reimer, 1918. 74pp.

Chaps. 1-6, pp. 10-53, give brief factual accounts of the African colonies.

46
Galvão, H. & Selvagem, C. **Império ultramarino Português (Monografia do Império).** Lisbon, Empresa Nacional, 1950. 4 vols. illus. maps.

Vol. 1, pp. 69-358, Cape Verde; pp. 359-402, Guinea; vol. 2, pp. 11-180, Guinea; pp. 181-416, São Tomé e Principe; vol. 3, Pp. 1-474, Angola; vol. 4, pp. 8-272, Mozambique (pp.273-440 cover Asian colonies). Encyclopedic work with sections for each country on its exploration and history, peoples, politics and administration, the economy, communications and finance.

47

Portugal. Agência-Geral do Ultramar. **Portugal overseas provinces, facts and figures.** Lisbon, 1965. 179pp.

African provinces are covered on pp. 5-112 with data on topography, climate, population, administration and history.

48

Abshire, D.M. & Samuels, M.A. *eds.* **Portuguese Africa: a handbook.** London, Pall Mall Press, 1969. xiii, 480pp. 25 maps.

Pt. 1, Background: topography, history, peoples; pt. 2, Government and society; pt. 3, Economy; pt. 4, Political and international issues. Review in *AHS* 4, 1971, 186-189 is critical of the emphasis on the interests of Portugal, with little attention to African activities.

49

Almeida, P.R. de. **Historia do colonialismo português em Africa: cronologia.** Lisbon, Estampa, 1978-79. 3 vols.

Vol. 1 covers 15th to 18th centuries; vol. 2, 19th century; vol. 3, 1900-1961. Extensive bibliography in vol. 3, pp.393-476. No index. For each year covers events in general, in Africa, and in each colony.

50

Nunez, B. **Dictionary of Portuguese-African civilization.** Oxford, Hans Zell, forthcoming 1993. 2 vols.

Vol. 1 includes some 3,000 terms relating to the Portuguese in Africa, and background data on individual states. Vol. 2, biographical articles.

See also 7.

> *For general works on former Belgian Africa see under* **CENTRAL AFRICA;** *for former Italian Africa see under* **NORTH-EAST AFRICA;** *for former Spanish Africa see under* **WEST AFRICA.**

Special subjects

Ethnography

51
Frobenius, L. & Wilm, L. von R. **Atlas Africanus: Belege zur Morphologie der Afrikanischen Kulturen.** Munich, C.H. Beck, 1921-1931. Pts 1-8, 39 col. maps. 37 x 27 cm.

Comp. at Forschungsinstitut für Kulturmorphologie. Each part issued in a portfolio. Pts. 4-8 have imprint Berlin, de Gruyter.

52
Baumann, H. *et al.* **Völkerkunde von Afrika: mit besonderer Berücksichtigung der kolonialen Aufgabe.** Essen, Essener Verlagsanstalt, 1940. xv, 665pp. 461 illus. 23 maps in pocket.

Pt. 1: "Völker und Kulturen Afrikas" by Baumann; pt. 2 : "Sprache und Erzebung" by D. Westermann. Part 3 by R. Thurnwald looks at various aspects of European contact. For the extensively revised **Die Völker Afrikas** (1975-79) *see* 60.

- - French trans. **Les peuples et les civilisations de l'Afrique, suivi de les langues et l'éducation.** Paris, Payot, 1948. (Bibliothèque scientifique). 605pp. (Reprint, Paris, 1967).

Trans. by L. Homburger. Omits part 3 of German original.

53
Bernatzik, H.A. *ed.* **Afrika: Handbuch der angewandten Völkerkunde.** Innsbruck, Schlüsselverlag, 1947. 2 vols. (xxi, 1429pp.)

Vol. 1, North Africa, Sudan, west Africa; vol. 2: Congo, eastern Africa, southern Africa. Each vol. has general introductory chapters, then country by country surveys (e.g. "Kenia", pp. 888-925, including 3pp. bibliography) with detailed accounts of each ethnic group. 33 contributors. Work in planning since 1937.

54
Ethnographic survey of Africa. London, International African Institute, 1950-1977. 60 vols.

French series pub. for IAI by Presses Universitaires, Paris as "Monographies ethnologiques africaines". The most extensive collection of ethnographic data on Africa, based on the literature and on field studies. A series of monographs on individual peoples, but with a largely consistent structure of presenting information on geographical distribution, size of population, social and political organization, religious beliefs, and economic and cultural activities. Issued in 7 sub-series: **North-Eastern Africa**, 3 vols (*see* 412); **East Central Africa**, 18 vols (*see* 527); **West Central Africa**, 4 vols (*see* 655); **Belgian Congo** later **Congo** later **Zaire**, 5 vols. (also published as "Monographies ethnographiques" by Musée Royale du Congo Belge/de l'Afrique Centrale; *see* 827); **Western Africa**, English series, 15 vols; French series, 10 vols (*see* 897); **Southern Africa**, 4 vols (*see* 1405); **Madagascar**, 1 vol. (*see* 1652).

55

Akademiia nauk, SSSR. Instituti Etnografii. **Narody Afriki**. Moscow, 1954. (Narody Mira; etnograficheski-ocherki). 731pp. illus.

- - rev. & updated German trans. **Die Völker Afrikas: ihre Vergangenheit und Gegenwart**. Berlin, VEB Deutscher Verlag der Wissenschaften, 1961. 2 vols.

Ed. D.A. Ol'derogge & I.I. Potekhin.

56

Froelich, J.-C. **Carte des populations de l'Afrique noire**. Paris, La documentation française, 1955. (Carte 71). col. map. 76 x 111 cm.
- - **Notice et catalogue**. Paris, 1955. xxx, 113pp.

Map at 1:5M. The accompanying text lists 1,540 tribal groups with map locations. Coverage is of west and central Africa.

57

American Museum of Natural History. **Tribal map of Negro Africa: Map N and Tribal Key**. New York, Man & Nature Publications, American Museum of Natural History, 1956. 56pp. folded map.

"Research and preparation" by C.B. Hunter. Lists 1,016 tribes giving for each a map location and a reference to one of the items in the bibliography of 49 items. No cross references from alternative names.

58

Johannesburg Public Library. **African native tribes**: rules for the classification of works on African ethnology in the Strange collection of Africana with an index of tribal names and their variants. Johannesburg, 1956. a-f, xxvii, 142pp.

Comprises a classification schedule, an expanded version of the Dewey Decimal Classification's class 572 which basically arranges tribes by geographical region, followed by an alphabetical index of names.

59

Murdock, J.P. **Africa: its peoples and their culture history.** New York, McGraw-Hill, 1959. xii, 456pp. illus. maps.

General introduction, followed by systematic surveys by cultural area. Index of c.5,000 names of ethnic groups, and folding map of culture areas. Reviews, *Africa*, 30, 1960, 277-278 and *JAH* 2, 1961, 299-309 where J.D. Fage ultimately compares the work unfavourably with Baumann (*see* 52) as the "standard handbook to the peoples of Africa".

60

Baumann, H. ed. **Die Völker Afrikas und ihre tradionellen Kulturen.** Wiesbaden, Franz Steiner, 1975-1979. 2 vols.

Vol. 1, 1975. ix, 815pp. 41 maps, 7 diagrs., covers 8 "cultural provinces" in southern Africa, together with a general introduction; vol. 2, 1979. ix, 734pp. 25 maps, covers 14 "cultural provinces" in east, west and north Africa. An extensively revised version of **Völkerkunde von Afrika** (*see* 52). Baumann himself had died in 1972. D. McCall in a review in *IJAHS*, 13, 1980, 753-757 concludes that "the only thing in English that can be compared is the **Ethnographic survey of Africa**" (*see* 54) but that this had the disadvantage of being a series of individual local volumes appearing over a number of years.

61

Hrbek, I. 'A list of African ethonyms', pp. 141-186 *in* **African ethonyms & toponyms**: report and papers of the meeting of experts organized by Unesco, Paris, 3-7 July, 1978. Paris, Unesco, 1984. (General History of Africa: studies and documents, 6).

Over 1,500 names of African peoples, giving alternative forms, relationships, and geographical location.

62

Knappert, J. **The Aquarian guide to African mythology**. Wellingborough, Aquarian Press, 1990. 272pp. illus.

"This modest guide ... does not pretend to give more than an anthology of myths and mythological figures" (preface). Alphabetically arranged, including general entries for e.g. "astrology", "gods", "sin", "sorcery" and specific entries for peoples, animals and objects.

See also 19

History

63

Freeman-Grenville, G.S.P. **Chronology of African history**. London, Oxford University Press, 1973. xxii, 312pp.

Consists of columns for different regions of Africa (together with one for "other countries") listing events year by year. Four principal sections, 1300 B.C.-600 A.D.; 600-1300; 1300-1800; 1800 to date, with headings for regions varying in each section. Reviews in *JAH* 15, 1974, 489-490; *GJ* 140, 1974, 497.

64

Mitchell, B.R. **International historical statistics: Africa and Asia**. London, Macmillan/New York, New York University Press, 1982. xx, 761pp.

Arranged in 11 major sections: climate, population, labour force, agriculture, industry, external trade, transport and communications, finance, prices, education, and national accounts. Lists major statistical series for each country with other sources footnoted under appropriate tables. Reviews in *IJAHS* 17, 1984, 127 and in *JAH* 24, 1983, 411-413 which praises the wide range of data assembled and the care taken to help users in assessing their reliability and comparability; "a mine of well-ordered information".

For historical atlases see 356-395.

Language

65

Cust, R.N. **A sketch of the modern languages of Africa**. London, Trübner, 1883. (Trübner's Oriental series). 2 vols. illus. maps in pocket.

First major study in English of African languages, following the classification of F.W. Müller of Vienna. Includes distribution map, list of 438 languages and 151 dialects.

66
Handbook of African languages. London, Oxford University Press for International African Institute, 1952-1959. 4 vols.

Pt. 1.'La langue berbère', by A.Bassett. 1952. v, 72pp; pt. 2, 'Languages of West Africa' by D. Westermann & M.A. Bryan. 1952. 215pp. (*see* 898); pt. 3, 'The non-Bantu languages of North Eastern Africa' by A.N. Tucker & M.A. Bryan. 1956. xvi, 228pp. (*see* 415); pt. 4, 'The Bantu languages of Africa' by M.A. Bryan. 1959. xi, 170pp. Although a number of additional studies are listed in bibliographies, library catalogues, and the IAI's own lists of publications as parts of the "Handbook", the 4 volumes above in fact represent the Institute's original concept of a four volume general survey covering all the languages of Africa, recording language groups, and estimates of numbers of speakers and their topographical distribution (*see* foreword by D. Forde, Director of the IAI, to pt. 4 *above*). Among the various other volumes issued by the Institute "in connection with the **Handbook**" note especially **The classification of the Bantu languages** by M. Guthrie. 1948. 91pp, a standard work of one school of thought on African language classification. A slightly modified outline appears as "Key list of Bantu languages", in vol. 2, pp. 11-15 of M. Guthrie **Comparative Bantu**, Farnborough, Gregg, 1970.

67
Greenberg, J.H. 'The languages of Africa', *International journal of American linguistics* 29(1) part 2, 1963, 1-171.

- - 2nd ed. Bloomington, IN, Indiana University, 1966. 180pp.

- - 3rd ed. Bloomington, IN, 1970. (Research Center for the Language Sciences, 25). 180pp. 5 maps.

"A complete genetic classification of the languages of Africa" (p. 1). Lists 730 languages classified into Niger-Congo, Afroasiatic, Khoisan, Chari-Nile, Nilo-Saharan and Niger-Kordofanian groups. Alphabetical index of languages, pp. 163-171. Remains one of the most widely followed systems of arranging African languages. Lengthy reviews in *Word*, 19, 1963, 407-417; *African language studies* 7, 1966, 160-170. Critical review of 1st ed. by M. Guthrie, *JAH* 5, 1964, 135-136 which "looks in vain for an admission that in respect to most of the problems discussed, more than one conclusion might be drawn".

68

Voegelin, C.F. & F.M. 'Languages of the world: Africa, fasciscle one', *Anthropological linguistics* 6(5) 1964, 1-339.

A general discussion of the problems of African language classification, followed by a structured list arranging individual languages under 47 families and five main groups (Niger-Congo, Nilo-Saharan, Nilo-Hamitic, Afro-Asiatic, Khoisan). Maps and detailed notes on topographic distribution and numbers of speakers. Data later revised and incorporated into the authors' **Classification and index of the world's languages**. New York, Elsevier, 1977, where however all languages and language groups are arranged alphabetically rather than by continent.

69

Welmers, W.E. 'Checklist of African language and dialect names', *Current trends in linguistics* 7, 1971, 759-900.

Useful quick-reference list.

70

Dalby, D. **Language map of Africa and the adjacent islands**. Provisional ed. London, International African Institute, 1977. 63pp.

Map at 1:5M on 4 sheets, with inset enlargements. Text includes discussion of principles of compilation, and a checklist of all languages shown on the map in both a structured and an alphabetical sequence.

71

Fivaz, D. & Scott, P.E. **African languages: a genetic and decimalised classification for bibliographic and general reference**. Boston, MA, G.K. Hall, 1977. xxxiv, 332pp.

A compilation by a linguist (Fivaz) and a librarian (Scott). "In general terms ... we have followed the most widely accepted genetic framework for Africa, that of Joseph H. Greenberg" (preface; *see* 67). Includes a classified schedule (pp. 3-82) of languages according to their perceived relationships; alphabetical list of preferred names for languages and dialects (pp. 83-256) with references from all traced alternative names and spellings; list of sources (pp. 257-304); language family charts and distribution maps (pp. 305-321). Gives comparative tables of the basic approach to classifying African languages offered by Greenberg (*see* 67) and the Bliss, Library of Congress, Universal Decimal Classification and Dewey classification schemes.

72

Jungraithmayr, H. & Moehlig, W.J.G. *eds.* **Lexikon der Afrikanistik: afrikanische Sprachen und ihre Erforschung.** Berlin, Reimer, 1983. 351pp.

Entries for language terms and names of languages, with maps.

73

Unesco. Regional Bureau for Education in Africa. **Les langues communautaires africaines et leur utilisation dans l'enseignement et l'alphabétisation: une enquête régionale.** Dakar, [1984]. 94pp.

Statistical data on the 23 most widely spoken African languages. Includes list of relevant research centres and journals.

74

Mann, M. & Dalby, D. **A thesaurus of African languages:** a classified and annotated inventory of the spoken languages of Africa, with an appendix on their written reproduction. Oxford, Hans Zell for International African Institute, 1988. 336pp.

Lists 2,550 languages classified into 315 sets and sub-sets. Follows system of Dalby, **Language map of Africa** (*see* 70). Sees many features of the classifications of Greenberg (*see* 67) and Fivaz and Scott (*see* 71) as "open to debate or already discredited" (preface). Notes language use in education and the media in each African country. Detailed bibliography, and index of 12,000 entries. Reproduces names of each language in phonetic script, the "African reference alphabet" as agreed at the Unesco Meeting of Experts on the Transcription and Harmonization of African Languages, Niamey, 17-21 July, 1978 (*see* **Final report.** Paris, Unesco, 1978). Typeset entirely in lower-case. The transcription and typesetting are among aspects singled out for comment in long reviews in *IJAHS* 21, 1988, 747-750 and *Journal of African languages & linguistics* 11, 1989, 175-182.

75

Bendor-Samuel, J. & Hartell, R.L. **A classification and description of Africa's largest language family.** Lanham, MD, University Press of America, 1989. 518pp.

The Niger-Congo family.

See also 409.

Etymology

76

Dalgish, G.M. **A dictionary of Africanisms: contributions of sub-Saharan Africa to the English language**. Westport, CT, Greenwood Press, 1982. 203pp.

"Terms from African languages that have entered into the general vocabulary of the English-speaking world" (preface). Long critical review in *Journal of African languages & linguistics* 8, 1986, 210-218.

Law

77

Allott, A.N. *ed.* **Judicial and legal systems in Africa**. London, Butterworth, 1962. (African law series, 4). xiii, 226pp.

Covers British territories (excluding South Africa) and Liberia. Sections for west, east and central Africa and the High Commission territories. For each country lists types of court, with outline of their constitution and powers.

78

Encyclopédie juridique de l'Afrique. Abidjan/Dakar/Lomé, Les Nouvelles éditions africains, 1982. 10 vols.

Vol. 1, "L'État et le droit"; vol. 2, "Droit international et relations internationales"; vol. 3, "Systèmes budgétaires etc."; vol. 4, "Organisations judicaires"; vol. 5, "Droit des biens"; vol. 6, "Droit des personnes"; vol. 7, "Droit des entreprises"; vol. 8, "Droit des relations professionelles"; vol. 9, "Droit des contrats"; vol. 10, "Droit pénal etc.; index thématique". A massive compilation of comparative data on African law and legal systems with over 100 French and African contributors.

79

Modern legal systems cyclopedia. Vol. 6: Africa. Buffalo, NY, William S. Hein, 1985. loose-leaf.

- - 2nd ed. Buffalo, NY, 1990.

Coverage in 2nd ed. is expanded to 2 vols; 6 & 6a, with material loose-leaf in folders. Intended for professional and academic use. Arranged alphabetically by country: for each provides an introductory section on geography, the economy and the peoples, followed by sections on the constitution, education and the legal profession. Includes an entry for Bophutatswana, one for the remainder of the "homelands" treated together, and an entry for Diego Garcia.

Literature

80
Zell, H.M. & Silver, H. **A reader's guide to African literature**. London, Heinemann, 1971. xxi, 218pp.

Includes biographies (pp. 113-199) of 51 authors.

- - 2nd ed. **A new reader's guide to African literature**. London, Heinemann, 1983. xvi, 553pp.

Comp. H.M. Zell, C. Bundy & V. Coulon. In addition to bibliographical sections, includes biographies (pp. 343-506) of 95 authors, 50 new to the 2nd ed. Both editions include lists of booksellers and publishers and 2nd ed. also lists libraries with Africana collections.

81
Jahn, J. *et al.* **Who's who in African literature: biographies, works, commentaries**. Tübingen, Horst Erdman, 1972. 412pp.

Comp. J. Jahn, U. Schild & A. Nordmann. Over 400 entries for Sub-Saharan African writers.

82
Herdeck, D.E. **African authors: a companion to Black African writing. Vol. 1**. Washington, DC, Black Orpheus Press, 1973.

No more published. Intended originally to be supplemented at two-yearly intervals with new eds. "about every six years" (preface). Entries for 594 authors, writing in 37 vernacular and European languages. Indexes by genre, date, country, language, gender. Also lists of relevant publishers, journals and booksellers and a bibliography.

83
Skurjat, E. **Afryka w twórezósci jej pisorgy**. Warsaw, University of Warsaw, 1973. (Kura szkolenia ekspertów-Studium Afrykanistygne Uniwersytetu Warszawskiego, 14). 133pp.

Bio-bibliography of African authors.

84

Page, J.A. & Jae Min Roh. **Selected Black American, African and Caribbean authors: a bio-bibliography.** Littleton, CO, Libraries Unlimited, 1985. xiii, 388pp.

Earlier version pub. as **Selected black American authors.** Boston, MA, G.K. Hall, 1977. Expanded version includes 48 African authors out of total 632, a number of them political (Kenyatta, Luthuli, Nkrumah).

85

African literatures in the twentieth century: a guide. New York, Ungar, 1986. 245pp.

General ed. L.S. Klein. Reprints articles on African countries and individual writers originally published in **Encyclopedia of world literature in the twentieth century** rev. ed. New York, Ungar, 1984. 5 vols. Entries for 38 national literatures and 42 individual authors.

86

Rouch, A. & Clavreuil, G. **Littératures nationales d'écriture française: Afrique noire, caraïbes, océan indien.** Paris, Bordas, 1986. 512pp.

By country. Each entry has a brief note on the historical and political background, an "histoire littéraire" and a selection of biographical entries. 17 African countries have 126 biographies.

Onomastics

Bibliography

87

Beers, H.D. 'African names and naming practices: a selected list of references in English', **Library of Congress information bulletin** 36, 25 March 1977, 206-207.

Lists of names

88

Chuks-Orji, O. **Names from Africa: their origin, meaning and pronunciation.** Chicago, IL, Johnson Publishing Co., 1972. 91pp.

Separate lists of male and female African personal names identifying their language and country of origin, and their meaning.

89

Madubuike, I. **A handbook of African names**. Washington, DC, Three
Continents Press, 1976. v, 233pp.

General discussion of names, followed by sections on the names given by
particular peoples. Emphasis on Nigerian names (e.g. Igbo, 48pp.).

Politics

90

Hertslet, *Sir* E. **The map of Africa by treaty**. London, HMSO, 1894. 2 vols.

- - 2nd ed. London, 1896. 3 vols.

- - 3rd ed. rev. & completed to the end of 1908 by R.W. Bryant & H.L.
Sherwood. London, 1909. 3 vols. (1,404pp.) & portfolio of maps. (Reprinted,
London, Frank Cass, 1967).

In 3rd ed. vol. 1 contains chronological list of relevant treaties, 1778 to 1908,
followed by discussion of the British possessions in Africa country by
country; vols. 2 & 3 cover relations between Britain and other foreign
countries active in Africa. Includes lists of treaties, conventions, proclamations
and other relevant documents, quotes of salient sections and references to
maps showing boundary decisions. Numerous maps in text and 44 maps in
accompanying portfolio. A major source for political history of the early
colonial period.

91

Bustin, E. **Guide des partis politiques africains: inventaire de 300 partis
recenses dans 45 pays africains**. Léopoldville, Éditions CRISP-IPC, 1962. 80pp.

First published in *Études congolaises* 7, 1962. Brief descriptions of history and
policies of each party. Country of origin index.

92

Decraene, P. **Tableau des partis politiques de l'Afrique au sud du Sahara**.
Paris, Fondation nationale des sciences politiques, Centre d'étude des relations
internationales, 1963. (Série C: recherches, 8). 137pp.

Includes country by country list of parties with information on their history,
objectives, and leaders.

93

Politisches Lexikon Schwarzafrika. Munich, C.H. Beck, 1978. (Beck'sche schwarze Reihe, 166). 540pp.

- - 2nd ed. **Politisches Lexikon Afrika.** Munich, 1985. (Beck'sche schwarze Reihe, 281). 510pp.

- - 3rd ed. Munich, 1987. (Beck'sche Reihe, 810). 530pp.

- - 4th ed. Munich, 1988. (Beck'sche Reihe, 810). 530pp.

Ed. R. Hofmeier & M.Schönborn (with J.M. Wérobèl-La Rochelle for 1st ed.). Covers Africa south of the Sahara. 1st ed. omits South Africa and includes Sudan. Subsequent eds. include South Africa and omit Sudan (covered in the publisher's companion volume **Politisches Lexikon Nahost**). 2nd and subsequent eds. include a chapter on African international organizations. Detailed and compact country accounts by individual authors with statistics.

94

Brownlie, I. **African boundaries: a legal and diplomatic encyclopedia.** London, C. Hurst for Royal Institute of International Affairs, 1979. xxxvi, 1355pp. maps.

A study of 105 separate boundary alignments involving 48 African states. For each, provides an historical account of its development, and detailed documentation of the currently agreed location, often reprinting the text of the appropriate documents. Each boundary is shown on a sketch-map.

95

Cook, C. & Killingray, D. **African political facts since 1945.** London, Macmillan, 1983. vii, 263pp.

- - 2nd ed. London, 1991. vii, 280pp.

Includes a chronology of main events, lists of governors, heads of state, and major ministerial appointments, lists of parliaments, political parties, trade unions, major conflicts and coups, demographic statistics, basic economic statistics, biographies (c. 150 figures). Very few sources quoted. 2nd ed. brings coverage up to the independence of Namibia in 1990. Similar but much briefer coverage of Commonwealth African countries with a wider time span, is given in the companion vol., **Commonwealth political facts, 1900-1977,** comp. C. Cook and J. Paxton. London, Macmillan, 1979.

96

Phillips, C.S. **The African political dictionary**. Santa Barbara, CA, & Oxford, Clio Press, 1984. (Clio Dictionaries in Political Science). xxviii, 245pp. maps.

Compiled originally for U.S. political science students. Arranged in broad sections (e.g. "Land and people", "Governmental institutions & processes") with discursive alphabetically arranged entries in each section. Tables with comparative data. Country and general indexes.

97

Ray, D.I. **Dictionary of the African Left: parties, movements and groups**. Aldershot, Dartmouth Publishing Company, 1989. vi, 273pp.

Introduction followed by "Chronology of Left states in Africa 1952-1988" and "Dictionary of the Left parties, movements and groups". Lists almost 300 parties with dates of activity, details of organization, membership, statutes, publications, history and leadership. Indexes by acronym and by country.

98

Shavit, D. **The United States in Africa: a historical dictionary**. New York, Greenwood Press, 1989. xxii, 298pp.

"Information about the persons, institutions and events that affected the relations between the U.S. and Africa, persons who have actually been in Africa ... organizations ... that functioned in Africa itself and events that occurred in that area" (preface). Brief entries (some four to a page). Includes references to sources. Index of individuals by profession and occupation. Review, *IJAHS*, 23, 1990, 733.

Lists of office holders

99

Henige, D. **Colonial governors from the fifteenth century to the present: a comprehensive list**. Madison, WI, University of Wisconsin Press, 1970. 461pp.

Lists of governors or other colonial administrators arranged by empire or "imperial system" then by colony. Historical notes on each empire, each colonial unit, and on sources used. Index of some 10,000 personal names. 81 out of the 412 listings provided refer to Africa. An essential source. Review, *AHS* 6, 1973, 128-130.

100

Sainty, J.C. **Colonial Office officials**. London, University of London, Institute of Historical Research, 1976. (Office-holders in modern Britain, 6). x, 52pp.

"Officials of the Secretary of State for War, 1794-1801, of the Secretary of State for War and Colonies, 1801-1854 and of the Secretary of State for Colonies, 1854-1870". 25 listings ranging from Secretaries of State down to Assistant Junior Clerks.

101
Bidwell, R.L. **Guide to African ministers**. London, Rex Collings, 1978. (Bidwell's guide to government ministers, 4). 79pp.

Basically covers the period post 1st Jan. 1950. Information on Ethiopia and Liberia pre-1950 is given in a note at the back of the vol. South Africa and Southern Rhodesia pre-1950 are covered in the companion **Bidwell's guide to government ministers. vol. 3: the British Empire and successor states, 1900-1974**, London, Cass, 1974. (The coverage of Gambia, Ghana, Kenya, Nigeria, Sierra Leone, Tanzania & Uganda in the 1974 volume is superseded by the present work, as is the coverage of the Sudan in **vol. 2: the Arab World**, London, 1973). States are arranged in eight groupings largely corresponding to colonial empires; for each state there is a chronological list (with actual day of appointment) of heads of state, prime ministers, and ministers for foreign affairs, defence, internal affairs and finance or their equivalents. No index of names.

102
Truhart, P. **Regents of nations: systematic chronology of states and their political representatives in past & present: a biographical reference book. Part 1: Africa/America**. Munich, Saur, 1984. xxx, 980pp.

Africa, pp. 1-465. Attempts extensive coverage of "all states and all state-like communities ... going back to the dawn of history" (preface). Cites some 250 sources for the data on Africa. For e.g. Ghana, contains lists for 32 African kingdoms, Dutch governors, Danish governors, governors of the British Company of Merchants Trading to Africa, governors of the Gold Coast, and heads of state, chiefs of government & foreign ministers since independence.

103
Stewart, J.D. **African states & rulers: an encyclopedia of native, colonial & independent states & rulers, past & present**. Jefferson, NC, McFarland, 1989. xx, 395pp.

Entries for 1139 separate administrative units with references to earlier, later, and related titles. Detailed cross references are provided from the names of contemporary political states (e.g. "Nigeria" refers to 96 separate relevant headings from Abeokuta to Zazzau). List of names and dates of office of principal officials (kings, governors, presidents, prime ministers etc.) are provided for each entry. Index of 10,500 personal names. "Not recommended" by "Africana reference works", *ABPR* 16, 1990, 89 but seen, with some reservations, as useful by *JAH* 31, 1990, 339.

See also 301, 302.

YEARBOOKS

General

104

Recueil des sociétés coloniales et maritimes. Brussels, Société d'études coloniales de Belgique, 1900-1901. Annual. 2 vols.

Basically concerned with listing financial and commercial organizations but includes a few colonial societies and learned institutions. Emphasis on Belgium and France and their colonies, with some coverage of Germany, U.K. and Portugal.

105

African annual & trader's yearbook. London, "African Commerce", 1901. 144pp.

"No more published" (BL catalogue). Covers some 42 African states with summarised statistics, a directory of mining firms, and miscellaneous commercial information.

106

South African advertising annual & press guide. Cape Town, National Publishing Co. Ltd., 1949- . Annual.

Title varies: **African press & advertising annual** (1950-1954/55); **Advertising & press annual of Africa** (1956-). Includes periodicals and newspapers arranged alphabetically by country, commercial radio and television stations, cinemas, and advertising agencies. Countries covered by the 1970s were Angola, Kenya, Malawi, South Africa, Tanzania, Uganda, Zimbabwe (with all categories of data); Burundi, Congo, Gabon, Ghana, Lesotho, Madagascar, Mauritius, Mozambique, Namibia, Nigeria, Réunion, St. Helena, Seychelles, Swaziland, Zaire, Zambia (basically press only).

107

Commercial directory of Africa, 1950/51. Nairobi, International Marketing Service Corporation, 1950. xxxv, 279pp.

"Believed to be the first commercial directory to cover Africa as a whole" (preface). Arranged under 487 headings for professions and industries.

108

Owen's African and Middle East commerce and travel and international

register 1953/54 [etc.]. London, Owen's Commerce and Travel (*later* Oxford, Owen's Worldwide Trade), 1953- . Annual.

Title varies: **Owens's trade directory and business travel guide: Middle East & Africa/Owen's business directory & travel guide/Owen's world trade Africa & Asia business directory/Owen's Africa business directory** (from 34th ed, 1988). Coverage of Africa south of the Sahara varies: 1971 ed. includes Angola, Cameroon, Central African Republic, Côte d'Ivoire, Dahomey, Djibouti, Ethiopia, Gabon, Gambia, Ghana, Kenya, Liberia, Malawi, Mauritania, Mauritius, Mozambique, Nigeria, Rhodesia, Senegal, Sierra Leone, Somalia, Sudan, Tanzania, Togo, Uganda, Zambia; 1985 ed. covers Cameroon, Côte d'Ivoire, Ethiopia, Gabon, Kenya, Malawi, Nigeria, Senegal, Seychelles, Somalia, Sudan, Tanzania, Togo. Includes general data on geography, population, communications, industry plus classified commercial directories.

109
Africa annual. London, Foreign Correspondents Ltd., 1958-1968. Annual (irreg.) 9 issues.

Ed. E.M. Crossley. Basic information with an emphasis on agriculture, mining, industry and trade. 140/160pp per issue. Up to 1966 arranged alphabetically by country, from 1967 arranged first by region.

110
Middle East and North Africa. London, Europa Publications, 11th ed. 1964- . Annual.

Commenced publication 1948 as **The Middle East**. Initial coverage of the Asian Middle East was extended to cover North Africa in 1964, including Chad, Ethiopia, French Somaliland, Mali, Mauritania, Niger, Somalia, Sudan. From 1971, all these countries are also covered by the same publisher's **Africa south of the Sahara** (*see* 115).

111
Année africaine 1963 [etc.]. Paris, Pedone, 1965- . Annual.

A joint compilation by CHEAM (Centre des hautes études administratives sur l'Afrique et l'Asie moderne), CERI (Centre d'étude des relations internationales de la Fondation des sciences politiques) and CEAN (Centre d'étude d'Afrique noire de l'Université de Bordeaux). Until issue for 1976 contains sections on Africa and the world, on inter-African relations and country by country surveys of all Africa south of the Sahara, with a narrative overview followed by a detailed chronology of events of the year. After 1976 changes format to emphasize general feature articles, and is no longer of the same value for quick reference purposes.

112
L'année politique africaine. Dakar, Société africaine d'édition, 1966-1979. Annual. 14 issues.

Issued in cyclostyled format, 1966-1970; from 1971 issued as Supplément to *Revue française d'études politiques africaines*. Country by country surveys for all Africa within five regions, covering major political events of the previous year. Merged in **L'année politique et économique Africaine** (*see* 122).

113
Afrique 1968 [-1982]. Paris, "Jeune Afrique", 1968-1982. Annual.

Pub. as "numéros spécial" of *Jeune Afrique*. Title and coverage vary. **Afrique 1968-Afrique '71/72**: thematic surveys, general articles, country surveys. **Afrique '73** contains no country surveys. **Afrique et Moyen-Orient '75-1976/77** expands coverage to include Middle East, and restores country surveys. **Annuaire de l'Afrique et du Moyen-Orient 1979; Annuaire ... 1980: les armées et la défence; Annuaire ... 1981/82: économie et développement**. Succeeded by **L'annuaire "Jeune afrique"** from 1991 (*see* 124).

- - English language ed. **Africa 1968-[1974/5]**. New York, Africana Publishing, 1969-1970. 6 issues.

Issues for 1968, 1969/70, 1971, 1972, 1973, 1974/75.

114
Africa contemporary record: annual survey & documents, 1968/69 [etc.]. New York, Holmes & Meier [etc.], 1969- . Annual.

Ed. C. Legum and J. Drysdale (to 1988), M. Doro (from 1989). Detailed reviews of the previous year's political, economic & social developments in each country, including statistics; also prints texts of significant documents issued during the year by international and regional organizations such as the UN and OAU. Review of vol. 6, 1973/74, *ASA review of books* 2, 1976, 8-9 is critical of variation in nature of coverage from year to year, and of the lack of good maps and historical background. Seen as "single best annual reference work on African affairs", (*IJAHS* 11, 1978, 728-730 on vol. 9, 1976/77) and as a marriage of "the highest standards of both scholarship and journalism" (*JAH* 21, 1980, 139 on vol. 10, 1977/78).

115
Africa south of the Sahara. London, Europa Publications, 1971-. Annual.

"Background to the continent" includes general articles, list of African regional organizations, who's who. Country by country surveys include background essays, economic, demographic and statistical data, directories of political cultural and commercial institutions. The most detailed continuing work of its kind.

116
Africa annual review, 1972 [-1974/75]. London, "Africa journal", 1972-1974. 3 issues.

Ed. R. Uwechue. General articles on economics and industry, followed by a country by country survey. Included loose wall map of Africa at 1:10M.

117
Almanach africain. Paris, Agence de coopération culturelle et technique, 1974- . Irreg. (Issue 6, 1984).

A general survey of African history, economics, communications, social services, literature, and religion.

118
Africa freedom annual. Sandton, S.A., Southern African Freedom Foundation, 1977- . Annual.

Ed. F.R. Metrowich. Includes "Africa in brief" with summary details of each country's politics, chronology of events during preceding year, and articles on themes (e.g. "Soviet involvement in Africa").

119
Africa guide. Saffron Walden, World of Information, 1977- . Annual.

15th ed. 1991. Title varies : **Africa review** (1985-). Economic and business survey covering all Africa, including North Africa. General articles, followed by country surveys with map, survey of recent events, "key facts", business directory, tourist information.

120 (*also entered at 298*)
Africa yearbook and who's who. London, "Africa journal", 1977. xlvii, 1364pp. No more published.

Ed. R. Uwechue. Comprises: diary of important events, 1975 & 1976; pt. 1, general: topography, peoples, economy etc.; pt. 2, regional organizations; pt. 3 (pp. 207-932) country by country surveys; pt. 4, Africa and international organizations; pt. 5, sport; pt. 6, who's who. A greatly expanded successor to 116 and one of the most detailed works of its kind. Although no further eds. followed, it formed the model for the "Know Africa series" from the same publishers, whose first editions were pub. in 1981 (*see* **Africa today, 25; Africa who's who,** 303; **Makers of modern Africa,** 304).

121
New African yearbook. London, IC Magazines Ltd., 1978- . Annual (irreg.)

1st ed. 1978, covers all Africa; 2nd to 4th eds. 1979 to 1981/82, cover south of the Sahara only. 5th & 6th eds. each issued in 2 volumes: **West and Central Africa** (1983/84, 1985/86), **East and Southern Africa** (1984/85, 1986/87). 7th ed., 1987/88 reverts to covering all countries south of the Sahara. 8th ed., 1991/92. Includes basic facts and statistics for each country.

122
L'année politique et économique africaine. Dakar, Société africaine d'édition, 1981-1985. Annual.

A merger of the former **Année politique africaine** (*see* 112) and **Économie africaine** (*see* 185). Economic and political data for the preceding year for 26 African states (Anglophone and Francophone west Africa and Francophone central Africa only).

123
Afrika Jahrbuch 1988 [etc.]: Politik, Wirtschaft und Gesellschaft in Afrika südlich der Sahara. Opladen, Institut für Afrika-Kunde, Hamburg, 1989- Annual.

General articles, chronology of major events, country by country survey.

124
L'annuaire "Jeune afrique" 1991 [etc.]: rapport annuel sur l'état de l'Afrique. Paris, "Jeune afrique", 1991- . Annual.

Initiated to mark 30th anniversary of the Groupe *Jeune Afrique*. Resumes the coverage previously provided by the same publishers in **Afrique 1968 [-1982]** *see* 113. Also available on disk. Provides "informations historiques, politiques, sociales, économiques et financières les plus récentes" with general sections, followed by country by country surveys of all 52 African countries.

Anglophone Africa

125

Colonial year book for the year 1890 [-1892]. London, Sampson Low, 1890-1892. 3 issues.

Ed. A.J.R. Trendall. Data "entirely derived from official sources" for each English colony, arranged alphabetically (e.g. "Gold Coast", 12pp. covering history, topography, and resources with summary statistics).

Francophone Africa

126

L'année coloniale, 1899 [-1902/03]. Paris, Charles Tallandier, 1899-1902. 4 issues.

Pub. under the direction of C. Mourey, Head of the Service de la statistique, l'Office colonial. Founded to simplify "la recherche d'un fait, d'un chiffre, d'un acte administratif". Pt. 1 in each issue provides articles on activities of the preceding year; pt. 2 gives a colony by colony account, with civil list, texts of legislation, statistics and maps; pt. 3, "Bibliographie coloniale de l'année ...".

127

Annuaire des entreprises d'outre-mer, des organismes officiels et professionnels d'outre-mer, etc. Paris, R. Moreux, 1912- . Annual. (69th ed., 1978).

Cover title: **Annuaire des entreprises et organismes d'outre-mer.** Includes 20 Francophone countries south of the Sahara. Administrative and commercial directories for each country, together with information on general commercial organizations of Francophone Africa.

128

France d'outre-mer. Paris, Société Didot-Bottin, 1946- . Annual.

Title varies: **Bottin de l'Union français d'états associés et térritoires d'outre-mer** (1953-56); **Bottin d'Afrique du nord et des térritoires d'outre-mer** (1959); **Bottin d'outre-mer** (1960-) Covers 21 countries (excluding Burundi, Mauritius, Rwanda, Seychelles, Zaire). Administrative and commercial directories for principal towns in each country. Street plans of Abidjan, Brazzaville, Dakar, Antananarivo.

129
Annuaire Noria: Afrique noire: guide économique. Limoges, 1950-1964.

Title varies: **Annuaire Noria: Afrique noire et océan indien** (1963-64) following the incorporation of the vol. for **Océan Indien** (*see* 129) previously published separately. Merged with **Annuaire économique des états d'Afrique noire** from 1965 (*see* 131).

130
L'Afrique d'expression française et Madagascar. Paris, Éditions France d'outremer, 1961- . Annual.

Issued as special numbers of the monthly *Europe d'outremer*. Preceded by a single vol. **Communauté zone franc d'Afrique et Marché commun** (1959) produced by the same publishers and giving identical coverage, but not counted by them in issue numbering. Country by country surveys with political, economic and statistical information. Includes Mauritius and Seychelles.

131
Annuaire économique des états d'Afrique noire. Paris, Ediafric-La documentation africaine [etc.], 1962- . Annual.

Title varies: **Sociétés et représentations industrielles et commerciales: Afrique noire, Madagascar** (1963); **Sociétés et fournisseurs d'Afrique noire et Madagascar** (1964); from 1965 amalgamated with **Annuaire Noria** (*see* 129) as **Sociétés et fournisseurs ... : guide économique Noria** (1965-) and adopted issue numbering of the earlier title. Later **France Afrique**, Paris, CIC Publications. Excludes Djibouti, Réunion. Commercial directory. 38th ed., 1989, 1240pp. has three sections for firms based in France, Africa south of the Sahara and North Africa.

132
La politique africaine en 1968 [etc.]. Paris, Ediafric-La documentation africaine, 1968-1969. 2 issues.

Special issues of *Bulletin de l'Afrique noire*. Covers 13 states of Francophone west and central Africa. Lists government officials, and political events of the year.

133
Répertoire de l'administration africaine. Paris, Ediafric-La documentation africaine, 1969- .

Special issues of *Bulletin de l'Afrique noire*. Covers Francophone west and central Africa. Lists chief political and civil service personnel.

134

Afrique noire politique et économique. Paris, Ediafric-La documentation africaine, 1977- . Annual. (5th issue 1983)

Issued as special numbers of *Bulletin de l'Afrique noire*. Covers 13 Francophone countries of west and central Africa in standardised format: politics, economics, agriculture, industry, finance communications. Essentially a continuation of **La politique africaine ...** (*see* 132).

135

Africascope: guide économique de la francophonie. Paris, Éditions Mermon, 1984- . Annual. (7th ed. 1989/90).

Sub-title varies: **Africascope: guide économique des pays francophones.** Available on MINITEL. Includes organizations in Francophone Europe (Belgium, France etc.) with African interests. Sections for west Africa, central Africa, and the Indian Ocean: within each, country by country surveys with standardised accounts of the economy, resources, and communications, and a commercial directory.

Former German Africa

136

Koloniales Jahrbuch: Beiträge und Mitteilungen aus dem Gebiete der Kolonialwissenschaft und Kolonialpraxis, 1888 [-1898]. Berlin, Deutsche Kolonial-Verlag, 1889-1899. Annual. 11 issues.

Ed. G. Meinecke.

137

Deutscher Kolonial-Kalendar. Leipzig, Klinkhardt/Berlin, Deutscher Kolonial-Verlag, 1889-1914. Annual.

Title varies: **... und Statistisches Handbuch** (1899-1915). Ed. G. Meinecke.

138

Die Entwicklung unserer Kolonien: sechs Denkschriften. Berlin, Mittler, 1892. 80pp.

Annual report for 1891, first part of 1892.

continued by:

Denkschriften betreffend I. Deutsch-Ostafrika; II. Kamerun [etc.] Berlin, Mittler, 1893-94.

Pub. as supplements to *Deutsches Kolonialblatt*, 4-5, 1893-1894. Annual reports for 1892-93/94.

continued by:

Jahresbericht über die Entwicklung unserer Kolonien 1894/95 [-1912/13]. Berlin, Mittler, 1896-1914.

Title varies : **Jahresberichte über die Entwicklung der deutschen Schutzgebiete** (1896/97-1907/08; pub. as supplements to *Deutsches Kolonialblatt*, 7-20, 1896-1909).

continued by:

Denkschrift über die Entwicklung der Schutzgebiete in Afrika und der Südsee im Jahre 1908/09. Berlin, Heymann, 1910.

continued by:

Die deutschen Schutzgebiete in Afrika und der Südsee: amtliche Jahresberichte, 1909/10 [-1912/13]. Berlin, Mittler, 1911-14.

139
Deutsches Kolonial-Handbuch. Berlin, Paetel, 1896-1913. Annual (irreg.) 13 issues.

Ed. R. Fitzner. Compilation of commercial and other information. Lists all government and mission stations with lists of European residents. Includes statistics. Sections for German East Africa also issued separately as **Adressbuch für Deutsch-Ostafrika.**

140
Deutsches Kolonial-Adressbuch. Berlin, Kolonial-Wirstchaftliches Komitee [etc.], 1897-1914, 1936.

Title varies: **Kolonial-Handels-Adressbuch** (1898-1915). Published as supplementary vols. to the *Deutsches Kolonialblatt* and contained the official reports of the German Colonial Office to the Reichstag on each colony with detailed statistics, lists of settlers, officials and businessmen.

141

Von der Heydt's Kolonial-Handbuch: Jahrbuch der deutschen Kolonial-und Übersee-Unternehmungen. Berlin, Verlag für Börsen-und Finanzliteratur, 1907-1914. Annual. 8 issues.

Commercial directory of German firms operating in the colonies.

142

Jahrbuch über die deutschen Kolonien. Essen, G.D. Baedeker, 1908-1914. Annual. 7 vols.

Ed. K. Schneider. Basically a series of individual articles on particular themes, but with a chronology of events of the previous year, and, from issue 3, 1910, statistical summaries.

143

Illustrierter Deutscher Kolonialkalender für 1909 [etc.]. Minden, Köhler, 1909/Berlin, Süssrott, 1910-1916. Annual.

Title varies: **Süssrott's illustrierten Kolonial-Kalender** (1910-1916).

See also 382.

Lusophone Africa

144

Anuário comercial de Portugal. Vol. 3, Ilhas e Ultramar. Lisbon, Anuário Comercial de Portugal, ?1934 - . Annual. (29th ed. 1963/64).

For each territory includes details on the civil and religious administration, and a directory of agricultural, commercial, industrial and professional enterprises.

145

Portugal. Agência-Geral das Colónias. **Anuário do Império Colonial Português**. Lisbon, 1935- . Annual.

Later **Anuário do Ultramar Português**.

STATISTICS

Bibliographies : economic statistics

146
United Nations Economic Commission for Africa (UNECA). **Bibliography of African statistical publications (Preliminary draft)**. Addis Ababa, 1962.

- - **Bibliography ..., 1950-1965**. Addis Ababa, 1966. 256pp.

- - **Bibliography ..., 1966-1973**. Addis Ababa, 1973. 45pp.

- - **Bibliography ..., 1969-1975**. Addis Ababa, 1975. 85pp.

- - **Bibliography ..., 1982-1985**. Addis Ababa, 1985. 63pp.

- - **Bibliography ..., 1985-1987**. Addis Ababa, 1987.

147
Ball, J. & Gardella, R. **Foreign statistical documents**, Stanford, Hoover Institution for War, Revolution & Peace, 1967. 173pp.

Limited to the holdings of the Hoover Institution, but with good coverage of African material.

148
Institute of Developing Economies, Tokyo. **Bibliography [later Catalogue] of statistical materials of developing countries**. Tokyo, 1968 etc..

Regularly revised. 8th ed. Tokyo, Asia Economic Press, 1983. xxxviii, 456pp.

149
Harvey, J. **Statistics - Africa: sources for market research**. Beckenham, CBD Research, 1970. xii, 175pp.

- - 2nd ed. Beckenham, 1978. 374pp.

For each country records the central statistical office and other official sources of government statistics; any non-official sources; libraries with statistical collections and bibliographies. Then lists major statistical series. Over 1,400 titles in 2nd ed., compared with 675 in 1st. The fullest source to its date, but limited almost entirely to series issued post independence.

150
Blauvelt, E. & Durlacher, J. **Sources of African and Middle Eastern economic information.** Aldershot, Gower, 1982. 2 vols.

Africa included in vol. 2 with country by country list of main contemporary statistical series.

151
Westfall, G. **Bibliography of official statistical yearbooks and bulletins.** Cambridge, Chadwyck-Healey, 1986. 247pp.

World-wide survey. Covers the major general statistical bulletins and annuals for each country, not including specialist series for specific topics (e.g. trade). For African countries, concentrates on post independence series with only brief mention of the colonial series.

152
Westfall, G. *ed.* **Guide to official publications of foreign countries.** Chicago, American Library Association, Government Documents Round Table, 1990. xxi, 359pp.

Arranged alphabetically by country, with a section on statistics, listing current statistical series, both general and special. Most references are for titles current in the 1980s. A useful up-date to item 151.

See also 159.

Bibliographies : demographic statistics

153
U.S. Library of Congress. Census Library Project. **Population censuses and other official demographic statistics of Africa (not including British Africa): an annotated bibliography.** Washington, 1950. 53pp.

Lists 198 censuses.

154
U.S. Library of Congress. Census Library Project. **Population censuses & other official demographic statistics of British Africa: an annotated bibliography.** Washington, 1950. 78pp.

Lists 285 censuses.

155

University of Texas. Population Research Center. **International population census bibliography**. Austin, 1965-68. 7 vols.

Vol. 2 (1965) Africa; vol. 7 (1968) Supplement (Africa, pp. 25-52).

continued by:

Goyer, D.S. **International population census bibliography, revision and update, 1945-1977**. New York, Academic Press, 1980. (Texas bibliography 2). 576pp.

Revises entries for post 1945 censuses in the original volumes, and extends coverage to 1977. Arranged alphabetically by country rather than by region.

156

Northwestern University Library. **Censuses in the Melville J. Herskovits Library of African Studies**, comp. J.L. McAfee. Evanston, Ill., 1975. 19pp.

- - rev ed. to 1978, comp. M.K. Cason. Evanston, Ill., 1978. 34pp.

157

France. Institut national de la statistiques et des études économiques. **Recensements et enquêtes démographiques dans les états africains et malgaches**. Paris, 1978.

158

Pinfold, J.R. **African population census reports: a bibliography and checklist**. Oxford, Hans Zell, 1984. 120pp.

Compiled for SCOLMA. Some 600 entries, with holdings in the U.K. (25 collections), Sweden (9 collections), France, Belgium, the Netherlands, and West Germany.

159

Evalds, V.K. **Union list of African censuses, development plans and statistical abstracts**. Oxford, Hans Zell, 1985. 180pp.

Covers material published 1945-1983 held in 12 U.S. collections.

160

Domschke, E.M. & Goyer, D.S. **The handbook of national population censuses: Africa & Asia**. New York, Greenwood Press, 1987. xiii, 1032pp.

A detailed analysis of the various methods of conducting censuses, the varieties of data included and details of all post 1945 censuses for each country. Africa covered on pp.35-545.

General

161
Africa-Vademecum: Grunddaten zur Wirtschaftsstruktur und Wirtschaftsentwicklung Afrikas. Munich, Weltforum Verlag for Afrika-Studienstelle, IFO Institut für Wirtschaftsforschung, 1968. 164pp. illus. maps.

"Statistical survey of the most important economical facts about Africa" (preface). Sections for Africa in the world, population, natural resources, agriculture, mining and manufacture, communications, trade, public finance, and development aid. 81 separate tables. Introductory sections also in English and French.

162
African economic handbook. London, Euromonitor Publications, 1986. 335pp.

Detailed statistics and commentary for the period 1973-1984.

163
African Development Bank. Statistics Division, Planning and Research Department. **Selected statistics on regional member countries.** Abidjan, 1987. 77pp.

54 tables, mostly covering data from 1975-1985.

164
United Nations. **Statistics and indicators on women in Africa, 1986.** New York, United Nations, 1989. xi, 255pp.

Extracted from the UN's "Compendium of statistics and indicators on the condition of women, 1986".

165
UNECA. Statistics Division. **African socio-economic indicators, 1986.** Addis Ababa, 1989. 79pp.

35 sets of statistical data, arranged by country.

166

World Bank Trade & Finance Division & United Nations Development Programme. **African economic and financial data**. Washington, DC, 1989. 204pp.

Data on 50 countries for 1980-87.

Bulletins & yearbooks

167

Statistik des Auslandes: Länderberichte. Wiesbaden, Statistisches Bundesamt, 1961- . Irreg.

Title varies : **Länderberichte** (1989-). Booklets (earlier issues 20/40pp. on average, expanding to 80pp. for many countries by late 1980s) issued separately and regularly revised for many countries of the world (*see* entries under each individual country below).

168

UNECA. **Statistical bulletin for Africa**. Addis Ababa, 1965-67. 2 issues.

Issue 1, Nov. 1965. 2 pts; issue 2, Mar. 1967. 3 pts. "Replaces the statistical annexes to *Economic bulletin for Africa*" (preface), issued 1962-1964.

169

UNECA. **Statistical yearbook**. Addis Ababa, 1970- . Irreg.

Title varies: **African statistical yearbook** (1976-). 1st ed., 1970; 2nd-4th eds, 1972-1974; 5th ed. 1976; 6th ed. 1980; 7th-11th eds., 1983-1987. 1st ed. comprises 7 vols., each devoted to a particular theme; subsequent eds. comprise 4 vols. each devoted to countries in a particular region (vol. 1, North Africa; vol. 2, West Africa; vol. 3, East & South Africa; vol. 4, Central Africa). UNECA also pub. **Quarterly statistical bulletin for Africa** (1969-71)/**Statistical & economic information bulletin for Africa** (1972-1977)/**Statistical information bulletin for Africa** (1978-1988) of which each issue contains statistical data and analysis on a particular theme or country.

170

UNECA. **Demographic handbook for Africa**. Addis Ababa, 1968- . Irreg.

Issues for 1968, 1971, 1975, 1980, 1982, 1988. "Major objective is to present in a consolidated form, demographic data and analysis from various sources pertaining to the principal demographic indicators of member states" (preface).

Anglophone Africa

General

171

Kuczynski, R.R. **Demographic survey of the British colonial empire**. London, Oxford University Press for Royal Institute of International Affairs, 1948. 4 vols.

Vol.1, West Africa; vol. 2, High Commission Territories, Central and East Africa, Mauritius and Seychelles. Compilation commenced in 1939 at the request of the Population Investigation Committee. For each country discusses methods of census taking, then provides a chronological account of demographic estimates and censuses, of provisions for registration of births and deaths with comments on fertility, mortality, and population growth together with extensive statistics. Reviews, *African affairs* 48, 1949, 162-163; 49, 1950, 76-77.

Bulletins & yearbooks

172

G.B. Board of Trade. **Statistical tables relating to the colonial and other possessions of the U.K.** London, HMSO, 1856-1912. Issues 1-37. Annual (irreg.).

Title varies: **Statistical tables relating to British colonies, possessions & protectorates ...** (issues 33-37, 1906-1912).

173

G.B. Board of Trade. **Statistical abstract for the several colonial and other possessions of the U.K., 1851/1863 [-1939/45]**. London, Board of Trade, 1865-1948. Irreg. Vols. 1-72.

Title varies: **Statistical abstract for the British self-governing Dominions, Possessions and Protectorates** (1917-1925); **... for the several British overseas Dominions and Protectorates** (1929-1938); **... for the British Commonwealth** (1946-48).

continued by:

G.B. Colonial Office. **The Commonwealth & the Sterling Area: statistical abstract, 1949/52 [-1967]**. London, HMSO, 1953-1968. Vols. 73-87.

174

G.B. Board of Trade. **Statistical abstract for the British Empire in each year from 1889 to 1903 [etc.].** London, HMSO, 1904-1915. Vols. 1-11.

Covers statistics up to and including 1913.

175

G.B. Colonial Office. **An economic survey of the colonial territories.** London, HMSO, 1932-1951. Irreg.

Issues for 1932-33, 1935-37, 1951. Presents a systematic account and statistics of each colony's economy with background data on topography, the administration, communications, etc. 1932-1937 issued in single vols.; 1951 issued in 7 vols (vol.1, The Central African and High Commission territories; vol. 2, The East African territories; vol. 3, The West African territories with St. Helena; vol. 7, colonies in general).

176

G.B. Colonial Office. **Digest of colonial statistics.** London, HMSO, 1952-1964. Quarterly/annual.

Annual 1963-64.

Francophone Africa

General

177

France. Ministère de la France d'outre-mer. Service de statistiques. **Inventaire social et économique des territoires d'outre-mer, 1950-1955.** Paris, 1957. 467pp.

Data on politics and administration, geography and climate, population, health, scientific organizations, justice, agriculture, forestry, mining, industry, communications, trade, and public finance.

178

France. Ministère de la France d'outre-mer. Service de statistiques. **Outre-mer 1958: tableau économique et social des états et territoires d'outre-mer à la veille de la mise en place des nouvelles institutions.** Paris, 1959. 862pp. maps.

Another collection of statistical data, updating the **Inventaire ...** (*see* 177).

Bulletins and yearbooks

179

France. Service coloniale de statistiques. **Tableaux et relevés de population ... sur les colonies françaises**. Paris, 1839-1896. Annual.

Title varies: **Tableaux de population ...** (1840-1881); **Bulletin de statistiques coloniales** (1882-1891); 1892/95 issued in 1 vol. as **Résumés des statistiques coloniales**. From 1897, this general statistical series was continued by a variety of specialized series: **Statistiques des finances des colonies françaises, ... du commerce, ... de l'industrie minière, ... de la navigation, ...de la population, ... des chemins de fer**.

180

France. Ministère des Colonies. **Bulletin mensuel des statistiques coloniales**. Paris, 1936-1939. Monthly.

continued by:

France. Institut national de la statistique et des études économiques. **Bulletin mensuel de statistique d'outre-mer**. Paris, 1945-1960. Vols. 1-16. Monthly.

continued by:

France. Institut national de la statistique et des études économiques. **Bulletin des statistiques des départements et territoires d'outre-mer**. Paris, 1959- . Quarterly.

181

France. Institut national de la statistique et des études économiques & Ministère de la France d'outre-mer, Service des statistiques. **Annuaire statistique des possessions françaises**. éd. provisoire. Paris, 1944-46.

Originally issued in fascs.

- - 2nd ed. **Annuaire statistique de l'Union française d'outre-mer, 1939/46**. Paris, 1949. 930pp.

Includes some data up to and including 1948/49.

- - 3rd ed. **Annuaire statistique ... 1939/49**. Paris, 1951. 2 vols. (453pp, 613pp.)

continued by:

France. Institut national de la statistique et des études économiques. **Annuaire statistique de l'Union française, 1949/54.** Paris, 1956. 2 vols. (138pp; 138pp.)

continued by:

Annuaire statistique de la Zone Franc, 1949/55. Paris, 1957-1958. 2 vols. (239pp.)

continued by:

France. Institut national des territoires d'outre-mer. **Annuaire statistique des territoires d'outre-mer.** Paris, 1959- . Annual.

182
France. Institut national de la statistique et des études économiques. **Données statistiques: africains et malgaches.** Paris, 1961-1972. Quarterly.

183
Mémento statistique de l'économie et de la planification africaines. Paris, Ediafric-La documentation africaine. 1964- . Irreg. (10th issue 1980).

Pub. as special numbers of *Bulletin de l'Afrique noire*. Title varies: **Mémento de l'économie africaine** (1965-). Covers 13 countries of Francophone West and Central Africa with economic statistics and tables.

184
OECD. Office statistique des Communautés Européennes. **Annuaire statistique des E.A.M.M. (États africaines et malgache associés).** Luxembourg, 1969- . Annual.

185
L'économie africaine, 1971 [etc.]. Dakar, Société africaine d'éditions, 1971-1979. Annual.

Issued as special numbers of *Moniteur africain*. Covers Francophone west and central Africa with statistical country by country surveys. Merged with **L'année politique et économique africaine** (*see* 122).

186
Organisation commune africaine, malgache et maurice (OCAMM). **Études et**

statistiques, Yaoundé, 1971- . Quarterly.

Covers Cameroon, Central African Republic, Chad, Gabon, Rwanda, Madagascar, Mauritius.

187
L'Économie des pays d'Afrique noire de la zone franc. Paris, Ediafric-La documentation africaine, 1973- . Irreg.

Issues for 1973, 1979. 1973 ed. "constitute en fait un mise à jour de la 7ième ed. (1972) de **Mémento ...** " (*see* 183). Covers Francophone west & central Africa.

188
La zone franc et l'Afrique. Paris, Ediafric-La documentation africaine, 1977- . Irreg.

Statistics, especially on trade between France and the Francophone countries of west and central Africa.

Former German Africa

Bibliography

189
'Kolonialstatistik', comp. R. Herrmann, pp. 940-979 *in* Zahn, F. ed. **Die Statistik in Deutschland nach ihrem heutigen Stand**. Munich & Berlin, J. Schweitzer, 1911.

- - 'Kolonialstatistik', comp. J. Rohrbach, pp. 525-530 *in* Burgdörfer, F. ed. **Die Statistik in Deutschland ...** 2nd ed. Berlin, Paul Schmidt, 1940.

Bibliographical listings of major German publications containing colonial statistics.

Bulletins & Yearbooks

190
Statistisches Jahrbuch für das Deutsche Reich. Berlin, Pottkammer & Mühlbrecht, 1880-1942.

Vols. 15 to 36, 1894-1915 include a section on the German colonies.

See also 136-143.

Lusophone Africa

191

Lopes de Lima, J.J. **Ensaios sobre a estatística das possessoes Portuguezas na Africa occidental e oriental, na Asia occidental, na China e na Oceania.** Lisbon, Imprensa Nacional, 1844-1862. 5 vols.

Vol. 1, Cape Verde Is.; vol. 2, São Tomé e Principe; vol. 3, Angola; vol. 4, Mozambique. (vol. 5 covers non-African colonies). First detailed survey produced of Portugal's overseas possessions.

192

Portugal. Ministério das Colónias [etc.]. **Anuário estatístico dos domínios ultramarinos portugueses.** Lisbon, 1875-1910. Irreg.

Includes a wide range of data: population, education, finance, commerce, shipping, communications etc.

193

Portugal. Ministério do Ultramar, Biblioteca e Arquivo Historico. **Estatística geral das colónias.** Lisbon, 1915. 2 vols.

194

Portugal. Instituto Nacional de Estatística. **Anuário estatístico do Império colonial/Annuaire statistique de l'empire colonial, 1943 [etc.].** Lisbon, 1945-1962. Annual.

Title varies: **Anuário estatístico do ultramar/Annuaire statistique d'outre-mer** (1949-1962).

195

Portugal. Instituto Nacional de Estatística. **Anuário estatístico. Vol. 2 : Ultramar.** Lisbon, 1961-1974. Annual.

Title varies : ... **Vol. 2 : Territórios Ultramarinos.** Following the cessation of **Anuário estatístico do Império colonial** (*see* 194) this general national Portuguese statistical annual added a second vol. covering colonial territories. Last volume pub. covers statistics of 1972.

DIRECTORIES OF ORGANIZATIONS

ORGANIZATIONS IN AFRICA

Some sources also include coverage of African related institutions located outside Africa.

General

196
International Council of Voluntary Agencies. **Africa's NGOs**. Geneva, 1968. 299pp.

Lists 1,839 non-governmental organizations arranged by country. Includes religious bodies, social welfare organizations, and a few research institutes. Detail varies, with often only name and address provided. Index by topic of activity, and by affiliation to international organizations.

197
Deutsche Afrika-Gesellschaft. **Abbreviations in Africa**. Bonn, 1969. ix, 260pp.

Some 4,000 abbreviations used by African organizations, research institutes, government agencies etc. Emphasis on Francophone Africa. No information on location or activities of organizations listed.

198
Abbreviations in the African press. New York, CCM Information, 1972. ix, 108pp.

Based on list compiled by Joint Publications Research Service (JPRS). Some 2,000 acronyms and abbreviations for organizations of all types. Covers all African countries, with entries also for organizations from Belgium, France, Italy, Portugal, Spain, Vatican, West Germany.

International organizations

199
UNECA. **Directory of intergovernmental co-operation organizations in Africa**. Addis Ababa, 1972.

- - 2nd ed. Addis Ababa, 1976. viii, 170pp.

200

African international organization directory and African participation in other international organizations, 1984/85. Munich & New York, K.G. Saur, 1984. (Guides to International Organizations, 1). 604pp.

Compiled by the Union of International Associations, and based upon their **Yearbook of international organizations**. Principal sections comprise a list of 817 individual organizations arranged under five categories (e.g. "Intercontinental membership", "regional membership"), and a country index. There are also indexes to subject keywords, acronyms and former names of organizations.

201

ROCIA: répertoire des organisations de coopération interafricaine. Yaoundé, Inter Media, 1984. 155pp.

Eight sections: politics, finance, development, agriculture, medicine, culture, and sport. Detailed accounts of the history and activities of some 50 organisations.

202

Belaouane-Gherari, S. & Gherari, H. **Les organisations régionales africaines: recueil de textes et documents [etc.].** Paris, Ministère de la coopération et du développement, La documentation française, 1988. 472pp.

Lists regional organizations, and reproduces their charters and other significant documents.

203

Fredland, R. **A guide to African international organizations**. London, Zell, 1990. vii, 316pp.

A wide variety of information including detailed treatment of eight major organizations (e.g. ECOWAS); alphabetical list of some 500 organizations, current and defunct; biographical data on some 120 miscellaneous individuals (including Africanus Horton, Nkrumah, Ali Mazrui); a chronology of significant dates in the founding and activities of organizations. Appendices include a list of acronyms, a list of organizations by date of foundation, individual country membership of organizations. Review, *ARD* 54, 1990, 43-44.

Administration

204

Duic, W.Z. **African administration: directory of public life, administration and justice for the African states. Vol. 1.** Munich, K.G. Saur, 1978. 1285pp. *No more published.*

Includes Benin, Cameroon, Gabon, Gambia, Ghana, Guinea, Guinea-Bissau, Ivory Coast, Liberia, Nigeria, Senegal, Sierra Leone, Togo, Upper Volta, Zaire, Zambia. Lists major government departments and business, financial, judicial, labour, social and religious organizations. Text in English, French, Dutch, German, Italian, Spanish and Serbo-Croat. Numerous maps including city plans.

205

Répertoire des pouvoirs publics africains. 2nd ed. Paris, Ediafric-La documentation africaine, 1975. 342pp.

Issued as special number of *Bulletin de l'Afrique noire.* Covers Francophone countries of west and central Africa. Lists government ministers, members of national assemblies, and senior government officials.

206

Guide permanent de l'administration africaine: institutions de l'Afrique noire. Paris, Ediafric-La documentation africaine, 1980.

207

International Federation of Library Associations and Institutions. International Office for Universal Bibliographic Control. **African legislative and ministerial bodies: list of uniform headings for higher legislative and ministerial bodies in African countries.** London, 1980. viii, 37pp.

Covers 15 countries: Benin, Botswana, Burundi, Côte d'Ivoire, Gabon, Gambia, Ghana, Kenya, Madagascar, Nigeria, Rwanda, Senegal, Sierra Leone, Tanzania, Togo. Lists headings used during the period 1970-1979. *See* Jover, B. 'The compilation of **African legislative and ministerial bodies**', *ARD* 26, 1981, 5-7.

Development

208

UNECA. **Directory of activities of international voluntary agencies in rural development in rural Africa.** 3rd ed. Addis Ababa, 1977. 173pp.

209

OECD. Development Centre. **Directory of development research and training institutes in Africa.** Paris, 1972. (*Liaison bulletin*, 1972, 1). 80pp.

Prepared in co-operation with CODESRIA. Covers 26 institutions in 15 African countries.

- - [rev. ed.] Paris, 1982. (*Liaison bulletin*, n.s. 8, 1982). xvi, 156pp. (*also pub.* Dakar, CODESRIA, 1983).

- - [rev. ed.] Paris, OECD Development Centre & CODESRIA, 1986. xxviii, 262pp.

1986 ed. lists 497 institutions in 46 African countries. Based upon a computerised database, using U.N. Macrothesaurus keywords, from which the compiling agencies offer specific subject searches and printouts.

210

Unesco. **Institutions engaged in social and economic planning in Africa.** Paris, 1967. 155pp.

Prepared by the International Committee for Social Science Documentation and CARDAN.

211

International Labour Office. **Directory of co-operative organizations: Africa south of the Sahara.** Geneva, 1975. (*Cooperative information*, suppl. 3). 273pp.

For each country gives a brief chronological outline of the development of co-operative organizations, then a directory of existing organizations and statistics on their operation.

212

Volunteers in Technical Assistance (VITA). **Directory of development resources: Africa.** Mt. Rainier, MD, 1979. [207]pp.

Comp. D. Culkin, ed. S. Breslin. Lists 187 African organizations by country with name and subject of interest indexes.

213

Agence de coopération culturelle et technique. **Recherche scientifique et développement 1980: répertoire des institutions francophones.** Paris, 1980. 2 vols.

A directory of institutions and scholars in Francophone countries involved in research into the Third World. Vol. 1 covers Africa.

214

African Centre for Applied Research and Training in Social Development (ACARTSOD). **Directory of social development institutions in Africa.** Tripoli, 1983. 167pp.

Comp. A. Guerma. Includes international, regional and national institutions.

215

Inventaire des sources africaines de conseil et d'assistance technique: répertoire. Levallois-Perret, Cités unies développement, 1990. 245pp.

Lists government and research organizations concerned with technical assistance.

216

UNECA. Pan African Development Information System (PADIS). **Directory of development institutions in Africa, 1991.** Addis Ababa, 1991. 112pp.

Lists 115 institutions. Country and subject indexes.

See also 234.

Education

217

Unesco Regional Office for Education in Africa. Documentation Centre. **Directory of adult education centres in Africa.** Dakar, 1974. iv, 130pp.

108 institutions, arranged by country, excluding North Africa and the Republic of South Africa.

218

African Council on Communication Education. **Directory of communication training institutions in Africa, 1988.** Nairobi, 1988. 66pp.

Some 100 entries for 25 countries.

219

Association of African Universities. Documentation Centre. **Directory of African universities.** Accra, 1974.

- - 2nd ed. Accra, 1976. 2 vols. (vi, 278, 9pp; vi, 111, 9pp).

Vol.1, Anglophone Universities; vol. 2, Universités francophones.

- - 3rd ed. Accra, 19??

- - 4th ed. Accra, 1986. x, 508pp.

- - 5th ed. Accra, 1988. 495pp.

All eds. maintain separate sequences for Anglophone and Francophone Africa.

Francophone Africa

220

Rupp, B. *et al.* **Études africaines: inventaire des enseignements dispensées dans les pays francophones, 1971-72: enquête avec l'appui de l'AUPELF.** Paris, Centre de recherche et documentation pour l'Afrique noire (CARDAN), 1972. (*Bulletin d'information et liaison CARDAN*, 4(1/2) 1972). ix, 273pp.

Covers institutions in 21 Francophone African countries (including North Africa), also in Belgium, Canada, France, Haiti, Switzerland. Bulk of coverage for France (pp. 123-229).

221

Association des universités partiellement ou entièrement de langue française (AUPELF). **Répertoire des enseignants et chercheurs africains; universités d'Afrique, membres de l'AUPELF.** Dakar/Montreal, AUPELF, 1984. 378pp.

Lists 886 researchers.

- - rev. ed. **Enseignants et chercheurs des institutions membres de l'AUPELF-UREF; Afrique, Caraïbe, Océan Indien.** Montreal, AUPELF, 1991.

Lists 2,203 researchers in total.

222

Association des universités partiellement ou entièrement de langue française (AUPELF). **Répertoire des instituts d'enseignement supérieur membres de** l'AUPELF 1986. 4th ed. Montreal, AUPELF, 1986.

Vol. 1, 420pp. "Algérie à Zaire (sauf France)", covers 32 institutions in 21 countries of Francophone Africa (excluding Chad).

- - rev ed. **Répertoire des établissements d'enseignement supérieur membres de l'AUPELF-UREF.** Montreal, 1991. 849pp.

Finance

223
African Economic Digest (AED). **The AED African financial directory.** London, Middle East Economic Digest Ltd., 1987. 289pp.

Based on data acquired during compilation of weekly *African economic digest* since 1980. Covers 52 member states of Organization of African Unity. General information on banking, and currencies, followed by directory of banks and other financial institutions by country.

Human rights

224
'Africa: human rights directory and bibliography', *Human rights internet reporter* 12(4) 1988/89. Special issue. 308pp.

Includes data on some 200 organizations and their publications arranged by country of location. Mostly African countries, but some indication of relevant organizations outside Africa is included. Also available on disk.

Libraries, archives and the book trade

225
Scientific Council for Africa South of the Sahara. **Directory of scientific and technical libraries in Africa South of the Sahara.** Kikwyu, 1953. (S.C.A. publication, 10). 61pp.

Lists 240 collections.

226
Dadzie, E.W. & Strickland, J.T. **Directory of archives, libraries & schools of librarianship in Africa.** Paris, Unesco, 1965. (Unesco bibliographic handbook, 10). 112pp.

Excludes North Africa and the Republic of South Africa. Lists 508 institutions (464 libraries and documentation centres, 36 archives, 8 schools of librarianship) in 39 countries. Annotations in English or French. Data up to 1963.

- - 2nd ed. **Directory of documentation, libraries and archives services in Africa,** ed. D. Zidouemba, comp. E. de Grolier. Paris, Unesco, 1977. 311pp.

Based on questionnaire circulated 1974/75 with a little up-dating. Only minimal information given on archives, with users referred to the **International directory of archives** (1975).

227
Gray, B. 'Selected directory of sources specialising in current Africana', *Current bibliography on African affairs* n.s. 3 (6) 1970, 5-20; n.s. 3(7) 1970, 4-21.

Covers book-trade sources within & outside Africa.

228
UNECA. **Directory of government printers and prominent bookshops in the African region.** Addis Ababa, 1970. 48pp.

229
Africa book-trade directory 1971. Munich, Verlag Dokumentation/New York, Bowker, 1971. 319pp.

Ed. S. Taubert. Covers 2,500 publishers, booksellers and other book-trade organizations in 54 African countries. Includes general background information on each country. Revised in **The book trade of the world** (*see* 233).

230
Centre africain de formation et de recherche administratives pour le développement (CAFRAD). **Directory of administrative information services in Africa.** Tangiers, CAFRAD, Centre de documentation, 1977. 123pp.

231
Zell, H.M. **The African book world and press: a directory.** Oxford, Hans Zell, 1977. xxvi, 299pp.

- - 2nd ed. Oxford, 1980. xxiv, 244pp.

- - 3rd ed. Oxford, 1983. xx, 285pp.

- - 4th ed. Oxford, 1989. xxi, 306pp.

Includes sequences listing university, college and public libraries; special libraries; booksellers; commercial and institutional publishers; periodicals and newspapers; book industry associations and literary societies; commercial and government printers (from 2nd ed.). Appendices list book-trade events, prizes, book clubs, news agencies (from 4th ed.), dealers in African studies material. Lists 2,347 organizations in 1st ed., over 4,400 in 4th. Reviews, *ARD* 15, 1977, 24-25; *ARD* 34, 1984, 50-51; *ARD* 49, 1989, 18-19. The standard guide.

232
Répertoire de centres de documentation modernes en Afrique noire francophone, à Madagascar et au Maghreb (développement rural). Paris, AGRIDOC International, 1981. 28pp.

233
The book trade of the world. vol. 4. Africa. Munich, Saur, 1984. 391pp.

Ed. S. Taubert and P. Weidhaas. A revised version of **Africa book trade directory** (*see* 229). Introduction (pp. 15-56) by Hans Zell with overview of the history and organization of the book trade. Chapters on each country.

234
Agence de coopération culturelle et technique. **Répertoire des sources d'information francophones pour le développement.** Paris, 1987. xi, 557pp.

Covers libraries and documentation centres in all Francophone African countries including Mauritius but excluding Madagascar; also relevant institutions in France, Belgium, Canada.

See also 255, 265.

Museums

235
Deutsche Afrika Gesellschaft. **Museums in Africa: a directory.** Bonn, 1970. xi, 594pp.

Lists 506 museums by country. Index by broad type of museum (e.g. "Art museums and galleries", "Botanical & zoological gardens"). Based on questionnaire, but detailed references given to other sources of information used.

236

Unesco/International Council of Museums Documentation Centre. **Directory of African museums**. 1981.

- - rev. ed. **Directory of museums in Africa**, ed. S. Peters, *et al*. London, Kegan Paul, 1990. 211pp.

1990 ed. lists 503 museums in 48 countries, including North Africa but excluding the Republic of South Africa. More than half the entries give name and address only, without further details. Review in *Africa* 61, 1991, 130-131 is very critical of obvious omissions: "this volume ... approaches the useless category".

Religion

237

Christian communication directory: Africa. Paderborn, Verlag Ferdinand Schöningh, 1980. 544pp.

Compiled jointly by the Catholic Media Council, Aachen, World Association for Christian Communication, London and Lutheran World Federation, Geneva. Lists Christian publishers, periodicals, printers, radio and television production studios.

238

Directory of theological institutions, associations, lay training centres in Africa. Geneva, Lutheran World Federation, 1984. 219pp.

Covers theological seminaries, university departments, Bible schools.

Research Centres

239

Scientific Council for Africa South of the Sahara. **Directory of scientific institutes, organizations and services in Africa south of the Sahara**. London, 1954. (Publication, 14). xiv, 133pp.

Arranged by country. Subject index.

240

Scientific Council for Africa South of the Sahara. **List of scientific societies south of the Sahara.** London, 1954. (Publication, 16). v, 32pp.

By country with subject index.

241

Deutsche Afrika Gesellschaft. **Wissenschaft in Afrika: Ein Verzeichnis der Institutionen.** Bonn, 1962. 168pp.

Lists principal research centres and scientific organizations arranged by country.

242

Food and Agricultural Organization (FAO). **Répertoire des institutions et stations de recherche agricole en Afrique.** Rome, 1966. 218pp.

243

International Conference on the Organization of Research & Training in Africa in Relation to the Study, Conservation and Utilization of Natural Resources. **Scientific research in Africa: national policies, research institutions.** Paris, Unesco, 1966. 214pp.

Basically a directory of research organizations.

244

Unesco. Field Science Office for Africa, Nairobi. **Survey on the scientific and technical potential of the countries of Africa.** Paris, Unesco, 1970. 296pp.

Principally an "Inventory of the scientific and research institutions in Africa" presented as an updated version of the list in **Scientific research in Africa ...** (*see* 243). Includes details of over 600 institutions in 40 African countries including North Africa.

245

OECD. **Directory of social science research and training units in Africa.** Paris, 1975. (*Liaison bulletin*, 1975, 2). xxiv, 170pp.

Covers 162 institutes in 37 African countries, including South Africa.

continued by:

CODESRIA. **Inventaire des chercheurs africains en sciences sociales.** Dakar,

1978- . Every 2/3 years.

3rd ed. 1983 includes 1,090 researchers from 305 institutions in 38 countries. 4th ed. 1986.

and:

CODESRIA. **Instituts de recherche en sciences sociales.** Dakar, 1983- . Every 2/3 years.

246
UNECA. Pan African Documentation & Information System (PADIS). **Directory of African experts, 1982.** New York, 1983. xviii, 457pp.
- - **Supplements** 1 to 4, New York, 1984.

Information on 3,600 experts from 46 African countries. Indexed by field of specialization and country of origin.

- - rev. ed. Addis Ababa, UNECA, 1989. 160pp.

Lists 400 specialists.

247
American Association for the Advancement of Science, Office of International Science, and African Regional Centre for Technology, Dakar. **Directory of scientific and engineering societies in Sub-Saharan Africa.** Washington, DC, 1985. 156pp.

- - 2nd ed. Washington, DC, 1987. x, 146pp.

1st ed. lists 245 societies, 2nd ed., 267 by region and country with subject index.

248
International Labour Office. **Directory of African technology institutions.** Geneva, 1985. 2 vols. (623pp; 577pp.)

Comp. J.C. Woilet & M. Allal. Describes 711 organizations including university departments, research centres, and technical departments of government ministries principally in the agricultural and building sectors.

249
African Regional Centre for Technology. **Directory of science and technology**

institutions, consulting organizations and experts in Africa. Dakar, 1986. 357pp.

Over 1,400 institutions by country.

250

African Academy of Sciences. **Profiles of African scientists.** Nairobi, 1990. x, 362pp.

 - - 2nd ed. Nairobi, 1991. xi, 661pp.

1st ed. includes some 400 from 32 countries; 2nd ed., over 600 from 40 countries.

251

International Association of Agricultural Librarians and Documentalists and Technical Centre for Agricultural and Rural Cooperation. **Agricultural information resource centers: a world directory 1990.** Urbana, IL, 1990. 641pp.

Arranged by country. 566 entries for 49 African countries.

See also 73, 213, 258, 260, 261, 264, 280.

Trade Unions

252

U.S. Department of Labor, Bureau of International Labor Affairs. **Directory of labor organizations: Africa.** Washington, DC, 1962.

 - - 2nd ed. Washington, 1966. 2 vols.

Country by country arrangement listing trade unions and trade union federations.

Women's Organizations

253

UNECA. African Training & Research Centre for Women. **Directory of African women's organizations.** Addis Ababa, 1978. 120pp.

254

UNECA. **Roster of African women experts.** Addis Ababa, 1988. 58pp.

AFRICAN-RELATED ORGANIZATIONS OUTSIDE AFRICA

General and international

255

'Collections of Africana', *Unesco bulletin for libraries* 15, 1961, 277-287; 16, 1962, 47-48; 17, 1963, 98-102; 18, 1964, 193.

An early attempt to bring together information on some 90 collections located in Europe (Belgium, France, West Germany, Italy, Netherlands, Poland, Portugal, U.K.) U.S.A., Japan, and Africa itself (Cameroon, Congo (Brazzaville), Congo (Léopoldville), Kenya, Rhodesia and Nyasaland, Portuguese possessions in Africa, Senegal, South Africa).

256

Institut africain de Genève & Centre de documentation de l'Institut universitaire de hautes études internationales. **Répertoire des principales institutions s'intéressant à l'Afrique noire.** Geneva, 1963. loose leaf.

Covers some 180 European and North American universities, research institutes, libraries, archives and museums with details of their activities and publications.

257

Unesco. **Social scientists specializing in African studies.** Paris, 1963. 375pp.

Lists 2072 individuals. Index by subject or region of specialization. Based on questionnaire circulated 1959/61.

258

International African Institute. **A preliminary register of African studies at universities, research centres and other institutions.** London, 1964. 33pp.

Based on a questionnaire sent out in 1963 as a preliminary to the Tropical African Studies Conference, Ibadan, 1964. Lists 147 institutions (67 in Africa, 47 in Europe, 26 in the U.S.A., 7 others).

259

U.S. Joint Publications Research Service. **Glossary of abbreviations relating to African affairs.** Washington, DC, 1966. 91pp.

Entirely concerned with organizations.

260

International African Institute. **International register of organizations undertaking Africanist research in the social sciences and humanities, 1970.** London, IAI Research Information Liaison Unit, 1971. v, 64pp.

Based on a questionnaire. Pp. 1-20, African countries, listing 174 institutions from 43 countries; pp. 21-58, other countries, listing 332 institutions from 28 countries (in addition to Europe and North America includes Brazil, India, Israel, Japan, Taiwan).

261

International African Institute. **International guide to African studies research.** London, 1975. x, 185pp.

Pp. 1-66, enlarged and revised ed. of **International register ...** (*see* 260). A total of 446 institutions from 41 African countries, and 26 others. Pp. 67-185 comprise the 4th issue in the series of guides to "Current Africanist research".

- - 2nd ed. London, Hans Zell, 1987. 276pp.

Comp. P. Baker. Covers over 1,100 institutions throughout the world, with details of courses offered, staff specialization, library resources and publications. Indexes by name of organization and scholar, and subjects and regions of specialization. Review, *ARD* 46, 1988, 53-55.

262

African Studies Association. **International directory of scholars and specialists in African studies.** Waltham, MA, 1978. viii, 355pp.

Some 2,700 entries, based upon a questionnaire.

263

U.N. Non-Governmental Liaison Service. **Non-Governmental organizations and Sub-Saharan Africa:** profiles of non-governmental organizations based in Western Europe, Australia and New Zealand, and their work for the development of Sub-Saharan Africa. Geneva, 1988. 284pp.

Lists organizations by country.

264

Dikomfu, L. *et al.* **Répertoire des institutions africanistes situées hors de l'Afrique sub-saharienne.** Kinshasa, Centre de co-ordination des recherches et de la documentation en sciences sociales en Afrique sub-saharienne

(CERDAS), 1989. 109pp.

Lists 184 institutions indicating activities and publications. Excludes the USA, but includes Egypt, South Africa and the Sudan. Index by country and subject.

265
Zell, H.M. **The African studies companion: a resource guide and directory**. Oxford, Hans Zell, 1989. x, 165pp.

Section 4, "Major libraries and documentation centres": 117 collections in 14 European countries, Canada and the USA, Australia, India and Japan; section 5, "Publishers with African studies lists": 66 in USA, UK, France, Germany, Netherlands and Sweden; 20 in 5 African countries; section 6, "Dealers and distributors of African studies materials": 100 organizations in 28 African and 6 non-African countries. There are also sections listing the major African regional and international organizations, African studies associations, and donor agencies.

See also 50, 73, 80.

Australasia

266
African Studies Association of Australia and the Pacific. **Directory of Africanists in Australia, New Zealand and Papua**. Geelong, Deakin University, 1979.

- - 2nd ed. Geelong, 1984. 37pp.

- - 3rd ed. Geelong, 1986.

- - 4th ed. Geelong, 1991. 72pp.

2nd ed. lists 120 individuals.

Europe

267
Agence de coopération culturelle et technique (ACCT). **Études africaines en Europe: bilan et inventaire**. Paris, Éditions Karthala, 1981. 2 vols. (655pp; 714pp.)

For each country includes essays on studies of particular subject fields followed by a directory. Vol. 1 includes Belgium, Denmark, Finland, West Germany, Italy, Netherlands, Norway, Portugal, Sweden, U.K. and essays on studies in France; vol. 2 is a directory of French organizations. Indexes by subject and country of interest.

268

The SCOLMA directory of libraries and special collections on Africa in the U.K. and Western Europe. 4th ed. Oxford, Zell, 1983. 183pp.

Comp. H. Hannam. Includes 275 entries of which 142 are for the U.K. Other countries covered are Austria, Belgium, Denmark, Finland, France, Germany, Iceland, Ireland, Italy, Netherlands, Norway, Portugal, Spain, Sweden, Switzerland. 1st to 3rd eds. of the SCOLMA directory covered the U.K. only (*see* 282). 5th ed. scheduled for publication 1992 will attempt to cover all Europe.

See also 198.

Belgium

269

Centre d'information et de documentation du Congo Belge et du Ruanda-Urundi. **Liste des sociétés, entreprises, associations et institutions d'activité coloniale ayant un siège en Belgique.** Brussels, 1952. 74pp.

270

Dauphin, J.C. 'Belgian centers of documentation and research on Africa', *African studies bulletin* 8, 1965, 21-39.

Includes some 50 organizations.

271

Simons, E. & Thijs, M. **Inventaire des études africaines en Belgique.** Brussels, Centre d'études et de documentation africaine, 1985. (*Cahiers du CEDAF*, 7/8, 1985). 303pp.

Details on 155 institutions arranged by city with indexes by discipline and region of study.

See also 234.

France

272

Dauphin, J.C. 'French provincial centers of documention and research on Africa', *African studies bulletin* 9, 1966, 48-65.

Checklist of some 40 organizations outside Paris.

273

Dauphin, J.C. *et al*. **Inventaire des resources documentaires africanistes à Paris.** Paris, Centre de recherche et documentation pour l'Afrique noire (CARDAN), 1969. (*Recherche, enseignement, documentation africanistes francophones, bulletin d'information et de liaison* 1(1) 1969). [102pp.].

Lists 129 libraries and research institutes. Indexes by acronym, subject and region of coverage, and by title of publications issued by each body.

274

France-Afrique subsaharienne: organisations culturelles et sociales; annuaire 1989. Paris, L'Harmattan, 1988- . Annual.

Ed. J.-M. M'Foumouangana & A.M. Passy. A directory of institutions in France with African interests. 1988 issue includes some 375 entries, alphabetically by title, including publishers and broadcasting services.

See also 220, 234

Germany

275

Deutsches Institut für Afrika-Forschung. **Institutionen der Afrika-Arbeit in der Bundesrepublik und Berlin (West).** Hamburg, 1971. (Dokumentationsdienst Afrika, 1). iv, 189pp.

Comp. U. Gerlach & T. Möller. 206 entries in sections for university and non-university institutes. Indexes by title, and subject and regional interest.

276

Deutsches Institut für Afrika-Forschung. **Afrika-bezogene Literatursammlungen in der Bundesrepublik und Berlin (West).** Hamburg, 1972. (Dokumentationsdienst Afrika, 2). xi, 214pp.

Comp. H. Henze. Lists 142 libraries.

277

Deutsches Übersee-Institut, Übersee-Dokumentation, Referat Afrika. **Institutionen der Afrika-Forschung und Afrika-Information in der Bundesrepublik Deutschland und Berlin (West).** Hamburg, 1990. (Dokumentationsdienst Afrika, Reihe B, 5). xi, 285pp.

Comp. M. Gebhardt. A revised version of the volumes of 1971 and 1972 (*see* 275, 276). In three sections for research institutes, libraries, and documentation centres and archives. Lists 210 institutions in total with indexes of acronyms, and areas of subject and regional interest.

Netherlands

278

Afrika-Studiecentrum. **Gids van Afrika-Collecties in Nederlandse bibliotheken en documentatiecentra.** Leiden, 1986. 153pp.

Ed. B. Hijma. Details of 123 collections.

Portugal

279

Portugal. Junta de Investigações do Ultramar. Centro de Documentação Científica Ultramarina. **Contribuçao para um dicionário de siglas de interesse ultramarino.** Lisbon, 1961. 70pp.

- - **1° Aditamento.** Lisbon, 1961. 10pp.

A list of abbreviations and acronyms for official, academic and political organizations concerned with activities in Portugal's overseas possessions.

280

Portugal. Junta de Investigações do Ultramar. Centro de Documentação Científica Ultramarina. **Istituições Portuguesas de interesse ultramarino.** Lisbon, 1964. 138pp.

Arranged by UDC. Gives only name of institution, address, and very brief details of its publications. Lists 147 institutions in Portugal, 165 in Angola, 138 in Mozambique, 47 in Portuguese Guinea, 38 in Cape Verde Islands, 35 in São Tomé e Principe.

Switzerland

281

Huber, H. **Die Afrika-Forschung in der Schweiz/Les recherches africaines en Suisse**. Berne, Schweizerische Afrika-Gesellschaft/Société suisse d'études africaines, 1976. 171pp.

Directory of some 100 scholars, and brief narrative account of major institutions.

- - rev. ed. Berne, 1985. 165pp.

Information on 125 individual scholars and directory of 29 institutions.

- - rev. ed. comp. C. von Graffenried & E. Schreyger. Berne, 1991. 188pp.

Covers 158 individual scholars and 27 institutions.

United Kingdom

282

The SCOLMA directory of libraries and special collections on Africa. London, SCOLMA, 1963. iii, 101, 18pp.

- - 2nd ed. comp. R.L. Collison. London, Crosby Lockwood, 1967. iv, 92pp.

- - 3rd ed. comp. R.L. Collison, rev. J. Roe. Frogmore, St. Albans, Crosby Lockwood, Staples, 1973. vii, 118pp.

1st ed. covers 128 institutions, 2nd ed., 159, 3rd ed., 141. The 4th ed., **The SCOLMA directory of libraries and special collections in the United Kingdom and Western Europe** (1983) expanded its regional coverage and is listed above under Europe (*see* 268).

283

Bradbury, R.E. **Directory of African studies in United Kingdom universities.** Birmingham, African Studies Association of the U.K., 1969. iv, 73pp.

Includes 38 universities and colleges listing relevant courses and staff, also 10 non-university institutions.

- - rev. ed. *ARD* 16/17, 1978, 39-87; 18, 1978, 37-59; 19, 1979, 8-15; 20, 1979, 22-24; 21, 1979, 35-44; 22, 1980, 31.

55 separate entries for universities and individual colleges, 11 for

polytechnics, and a section on Inter-University Council supported links between British and African universities.

284

Hodder-Williams, R. **A directory of British Africanists**. Bristol, University of Bristol for African Studies Association of the U.K., 1986. 85pp.

- - 2nd ed. Bristol, University of Bristol for Royal African Society, 1991. ii, 141pp.

1st ed. contains 443 entries, 2nd has 512 entries with details of career, interests and publications. Indexes by discipline and country of interest. 2nd ed. contains brief introductory essay analysing the data collected. "Africanists" are defined as "all those contributing either through active research or through teaching in the tertiary sector, to the study of Africa".

North America

Canada

285

Bullock, R.A. & Killam, G.D. **Resources for African studies in Canada**. Ottawa, Canadian Association of African Studies, 1976. vi, 139pp.

Bi-lingual English/French. Lists of both institutions and of individual researchers.

USA

286

Mithun, J.S. **African programs of U.S. organizations**. Washington, DC, U.S. Dept. of State, Bureau of Intelligence & Research, External Research Division, 1965. 132pp.

Details on 724 programmes, arranged under categories such as universities, business organizations, and private institutions.

287

Duignan, P. **Handbook of American resources for African studies**. Stanford, Hoover Institution, 1966. (Hoover Institution on War, Revolution and Peace, Bibliographical series, 29). 234pp.

Describes the holdings of 95 library and manuscript collections, 108 church and missionary libraries and archives, 95 art and ethnographic collections and 4 business archives.

288
African Studies Association. Research Liaison Committee. **Directory of African studies in the United States, Feb. 1971**. Waltham, MA, 1971. [143pp].

Covers 80 institutions.

- - [2nd ed.] Waltham, MA, 1972. 158pp.

- - [3rd ed.] Waltham, MA, 1973. 201pp. - - **Supplement ...** Waltham, Mass., 1973. iv, 28pp.

Main vol. lists 238 institutions; supplement adds corrections and details of a further 38.

- - 4th ed. ... **1974/75**. Waltham, MA, 1975. iii, 204pp.

268 full entries, with briefer details on 59 which did not answer questionnaire.

- - 5th ed. **Directory of African and Afro-American studies in the United States**. Waltham, MA, African Studies Association, 1976. v, 329pp.

908 entries.

- - 6th ed. Waltham, MA, Crossroads Press for African Studies Association, 1979. v, 306pp.

900+ entries.

- - 7th ed. Los Angeles, African Studies Association, 1987. vi, 273pp.

388 entries. Preface explains that reduction in entries since earlier eds. is partly explained by decision not to include entries for institutions not replying to questionnaire. 8th ed. announced for publication, 1992.

289
Yale University Library. **Directory of Southern Africanists in the U.S. and Canada**. Prelim. ed. New Haven, CT, 1978.

290
Thompson, E.D. **Directory of women in African studies**. Los Angeles, African

Studies Association, 1984. 45pp.

Lists 197 women: indexes by topographic and subject interests.

291
Gosebrink, J.E.M. **African studies information resources directory**. Oxford, Hans Zell for African Studies Asssociation, 1986. 572pp.

Entries for 437 U.S. institutions including libraries, archives, museums, documentation centres and learned societies. Separate sections for 86 church & mission organizations, 43 booksellers and distributors and 48 publishers. Conceived as a partial revision of **Handbook of American resources ...** (*see* 287). Review, *ARD* 43, 1987, 31-33. The standard guide to U.S. institutional interest in Africa.

BIOGRAPHICAL SOURCES

General

292

Segal, R. *ed*. **Political Africa: a who's who of political personalities and parties**. London, Stevens/New York, Praeger, 1961. xi, 475pp.

Pt. 1 includes c. 400 living figures. Preface notes that data are comparatively more complete for Kenya, Nigeria and South Africa. Pt. 2 (pp. 291-475) discusses contemporary political parties country by country.

- - Rev. & abridged ed. **African profiles**, Harmondsworth, Penguin, 1962. 351pp.

293

Deutsche Afrika-Gesellschaft. **Afrikanische Köpfe**. Bonn, Deutscher Wirtschaftsdienst, 1962. 2 vols. loose-leaf.

Biographies and portraits of contemporary African leaders.

294

Taylor, S. *ed*. **The new Africans: a guide to the contemporary history of emergent Africa and its leaders**. New York, Putnam, 1967. 504pp.

Written by some 50 Reuters News Agency correspondents. Includes some 600 entries for living figures in Africa south of the Sahara (excluding the Republic of South Africa).

295

Friedrich-Ebert-Stiftung. Forschungsinstitut. **Africa Biographien**. Hanover, Verlag für Literatur und Zeitgeschichte, 1967-1970. 4 vols. loose-leaf.

- - English trans. **African biographies**. Bad Godesberg, Verlag Neue Gesellschaft, [1971-1981]. 7 vols. loose-leaf.

The English translation is revised and updated. The plan was to issue supplementary pages. Coverage is of contemporary figures, mostly political.

296

Dictionary of African biography. London, Melrose Press, 1970-1971. Annual. 2 issues.

Ed. E. Kay. Some 2,500 entries in each issue for living figures in "free Africa" (excluding South Africa, Southern Rhodesia, and Portuguese colonies).

297

Dickie, J. & Rake, A. **Who's who in Africa: the political, military and business leaders of Africa**. London, "African development", 1973. 602pp.

610 entries grouped by country (with some countries, e.g. Burundi, Central African Republic, having only a single entry).

298 (*also entered at* 120)
Africa yearbook and who's who. London, "Africa journal", 1977. xlvii, 1364pp.

Ed. R. Uwechue. "Who's who in Africa today" section includes c. 2,400 biographies. No further vols. published, but later used as the model for the same editor and publisher's "Know Africa series": **Africa today** (*see* 25), **Africa who's who** (*see* 303) and **Makers of Modern Africa** (*see* 304).

299

Encyclopaedia Africana dictionary of African biography. Algonac, MI, Reference Publications, 1977- . To be published in 20 vols.

Vol. 1, Ethiopia and Ghana (1977, *see* 459, 979); vol. 2, Sierra Leone & Zaire (1979, *see* 885, 1079); vol. 3, South Africa, Botswana, Lesotho and Swaziland (forthcoming 1992). The only published product to date of the long established **Encyclopaedia Africana** project (*see* 31). Each vol. will cover two to three countries, with a very wide range of contributors. For specific details on vols. published to date see under the individual countries.

300

Les africains. Paris, Éditions "Jeune afrique", 1977-1978. 12 vols.

Ed. in chief, C.-A. Julien. Detailed biographies of 120 figures "qui ont marqué de leur empreinte l'histoire du continent" (preface). Includes portraits, illustrations, reproductions of texts of contemporary documents, and references to sources. Covers all periods with entries for figures from Hannibal to Lumumba. Emphasis on areas of Africa of French interest, with over half the entries coming from North Africa.

301

Lipschutz, M.R. & Rasmussen, R.K. **Dictionary of African historical biography**. Berkeley, CA, University of California Press/London, Heinemann,

1978. 304pp.

About 750 entries for figures, both living and dead, of significance in the history of Sub-Saharan Africa before 1960; also lists of rulers and office-holders, subject-index, detailed bibliography (c. 800 refs.). Includes some 120 non-Africans. Reviews in *JAH* 20, 1979, 311-312 and *ASA review of books* 5, 1979, 97-98, which notes relatively sparser coverage of Francophone Africa.

 - - 2nd ed. expanded & updated. Berkeley, CA, University of California Press, 1986. xi, 328pp.

Includes "Supplement" with entries for 57 post-1960 political leaders.

302
Burke's royal families of the world, vol. 2: Africa and the Middle East. London, Burke's Peerage, 1980. xvi, 320pp.

Comp. D. Williamson. Genealogical information on families reigning "in comparatively recent times" (i.e. since c. 1920). In addition to lists, contains brief essays on various North African dynasties, also on Ethiopia, Zanzibar and Zululand. Admits that Sub-Saharan Africa "presented severe problems which compilers ... have been unable to solve". Appendix contains much briefer notes on "Pre-colonial African states". Review, *JAH*, 22, 1981, 419-420.

303
Africa who's who. London, "Africa journal", 1981. (Know Africa series). vii, 1169 pp.

 - - 2nd ed. London, Africa Books, 1991. viii, 1863pp.

Ed.-in-chief, R. Uwechue. 1st ed. includes entries for c.7,000, 2nd ed. for c. 12,000 living figures. Developed from **Africa yearbook and who's who** (*see* 298).

304
Makers of modern Africa: profiles in history. London, "Africa journal", 1981. (Know Africa series). 591pp.

 - - 2nd ed. London, Africa Books, 1991. xvii, 797pp.

Ed.-in-chief R. Uwechue. 1st ed. includes c. 500 (2nd ed., 680) eminent dead African figures, mostly from 19th and 20th centuries. Numerous portraits.

305

Southern, E. **Biographical dictionary of Afro-American and African musicians.** Westport, CT, Greenwood Press, 1982. (Greenwood encyclopedia of black music). 478pp.

306

Seck, N. and Clerfeuille, S. **Musiciens africaines des années 80: guide.** Paris, l'Harmattan, 1986. 1676pp.

307

Wiseman, J.A. **Political leaders in Black Africa: a biographical dictionary of the major politicians since independence.** Aldershot, Edward Elgar, 1991. xxiii, 248pp.

485 brief biographies with a country index. No sources listed.

See also 80-86, 203, 1529.

Anglophone Africa

Bibliographies

308

Simpson, D.H. 'Biographical sources for colonial history in Africa', *ARD*, 29, 1982, 19-21.

General

309

Kirk-Greene, A.H.M. **A biographical dictionary of the British colonial governor. Vol. 1, Africa.** Brighton, Harvester Press/Stanford, Hoover Institution Press, 1980. 256pp.

Some 200 entries for the period 1875 to 1980. Includes strictly factual data on birth, education, career, publications with reference to sources. Review, *JAH* 23, 1982, 430-431.

310

Kirk-Greene, A.H.M. **A biographical dictionary of the British Colonial Service, 1939-1966.** Oxford, Hans Zell, 1991. xvii, 401pp.

Some 15,000 entries "being a cumulative and composite reproduction of all the biographical entries as they appeared in the *Colonial Office lists*" (preface).

Includes a detailed and valuable introduction covering the history of the British Colonial Service, the history and development of the *List* with lengthy notes on the ten major categories of information that each biographical entry comprises, and an indication of other biographical sources for the same officers in departmental service lists, Blue books etc. Kirk-Greene has also written of his work in compiling these lists and of sources for colonial officers in general in: 'The British colonial governor in the literature', *ARD* 12, 1977, 10-13; and in 'Colonial service biographical data: the published sources', *ARD* 46, 1988, 2-16.

Francophone Africa

311
Annuaire des états d'Afrique noire: gouvernements et cabinets ministériels, partis politiques. Paris, Ediafric-La documentation africaine, 1961. 443pp.

- - 2nd ed. Paris, 1962. 443pp.

Brief biographies of leading political officials in the 14 countries of Francophone west and central Africa, and in regional and international African organizations.

312
Annuaire parlementaire des états d'Afrique noire. Paris, "Annuaire afrique", 1962. 332pp.

1,100 brief biographies of political and administrative officials in the Francophone countries of west and central Africa.

313
Présidents, administrateurs et directeurs généraux des sociétés publiques et privées d'Afrique noire. Paris, Ediafric-La documentation africaine, 1969. 471pp.

Running title : **PDG afrique**. Special number of *Bulletin de l'Afrique noire*. Includes some 1,500 biographies of key officials in the economic sphere in Francophone west and central Africa.

314
Les élites africaines 1970/71 [etc.]. Paris, Ediafric-La documentation africaine, 1971- .

Published as special numbers of *Bulletin de l'Afrique noire*. Issues for 1970/71,

1972, 1974, 1977, 1979. Brief biographies of political leaders of Francophone west & central Africa. Over 5,000 entries per issue.

315

Hommes et destins (Dictionnaire biographique d'outre-mer). Paris, Académie des sciences d'outre-Mer, 1975- .

8 vols. pub. to 1988. Ed. R. Cornevin. Each vol. contains an individual alphabetical sequence (and a cumulative index to earlier vols.) with 250 detailed entries for individuals of significance in French colonial history. Entries are signed and provided with bibliographies. Vol. 8, 1988, "Gouverneurs, administrateurs, magistrats". A large scale project originally founded in 1971, which acknowledges the example of the **Biographie belge d'outre-mer** (*see* 833).

316

Broc, N. **Dictionnaire illustré des explorateurs et grands voyageurs français du XIXe siècle. 1, Afrique.** Paris, Comité des travaux historiques et scientifiques, Ministère de l'éducation nationale, 1988. xxxi, 346pp. illus. 5 maps in pocket.

389 biographies with refs. to sources. Numerous illus. from the photographic collections of the Société de géographie. "An erudite and judicious compilation" (*JAH*, 32, 1991, 169).

See also 133.

Former German Africa

317

Weidmann, C. **Deutsche Männer in Afrika: Lexikon der hervorragendsten deutschen Afrika-Forscher, Missionare, [etc.].** Lübeck, B. Nöhring, 1894. viii, 194pp. illus.

An alphabetical biographical dictionary covering some 500 individuals, together with entries for organizations, and a particularly lengthy entry under "Missionen" (pp. 87-127, double column) with sections for each missionary society, and long lists of missionaries and their stations.

See also 387.

Lusophone Africa

318
Colecçao pelo império. Lisbon, Agência-Geral do Ultramar, Divisão de Publicações e Biblioteca, 1935-61. Fascs. 1-131.

A collection of biographies of those active in the Portuguese colonies: governors, administrators, missionaries, military leaders.

See also 50.

ATLASES & GAZETTEERS

ATLASES

Bibliographies

319
Library of Congress. **List of geographical atlases in the Library of Congress.**
Washington, DC, 1909-1974. 8 vols.

Vols. 1-4 cover material published before 1920 (Africa, vol. 1, pp. 1189-1192;
vol. 2, pp. 686-691); vols. 5-8 cover material published 1920-1960 (Africa, vol.
6, pp. 426-475; also sections under European countries, e.g. "France: colonies",
pp. 159-161).

320
Dahlberg, R.E. & Thomas, B.E. 'An analysis and bibliography of recent
African atlases', *African studies bulletin* 5, 1962, 22-32.

- - Supplement 1, *ibid.* 6, 1963, 6-9.

Original article lists 92 items, supplement adds 25. Covers material published
since 1945.

321
Dahlberg, R.E. 'A preliminary bibliography of African atlases', *Bulletin of the
Geography & Map Division of the Special Libraries Association* 59, 1965, 3-9,
32-37.

Lists 175 items, incorporating the majority of entries from Dahlberg and
Thomas (*see* 320) and adding 62 new items, most published before 1945.
Includes refs. to entries in Library of Congress, **List of geographical atlases
...** (*see* 319). Covers a wide range including school atlases and some world
atlases with good African coverage.

322
Stams, W. **National and regional atlases: a bibliographic survey, up to and
including 1978.** Amsterdam, International Cartographic Association, 1984.
249pp.

Africa, pp. 149-164 and 225-227. No annotations.

General

323

Atlas von Afrika; mit einem geographisch-statistischen Text. Vienna & Budapest, Hartleben, 1886. 16pp. 18 plates. 24 x 17 cm.

Comp. A. Hartleben. 50 coloured maps on 18 plates showing political divisions, topography, vegetation and ethnography.

324

Universities Mission to Central Africa. **The UMCA atlas**. London, 1903. 40pp. 8 plates. col. maps.

325

Ghisleri, A. **Atlante d'Africa**. Bergamo, Istituto Italiano d'Arti Grafiche, 1909. 238pp. 20 plates.

Includes 36 coloured maps on plates, and 160 maps and plans in the text, covering topography, economics and statistics.

326

Dardano, A. & Riccardi, R. **Atlante d'Africa**. Milan, Hoepli, 1936. 132pp. 24 col. maps on 16 plates, 120 photos. 41 x 32cm.

Maps compiled by Istituto Italiano d'Arti Grafiche di Bergamo. Essentially a revised ed. of Ghisleri (*see* 325). Maps by Dardano, text by Riccardi.

327

Parry, R.E. & Midgley, C. *eds*. **Wheaton's modern atlas of Africa**. Exeter, A. Wheaton, 1937. 16pp.

328

Pfrommer, F. **Afrika-Atlas**. Karlsruhe, Kunstdruckerei Künsterbund, [194?]. 8pp. incl. col. maps. 32 x 24cm.

Comp. by Reichskolonialbund Bundesführung. Covers topography, vegetation, agriculture, communications, natural resources, population, ethnography, and emphasizes the former German colonies.

329

The Times atlas of the world, mid-century edition. Vol. 4, Southern Europe and Africa. London, Times Publishing, 1956. 96 plates.

Plates 85-95 cover Africa, mostly at 1:5m. Later revisions of this atlas as **The Times atlas of the world: comprehensive edition** are issued as a one vol. work. The 1956 ed. remains convenient and useful for coverage of Africa towards the end of the colonial period.

330
Horrabin, J.F. **An atlas of Africa**. London, Gollancz/New York, Praeger, 1960. 162pp.

50 small black and white sketch-maps each with a facing page of interpretation. "For the intelligent newspaper reader" (preface). Emphasis on historical maps.

331
Boyd, A. & van Rensburg, P. **An atlas of African affairs**. London, Methuen/New York, Praeger, 1962. 133pp.

- - 2nd ed. London/New York, 1965. 133pp.

37 black and white sketch maps of contemporary Africa, with supporting text.

332
Martin, G.J. **Africa in maps**. Dubuque, IA, W.C. Brown, 1962. 124pp.

58 black and white thematic maps covering climate, political history, population, ethnography, public health, agriculture, communications, and industry.

333
Africa: maps and statistics/Kaarte en statistic Afrika. Pretoria, Africa Institute, 1962-65. 10pts. 194pp. 87 maps. 74 tables. 6 figs. 32x35 cm.

Originally announced as 12 pts. and so referred to in pts. 1-9. Pt. 10 notes change of policy. Parallel English/Afrikaans text, with statistical tables, and colour maps. Scales 1:30M & 1:60M. Pt. 1, Population; pt. 2, Vital and medical aspects; pt. 3, Cultural and educational aspects; pt. 4, Transport and communication; pt. 5, Energy resources, production and consumption; pt. 6, Agriculture and forestry; pt. 7, Livestock, farming and fishing; pt. 8: Mining, industry and labour; pt. 9, Trade, income and aid; pt. 10, Political development.

334
Shorter Oxford atlas of Africa. Oxford, Clarendon Press, 1966. 96pp. incl.

48pp. topographic maps.

Derived from topographic section of **Oxford regional economic atlas: Africa** (*see* 355). Index of 18,000 names.

335
Atlas Afriki/Atlas of Africa. Moscow, Glavnoe Upravienie Geodezii i Kartographie, 1968. 118pp. 32 x 27cm.

Text in Russian with separate 39pp. pamphlet containing English translations of map titles, legends and reference data. Includes thematic maps of Africa as a whole covering history, climate, geology, vegetation, fauna, peoples, language, agriculture, industry, communications, and regional maps (pp. 20-45).

336
Davies, H.R.J. **Tropical Africa: an atlas for rural development**. Cardiff, University of Wales Press, 1973. xiv, 81pp. 40pp. of maps. 41 x 24 cm.

Basically west, central and east Africa from Senegal east to Somalia, south to Zaire and Tanzania. 40 thematic maps at 1:20M and 1:40M. Compiled by Department of Geography, University College of Swansea for Unesco Agricultural Education and Science Division. Covers climate, population, communications, subsistence agriculture and cash crops.

337
Grand atlas du continent africain. Paris, "Jeune Afrique", 336pp. 140 maps.

Also pub. in English as **Atlas of the African continent**. New York, Hippocrene, 1973. 336pp. 140 maps. Editorial director, R. Nguyen Van Chi-Bonnardel. Prepared jointly by publishers of *Jeune Afrique* and *Africa magazine*. Maps prepared by L'Institut géographique national in Paris. Coloured maps at scales of 1:1M to 1:10M. Each country covered on 2 maps with accompanying text and statistics. Index-gazetteer of 6,000 entries. The standard modern atlas of Africa.

338
L'Afrique historique et géographique, St. Germain-en-Laye, Editions M.D.I., 1977. 32pp. 30 x 35cm.

Cover-title: **Atlas de l'Afrique**. Comp. A. Auger *et al*. 30 thematic maps at 1:30M.

339
U.S. Central Intelligence Agency. **Maps of the world's nations. Vol. 2, Africa.**
Washington, DC, 1977. 53pp.

One page map for each country showing only major cities, road and rail
routes and airports.

340
Cultural atlas of Africa. Oxford, Phaidon/New York, Facts on File, 1981.
240pp. col. maps. illus.

Ed. J. Murray. 84 maps with accompanying text and over 300 photos. Pt. 1,
physical background; pt. 2, cultural; pt. 3, nations of Africa, arranged by 8
regions, then country by country. Bibliography and gazetteer. Review, *Africa*,
52, 1982, 90-92.

341
Africa today: an atlas of reproducible pages. Wellesley, MA, "World Eagle",
1983. Loose leaf. 153pp. maps.

- - rev. ed. Wellesley, MA, 1990.

Includes 100 thematic maps with accompanying statistical data, and 53 maps
of individual countries reprinted from those issued by the U.S. Central
Intelligence Agency and Department of State.

342
Griffiths, I.L. **An atlas of African affairs.** London, Methuen, 1984. vii, 200pp.
maps.

Text discusses 55 themes, broadly divided into "environmental", "historical",
"political", "economic", and "the South", with a total of 121 black and white
maps. Appendices give a chronology of African independence, with notes on
major administrative changes and political leaders post independence.

343
Feizhou Dituji. Beijing, Ditu Chubanche, 1985. 250pp. 37 x 53cm.

Large scale general atlas of Africa. 41 plates with 72 thematic maps, the
majority at 1:40M or 1:60M; 55 plates with 94 topographic regional maps.
Contents list in English, index arranged by Chinese characters, but with
romanized equivalents added. All other information in Chinese.

344

Soviet Union. Glavnoe Upravienie Geodezii i Kartographie. **Atlas mira: Africa**. Moscow, 1985.

See also 25, 51, 90, 94.

Facsimiles

345

Yusuf Kamal, *Prince*. **Monumenta cartographica Africae et Aegypti**. Cairo, author, 1926-51. 5 vols. in 16.

Privately printed in the Netherlands in an edition of 75 copies. Much of the work on assembling the plates was undertaken by F.C. Wieder and J.H. Kramers in the Netherlands. Pts. 1-14 pub. 1926-1939; pts. 15-16 pub. 1951, delayed by the war and the death of Wieder. A complete set is claimed to weigh over 500lbs. Comprises 1,652 high quality collotype reproductions of maps from earliest times to the 19th century. Also reproduces many relevant texts in the original language with accompanying French translation. Vol. 1, 1926, "Époque avant Ptolémée"; vol. 2, 1928-1933, "Ptolémée et époque gréco-romain"; vol. 3, 1930-1935, "Époque arabe"; vol. 4, 1936-1939, "Époque des portulans, suivie par l'époque des découvertes"; vol. 5, 1951, "Additamenta (naissance et évolution de la cartographie moderne)". Use of this vast and valuable collection of material is facilitated by the author's **Quelques éclaircissements épars sur mes "Monumenta ... "**, Cairo, author, 1935. 216pp. *A list of geographical atlases in the Library of Congress*, vol.6, Washington, DC, Library of Congress, 1963, pp. 426-458 lists the subject of every plate. Reviews in *GJ*, 73, 1929, 549-550; 79, 1932, 143-144; 91, 1938, 558-559; *Geographical review*, 24, 1934, 175-176; 27, 1937, 686-687; 41, 1951, 670.

346

Klemp, E. **Africa on maps dating from the twelfth to the eighteenth century**. Leipzig, Edition Leipzig, 1968. 77 maps. 60pp. booklet in pocket.

High quality coloured facsimiles, reproducing originals located in 14 libraries and archives. The booklet provides a description of each plate.

347

Tooley, R.V. **Collectors' guide to maps of the African continent and Southern Africa**. London, Carta Press, 1969. xvi, 132, 100pp.

Includes reproductions of some 120 maps dating from 1540 to 1872 in black and white, with 6 in colour.

348

Norwich, I. **Maps of Africa: an illustrated and annotated carto-bibliography.**
Johannesburg, Donker, 1983. 444pp.

Bibliographical descriptions by P. Kolbe. Lists and describes 345 maps of
Africa dating from 1486 to 1886, arranged by region. Each map is reproduced
in black and white, with ten also being reproduced in colour.

Thematic

Agriculture

349

World atlas of agriculture. Vol. 4, Africa. Novara, Istituto Geografico de
Agostini for Committee for the World Atlas, 1976. xi, 761pp.

Small black and white maps, mostly in text, with comment and statistics.
Arrangement is alphabetical by country, followed by subdivisions for physical
environment and communication; population; exploitation of resources,
ownership and local tenure; land utilization, crops and communal husbandry;
and agricultural economy.

350

Clarke, R., *et al.* **African agriculture: the next twenty five years. Annex 5:
atlas of African agriculture.** Rome, Food and Agricultural Organization of the
U.N., 1986. 72pp. 22 x 32cm.

Maps on production, population and the economy. Text includes numerous
statistical tables and diagrams.

Climate

351

Conseil de co-operation technique en Afrique/Conseil scientifique d'Afrique
(CCTA/CSA). **Climatological atlas of Africa.** Lagos & Nairobi, 1961. viii,
110pp.

Comp. and ed. by S.P. Jackson at the African Climatology Unit, University of
the Witwatersrand, Johannesburg. Text in English, French and Portuguese. 55
double page plates, mostly at 1:5M. General and regional maps showing
annual and monthly data for rainfall, temperature and humidity.

352

Thomson, B.W. **Atlas of the climate of Africa**. London, Oxford University Press, 1965. 15pp. 132 maps. 46 x 52cm.

Black and white maps (1:22M to 1:30M) based on 1956-60 data. "A most valuable store of information ... not readily available from any other source", (*GJ*, 132, 1966, 291-292).

353

Klimatichesky atlas Afriki. Leningrad, Gidrometeoizdat, 1978. 2 vols. 30 x 40cm.

Ed. A. N. Lebedeva. 165 maps in total.

354

Leroux, M. **Le climat de l'Afrique tropicale/The climate of tropical Africa**. Paris, Éditions Champion, 1983. 2 vols. maps.

Vol. 1, Text. 633pp; vol. 2, Maps. 24pp., 247 plates including maps and diagrams. Parallel French and English text.

Economics

355

Oxford Regional Economic atlas: Africa. Oxford, Clarendon Press, 1965. 64, 164pp. incl. 112 pp. col. maps.

45pp. topographical maps (later revised and issued as **Shorter atlas of Africa**, *see* 334), remainder thematic. Critical review, *GJ* 131, 1965, 400-401.

History

356

Bartholomew, J.G. **A literary and historical atlas of Africa and Australasia**. London, Dent/New York, Dutton, 1913. (Everyman's library). xi, 218pp. maps.

Includes maps of notable battles, districts etc. connected with famous authors and their books.

357

Fage, J.D. **An atlas of African history**. London, Arnold, 1958. 64pp. maps.

Contains 62 black and white maps, covering 410-1957 A.D. Detailed legends.

Review, *Africa*, 29, 1959, 98-100.

- - 2nd ed. London, 1978. Maps by M. Verity.

71 maps. Uses two tones of brown shading to improve clarity. New maps are for pre 19th century period. Reviews, *GJ* 144, 1978, 521-522; *JAH* 20, 1979, 377.

358
Gray, R. 'Eclipse maps', *Journal of African history* 6, 1965, 251-262; 'Annular eclipse maps', *ibid.* 9, 1968, 147-157.

Together the two articles reproduce 9 maps (which were also advertised as being available in enlarged size 1:10M on plastic from the journal) showing the actual paths taken across the continent by 164 total solar eclipses visible in Africa, 1000-2000 AD. The intention is to aid in identifying oral traditions with particular eclipses. Much of the data are drawn from that originally published in T. von Oppolzer, **Canon der Firslinissi**, Vienna, 1887; English trans. by O. Gingerich, New York, Door, 1902.

359
Gailey, H.A. **The history of Africa in maps**. Chicago, IL, Denoyer-Gappert, 1967. 96pp. maps.

47 hand-drawn and lettered black and white maps with accompanying text. "For schools and colleges" (introduction).

360
Clark, J.D. **Atlas of African prehistory**. Chicago, IL, University of Chicago, 1967. 62pp. maps.

Comp. under the auspices of the Pan African Congress on Prehistory and Quaternary Studies. 12 base maps, 38 transparent overlays (25 at 1:20M, 13 at 1:38M). Includes maps showing rainfall, vegetation, soils etc. of modern Africa, together with maps showing similar hypothetical data for prehistoric times, accompanied by transparent "cultural overlays" for various periods of prehistory from the Earlier Stone Age to the Neolithic. 62pp "handbook" section of explanatory notes includes a gazetteer of prehistoric sites. Reviews in *GJ*, 137, 1971, 592-593; *AHS*, 1, 1968, 111-112

361
Freeman-Grenville, G.S.P. **A modern atlas of African history**. London, Rex Collings, 1976. 63 pp. maps.

Maps by E. Hausman. Includes 70 two-colour maps, about half concerned with Africa pre 1500. Intended as a companion to the author's **Chronology of African history** (*see* 63). Review, *IJAHS*, 11, 1978, 134-135.

362
McEvedy, C. **The Penguin atlas of African history**. Harmondsworth, Penguin Books/New York, Facts on File, 1980. 142pp. maps.

59 black and white plates with facing text; 21 covering the period pre 1000 A.D., 19 covering post 1800. Outline schematic maps as in the author's earlier series of world history atlases. Excludes the Indian Ocean islands of Mauritius, Seychelles and Réunion.

363
Kwamewa-Poh, M. *et al.* **African history in maps**. Harlow, Longmans, 1982. 80pp. 36 col. maps.

364
Historical atlas of Africa. London, Longman, 1985. 168pp. col.maps.

Ed. by J.F.A. Ajayi & M. Crowder, with over 50 contributors. Represents a ten year project of compilation. Includes 72 "map-sets", altogether comprising over 300 individual maps. 5,000 entry index provides a "unique guide to name changes over 3,000 years of African history" (preface). "Difficult to find anything negative to say ... unlikely to be surpassed as the standard work for years to come" (*JAH* 28, 1987, 151-152).

365
Freeman-Grenville, G.S.P. **The new atlas of African history**. London/New York, Simon & Schuster, 1991. 144pp. maps.

103 maps accompanied by 64pp. text.

   Colonies: general

366
Supan, A.G. **Die territoriale Entwicklung der europäische Kolonien; mit einem kolonialgeschichtlichen Atlas von 12 Karten und 40 Karten im Text.** Gotha, J. Perthes, 1906. xi, 344pp.

Covers the individual colonial empires. Review in *Bulletin of the American Geographical Society* 1908, 699-702.

British

367

Oxford atlas of the British colonies. Pt. 1, British Africa. Oxford, William Stanford, 1905. ii, 17pp.

17 maps: rainfall, temperature, physical Africa in general, regional maps of the Cape, Natal, Transvaal, Rhodesia, West Africa, East Africa and Central Africa.

368

Robertson, C.G. & Bartholomew, J.G. **Historical and modern atlas of the British Empire specially prepared for students.** London, Methuen, 1905. 15, 64pp.

369

Philip's atlas of the British Empire. London, G.Philip & Sons, 1924. iv, 64pp. incl. 32 col. maps. illus. diagrs. 26 x 21cm.

370

Stembridge, J.H. **An atlas of British Empire.** London, Oxford University Press, 1944. (Oxford pamphlets on world affairs, 65). 45pp. incl. col. maps.

Also pub as: **Atlas of the British Commonwealth and Empire.** New York, OUP, 1944. (America in a world at war, 29).

371

G.B. Colonial Office. **Colonial Office list. Map supplement.** London, HMSO, 1948. 2pp. 39 colour maps. 23 x 15 cm.

Comp. by Directorate of Colonial Survey. Includes individual plates for each African colony.

French

372

France. Ministère de la Marine et des Colonies. **Atlas des colonies françaises.** Paris, A. Challamel, 1866. 14 maps.

373

Mager, H. **Atlas colonial.** Paris, C. Bayle, 1885. 432pp. incl. 30 col. maps.

374

Mager, H. & Jacquemart, A. **Atlas colonial: éd. populaire et classique.** Paris, C. Bayle, 1890. 20pp. incl. 19 maps.

375

Pelet, P. **Nouvel atlas des colonies françaises, dressé par ordre de l'Administration des Colonies.** Paris, A. Challamel, 1891. iv, 70pp. 22 col. maps. 27 x 20cm.

- - new ed. **Atlas des colonies françaises.** Paris, Colin, 1902. ii, 74, 26pp. 27 col. maps.

- - new ed. Paris, [1914?] iv, 74, 27pp. 27 col. maps.

1902 ed. orig. pub. in parts, 1898-1902, and described by Pelet in *Annales de géographie* 9, 1900, 229-232.

376

Malleterre, G. & Legendre, P. **Livre-atlas des colonies françaises à l'usage de l'enseignement des colonies.** Paris, C. Delagrave, 1900. 6 vols.

Vol. 6, Africa.

377

France. Ministère de l'éducation nationale. **Atlas des térritoires français d'outre-mer.** Paris, Service de coordination de l'enseignement dans la France d'outre-mer, [1912?]. (Carnet de documentation, 21). 19pp. incl. 14pp. maps. 28 x 22cm.

378

Atlas colonial français: colonies, protectorats et pays sous mandat. Paris, L'Illustration, 1929. 318pp. incl. 56 plates of colour maps. 42 x 33cm.

Maps and text by P. Pollacchi. Maps 4-25 and 27 cover Africa, including inset city plans.

379

Grandidier, G. *ed.* **Atlas des colonies françaises, protectorats et territoires sous mandat de la France, publié sous la direction de G. Grandidier.** Paris, Societé d'éditions géographiques, maritimes et coloniales, 1934. iii, 236 pp. incl. maps. 39 colour map plates. 56 x 41cm. Loose-leaf (issued in parts).

Plates 2-29, Africa. Scales from 1:1M to 1:8M. Thematic maps covering geology, rainfall, population, and the economy. Text covers geography and ethnography, and includes descriptions of major cities. Section for West Africa by H. Hubert, for Equatorial Africa and Cameroon by G. Bruel, for Madagascar by G. Grandidier. Review, *Annales de Géographie*, 44, 1935, 80-86.

380
Les atlas de Jeune Afrique. Paris, "Jeune Afrique", 1975-

A series of standardised thematic atlases with accompanying text. Vols. for sub Saharan Africa include Cameroon, Central African Republic, Congo, Côte d'Ivoire, Mali, Mauritania, Niger, Senegal, Togo, Upper Volta/Burkina Faso, Zaire. *See* more detailed entries under the appropriate country.

German

381
Deutscher Kolonial-Atlas für den amtlichen Gebrauch in den Schutzgebieten. Berlin, D. Reimer, 1893. ii, [84]pp. 5 plates.

Pp. 1-32, "Die Schutzgebeite des deutschen Reiches" by J. Partsch; pp. 35-84, notes on each plate by R. Keipart, discussing sources, with an index to names shown. Detailed bibliography of 150 items for maps of west Africa. Plate 2, West Africa; plate 3, South West Africa; plate 4, East Africa (all at 1:3M).

382
Deutsche Kolonialgesellschaft. **Kleiner deutscher Kolonialatlas**. Berlin, D. Reimer, 1896. 4pp. 7 col. maps. 32 x 16 cm.

- - 2nd to 6th eds. pub. Berlin, 1898-1904.

continued by:

Deutsche Kolonialgesellschaft. **Deutscher Kolonialatlas mit Jahrbuch**. Berlin, D. Reimer, 1905-1941. Irreg. 22 issues.

Each issue contains 8 (later 9) maps, of which sheets 2 to 6 (later 2 to 7) cover Africa.

383
P. Langhans, *ed*. **Deutscher Kolonial Atlas**. Gotha, J.Perthes, 1897. 3, 18pp. 30 col. maps.

384
Sprigade, P. & Moisel, M. **Grosser deutscher Kolonialatlas; herausg. von der Kolonial-Abtheilung des auswärtigen Amts.** Berlin, D. Reimer, 1901-1914. 8 pts. col. maps. 57 x 35cm.

- - **Ergänzungs-Lieferung[en].** Berlin, 1909-1914. 3 pts.

Maps 9 to 15, which would have included South-West Africa were announced as forthcoming but never pub. Maps 2a-b (1906-07), Togo, 2 sheets at 1:500,000; maps 3-8d (1901-14) Kamerun, 10 sheets at 1:1M; maps 16-24 (1903-11) Deutsch Ostafrika, 9 sheets at 1:1M. Supplement includes revised issues of maps 3-6 and 8.

385
Deutsche Kolonialgesellschaft. **Wirtschafts-Atlas der deutschen Kolonien.** Berlin, D. Reimer, 1906. 24pp. incl. 10 col. maps. 44 x 34cm.

- - 2nd ed. Berlin, 1907.

386
M. Eckert. **Wirtschaftsatlas der deutschen Kolonien: auf Veranlassung der deutschen Kolonialgesellschaft ... topographische Grundlagen von P. Sprigade und M. Moisel.** Berlin, D. Reimer, [1912]. viii, 52pp. incl. 53 colour maps and 65 tables.

Shows routes of navigation and includes much statistical information. Plans of Lomé, Douala, Swakopmund, Lüderitzkircht, Windhoek, Dar es Salaam.

Gazetteers

387
Deutsches Kolonial-Lexikon. Dresden, Kühtman, 1903. 165pp.

Ed. O. Kausch. Alphabetical list of locations in German colonies. Also includes lists of German explorers and missionaries.

Portuguese

388
Silveira, L. **Ensaio de iconografia dos cidades portuguesas do ultramar.** Lisbon, Junta de Investigações do Ultramar, [1952]. 4 vols. illus. maps.

Vol. 2, pp. 125-301, Africa; pp. 243-299, eastern Africa. Reproductions and descriptions of maps, drawings, city plans, fortifications, etc. P. 301: English summary, "Portuguese towns in Africa".

389
Portugal. Ministério da Marinha e Ultramar. Commissão de Cartografia. **Atlas colonial Português**. Edição reduzida. Lisbon, 1903. 10 maps.

- - 2nd ed. Lisbon, 1909. 13 maps.

390
Atlas de Portugal e colónias: descriptivo e illustrado. Lisbon, Empresa Editora do Atlas de Geografia Universal, 1906. [n.p.]

Comp. by J.G. Ferreira da Costa.

391
Portugal. Ministério das Colónias. Commissão de Cartografia. **Atlas colonial Português**. Lisbon, 1914. 2pp. 22 plates col. maps. 41 x 29cm.

392
Portugal. Ministério das Colónias. Junta das Missões Geográficas e de Investigações do Ultramar. **Atlas de Portugal ultramarino e das grandes viagens Portuguesas de descobrimento e expansão**. Lisbon, 1948. viiipp. 110 colour maps on 118pp. 49 x 37cm.

- - [Index], *Garcia de Orta* 2, 1954, 257-261.

Rev. ed. of **Atlas colonial Português** (*see* 391). Maps 2 and 8 show voyages and travels exploring Africa, 15th-19th centuries; maps 12-86, Africa. Thematic maps for Cape Verde, Guinea, São Tomé & Principe, Angola and Mozambique, covering ethnography, linguistics, geology, the economy, and communications.

393
Atlas missionário português. Lisbon, Missão para o Estudo da Missionologia Africana, Centro de Estudos Políticos e Socias, 1962. 177pp.

- - 2nd ed. Lisbon, Centro de Estudos Históricos Ultramarinos, Junta de Investigações do Ultramar, 1964. vii, 198pp.

Comp. by A. da Silva Rego and E. dos Santos. High quality colour production. Covers Roman Catholic and Protestant missions and activities in the Portuguese Empire. 2nd ed. includes additional maps on non-missionary activities such as administrative divisions, ethnography, languages, and demography.

For atlases of **Italian** *colonies, see 416, 417; for* **Spanish** *colonies see 1335.*

GAZETTEERS

Bibliographies

394
Meynen, E. **Gazetteers and glossaries of geographical names of the member-countries of the United Nations: ... bibliography, 1946-1976.** Wiesbaden, Steiner, 1984. xiv, 518pp.

Arranged by country. The fullest available listing for its period of coverage.

See also 399.

General discussions of African toponymy

395
Martonne, E. de. 'Aspects de la toponymie africaine', *Bulletin commercial, historique et scientifique de l'Afrique occidentale française,* 1930, 400-423.

Comments by the Director of the survey and mapping activities of A.O.F.

396
Aurousseau, M. **The spelling of African place names**. London, Royal Geographical Society, Permanent Committee on Geographic Names, 1950-1953. (PGCN leaflets 6, 6a, 6c).

397
Tucker, A.N. 'Towards place name gazetteers in Africa - some problems of standardization', **Sixth International Congress of Onomastic Sciences, Munich 24-28 Aug., 1958, Report**. Munich, Bayerische Akademie der Wissenchaften, 1961. Vol.3, Paper 92, pp. 744-749.

Discusses problems relating to the colonial presence, the multi-lingual nature of many countries, and whether standardization should be on a political, linguistic or regional basis. Among a number of earlier articles by Tucker, *see* especially 'The spelling of African place-names on maps', *Bulletin of the School of Oriental and African Studies,* 12, 1948, 824-830 and 'Conflicting principles in the spelling of African place-names', *Onoma* 7, 1956/57, 215-228.

398

Institut géographique national. **Principes de transcription des toponymes africaines.** Paris, 1963.

399

African ethonyms and toponyms: report and papers of the meeting of experts organized by Unesco, Paris, 3-7 July, 1978. Paris, Unesco, 1984. (General History of Africa: studies and documents, 6).

Includes 8 papers on problems of choice of appropriate forms and spelling of names of African peoples and places (*see* paper by Hrbek entered at 61). Pp. 187-196, "African toponymy: a bibliography". A footnote indicates that the bibliography was originally prepared by C.V. Taylor in 1967, and had not been updated.

400

Kake, B.I. **Glossaire critique des expressions géographiques concernant le pay des noirs, d'après les sources de langue arabe du milieu du VIIIe à la fin du XIIIe siècle.** Paris, "Présence Africaine", 1965. 157pp.

Gazetteers & placename directories

401

Gross, A. **Gazetteer of central and south Africa.** London, "Geographia", [1926?]. 271pp.

Despite title, includes all Africa south of the Sahara. Some 10,000 entries of one or two lines for towns and natural features with up to twelve lines for states and territories.

402

G.B. Army. G.H.Q. Middle East. Survey Directorate. **Africa: index gazetteer showing place-names on 1:2M map series.** Fayid, 1947. iv, 501pp.

Contains over 50,000 names derived from 37 sheets, compiled by various mapping agencies. References given to sheet and degree square together with abbreviated indication of the feature named. Lists of "meanings of terms in local languages".

403

Kirchherr, E.C. **Abyssinia to Zona Al Sur Del Draa: an index to the political units of Africa in the period 1951-1967**: a gazetteer of former and current names of African territories. Kalamazoo, MI, Western Michigan University,

Institute of International & Area Studies & School of Graduate Studies, 1968. (Monographic Series on Cultural Changes, 2). 32pp. maps.

- - 2nd ed. ... **1950-1974**. Athens, OH, Ohio University, Center of International Studies, 1975. (Papers in International Studies, Africa series, 25). x, 40pp. maps.

- - 3rd ed. **Abyssinia to Zimbabwe: a guide to the political units of Africa in the period 1947-1978**. Athens, 1979. x, 80pp.

A guide to name changes of African states. Each ed. is considerably expanded in depth of coverage. Later completely revised and published as **Place names of Africa, 1935-1986** (*see* 406).

404
U.S. Board on Geographic Names. **Africa and South West Asia: official standard names approved by the U.S.B.G.N: gazetteer supplement, Aug. 1972**. Washington, DC, 1972. 182pp.

Contains supplementary lists to vols. for individual countries issued by the U.S.B.G.N. Refs. to specific sections are given below under each country.

405
Cities of the world: vol. 1, Africa. Detroit, MI, Gale Research, 1985. 788pp.

- - 2nd ed. Detroit, 1986. 788pp.

- - 3rd ed. Detroit, 1987. 842pp.

Ed. M.W. Young and S.L. Stetler. Based on the diplomatic "Post reports" issued by the U.S. Department of State, and so only includes countries with which the U.S.A. had diplomatic relations at the time of compilation (e.g. omits Angola). Arranged by country with general "country profile", followed by long entries for major cities (75 in 1st and 2nd eds., 84 in 3rd) and very brief comments on some 600 others.

406
Kirchherr, E.C. **Place names of Africa, 1935-1986: a political gazetteer**. Metuchen, NJ, Scarecrow Press, 1987. viii, 136pp.

"Completely revised, updated and enlarged ed." of **Abyssinia to Zona Al Sur Del Draa [etc]** (*see* 403). Alphabetical list of current and past names of African states, with detailed notes on name and boundary changes, illus. by

23 maps. Detailed supplementary notes on: mandates & trusteeships; French colonial federations in west & central Africa; former Italian colonies; Northwest Africa; former British territories of central & southern Africa; African islands; secessionist states; "independent homelands". Review, *IJAHS* 21, 1988, 759-760.

407
Lieux et peuples d'Afrique. Paris, Éditions Nathan for Radio France internationale service co-opération, 1987. 276pp.

Originally prepared by J. Sorel and B.I. Kake for the broadcast "Mémoire d'un continent". Alphabetical list of 740 place names (and a few ethnic names) with notes on their origins, and references to sources. Index by country.

See also 103, 387.

NORTH-EAST AFRICA

Djibouti
Ethiopia
Somalia
Sudan

HANDBOOKS

408

Bertarelli, L.V. **Possedementi e colonie; Isole Egee, Tripolitania, Cirenaica, Eritrea, Somalia**. Milan, Touring Club Italiano, 1929. (Guida d'Italia). 852pp. 91 maps & plans.

Pp. 519-686, Eritrea (with 6 maps); pp. 687-808, Somalia (with 6 maps). Detailed guide book, which, in addition to itineraries, includes coverage of topography, fauna and flora, history and exploration, peoples and languages, agriculture and industry, and politics and administration.

409

Piccioli, A. **La nuova Italia d'oltremare**; l'opera del fascismo nelle colonie iteliane; noticie, dati, documenti. Milan, Mondadori, 1933. xxxi, 1776pp. illus.

- - 2nd ed. Milan, 1934. 2 vols.

Includes Ethiopia, Eritrea, Somaliland, also Libya. Sections on history and politics, agriculture, public works, education, communications, law, public health. Numerous photographs and statistical tables. No index. Bibliography, pp. xvii-xxxi.

410

Africa orientale italiana. Milan, Touring Club Italiano, 1938. (Guida d'Italia, 24). 640pp. 15 maps. 16 city plans.

Covers Ethiopia, Eritrea, Italian Somaliland. Pp. 33-174 contain general information on geography, natural resources, history, peoples and communications; pp. 175-623 treat each district individually, with detail based upon itineraries; pp. 623-640, index-gazetteer. Coloured folding maps at 1:6M; regional maps at 1:1M. "Excellent work ... much more than a mere guide" (Duignan).

411

G.B. War Office. **A gazetteer of Abyssinia (including Eritrea, Italian, British and French Somaliland)**. Khartoum, Directorate of Army Printing and Stationery Service, 1940. [137pp.]

Despite title, basically a handbook. Comp. Capt. G.C. Shortridge. Pt. 1 (pp. 1-38), geographical; pt. 2 (pp. 1-45), political ; pt. 3 (pp. 1-54), diplomatic and military history.

412

Ethnographic survey of Africa: North-Eastern Africa. London, International Institute, 1955-1974. 4 vols. illus. maps.

Sub-series of the **Ethnographic survey** (*see* 54). Vol. 1, 'Peoples of the Horn of Africa; Somali, Afar and Saho', by I.M. Lewis. 1955. 199pp; vol. 2, 'The Galla of Ethiopia; the kingdoms of Kafa and Janjero' by G.W.B. Huntingford. 1955. 156pp; vol. 3, 'Peoples of South-West Ethiopia and its borderland', by E. Cerulli. 1956. 148pp; vol. 4, 'The central Ethiopians: Amhara, Tigrina and related peoples', by W.A. Shack. 1974. 152pp.

413

Tucker, A.N. & Bryan, M.A. **The non-Bantu languages of North Eastern Africa**; with a supplement on the non-Bantu languages of southern Africa by E.O.J. Westphal. London, Oxford University Press for International African Institute, 1956. (Handbook of African languages pt. 3). xvi, 228pp. maps.

A systematic survey of languages, speakers and their location. *See* 66 for note on the **Handbook**. Review, *Africa*, 27, 1957, 298-300.

YEARBOOKS

414

Annuario delle colonie italiane [e dei paesi vicini]. Rome, Istituto Fascista dell'Africa Italiana [etc.], 1926-1940. Annual. 14 issues (1938/39 issued as 1 vol.)

Title varies: **Annuario dell'Impero** (1937); **Annuario dell'Africa italiana** (1938/39-1940). Ed. for 1938/39 includes list of events of 1937 and other general political and administrative information; pt. 3. "Africa Orientale Italiana" (pp. 443-814) covers historical, geographical, administrative and economic data. Detailed index.

415

Italy. Ministero della Cultura Popolare. **Guida amministrativa e delle attività economiche dell'impero Africa orientale italiana, 1938/39.** Turin, Briscioli, 1938. 612pp. illus.

Covers administrative districts of Addis Ababa, Amara, Eritrea, Galla-Sudan, Harar, Somalia. Essays on the empire in general, and data on major relevant societies, libraries etc. in Italy, followed by details of the administration, judiciary, military, communications, trade, finance, and professional and commercial directories for each district.

ATLASES & GAZETTEERS

Atlases

416

Baratta, M. & Visintin, L. **Atlante delle colonie italiane con notizie geografiche ed economiche.** Novara, Istituto Geografico de Agostini, [1928]. xv, 87 pp. 36 col. maps. 113 illus.

417

Agostini, G. de. **Italy and her Empire: perforated pocket atlas.** Trans. E. Cope. Genoa, E.E. Ortelli, 1937. 34pp.

Includes 16 col. maps with accompanying text.

Gazetteers

418

Italy. Istituto Geografico Militare. **[Index gazetteer to] Carta dell'Africa orientale, scala 1:1,000,000.** Florence, 1935. 8 pts.

Covers Ethiopia and Italian Somaliland with pamphlets for Addis Ababa, 30pp; Alula, 20pp; Asmara, 44pp; Belet Uen, 24pp; Harrar, 25pp; Lago Margherita, 28pp; Mogadiscio, 25pp; Obbia, 10pp.

419 (*also entered at* 560, 1673)
G.B. Army. G.H.Q. Middle East. Survey Directorate. **East Africa: index gazetteer showing place names on 1:500,000 map series.** Cairo, 1946-1948. 3 vols. in 4.

Vols. 2, 2A (1946-47). vii, 474pp. "Abyssinia, Eritrea, British, French and Italian

Somaliland and part of the Sudan". Sudan included only where it appears on edges of sheets covering other countries.

420
U.S. Board on Geographic Names. **Ethiopia, Eritrea and the Somalilands; official names approved by the U.S.B.G.N.** Washington, DC, 1950. v, 498pp.

Pp. 1-250, Ethiopia; pp.251-308, Eritrea; pp. 309-380, British Somaliland; pp. 403-498, Italian Somaliland; pp. 381-401, French Somaliland. For later eds. covering individual countries *see* 430, 465, 489.

- - **Gazetteer supplement: Africa and South-West Asia.** Washington, DC, 1972. (Pp. 55-60, Ethiopia; p. 55, Somalia).

DJIBOUTI

HANDBOOKS

421
India. Intelligence Branch. **French possessions in the Gulf of Aden**. Simla, 1895. 51pp. maps.

Comp. Capt. E.J.E. Swayne. Follows standard pattern of the British War Office "précis" volumes. Map of the region at 1:1M.

422
G.B. War Office. General Staff. **Military report on French Somaliland**. London, 1909. (A. 1317). viii, 91pp. illus. maps in pocket.

History, administration, geography, climate, and local tribes.

423
G.B. Foreign Office. Historical Section. **French Somaliland**. London, 1920. (F.O. Handbook, 109). 28pp.
Also pub. in F.O. **Peace handbooks**, vol. 17. London, 1920.

424
Île de la Réunion; Côte française des Somalis; Établissements français dans l'Inde. Paris, Société d'éditions géographiques, maritimes et coloniales, 1931. (Exposition coloniale internationale de Paris). various paging. illus. maps.

'La Côte française des Somalis', comp. A.D. Martineau, 66pp., includes an account of the geography, history, peoples and economic structure, with statistics. (The section on Réunion is discursive and with little specific fact, and has not been noted below).

425
Africa Orientale Italiana. Governo Generale. **Costa francese dei Somali**. Addis Ababa, 1939. 3 vols. illus. maps.

Comp. G. Adami. Vol. 1, 154pp. Topography, climate, flora and fauna, communications; vol. 2, 70pp. Tribes, administration, economics and politics; vol. 3, 21pp. Supplement to vol. 2 specifically regarding the contemporary military situation.

See also 1634.

YEARBOOKS

426

French Somaliland. Service d'information de la Côte française des Somalis. **Annuaire de la Côte française des Somalis.** Djibouti, 1955-1959?

Title varies: **Guide-annuaire ...**

See also 1662.

STATISTICS

427

French Territory of the Afars & Issas. Service de statistique et documentation/Djibouti. Direction nationale de la Statistique [etc.]. **Bulletin de statistique et de documentation,** Djibouti, 1970- . Quarterly (irreg.)

Title varies: **Bulletin trimestriel de statistique** (issues 32-36)/**Bulletin semestriel de statistique** (issue 37, 1981-). Issue 41, 1987.

428

Djibouti. Direction nationale de la Statistique [etc.]. **Annuaire statistique de Djibouti 1975/78** [etc.]. Djibouti, 1981- . Annual.

429

Statistik des Auslandes: Länderberichte: Dschibuti. Wiesbaden, Statistisches Bundesamt, 1983- . Irreg.

Issue for 1983.

ATLASES & GAZETTEERS

Gazetteers

430

U.S. Board on Geographic Names. **Gazetteer of Djibouti.** Washington, DC, 1983. 151pp.

Revised version of the appropriate section in **Ethiopia, Eritrea and the Somalilands ...** (*see* 420). Includes 6,750 entries from maps at scale of 1:100,000.

ETHIOPIA

HANDBOOKS

431

G.B. War Office. Topographical & Statistical Department. **Routes in Abyssinia**. London, 1867. ii, 239pp. maps in pocket.

Comp. Lt. Col. A.C. Cooke. Unlike other vols. issued by the War Office as "Routes" this vol. consists of reprints of the texts of some 30 travel accounts ranging from James Bruce (1771) to the mid 19th century. Includes two reproductions of maps from the original accounts, and a new map indicating the various routes included. Arranged as a basic sequence, with two appendices.

- - [2nd ed.] **Col. Cooke's general description of Abyssinia and the different routes leading into it; presented to the House of Commons in pursuance of their address dated 26 Nov. 1867**. London, HMSO, 1867. (Command paper 3964). 252pp.

Rearranges text into a single sequence, and includes only the map specially drawn for the 1867 ed.

432

G.B. War Office. Intelligence Division. **Précis of information obtained by the British mission to Abyssinia (March to June 1897)**. London, 1897. (A. 508). 144pp. 5 maps in pocket.

Comp. F.R. Wingate and A.W. Gleichen of the mission. Usual "précis" coverage of topography, history and the administration with additional data on religion, education, literature and art. Appendices include texts of documents relating to boundaries. Maps include 1:63,360 of Addis Ababa, and three 1:250,000 route maps of the expedition.

433

G.B. War Office. Intelligence Department. **Military report on Abyssinia (Provisional)**. London, 1902. (A. 762). xiii, 162pp.

Comp. Capt. C.C. Bigham. Includes coverage of history, geography and peoples for the whole country, together with sections for each sub-region. 14 routes described in detail.

434
G.B. War Office. General Staff. **Military report on Eritrea**. London, 1906. (A. 1120). iv, 43pp. map.

Includes map at 1:3M.

435
G.B. Admiralty. Naval Intelligence Division. **A handbook of Abyssinia**. London, 1917. (C.B. 447). Vol. 1, General. 551pp. *No more published.*

Pt. 1, General; geography, climate, population, health, communications; pt. 2, Abyssinia; history, social conditions, religion, administration, trade and resources; part 3, brief treatments of Eritrea, British, French & Italian Somalilands. Appendices include a bibliography, "recent military information", and a very extensive (pp. 361-532) language section providing notes on grammar, vocabularies, and phrases in Amharic, Tigrine, Galla and Somali. Vol. 2 was to cover "routes ... and towns".

436
G.B. Foreign Office. Historical Section. **Abyssinia**. London, 1920. (F.O. Handbook, 129). 109pp.

- - **Eritrea**. London, 1920. (F.O. Handbook, 126). 32pp.

Both also pub. in F.O. **Peace handbooks**, vol. 20. London, 1920.

437
G.B. War Office. General Staff. **A handbook of Abyssinia: communications**. London, 1922. (B. 133). 559pp. 2 maps in pocket.

Sections on roads, railways, and telegraphs with detailed information on 121 routes, containing much miscellaneous topographical and ethnographic data. Descriptive gazetteer of about 100 localities; glossary of "native topographical words". Essentially provides the coverage of the proposed vol. 2 of the Admiralty **Handbook ...** (*see* 435) which was never issued.

438
G.B. War Office. General Staff. Intelligence Division. **A handbook of Ethiopia;** provisional ed. Khartoum, 1941. 150pp.

439
G.B. War Office. General Staff (Intelligence). Headquarters Troops in the Sudan. **Handbook of Western Italian East Africa**. Khartoum, 1941. 2 vols.

(B.1214, B.1214-1).

Covers Abyssinia and Eritrea to the north and west of Addis Ababa. Vol. 1, General. iv, 195pp. maps. Includes gazetteer of 71 settlements. Vol. 2, Communications. ii, 263pp. illus. maps. Includes itineraries for some 60 road routes with the "greater part of information taken from **Africa orientale italiana**" (*see* 412). Maps of whole region at 1:6M and of western region at 1:2M.

440

G.B. War Office. General Staff (Intelligence). Headquarters Troops in the Sudan. **Handbook of Eritrea: vol. 2. Communications.** Khartoum, 1943. iii, 195pp. illus. maps.

Revised version of vol. 2 of the **Handbook of Western Italian East Africa** (*see* 439), omitting Abyssinia and giving greatly increased detail on each route and more illustrations. Map at 1:1M.

441

Ethiopia. Ministry of Commerce & Industry. **Economic handbook of Ethiopia.** Addis Ababa, 1951.

- - rev. ed. Addis Ababa, 1958. xii, 171pp. illus. map.

442

Guide book of Ethiopia. Addis Ababa, Ethiopian Chamber of Commerce, 1954. xxx, 443pp. illus. maps.

Includes sections on "government, people, culture", "physiography, climate, geology", "agriculture", "commerce, industry & finance" together with much general information and statistics and notes on each province. Bibliography, pp. 417-433. Numerous photos and maps.

443

Ewert, K. **Äethiopien.** Bonn, Schroeder for Deutsche Afrika-Gesellschaft, 1959. (Die Länder Afrikas, 22). 99pp.

444

Area handbook for Ethiopia, comp. G.A. Lipsky, *et al.* Washington, DC, U.S. Department of Defence, 1960. xi, 621pp. maps. (Reprinted, 1964).

- - 2nd ed. comp. I. Kaplan, *et al.* Washington, DC, 1971. xiv, 543pp. maps.

- - 3rd ed. **Ethiopia: a country study**; comp. I. Kaplan & H.D. Nelson. Washington DC, 1981. xxix, 366pp. illus. maps.

445

Lipsky, G.A., *et al.* **Ethiopia: its people, its society, its culture**. New Haven, CN, Human Relations Area Files Press, 1962. (Survey of world cultures, 9). xii, 376pp. illus. maps.

"Prepared under the auspices of the American University, Washington". Detailed survey with sections on history, geography, ethnic groups, languages, literature, administration and the economy.

446

Ethiopia. Ministry of Information. **The handbook for Ethiopia**. Nairobi, University Press of Africa, 1969. 328pp. illus. maps.

Topographic, political & economic information. Includes economic statistics and business directory.

447

Prouty, C. & Rosenfeld, E. **Historical dictionary of Ethiopia**. Metuchen, NJ, Scarecrow Press, 1982. (African historical dictionaries, 32). xv, 431pp.

Includes a bibliography of 213pp. Review, *JAH*, 23, 1983, 425.

Date-conversion tables

448

Conti-Rossini, C. **Tabelle comparative del Calendario Etiopico col Calendario Romano**. Rome, Istituto per l'Oriente, 1948. 47pp.

Comparative date tables from 1341 to 2000 A.D.

449

Hammerschmidt, E. **Äthiopische Kalendartafeln**. Wiesbaden, Franz Steiner, 1977. 21pp.

Tables for converting days of each month from the Ethiopian calendar to the Julian and Gregorian calendars.

YEARBOOKS

450

Trade directory and guide book to Ethiopia. Addis Ababa, Ethiopian Chamber of Commerce, 1954- . Irreg.

Title varies : **Ethiopian trade directory.** 1st issue, 1954; 2nd issue 1967; 3rd issue, 1971/72; issue for 1990. Includes general geographical and economic information, and a commercial directory.

451

Trade directory of the Empire of Ethiopia. London, Diplomatic Press & Publishing Co., 1965. ? 1 issue.

See also 539, 541, 544.

STATISTICS

452

Ethiopia. Central Statistical Office [etc.]. **Statistical abstract.** Addis Ababa, 1963- . Annual (bi-annual, 1980-).

Text in English and Amharic. 1967/68 issued as one vol. Not issued for 1973-74. Abbreviated version issued as **Statistical pocket book** (later **People's Democratic Republic of Ethiopia in facts & figures**) Addis Ababa, 1963- .

453

Statistik des Auslandes: Länderberichte: Äthiopien. Wiesbaden, Statistisches Bundesamt, 1965- Irreg.

Issues for 1965, 1972, 1982, 1990.

454

Ethiopia. Central Statistical Authority. **Statistical bulletin.** Addis Ababa, 1968- . Irreg. (issue 47, October 1985).

DIRECTORIES OF ORGANIZATIONS

455

Ethiopian Library Association. **Directory of Ethiopian libraries.** Addis Ababa, 1968. 76pp.

Comp. G. Amos. Lists 94 libraries.

456

Ethiopian Library Association. **Directory of special libraries in Ethiopia.** Addis Ababa, 1976.

BIOGRAPHICAL SOURCES

457

Puglisi, G. **Chi é? Dell'Eritrea: dizionario biografico.** Asmara, Agenzia Regina, 1952. xxiii, 304pp.

Basically concerned with resident Italians.

458

Dictionary of Ethiopian biography. Addis Ababa, Addis Ababa University, Institute of Ethiopian Studies, 1975- .

Eds. B. Mikael, S. Chojnacki, R. Pankhurst. Vol. 1. Early times to c.1270 A.D. Review, *IJAHS*, 10, 1977, 517-519. *No more published?*

459 (*also entered at* 979)
Encyclopedia Africana dictionary of African biography. Vol. 1. Ethiopia and Ghana. Algonac, MI, Reference Publications, 1977. 367pp.

Ethiopia, pp. 22-166. Ed. R.L. Haas. Historical introduction (pp. 22-41) by R. Pankhurst. 152 entries, many with portraits, and bibliographies. Includes entries for Europeans (e.g. James Bruce, Orde Wingate). Reviews in *IJAHS*, 11, 1978, 546-550, and in *JAH*, 20, 1979, 310-312 which praises "solid scholarship ... unquestionably a work of major importance". For the planned encyclopedia as a whole *see* 31; for the dictionary of biography *see* 299.

ATLASES & GAZETTEERS

Atlases

460

Padoan, L. **L'Abissinia nella geografia dell'Africa orientale.** Milan, Il Mondo Geografico, [1936]. 49pp. 14 x 18cm.

26 coloured maps and diagrams.

461

Ethiopia. Ministry of Education. **Preliminary atlas of Ethiopia**. Addis Ababa, 1962.

- - rev. ed. **An atlas of Ethiopia**. Addis Ababa, 1969. x, 84pp.

Comp. M. Wolde-Mariam. 1969 ed. contains 53 black and white maps, plus text, diagrams and reproductions of aerial photos. Majority of maps at 1:9M. "The boundaries shown on these maps are not necessarily those recognized by the Imperial Ethiopian Government" (preface). Review, *GJ*, 139, 1973, 381.

462

Ethiopia. Ethiopian Mapping Agency. **National atlas of Ethiopia**. Preliminary ed. Addis Ababa, 1981. 93pp. incl. 90 black and white maps.

- - 1st ed. Addis Ababa, 1988. viii, 156pp. 39 x 39cm.

1988 ed. contains 76 thematic coloured maps, including 12 on historical themes, with accompanying text. Principal scale 1:5M.

Gazetteers

463

Conti-Rossini, C. 'Catalogo dei nomi propri de luogo dell'Etiopia, contenuti nei testi gi'iz ed amharica finora pubblicati', pp. 387-439 in **Primo Congresso Geografico Italiano**, Genoa, 18-25 Sept., 1892. **Atti, vol. 2: Memorie della sezione scientifica**. Genoa, R. Istituto Sordo-Muti, 1894.

A list which cites use of the place names in some 25 sources. See also G.W.B. Huntingford,'Ethiopian place names', *African language studies*, 3, 1962, 182-194.

464

Italy. Istituto Geografico Militare. **Indice dei nomi contenuti nella carta demostrativa della colonie Eritrea e regioni adiacenti alla scala di 1:400,000**. [Florence, ?1940] 128pp.

465

U.S. Board on Geographic Names. **Gazetteer of Ethiopia**. Washington, DC, 1982. xxii, 663pp.

Revised version of appropriate section of **Ethiopia, Eritrea and the Somalilands ...** (*see* 420). Includes 30,500 names from maps at 1:250,000.

SOMALIA

HANDBOOKS

466

Cox, P.Z. **Genealogies of the Somali, including those of the Äysa and Gadabürsi.** London, Indian Army Staff Corps, 1896. 47pp.

Includes general data on distribution of ethnic groups.

467

G.B. War Office. Intelligence Division. **Précis of information concerning Somaliland, 1902.** London, 1902-1903. 2 vols. maps.

Vol. 1, 1902. iv, 160pp. Covers topography, history, inhabitants, communications and the administration. Appendices include lists of tribes with their location and population and genealogies of local chiefs. Vol. 2, 1903. 209pp. Route & river reports. Includes details of 77 land routes and the Juba river.

468

G.B. War Office. General Staff. **Military report on Somaliland, 1907.** London, 1907-1908. 2 vols. illus. maps in pocket.

"This report is based upon the **Précis** ... [*see* 467] revised ... by Lt.Col. M.L. Hornby", (preface). Vol. 1, 1907. vi, 279pp. Geographical, descriptive and historical. Subdivides each topical section by British, French, Abyssinian and Italian Somalilands. Includes descriptive gazetteer of c.60 ports, and settlements. Appendices include lists of tribes and clans, and selected genealogies. Vol. 2, 1908. xix, 652pp. Routes. Includes descriptions of 169 itineraries.

469

G.B. Foreign Office. Historical Section. **British Somaliland & Sokotra.** London, 1920. (F.O. Handbook, 97). 39pp.
Also pub. in F.O. **Peace handbooks**, vol. 16. London, 1920.

470

G.B. Foreign Office. Historical Section. **Italian Somaliland.** London, 1920. (F.O. Handbook, 128). 27pp.
Also pub. in F.O. **Peace handbooks**, vol. 20. London, 1920.

471

G.B. War Office. General Staff. **Military report on British Somaliland (including notes on French and Italian Somaliland).** London, 1925-1926. 2 vols. maps in pocket.

Vol. 1, 1925. 115pp. General. Topographic description, geography, peoples, communications, trade; vol. 2, 1926. 412pp. Routes. Details of 179 routes arranged by district, with a gazetteer of 44 settlements.

472

Corni, G. *ed.* **Somalia italiana.** Milan, Editoriale Arte e Storia, 1937. 2 vols. illus. maps.

Ed. by former governor of Italian Somaliland with numerous contributors. Vol. 1 covers natural resources, history and peoples; vol. 2 describes the Italian administration.

473

G.B. War Office. General Staff. **Military report on Somaliland, 1940.** London, 1940. (B. 454). iii, 83pp. map.

Covers history, geography, ethnography, communications. Map at 1:2M.

474

Hunt, J.A. **A general survey of the Somaliland Protectorate, 1944-1950**: Final report on "An economic survey and reconnaissance of the British Somaliland Protectorate, 1944-1950", Colonial Development and Welfare Scheme D. 484. London, Crown Agent for the Colonies, 1951. 203pp. maps.

Includes information on topography, climate, resources, with accounts of tribes and genealogies and a gazetteer (pp. 16-39).

475

Zöhrer, L.G.A. **Somaliländer.** Bonn, Schroeder for Deutsche Afrika-Gesellschaft, 1959. (Die Länder Afrikas, 17). 194pp. illus. maps.

476

Area handbook for Somalia, comp. I. Kaplan, *et al.* Washington, DC, U.S. Department of Defense, 1969. xiv, 455pp. maps.

- - 2nd ed. comp. I. Kaplan, *et al.* Washington, DC, 1977. xvi, 392pp. maps.

- - 3rd ed. **Somalia: a country study,** comp. H.D. Nelson. Washington, DC,

1982. 346pp. illus. maps.

477

Somalia. Ministry of Information & National Guidance. **Somalia today: general information**. rev. ed. Mogadishu, 1970. vii, 311pp.

Comp. Ismail Mohamed Ali.

478

Castagno, M. **Historical dictionary of Somalia**. Metuchen, NJ, Scarecrow Press, 1975. (African historical dictionaries, 6). 213pp.

YEARBOOKS

479

G.B. Colonial Office. **[Annual reports]: Somaliland, 1904-1959**. London, 1906-1960.

As **Annual report on Somaliland**, 1904/05-1919/20 (as Command papers); **Colonial Office annual report**, 1920-1958 (not pub. 1938-1947). From 1950/1951-1958/1959 pub. biennially. *For fuller details see Appendix.*

480

Italy. Ministero degli Affari Esteri. **Rapport du gouvernement italien à l'assemblée générale des Nations Unies sur l'administration de tutelle de la Somalie, 1951 [-1959]**. Rome, 1952-60. Annual. 9 issues.

Each vol. has a large range of statistics and administrative information.

481

The Somali business community guide, July 1987. Mogadishu, Halane Marketing & Advertising, 1987. 41pp.

Alphabetical by company: no index.

See also 541, 544.

STATISTICS

482

Italy. Ministero degli Affari Esteri. **Statistique de la Somalie sous tutelle**

italienne, 1958. Rome, 1959.

483

Somalia. Planning Directorate. Statistical Department. **Quarterly statistical bulletin.** Mogadishu, 1965-1966.

continued by:

Somalia. Ministry of Planning & Co-ordination. **Somali statistics: monthly bulletin.** Mogadishu, 1967- .

Title varies: later **Monthly statistical bulletin.**

484

Somalia. Central Statistical Department [etc.]. **Somalia in figures.** Mogadishu, 1964- . Every 3 years.

6 issues for 1964-1979 recorded in *ALEA* 1980.

485

Somalia. Central Statistical Department [etc.]. **Statistical abstract.** Mogadishu, 1964- . Annual.

From 1964-1971 had added title **Compendio statistico** with text in English & Italian; from 1972 text in English and Somali, with added title **Koobaha istaatistikada.**

486

Statistik des Auslandes: Länderberichte: Somalia. Wiesbaden, Statistisches Bundesamt, 1966- . Irreg.

Issues for 1966, 1967, 1970, 1974, 1984, 1986, 1988, 1991.

ATLASES & GAZETTEERS

Atlases

487

Johnson, J.W. **Historical atlas of the Horn of Africa.** Mogadishu, 1967. 15 pp.

Author was a U.S. Peace Corps volunteer in Somalia, 1966-69. 15 hand-drawn, cyclostyled maps showing changing boundaries between Somalia and its neighbours, 1888-1967.

Gazetteers

488
Somaliland Protectorate. Survey Department. **Gazetteer of place names, British Somaliland and grazing areas**. [Hargeisa], 1945. 45pp.

- - rev. ed. Hargeisa, 1946. 45pp.

489
U.S. Board on Geographic Names. **Gazetteer of Somalia**. Washington, DC, 1987. xviii, 519pp.

Revised version of the appropriate sections of **Ethiopia, Eritrea and the Somalilands ...** (*see* 420). 23,000 entries based on maps at 1:200,000.

SUDAN

HANDBOOKS

490

Egypt. General Staff. **General report on the province of Kordofan.** Cairo, 1877. xii, 211pp. illus. maps.

Comp. Maj. H.G. Prout. Covers topography, peoples, climate, natural resources and communications in the style of the British War Office reports.

491

G.B. War Office. Intelligence Branch. **Report on the Egyptian provinces of the Sudan, Red Sea and Equator.** London, 1883. 210pp. map (in pocket).

- - rev. ed. ... **revised to July 1884.** London, 1884. 275pp. map.

Includes history, topography, climate, and ethnography, with some 35 itineraries. Map at 1:2,255,080.

492

G.B. War Office. Intelligence Branch. **The Nile above the Second Cataract: précis of information.** London, 1884. 60pp. illus. maps.

Comp. Lt. Col. R.H. O'Grady-Haly. Pt. 1, Sarras to New Dongola; pt. 2, New Dongola to Aby Hamed and Khartoum. Route descriptions. 15 coloured maps of each rapid or cataract at 1:100,000.

493

G.B. War Office. Intelligence Division. **Report on the Nile and country between Dongola, Suakin, Kassala and Omdurman**, describing the various routes bearing on this country. London, 1897. viii, 267pp. maps.

- - 2nd ed. London, 1898. viii, 338pp.

Comp. A.E.W. Gleichen. Basically a series of itineraries, some 30 in 2nd ed. which has increased coverage of the area between Massawa and Omdurman. Maps include Khartoum and Omdurman at 1:25,000.

494

Gleichen, *Lord* A.E.W. **Handbook of the Sudan.** London, War Office,

Pt. 1, Topographical: the White Nile & its tributaries, lands on either bank, Bahr el Ghazal country, based upon **Report ...** (*see* 491). Pt. 2, Historical: general to 1882 then by region.

- - **Supplement**. London, War Office, Intelligence Division, 1899. vii, 219pp. maps.

Arranged as the **Handbook** with "material... by numerous officers written since the Omdurman campaign". Maps at 1:3M.

495
Gleichen, *Lord* A.E.W. **The Anglo-Egyptian Sudan: a compendium prepared by officers of the Sudan Government**. London, HMSO, 1905. 2 vols. (xiii, 371pp; viii, 236pp.). illus. maps.

"A comprehensive description of the Anglo-Egyptian Sudan in 1905 ... includes revision & amplification of the **Handbook of the Sudan** (1898) and of the **Supplement** (1899)" *see* 494. Vol. 1. pt. 1, Geographical and descriptive, by region; pt. 2, Historical. Appendices include lists of tribes (over 250 groupings), texts of 19 treaties and agreements, notes on boundaries, bibliography and cartography. 67 photos. Vol. 2, Routes, following arrangement of regions in vol. 1.

- - **The Anglo-Egyptian Sudan**. Vol. 2, chapter 7 - Supplement. Bahr el Ghazal. London, HMSO, 1906. 34pp.

Adds an additional 21 itineraries.

496
Sudan. Intelligence Department. **Anglo-Egyptian Sudan handbook**. Khartoum & London, 1911-1912. 2 vols. illus. maps.

Vol. 1, 1911. 164pp. map. Bahr el Ghazal; vol. 2, 1912. 215pp. map. Kordofan and the region to the west of the White Nile. Standard format of the British War Office reports, covering topography, ethnography, administration, history and finance. Maps at 1:2M.

497
G.B. Foreign Office. Historical Section. **Anglo-Egyptian Sudan**. London, 1920. (F.O. Handbook, 98). 174pp.
Also pub. in F.O. **Peace handbooks**, Vol. 16. London, 1920.

498

G.B. Admiralty. Naval Intelligence Division. **A handbook of the Anglo-Egyptian Sudan**. London, 1922. (I.D. 1218). viii, 776pp. 5 maps.

A very wide-ranging collection of data, mostly compiled before the end of World War I. Sections for geography, fauna, history, population, religion, government and administration, resources, trade and industry, health and communications. Gazetteer of 27 towns.

499

G.B. War Office. General Staff. **Military report on the Sudan**. London, 1927. (A. 2996). 338pp.

- - **Amendments 1-3**. London, 1930-32.

General coverage of the whole country with detailed sections on each province (pp. 81-203). Appendices with texts of treaties and boundary agreements.

500

Sudan. **Equatorial Province handbook**. [Khartoum], 1936- .

Vol. 1, 1936. 168pp. maps. Mongalla, comp. by L.F. Nalder. "Compiled before the amalgamation of Mongalla province with Bahr el Ghazal province into the Equatoria province, 1st Jan 1936". Includes data on topography, peoples (including list of tribes), administration, natural resources and communications. List of British officials past and present. *?More vols. published*.

501

G.B. War Office. General Staff (Intelligence). Headquarters Troops in the Sudan. **The Anglo-Egyptian Sudan: handbook of topographical intelligence**. Khartoum, 1940. (B. 1215). vi, 229pp. illus. maps.

Detailed information in standard "military report" presentation. Includes descriptive gazetteer of 32 settlements. Plans of Port Sudan (1:10,000) and Khartoum (1:20,000).

502

Herzog, R. **Sudan**. Bonn, Schroeder for Deutsche Afrika-Gesellschaft, 1958. (Die Länder Afrikas, 8). 85pp. illus. maps.

- - 2nd ed. Bonn, 1961. 101pp.

503

Area handbook for the Republic of the Sudan, comp. J.A. Cookson, *et al.* Washington, DC, U.S. Department of Defense, 1960. viii, 473pp. maps.

- - 2nd ed. **Area handbook for the Democratic Republic of Sudan** comp. H.D. Nelson, *et al.* Washington, DC, 1973. xiv, 351 pp. maps.

- - 3rd ed. **Sudan: a country study**, comp. H.D. Nelson, *et al.* Washington, DC, 1982. 365pp. illus. maps.

504

Voll, J.O. **Historical dictionary of the Sudan**. Metuchen, NJ, Scarecrow Press, 1978. (African historical dictionaries, 17). xvii, 175pp.

Review, *IJAHS*, 14, 1981, 770-772.

See also 93, 527.

YEARBOOKS

505

Sudan almanac 1884/85 [etc.]. London, Khartoum etc., Sudan Central Office of Information, 1884- . Annual.

Issuing body varies : pre-independence issued by G.B. War Office, Intelligence Department, *later* Egypt. Intelligence Department, *later* Sudan. Intelligence Department; post-independence by Sudan. Public Relations Office, etc. Long-running title growing from a first issue containing 14pp. of purely calendrical information to issues of 350+ pages by 1960s including detailed background historical, administrative and topographical information, statistics, lists of government departments and agencies and other institutions, and a directory of newspapers and periodicals.

506

G.B. Foreign Office. **[Annual reports]: Sudan, 1899-1952.** London, 1899-1956. Annual.

As **Report by HM Agent and ConsulGeneral on the finances, administration and condition of Egypt and the Soudan**, 1899-1920, **Report on the finances, administration and condition of the Sudan**, 1921-52 (all as Command papers). 1914-1919 covered in one report, reports for 1939/41 and 1942/44 issued 1950/51. *For fuller details see Appendix.*

507
Sudan directory. Khartoum, Sudan Advertising & Publishing Co., 1921-1950?
Annual.

"Patronized by the Sudan Government". Substantial work; 1921 ed. 726pp.,
includes civil list, directory of British residents, texts of ordinances, statistics,
and a commercial directory.

508
Trade directory of the Republic of the Sudan 1957/58 [-1966/67]. London,
Diplomatic Press & Publishing Co., (Diprepu Co.) Ltd., 1958-1966. Annual
(irreg.) 8 issues.

Title varies: **Sudan trade directory** (1966-67). Includes lists of officials,
statistics, commercial directory. 1st to 5th eds., 1957-58 to 1963, include
"Who's who" (120+ entries).

See also 544.

STATISTICS

509
Sudan. Ministry of Planning. Department of Statistics. **Statistical abstract.**
Khartoum, 1970- . Annual.

Title varies: **Statistical yearbook** (1973-).

510
Statistik des Auslandes: Länderberichte: Sudan. Wiesbaden, Statistisches
Bundesamt, 1966- . Irreg.

Issues for 1966, 1976, 1985, 1987, 1990.

DIRECTORIES OF ORGANIZATIONS

511
Sudan. National Council for Research. Council of Scientific & Technical
Research. **Directory of research centres, institutes and related bodies
engaged in scientific and technical research.** Khartoum, 1974. 77pp.

Comp. L.A. Gadir & A. Hassib.

512
Sudan. National Council for Research. Sudan National Documentation Centre.
Directory of information sources: provisional list. Khartoum, 1979.

BIOGRAPHICAL SOURCES

513
Sudan. Civil Secretary's Office. **Sudan Political Service, 1899-1929.** Khartoum,
1930. 66pp.

Brief details of service of some 200 officers, arranged chronologically by date
of commencement of service.

514
Hill, R.L. **A biographical dictionary of the Anglo-Egyptian Sudan.** Oxford,
Clarendon Press, 1951. xvi, 392pp.

- - 2nd ed. **A biographical dictionary of the Sudan.** London, Frank Cass,
1967. xvi, 409pp.

Includes some 1,900 entries for those dead before 1948. 2nd ed. reproduces the
original text with a new introduction and additional notes.

See also 508.

ATLASES & GAZETTEERS

Atlases

515
Sudan. Ministry of Education. **Atlas Jumhuriyat al-Sudan al-Dimiqiratiyah.**
Khartoum, 1973. 49pp.

World atlas with 13pp. (21 maps) devoted to Sudan. All text in Arabic.

516
Hinkel, F.W. **The archaeological map of the Sudan (AMS).** Berlin, Akademie
Verlag, 1979-

To appear in 10 fascs. Sponsored by Akademie der Wissenschaft der Deutsche
Demokratische Republik, Zentralinstitut für alte Geschichte und Archaologie.

Accompanied by **The archaeological map of the Sudan: a guide to its use and explanation of its principles.** Berlin, 1977. Review, *IJAHS*, 15, 1982, 295-296.

517

Sudan. Survey Department. **National atlas of the Sudan.** Khartoum, 1987.

Gazetteers

518

'Glossary of Arabic geographical terms used in maps and route reports in the Anglo-Egyptian Sudan', *Journal of the African Society*, 11, 1912, 201-205.

519

Sudan. Survey Department. **Index gazetteer of the Anglo-Egyptian Sudan showing place names.** Khartoum & London, 1921. vi, 220pp. map.

- - rev. ed. Khartoum, 1932. 360pp.

- - rev. ed. London, HMSO, 1952. 360pp.

Based on the coverage of the 1:250,000 map series. 1921 ed. includes c.22,000 names. See also J.W. Wright & G. Janson-Smith, 'The spelling of place names in the Sudan', *Sudan notes & records* 32, 1951, 311-324.

520

U.S. Department of the Interior. Division of Geography. **Preliminary N.I.S Gazetteer, Anglo-Egyptian Sudan.** Washington, DC, Central Intelligence Agency, 1949. 11, 136pp.

521

U.S. Board on Geographic Names. **Sudan: official standard names approved by the U.S.B.G.N.** Washington, DC, 1962. (Gazetteer, 68). xi, 358pp.

Rev. version of **Preliminary N.I.S Gazetteer ...** (*see* 520). c.25,000 entries from maps at 1:100,000.

- - **Gazetteer supplement: Africa and South-West Asia.** Washington, DC, 1972. (Sudan, pp. 149-152)

EAST AFRICA

Kenya
Tanzania
Uganda

HANDBOOKS

522

G.B. War Office. Intelligence Department. **Handbook of British East Africa,** including Zanzibar, Uganda and the territory of the Imperial British East Africa Company. London, 1893. 176pp. 2 maps in pocket.

Comp. Capt. H. Foster. Separate sections for each territory. Revised eds. published as **Précis of information ... British East Africa Protectorate and Zanzibar** (1901, *see* 563) and **Précis of information ... Uganda Protectorate** (1902, *see* 627).

523

G.B. Foreign Office. Historical Section. **Kenya, Uganda and Zanzibar.** London, 1920. (F.O. Handbook, 96). 110pp.
Also published in F.O. **Peace handbooks,** vol. 16. London, 1920.

524

The East African manual, dealing with the governments, etc. in Kenya Colony, Tanganyika Territory, Nyasaland, Uganda and Zanzibar Protectorate and Portuguese East Africa, 1929/30. London & Johannesburg, Mining & Industrial Publications of Africa, 1929. cix, 960pp. illus.

- - 2nd ed. London, 1932. xcv, 877pp.

Ed. C. Carlyle-Gall. Contents of 1929/30 ed: pp. 1-360, Kenya; pp. 362-508, Tanganyika Territory; pp. 509-686, Nyasaland Protectorate; pp. 686-710, Uganda Protectorate; pp. 711-758, Zanzibar Protectorate; pp. 771-960, Portuguese East Africa. Emphasis of coverage is on commerce, manufacturing and agriculture.

525

Macmillan, A. *ed.* **Eastern Africa and Rhodesia: historical and descriptive, commercial and industrial, facts, figures and resources.** London, W.H. & L. Collingridge, 1930. 504pp. illus.

Numerous contributors drawn from the local press. Sections for Kenya, Uganda, Tanganyika, Zanzibar, Nyasaland, Portuguese East Africa and Rhodesia, each with a general account of history, topography, and resources, followed by a commercial directory. Many black and white illus.

526
Road book of East Africa. Nairobi, Royal East African Automobile Association, 1930. 192pp. folding map.

Includes itineraries and details of communications. For the Association's **Handbook**, first published in 1939 and regularly revised, *see* 559.

527
Ethnographic survey of Africa: East Central Africa. London, International Institute, 1950-1977. 18 vols.

Sub-series of **Ethnographic survey** (*see* 54). Vol. 1, 'The peoples of the Lake Nyasa Region' by M. Tew. 1950. 156pp; vol.2, 'Bemba and related peoples of Northern Rhodesia etc.', by W. Whiteley & J. Slaski. 1951. 100pp; vol.3, 'The coastal tribes of the north-eastern Bantu', by A.H.J. Prins. 1952. 138pp; vol.4, 'The Nilotes of the Anglo-Egyptian Sudan and Uganda', by A.J. Butt. 1952. 198pp; vol.5, 'The Kikuyu and Kamba of Kenya', by J. Middleton. 1953. 107pp; vol. 6, 'The northern Nilo-Hamites', by G.W.B. Huntingford. 1953. 108pp; vol. 7, 'The central Nilo-Hamites', by P. & P.H. Gulliver. 1953. 106pp; vol. 8, 'The southern Nilo-Hamites', by G.W.B. Huntingford. 1953. 152pp; vol. 9, 'The Azande and related peoples of the Anglo-Egyptian Sudan and Belgian Congo', by P.T.W. Baxter & A.J. Butt. 1953. 152pp; vol.10, 'The Gisu of Uganda', by J.S. La Fontaine. 1959. 68pp; vol. 11, 'The eastern lacustrine Bantu', by M.C. Fallers. 1960. 86pp; vol. 12, 'The Swahili-speaking peoples of Zanzibar and the East African coast', by A.H.J. Prins. 1961. 143pp; vol. 13, 'The western lacustrine Bantu', by B.K. Taylor. 1962. 159pp; vol. 14, 'Les anciens royaumes de la zone interlacustrine méridionale (Rwanda, Burundi, Buha)' by M. d'Hertefelt *et al*. 1962. 252pp; vol. 15, 'The Fipa and related peoples of South-west Tanzania and North-eastern Zambia' by R.G. Willis. 1966. xvi, 82pp; vol. 16, 'The matrilineal peoples of Eastern Tanzania', by T.O. Beidelman. 1967. 94pp; vol. 17, 'The peoples of Greater Unyamwezi, Tanzania' by R.G. Abrahams. 1967. 95pp; vol. 18, 'The Chagga and Meru of Tanzania', by S.F. Moore & P. Puritt, 1977. xiv, 140pp.

528
Roux, L. **L'Est Africain Brittanique: Kenya, Tanganyika, Uganda et Zanzibar**. Paris, Société d'études géographiques, maritimes et coloniales, 1950. (Terres lointaines, 5). 223pp. 4 maps.

Covers topography, peoples, history, politics and administration, resources and communications.

529
Weigt, E. **Kenya und Uganda**. Bonn, Schroeder for Deutsche Afrika-Gesellschaft, 1958. (Die Länder Afrikas, 10). 103pp.

530
Guide to the East African territories of Kenya, Tanganyika, Uganda and Zanzibar. Nairobi, East African Airways, 1959. 356pp. illus. map.

Comp. L.S. Levin. "First attempt ever made to publish a comprehensive guide dealing solely with these territories" (preface). Based on pattern of the author's guide to Rhodesia and Nyasaland (*see* 656). General section followed by country surveys. Covers historical background as well as current political, social and economic data with statistics.

531
Ostafrika: Reisehandbuch Kenya und Tanzania. Bonn, Deutsche Afrika-Gesellschaft, 1973. 570pp. illus. maps.

- - 2nd ed. Frankfurt-am-Main, Otto Lembek, 1975. 570p. illus. maps.

- - 3rd ed. Frankfurt-am-Main, 1981. 796pp. illus. maps.

Comp. G. Baumhögger, *et al*. A very detailed traveller's guide which includes background essays on history, politics, geography and peoples followed by itineraries.

See also 1368.

YEARBOOKS

532
East African diary. Mombasa, "East African Standard", 1902-1903. 2 issues.

Title varies: **East African and Uganda diary** (1903).

continued by:

Handbook for East Africa, Uganda and Zanzibar. Mombasa, "East African Standard"/Government Printing Press, 1904-1907. Annual. 4 issues.

Ed. H.F.G. Bell, First Assistant Secretary, East African Protectorate. Includes civil list with histories of service, historical and topographical information, statistics, "list of European residents in East Africa" (c.650/700 names).

533
Drumkey's year book for East Africa, 1909. Bombay, "Times of India", 1909. vi, 394pp.

Comp. Y.S.A. Drumkey, "late Permanent Secretary to H.H. the Sultan of Zanzibar". Covers British East Africa Protectorate, Zanzibar, Uganda, with 4pp. on German East Africa. Includes civil list (with some brief histories of service), detailed historical, economic, topographic and social information, commercial directory, list of residents.

534
The "Red book": the directory of East Africa, Uganda and Zanzibar. Mombasa & Nairobi, "East African Standard", 1909-1930/31. Irreg. 6 issues.

Issues for 1909, 1912, 1919, 1922/23, 1925/26, 1930/31. Title varies: **The "Red book" :the "Standard" British East Africa & Uganda handbook & directory** (1919); **The East African Red book** (cover title 1922/23, title page 1925/26, 1930/31)." Modelled on the **Handbook ...** [*see* 532]" (preface to 1909 volume). Information much expanded from 1919 issue onwards with "who's who" and classified trade directory. Coverage of Zanzibar omitted from 1919 issue, but restored, together with Tanganyika from 1922/23 onwards.

535
Ward, H.F. & Milligan, J.W. **Handbook of British East Africa, 1912/13.** Nairobi, Caxton Printing and Publishing Co., 1912. 278pp. 2 folding maps.

Produced by publishers of the "Leader", and in many ways a forerunner of the **"Leader" annual** (*see* 536), though omitting Uganda and Zanzibar. Includes historical, topographical and economic background, statistics, civil list, trade directory, register of European residents.

536
"Leader" annual and gazetteer of British East Africa 1914: a descriptive, official and statistical account and directory of British East Africa and Uganda. Nairobi, Caxton Printing & Publishing Co., 1914. 286pp.

Comp. W.T. Moroney. Includes historical, topographical, and economic information, civil lists, commercial directory, list of residents. Separate sections for Uganda and Zanzibar.

537
The Swift directory of British East Africa, Uganda and Zanzibar. Calcutta, Thacker, Spink & Co., 1915. lii, 292pp. folding map.

Comp. J.G. Harris. Emphasis on listing European residents and providing a commercial directory, arranged by city.

538
The Kenya annual and directory; including Uganda section: a descriptive, official and statistical account. Nairobi, Caxton Printing & Publishing Co., The "Leader" Office, 1921-1922. Annual. 2 issues.

Includes civil list, commercial directory, gazetteer covering some 50 settlements, directory of residents (c.4,000 names). Preface to the 2nd issue of 1922 calls it "the fifth annual publication issued from the "Leader" office in the shape of an annual or directory" - *see* 535, 536; the fifth title has not been identified.

539
Kenya-Uganda-Tanganyika and Zanzibar directory: trade and commercial index. Nairobi, East African Directory Co., 1936- . Irreg.

Title varies: **Kenya, Uganda, Tanzania, Zambia, Malawi and Ethiopia directory ...** (1968-). Section for each country with trade and agricultural statistics, lists of residents, and commercial directory.

540
G.B. Colonial Office. **[Annual reports]: East Africa High Commission, 1948-68.** London etc., 1949-1969. Annual.

As **Annual report on the East Africa High Commission,** 1948-60; **Annual report on the East African Common Services Organization,** 1961-67; **East African Community annual report,** 1968. 1949-53 pub in Colonial series. Reports for 1956 and 1961-68 pub. in Nairobi. *For fuller details see Appendix.*

541
The Year Book & Guide to East Africa. London, Robert Hale, 1950-1965. Annual. 16 issues.

Sponsored by the Union-Castle Mail Steamship Co. Formerly incorporated in **Brown's South Africa** etc. (1893-1949, *see* 1432). Emphasis on information for traveller and potential settler. First issue covers Belgian Congo, British and French Somaliland, Egypt, Eritrea, Ethiopia, Kenya, Nyasaland (to 1954, thereafter transferred to **Yearbook and guide to Southern Africa** *see 1448*), Portuguese East Africa, Somalia, Tanganyika, Uganda, Zanzibar. From 1955 coverage extends to Madagascar, Mauritius, Réunion, and the Seychelles.

542
British Africa trade directory, 1952/53: East African edition. Nairobi, S.H. Abid, 1952. 266pp.

Kenya has 28pp. of general information and statistics followed by a commercial directory; Tanganyika, Uganda and Zanzibar have only a commercial directory.

543
A year book of East Africa 1953/54. Nairobi, English Press Ltd., 1954. 480pp. illus.

Well illustrated. Includes various signed contributions on special topics. Lacks normal directory structure and an index, but contains much miscellaneous information on politics, administration, education, and agriculture.

544
Directory: trade, commerce and local manufacturers index, 1971/72 [etc.]. Nairobi, East African Directory Co. Ltd., 1971- . Annual.

Detailed coverage of Kenya, Tanzania, Uganda, Ethiopia, Zambia; briefer coverage of Congo, Central African Republic, Chad, Malawi, Somalia, Sudan, Zaire. Includes general economic & administrative information.

545
New African yearbook: East & Southern Africa, 1984/85 [-1986/87]. London, IC Magazines Ltd., 1984-1986. 2 issues.

Issued as vol. [2] of 5th and 6th editions of **New African yearbook** (*see* 121 for publishing history).

See also 1445.

STATISTICS

546
East Africa High Commission. East Africa Statistical Department. **Economic and statistical bulletin.** Nairobi, 1948-1961. Quarterly. Issues 1-52.

continued by:

East African Common Services Organization. East African Statistical Department. **Economic and statistical review**. Nairobi, 1961-?1977. Quarterly.

547

Statistik des Auslandes: Länderberichte: Ostafrika. Wiesbaden, Statistisches Bundesamt, 1971.

There are also volumes for individual countries (*see below*).

548

Netherlands. Ministerie van Landbouw en Visserij. Directoraat-General de Landbouw en de Voedselvoorziening. Afdeling Statistik en Documentatie. **Basesreeksen Kenya, Tanzania, Uganda**. Hague, 1972. 82pp.

A collection of basic demographic and economic statistics.

DIRECTORIES OF ORGANIZATIONS

549

Makerere University College. Library. **Directory of East African libraries**. Kampala, 1961. 84pp.

- - 2nd ed. Kampala, 1969. 113pp.

1st ed. comp. by E.J. Belton contains 90 entries. 2nd ed. comp. M.E.C. Kibwika-Bagunda, includes some 110 entries, arranged by country and title with subject and city indexes.

550

East African Academy. **Research services in East Africa**. Nairobi, East African Publishing House, 1966. 239pp.

Based on information gathered by Marco Surveys Ltd. Covers government, commercial and private research organizations in some thirty subject fields.

551

Makerere University College. East African School of Librarianship. **A preliminary directory of documentation centres in Kenya, Malawi, Tanzania, Uganda and Zambia**. Kampala, 1969. 15pp.

Comp. S.W. Davis.

BIOGRAPHICAL SOURCES

552

[Dictionary of East African biography]. Project commenced in 1961 by D.H. Simpson, Librarian, Royal Commonwealth Society, Sir John Gray & H.B. Thomas, with later participation by A.T. Matson and the History Department, University of Makerere. The data available in the Society Library consist of lists of names under various categories, e.g. missionaries (by denomination), doctors, Uganda Railway staff, etc., together with a card index of individual names which contains references to the lists and to published biographical sources, and short entries for persons for whom no other source exists. Coverage is limited to those who had made some public impact on East Africa by 1900.

Lists of the names collected to date (a total of 5,370) were published in a number of cyclostyled pamphlets, comp. D.H. Simpson, *et al.* **Dictionary of East African Biography project**. London, 1965. 7 parts. General introduction (6pp); UMCA missionaries (12pp); Roman catholic missionaries (17pp); Other missionaries (15pp); Royal Naval personnel (22pp); Germans (23pp); Miscellaneous (74pp). D.H. Simpson, 'The DEAB project', *Library materials on Africa* 9, 1971, 98-101 estimated the file at that time as containing 6,000 to 6,500 entries, of whom some 1,500 were missionaries. In 1992, the total number of entries was approaching 10,000. Proposals to publish the file in its entirety have so far proved unsuccessful.

553

Who's who in East Africa 1963/64 [-1967/68]. Nairobi, Marco Publishers (Africa) Ltd., 1963-1967. Bi-annual. 3 issues.

Separate sequences for Kenya, Uganda, Tanganyika, Zanzibar (Tanzania in 1967/68 issue). About 4,500 entries in 1967/68 issue. Includes portraits.

554

Gillett, M. **Tribute to pioneers: Mary Gillett's index of many of the pioneers of East Africa**. Oxford, author, 1986. [250]pp. + 3 supplements.

Biographical dictionary of Europeans reaching East Africa pre 1914. Details often very brief, and no sources given.

See also 665.

ATLASES & GAZETTEERS

Atlases

555
Goldthorpe, J.E. & Wilson, F.B. **Tribal maps of East Africa and Zanzibar.** Kampala, East African Institute of Social Research, 1960. (East Africa Studies, 13). vi, 14pp. 8 maps.

Ethnic maps for East Africa in general, Uganda and Kenya; population maps for Zanzibar and Pemba.

556
Oxford Atlas for East Africa. London & Nairobi, Oxford University Press, 1966. 65, 11pp. 20 x 26cm.

Comp. by Cartographic Department, Clarendon Press, with advice from F.C.A. McBain. 13 maps cover East Africa, 9 the remainder of Africa, 43 the rest of the world.

557
East African secondary school atlas. Nairobi, Trans Africa, 1974. 100pp.

Comp. B.L. Boorman & T. Treadaway. Maps 2-19, East Africa; 20-30, rest of Africa; 31-84, rest of the world.

See also 1432.

Gazetteers

558
British East Africa. Postmaster General. **East Africa and Uganda post office guide.** Nairobi, 1917. 242pp.

559
Royal East African Automobile Association. **Handbook.** Nairobi, 1939- . Irreg.

Titles of eds. vary: **Handbook and gazeteer** [sic] **of East Africa, 1952.** "Modelled on **Handbook** of the Automobile Association of South Africa" (preface to 1939 ed.). Includes city plans and itineraries, and always a substantial gazetteer section. 1956/57 ed. xii, 208pp. has "Shorter gazetteer of East Africa", pp. 59-208 with grid references and brief descriptions. Also includes 12 town plans.

560 (*also entered at* 419, 1673)
G.B. Army. G.H.Q. Middle East. Survey Directorate. **East Africa: index gazetteer showing place-names on 1:500,000 map series.** Cairo, 1946-48. 3 vols. in 4.

Vol. 1, 1946. vi, 173pp. Kenya, Uganda, Tanganyika. Vol. 2 covers North-East Africa (*see* 419), vol. 3 covers Madagascar and Mozambique (*see* 1673).

561
U.S. Board on Geographic Names. **British East Africa: official standard names approved by the U.S.B.G.N.** Washington, DC, 1955. (Gazetteer, 1). ii, 601pp.

Pp. 1-170, Kenya; pp. 171-247, Tanganyika; pp. 429-558, Uganda; pp. 559-601, Zanzibar. 24,700 names. Rev. eds. later published for each territory; **Kenya** (*see* 582); **Tanzania** (*see* 624); **Uganda** (*see* 652).

562
East African Posts and Telecommunications Corporation. **List of post offices in East Africa.** Nairobi, 1973. 47pp.

KENYA

HANDBOOKS

563
G.B. War Office. Intelligence Division. **Précis of information concerning the British East Africa Protectorate and Zanzibar** (revised December 1900). London, 1901. 133pp. 2 maps in pocket.

Comp. by Sir J.C. Ardagh. Rev. ed. of appropriate sections of **Handbook of East Africa** (*see* 532). Title at start of text: "Handbook of the B.E.A. Protectorate ...". Includes historical, topographical, economic and social data, and a genealogy of Somali tribes.

564
G.B. War Office. General Staff. **Military report on the East Africa Protectorate and Zanzibar**. London, 1910.

Vol. 1, General. iv, 247pp. map in pocket. "Based on **Précis** ... originally issued 1893, revised 1900". Sections for geography, ethnography and government, history, finance, trade and resources, communications, and military affairs. Appendices include the report on Zanzibar (pp. 189-201), genealogical tables and trade statistics. Vol. 2 *never published*.

565
G.B. Admiralty. Naval Intelligence Division. **A handbook of Kenya Colony (British East Africa) and the Kenya Protectorate (Protectorate of Zanzibar)**. London, 1920. (I.D. 1216). 680pp. map.

Pp. 1-508, Kenya Colony; pp. 509-580, Kenya Protectorate. Detailed account emphasising topography, peoples, natural resources. Includes descriptive gazetteer of some 60 major townships and ports, and lists of administrative divisions.

566
Kenya: descriptive handbook. London, [1928]. 105pp. (RCS catalogue. Now missing)

567
G.B. War Office. General Staff. **Kenya: military report**. London, 1939. (B. 433). iv, 140pp. map in pocket.

Covers history, administration, peoples, topography and communications. Detailed accounts of 6 settlements: Eldoret, Kisumu, Kitwe, Mombasa, Nairobi, Nakuru. Map at 1:2M.

568
Area handbook for Kenya, comp. I. Kaplan, *et al*. Washington, DC, U.S. Department of Defense, 1967. xii, 707pp. maps.

- - 2nd ed. comp. I. Kaplan, *et al*. Washington, DC, 1976. xiv, 472pp. maps.

- - 3rd ed. **Kenya: a country study**, comp. H.D. Nelson, *et al*. Washington, DC, 1984. 340pp. illus. maps.

569
Kenya: an official handbook. Nairobi, East African Publishing House for Government of Kenya, 1973. 208pp. illus.

Coloured and black and white illus. 5 maps at 1:3M. "First of its kind to be published by our government" (preface).

- - rev. ed. Nairobi, Kenya Literature Bureau, 1983. 336pp. illus.

Issued to mark 20th anniversary of Kenyan independence.

- - rev. ed. Nairobi, Ministry of Information & Broadcasting, 1988. 309pp. illus.

Produced to mark 25th anniversary of Kenyan independence.

570
Ogot, B.A. **Historical dictionary of Kenya**. Metuchen, NJ, Scarecrow Press, 1981. (African historical dictionaries, 29). 279pp.

Critical reviews in *African affairs* 81, 1982, 444-446; *JAH* 23, 1982, 431.

YEARBOOKS

571
G.B. Colonial Office. **[Annual reports]: Kenya, 1891-1962**. London, 1894-1966.

As **Report ... on the East African Protectorate**, 1891/94, 1895/97-1903/04 (not issued 1898/99, 1902/03), **Report on the East Africa Protectorate**, 1904/05-

1917/18, (all as Command papers); **Colonial Office annual report on the East African Protectorate**, 1918-19, **Colonial Office annual report for Kenya Colony and Protectorate,** [title varies], 1919/20-1962 (not issued 1939-45). Prior to 1904/05 issued by the Foreign Office. *For fuller details see Appendix.*

572
Kenya yearbook : Uhuru 10 [etc.]. Nairobi, Newspread International, 1974- Annual (irreg.).

Title varies : **Kenya factbook** (10th ed. 1986/87-). Not pub. 1975, 1982/83, 1983/84, 1986/87, 1990. 12th ed. 1991. Ed. Kul Bhushan. Magazine style format. Title refers to number of years since independence. Includes lengthy chronology of events in Kenyan history, sections on the people, the economy, finance, industry, natural resources, communications, medicine, education and a commercial directory.

See also 662.

STATISTICS

573
East Africa High Commission, East African Statistical Department (Kenya Unit). **Statistical abstract**. Nairobi, 1955-1960. Annual.

1956/57 issued as one vol.

continued by:

Kenya. Central Bureau of Statistics [etc.]. **Statistical abstract**. Nairobi, 1961- . Annual.

574
Kenya. Central Bureau of Statistics, [etc.]. **Kenya statistical digest**. Nairobi, 1963-1986. Quarterly.

continued by:

Monthly statistical bulletin, Nairobi, 1986- .

575
Statistik des Auslandes: Länderberichte: Kenia. Wiesbaden, Statistisches Bundesamt, 1964- . Irreg.

Issues for 1964, 1969, 1982, 1983, 1985, 1987, 1989. Also included in East Africa vol. for 1971 (*see* 547).

DIRECTORIES OF ORGANIZATIONS

576
Directory of libraries in Kenya. Nairobi, Gazelle Books, 1977. iii, 102pp.

Comp. J.R. Njuguna. Lists 96 libraries. Includes subject but not geographical index.

577
Kenya. National Academy for Advancement of Arts and Sciences. **Directory of associations in Kenya**. Nairobi, 1980. 113pp.

Comp. P.G. Mwathi.

578
Kenya Library Association and National Council for Science and Technology. **Subject guide to information sources in Kenya**. Nairobi, 1984. 207pp.

Comp. A.R. Mulaha. A guide to Kenyan libraries.

579
Kenya. National Council of Social Service. **A directory of non-government (voluntary) organizations in Kenya**. Nairobi, [1988]. 485pp.

Comp. C.M. Lekyo & A. Mirikau. Lists nearly 300 organizations according to their area of activity.

BIOGRAPHICAL SOURCES

580
Who's who in Kenya, 1982-83. Nairobi, African Book Services, 1982. vii, 376pp.

Ed. M. Nzioki and M.B. Dar.

ATLASES & GAZETTEERS

Atlases

581
Kenya. Survey of Kenya. **Atlas of Kenya:** a comprehensive series of new and authentic maps prepared from the National Survey and other governmental sources with gazetteer and notes on pronunciation and spelling. Nairobi, 1959. ix, 44pp. 46 x 49cm.

Detailed coloured maps. 24 thematic maps at 1:3M show the whole country and cover climate, geology, soils, agriculture, medicine, ethnography, industry, and commerce. 5 provincial maps at 1:1M. Plans of Nairobi and Mombasa (1:20,000), smaller townships (1:50,000). Historical maps: 6 reproductions of maps of 1564, 1596, 1662, 1809, 1850, 1856. Gazetteer has some 2,000 entries. Review, *GJ*, 127(4) 1961, 554.

- - [2nd ed.] Nairobi, [1962]. ix, 46pp. 45 x 47cm.

Basically an updated reprint of the 1959 ed. with a few corrections.

- - 3rd ed. **National atlas of Kenya.** Nairobi, 1970. iv, 103pp. 43 plates. 38 x 40cm.

Substantially "rearranged, enlarged, recompiled and redrawn" (foreword). Retains only basic topographic and historical maps from 1st and 2nd eds. Review, *GJ*, 137, 1971, 590-591.

- - 4th ed. **National atlas of Kenya.** Nairobi, 1985.

Gazetteers

582
U.S. Board on Geographic Names. **Kenya: official standard names approved by the U.S.B.G.N.** Washington, DC, 1964. (Gazetteer, 78). vi, 467pp.

Replaces the appropriate section of **British East Africa ...** (*see* 561). Includes 27,000 names.

- - 2nd ed. Washington, DC, 1978. vii, 470pp.

Includes c. 30,000 names from maps at 1:50,000 (for south and south-west), 1:100,000 (for rest of country).

TANZANIA

HANDBOOKS

583

G.B. War Office. General Staff. **Military report on German East Africa.**
London, 1902. (A. 771).

- - [rev. ed.]. London, 1905. (A. 956). vii, 75pp. 2 maps in pocket.

- - **Addendum 1, May 1906** (A. 1187). 16pp ; - - **Addendum 2, May 1907** (A.
1188) 14pp. - - **Addendum 3, May 1908** (A. 1275). 18pp.

Comp. H.C. Lowther. Covers topography, communications, principal towns
(with notes on 22), harbours and military stations, natural resources,
ethnography. Includes a brief commercial directory, and a description of 9
routes. Maps include region at 1:5M, Dar-es-Salaam at 1:12,092. Addenda
follow same pattern as the parent work and cover recent events.

584

India. General Staff. **Field notes on German East Africa.** Simla, 1914. (A. 67).
vi, 107pp.

Compiled on a similar pattern to the "Military reports" of the War Office
Intelligence Branch. Appendices include list of tribes by district.

585

Karstedt, O. **Deutsch Ostafrika und seine Nachbargebiete: ein Handbuch für
Reisende.** Berlin, D. Reimer, 1914. xi, 319pp. illus. maps.

General sections on history and topography, followed by regional sections on
Dar es Salaam, Tanga, Zanzibar. Compiled for the traveller, but includes
considerable general detail.

586

G.B. Admiralty. Naval Intelligence Division. **A handbook of German East
Africa.** London, 1916. (I.D. 1055). 440pp. map. (Re-issued 1920, 1923).

Detailed historical, administrative and economic information. Includes (pp. 28-
113) substantial list of all ethnic groups.
- - **Hygiene & disease in Eastern tropical Africa:** the protection of aircraft
from the attacks of insects. Issued as a supplement to the "Handbook of

German East Africa". London, 1916. 56pp.

587

G.B. Admiralty. Naval Staff. Intelligence Department. **East African Protectorate, March 1919**. London, 1919. (I.D. 1174 KK). 38pp.

Covers German East Africa with data on topography and peoples.

588

G.B. Foreign Office. Historical Section. **Tanganyika (German East Africa)**. London, 1920. (F.O. Handbook, 113). 115pp.
Also published in F.O. **Peace handbooks**, vol. 18. London, 1920.

589

British Empire Exhibition. Central Committee of Tanganyika. **Tanganyika Territory handbook**. London, 1925. xiv, 178pp. 2 maps.

Descriptive and historical.

590

Sayers, G.F. *ed.* **The handbook of Tanganyika**. London, Macmillan, 1930. x, 636pp. 32 photos. 9 maps.

Author was Assistant Secretary in the Chief Secretary's Office. "This handbook, although in part compiled from official records, is not an official publication" (title-page). Very detailed account of the administration with supporting historical and topographical information. For the "2nd ed." by J.P. Moffett (1958) basically a completely new work, *see* 594.

591

Tanganyika guide. Nairobi, "East African Standard", 1936. 136pp. illus. map.

- - 2nd ed. Letchworth, 1948, 160pp.

- - 3rd ed. Letchworth, 1953, 180pp.

Covers history, topography, natural resources, tourism, statistics.

592

Arning, W. **Deutsch-Ostafrika: gestern und heute**. Berlin, D. Reimer, 1936. 388pp. illus.

- - 2nd ed. Berlin, 1942. viii, 425pp.

Sections for the former German East Africa in general, Tanganyika and Ruanda-Urundi. Detailed account of topography, history, politics, industry, and agriculture. Essentially an up-dated version of 585.

593
Moffett, J.P. *ed.* **Tanganyika: a review of its resources and their development.** Dar es Salaam, Government of Tanganyika, 1955. xviii, 924pp. maps.

Extremely detailed account devoted largely to the economic situation of the country. Numerous statistics, and 61 tables of data. 12 maps.

594
Moffett, J.P. *ed.* **Handbook of Tanganyika.** 2nd ed. Dar es Salaam, Government of Tanganyika, 1958. xi, 703pp. illus. maps.

A completely recast 2nd ed. of Sayers **Handbook ...** of 1930 (*see* 590). "Mainly historical and descriptive ... complementary to **Tanganyika: a review** [*see* 593] which was primarily economic" (preface). Author was Commissioner for Social Development. Numerous statistics, 12 maps, extensive bibliography (pp. 567-677).

595
Scheel, J.O.W. **Tanganyika und Sansibar.** Bonn, Schroeder for Deutsche Afrika-Gesellschaft, 1959. (Die Länder Afrikas, 20). 136pp.

596
Tanganyika. Information Services. **Tanganyika data book.** Dar es Salaam, 1961. issued loose leaf with binder. *No revisions traced.*

Sections for the administration, agriculture, commerce, local government, social services, etc.

597
Area handbook for Tanzania, comp. A.B. Herrick, *et al.,* Washington, DC, U.S. Department of Defense, 1968. xvi, 522pp. maps.

- - 2nd ed. **Tanzania: a country study,** comp. I. Kaplan, *et al.* Washington, DC, 1978. xix, 344pp. illus. maps.

598
Tanzania. Ministry of Information and Tourism. **Tanzania today.** Nairobi, University Press of Africa, 1968. vii, 316pp.

Topographical, economic and statistical information.

599
Kurtz, L.S. **Historical dictionary of Tanzania**. Metuchen, NJ Scarecrow Press, 1978. (African historical dictionaries, 15). 331pp.

See pp. xxiv-xxv for details of reviews.

See also 1415.

Zanzibar

600
Zanzibar. **A handbook of Zanzibar**. Zanzibar, 1912. 49pp.

Largely addressed to the traveller walking round the city, with information related to the route. Includes brief civil list.

601
Shelswell-White, G.H. **A guide to Zanzibar**. Zanzibar, Government Printer, 1932. 73pp.

- - 2nd ed. Zanzibar, 1939. 74pp.

- - 3rd ed. rev. J.O'Brien, *et al.* Zanzibar, 1949. xii, 109pp.

- - 4th ed. rev. K.S.Madan. Zanzibar, 1952. x, 146pp. photos, maps.

The standard guide, originally compiled by the private secretary to the Sultan and regularly revised, with historical, topographical, and tourist information.

YEARBOOKS

602
G.B. Colonial Office. **[Annual reports]: Tanganyika, 1918-60**. London, 1921-1961.

As **Report to the Council of the League of Nations on the administration of Tanganyika Territory**, 1918/20, 1921, (as Command papers); **Report by H.B.M. Government to the League of Nations**, [title varies], 1922-1938 (not pub. 1939/46), **Report ... to the Trusteeship Council of the UN**, 1947, **Report ... to the General Assembly of the UN**, 1948-60 (in Colonial series). *For fuller* *details see Appendix.*

603

Tanganyika and Zanzibar directory. Tanga, 1935. xvi, 246pp.

604

Tanganyika. Department of Commerce and Industry. **Commerce and industry in Tanganyika.** Dar es Salaam, 1957-1961. 2 issues.

Includes information on topography, natural resources, communications, and trade with statistics.

Zanzibar

605

G.B. Colonial Office. **[Annual reports]: Zanzibar, 1913-1960.** London, 1914-1963.

As **Annual report on Zanzibar**, 1913-19, (as Command papers); **Colonial Office annual report** 1920-60, (not pub. 1939-45). Pub. biennially from 1949/50-1959/60. Preceded by four reports issued by the Foreign Office: **Reports on Zanzibar Protectorate**, 1893-94 (C.6955); **Report on the revenue and administration in Zanzibar in 1894** (C.7706); **Report ... on Island of Pemba**, 1896-97 (C.8701); **Despatch from H.M.'s Agent and ConsulGeneral furnishing a report on the administration, finance and general condition of the Zanzibar Protectorate**, 1909 (Cd.4816). *For fuller details see Appendix.*

STATISTICS

Bibliography

606

Tanzania. Statistical Bureau. **A bibliography of economic and statistical publications on Tanzania.** Dar es Salaam, 1967. 23pp.

- - 2nd ed. Dar es Salaam, 1975.

607

Tanzania. Central Bureau of Statistics. **A guide to Tanzania statistics.** Dar es Salaam, 1968. 51pp.

Includes an account of the organizations responsible for collecting the data.

608

Tanzania. Central Bureau of Statistics. **A guide to official statistics of Tanzania, January 1985.** Dar es Salaam, 1985. 20pp.

Covers 16 different areas of statistics.

Bulletins

609

East Africa High Commission. East African Statistical Department (Tanganyika Unit). **Tanganyika monthly statistical bulletin.** Dar es Salaam, 1951-1964.

continued by:

Tanzania. Bureau of Statistics [etc.]. **Monthly statistical bulletin.** Dar es Salaam, 1964- .

Title varies: **Quarterly statistical bulletin** (1971-).

Yearbooks

610

East Africa High Commission, East African Statistical Department (Tanganyika Unit). **Statistical abstract 1938/51** [etc.]. Nairobi, 1953-1960. Irreg.

Issues for 1951-52, 1954-1958, 1960.

continued by:

Tanzania. Bureau of Statistics [etc.]. **Statistical abstract.** Dar es Salaam, 1961- . Annual (irreg.)

No issues published for 1967-69, 1974-78. Vols. for 1973/79 (1983); 1979 (1981); 1982 (1983); 1984 (1986).

611

Statistik des Auslandes: Länderberichte: Tansania. Wiesbaden, Statistisches Bundesamt, 1965- . Irreg.

Issues for 1965, 1987, 1989. Also included in vol. for East Africa, 1971 (*see* 547).

Zanzibar

612

Crofton, R.H. **Statistics of the Zanzibar Protectorate, 1893-1920.** Zanzibar, Government Printer, 1921. 36pp.

- - 2nd ed. **Statistics ... 1893-1927.** Zanzibar, 1928. Then annual editions, 3rd to 9th, 1929-1936.

613

Zanzibar. Department of Statistics. **Summary digest of useful statistics.** Zanzibar, 1961.

614

Zanzibar. Department of Statistics. **Statistical abstract of Zanzibar.** Zanzibar, 1981- . Annual.

DIRECTORIES OF ORGANIZATIONS

615

Tanganyika Library Service. **Directory of libraries in Tanzania.** Dar es Salaam, 1972. 52pp.

- - [rev. ed.] **Directory of libraries, museums and archives in Tanzania.** Dar es Salaam, Tanzania Library Service, 1978.

1972 ed. comp. C.S. Ilomo.

616

Tanzania. Ministry of Agriculture. Research & Disease Control Section. **Directory of agricultural research institutes in Tanzania: with special reference to crop research.** Dar es Salaam, 1974. iv, 73pp.

617

Tanzania. Ministry of Manpower Development. **Directory of training institutions.** Dar es Salaam, 1977. 130pp.

Lists 132 institutions by ministry responsible, plus 47 "Folk Development Colleges" and very brief details on another 98 organizations.

618

Tanzania Research & Information Service (TANRIS). **Directory of technical information resources in Tanzania.** Dar es Salaam, 1981. 11, 60pp.

BIOGRAPHICAL SOURCES

619
Ingrams, W.H. **Chronology and genealogies of Zanzibar rulers.** Zanzibar, 1926. 10pp.

ATLASES & GAZETTEERS

Atlases

620
Tanganyika. Department of Lands & Mines, Survey Division. **Atlas of the Tanganyika Territory.** Dar es Salaam, 1942. 31pp. incl. part col. maps. 46 x 48cm.

Text on verso of some maps. Thematic maps showing geology, rainfall, temperature, forest resources, game, population, agriculture, minerals and communications. Maps 19-27 show development of cartographic knowledge of East Africa and routes of explorers. Majority of sheets at 1:4M.

- - 2nd ed. Dar es Salaam, 1948. 35pp. incl. part col. maps.

Adds maps for soils, vegetation, drainage basins, mines. Review, *Geographical review* 41, 1951, 483-484.

- - 3rd ed. Tanganyika. Department of Lands and Surveys. Survey Division. **Atlas of Tanganyika, East Africa.** Dar es Salaam, 1957. iv, 30pp. incl. col. maps. 56 x 59 cm.

Text and tables on verso of most maps. Omits historical maps of earlier eds., adds maps of mean rainfall, labour distribution, water supply. Maps are now at the larger scale of 1:3M. Includes plans of Dar es Salaam (1:25,000), Tanga (1:10,000), Dodoma (1:5,000), Morozoro (1:2,500).

- - [4th ed.] Tanzania. Ministry of Lands, Housing & Urban Development. Surveys & Mapping Division. **Atlas of Tanzania.** Dar es Salaam, 1969. iii, 61pp.

Includes 24 map plates and the 4 plans. Sections for topography, climate, flora and fauna and human geography. Reviews in *GJ*, 136, 1970, 311-312; *Tanzania notes and records* 72, 1973, 81-87.

621

Jensen, S.B. **Regional economic atlas, mainland Tanzania.** Dar es Salaam, University College of Dar es Salaam, Bureau of Resource Assessment & Land Use Planning, 1968. 74pp.

18 black and white maps at 1:6,500,000, featuring population, industry, trade, education and natural resources, with accompanying text and statistical tables.

622

Berry, L., *ed.* **Tanzania in maps.** London, University of London Press, 1971/New York, Africana Publishing Corporation, 1972. 172pp.

Compiled by Tanzania Bureau of Resource Development and Land Use Planning and Department of Geography at University of Dar es Salaam. 61 black & white thematic maps, with text. Statistical tables, pp.153-176. "Single most valuable reference work available on Tanzania" (*ASA review of books* 1, 1975, 109-110). Also reviewed *GJ*, 138, 1972, 525.

623

Soil atlas of Tanzania. Dar es Salaam, Tanzania Publishing House, 1983. 56pp. 39 x 39cm.

Comp. A.S. Hathout. 49 maps.

See also 753, 1642.

Gazetteers

624

U.S. Board on Geographic Names. **Tanzania: official standard names approved by the U.S.B.G.N.** Washington, DC, 1965. (Gazetteer, 92). v, 236pp.

Pp. 1-199, Tanganyika (14,150 entries from 1:100,000/1:500,000 series); pp. 201-236, Zanzibar (incorporating text from separately published **Zanzibar: official standard names ...** , *see* 626). Replaces appropriate sections in **British East Africa ...** (*see* 561).

- - **Gazetteer supplement: Africa and South-West Asia.** Washington, DC, 1972. (pp. 155-159, Tanzania)

Zanzibar

625

Piggott, P.H. **The gazetteer of Zanzibar Island**. Zanzibar, Government Printer, 1962. ii, 17pp.

Some 650 entries. Based on sheets 1 and 2 of 1:63,360 series produced by 89 Field Survey Squadron, Royal Engineers.

626

U.S. Board on Geographic Names. **Zanzibar: official standard names approved by the U.S.B.G.N.** Washington, DC, 1964. (Gazetteer, 76). iii, 36pp.

Some 2,400 names from maps at 1:63,360. Text also incorporated into **Tanzania: official standard names ...** (*see* 624).

UGANDA

HANDBOOKS

627

G.B. War Office. General Staff. **Précis of information on the Uganda Protectorate**. London, 1902. iv, 159pp. 5 maps in pocket.

Comp. E.M. Woodward. Title on first page of text "Handbook of the Uganda Protectorate". A revised ed. of the appropriate sections of **Handbook of British East Africa ...** (*see* 522). Includes separate chapters on each province, including Eastern Province, not previously covered. Standard "précis" coverage. Appendix describes 21 routes.

628

Johnston, *Sir* H.H. **The Uganda Protectorate**: an attempt to give some description of the physical geography, botany, zoology, anthropology, languages and history of the territories under British Protectorate in East Central Africa [etc.]. London, Hutchinson, 1902. 2 vols. 510 illus. 48 col. plates. 9 maps.

 - - 2nd ed. New York, Dodd, Mead, 1904. 2 vols.

Detailed wide-ranging account by the Special Commissioner to the Uganda Protectorate, 1899-1902. Sections on anthropology by F. Shrubsall. 2nd ed. is a reprint "with prefatory chapter giving additional matter" (title-page).

629

G.B. War Office. General Staff. **Military report on the Uganda Protectorate, 1909**. London, 1908. (B. 124). xi, 337pp.

Comp. Capt. A.H.C. MacGregor & Lt. S.W.H. Rawlins. Based on **Précis ...** (*see* 627). Information arranged by province. Appendix 1 (pp. 193-283) lists 48 routes.

630

Wallis, H.R. **Handbook of Uganda**. London, Crown Agents for Government of Uganda, 1913. xix, 220pp.

 - - 2nd ed. London, 1920. xxi, 316pp.

Author was Chief Secretary to the Governor, later Acting Governor. Includes historical and topographical surveys, detailed account of natural resources, trade and industry, with statistics. 2nd ed. has extended treatment of anthropology and botany, and includes a bibliography.

631
G.B. Admiralty. Intelligence Division. Geographical Section. **A handbook of the Uganda Protectorate**. London, 1920. (I.D. 1217). viii, 447pp.

Acknowledges Wallis (*see* 630) as a major source. Data included were gathered during the war and not updated. Covers topography, natural resources, agriculture, commerce and industry, administration, communications and history, and includes annual surveys of economic data, 1893/94 to 1916/17.

632
G.B. War Office. General Staff. **Military report on Uganda**. London, 1927. 2 vols.

Vol. 1 *not traced.*; vol. 2, Routes, 1927. 322pp. Lists 214 itineraries.

633
Thomas, H.B. & Scott, R. **Uganda**. London, Oxford University Press, 1935. xx, 559pp.

"Although produced with the assistance ... of the Uganda Government ... is not to be regarded as an 'official' publication. It is ... in effect, a third edition of the **Handbook of Uganda**" (*see* 630). Detailed survey of every aspect of the country with statistics.

634
G.B. War Office. General Staff. **Uganda military report**. London, 1940. (B. 140). iii, 135pp. maps.

Covers history, administration, topography, ethnography, communications. Detailed treatment for Entebbe, Jinja, Kampala.

635
Berger, H. **Uganda**. Bonn, Schroeder for Deutsche Afrika-Gesellschaft, 1964. (Die Länder Afrikas, 27). 80pp.

636
Area handbook for Uganda, comp. A.B. Herrick, *et al.* Washington, DC, U.S. Department of Defense, 1969. xvi, 456pp. maps.

YEARBOOKS

637

G.B. Colonial Office. [**Annual reports**]: **Uganda, 1901-1961**. London, 1901-1963.

As **Preliminary report by Her Majesty's special Commissioner on the Protectorate of Uganda**, 1900, (Cd.256) with maps (Cd.361), **Annual report on Uganda**, [title varies], 1902/03-1918/19 (as Command papers); **Colonial Office annual report**, 1919/20, 1920-1961 (not pub. 1939-45). Reports prior to 1904/05 issued by the Foreign Office. *For fuller details see Appendix.*

638

Saben's commercial directory and handbook of Uganda. Kampala, Saben and Co., 1947/48- . Annual.

9th issue for 1955/56 last traced. General topographical and economic information, directories of residents and institutions. 1955/56 issue is "the first to include a classified commercial directory" (preface).

639

Uganda. Ministry of Information, Broadcasting and Tourism. **Uganda 1962/63** [etc.]. Kampala, 1964-1970. Annual (irreg). 3 issues.

Issues for 1962/63, 1964, 1967. Running title : "Uganda report". A post-independence continuation of 637.

640

Uganda trade directory 1966/67. London, Diplomatic Press & Publishing Co. (Diprepu Co.) Ltd., 1966. *No more published?*

641

Uganda. Ministry of Information & Broadcasting. **Uganda 1983** [etc.] **yearbook**. Kampala, 1983- . Annual.

"First publication of its kind to be issued since ... liberation of 1979" (preface to 1983 ed.). Largely economic and statistical data.

STATISTICS

642

East Africa High Commission, East African Statistical Department (Uganda Unit). **Statistical abstract**. Entebbe, 1957-1960. Annual.

continued by:

Uganda. Statistics Division [etc.]. **Statistical abstract**. Entebbe, 1960-1979. Annual.

Last issue pub. 1979 covers 1974.

643

Uganda. Statistics Division. **Quarterly economic and statistical bulletin.** Entebbe, 1965- .

644

Statistik des Auslandes: Länderberichte: Uganda. Wiesbaden, Statistisches Bundesamt, 1965- . Irreg.

Issues for 1965, 1986, 1988. Also included in vol. for East Africa, 1971 (*see* 547).

DIRECTORIES OF ORGANIZATIONS

645

Trowell, K.M. **A handbook of the museums and libraries of Uganda.** Kampala, Uganda Museum, 1957. (Museum occasional paper, 3)

646

Makerere University. Centre for Continuing Education & Unesco. **Directory of adult education agencies in Uganda**. Kampala, 1984. 123pp.

Comp. A. Okech.

BIOGRAPHICAL SOURCES

647

Who's who in Uganda, 1988/89 [etc.]. Kampala, Fountain Publishers Ltd., 1989- . Annual.

1988/89 ed. includes some 1,500 biographies with a selection of portraits under headings according to activity (e.g. "Government", "Politics", "Sport and entertainment" etc.)

ATLASES & GAZETTEERS

Atlases

648

Uganda. Department of Lands & Surveys. **Atlas of Uganda**. Entebbe, 1962. 83pp. 49 x 51cm.

- - 2nd ed. Entebbe, 1967. 81pp. 49 x 51cm.

37 coloured maps and text. Thematic coverage of physical features, climate, flora & fauna, human geography, agriculture, industry, trade, communications, and historical themes (archaeological sites, early travels, evolution of borders). Main maps at 1:1,500,000, town plans of Kampala and Jinja at 1:10,000. Gazetteer. 2nd ed. extensively revised but contains reduced scale coverage of crop distribution.

649

Makerere University. Department of Geography. **Atlas of population census 1969 for Uganda**. Kampala, 1974. 184pp. maps.

Comp. B.W. Langlands. Includes 60 maps, and 31 tables of data. "Aims to present key findings of the census in the visual form of maps" (introduction).

650

Uganda atlas of disease distribution. Nairobi, East Africa Publishing House, 1975. xvi, 165pp.

Ed. S.A. Hall & B.W. Langlands.

Gazetteers

651

Richardson, E. **Index to maps of Uganda Protectorate**. Entebbe, Uganda Land & Survey Department, 1922. 141pp.

Based on G.S.G.S. Series 1764 "Africa" at 1:250,000.

652

U.S. Board on Geographic Names. **Uganda: official standard names approved by the U.S.B.G.N.** Washington, DC, 1964. (Gazetteer, 82). iii, 167pp.

Includes 11,900 names from maps at 1:250,000. Replaces appropriate section in **British East Africa ...** (*see* 561)

- - **Gazetteer supplement: Africa and South-West Asia.** Washington, DC, 1972. (p. 179, Uganda).

653
Uganda. Department of Lands & Surveys. **Gazetteer of Uganda.** Kampala, 1971. vi, 203pp.

CENTRAL AFRICA

Anglophone Central Africa
Malawi
Zambia
Zimbabwe

Francophone Central Africa

Former French Equatorial Africa
Central African Republic
Chad
Congo
Gabon

Former Belgian Africa
Burundi & Rwanda
Burundi
Rwanda
Zaire

ANGLOPHONE CENTRAL AFRICA

Note that many sources, particularly those published during the colonial period, whose main emphasis is on Southern Africa, and are listed in that section, will often include coverage of the countries of this region.

HANDBOOKS

654
Johnston, *Sir* H.H. **British Central Africa**: an attempt to give some account of a portion of the territories under British influence north of the Zambesi. London, Methuen, 1897. xxi, 544pp. 220 illus. 6 maps.

- - 2nd ed. London, 1898. xix, 544pp.

Principally concerned with the regions bordering on Lakes Tanganyika and Nyasa, and the river Shiré. Systematic treatment of topography, history, peoples, flora and fauna. Author was Commissioner in British Central Africa, 1891-1896.

655
Ethnographic survey of Africa: West Central Africa. London, International African Institute, 1951-1953. 4 vols. maps.

Sub-series of **Ethnographic survey** (*see* 54). Vol. 1, 'The southern Lunda and related peoples (Northern Rhodesia, Angola, Belgian Congo)' by M. McCulloch. 1951. 110pp; vol. 2, 'The Ovimbundu of Angola', by M. McCulloch. 1952. 50pp; vol. 3, 'The Lozi peoples of North-Western Rhodesia' by V.W. Turner. 1952. 64pp; vol. 4, 'The Ila-Tonga peoples of North-Western Rhodesia' by M.A. Jaspan. 1953. 72pp.

656
Central African Airways guide to the Federation of Rhodesia and Nyasaland. Salisbury, A.J. Levin, 1957. 264pp.

- - 2nd ed. Salisbury, 1958. 298pp.

- - 3rd ed. Salisbury, 1961. 661pp.

Cover title : **Guide ...** Comp. L.S. Levin. Popular layout with photographs, but very detailed information, greatly increased in 1961 ed. Covers topography, government and administration, communications, economics, with civil list and descriptive gazetteer of over 120 locations.

657
Schmidt, W. **Föderation von Rhodesien und Nyasaland**. Bonn, Schroeder for Deutsche Afrika-Gesellschaft, 1959. (Die Länder Afrikas, 16). 139pp. illus. maps.

Later expanded to individual vols. in the series for **Malawi** (*see* 674), **Rhodesien** (*see* 724) and **Zambia** (*see* 694).

658
Handbook to the Federation of Rhodesia and Nyasaland. London, Cassell for Federation Information Department, 1960. xii, 803pp. 180 photos. maps in text & folding maps.

- - **Index to the Handbook ...** Comp. A.S.C. Hooper, M.S. in Library Science, Catholic University of America, 1969.

Ed. W.V. Brelsford, Director of Information of the Federation with 25 contributors. An immensely detailed work covering all aspects of topography, history, and the social, administrative and economic structure of the region.

See also 1366, 1415.

YEARBOOKS

659

The Rhodesia directory. Bulawayo, Publications (Central Africa) (*later* Ndola, Directory Publishers of Zambia), 1910- . Annual.

76th issue 1986. Title varies : **Rhodesia-Zambia-Malawi directory; Directory for Zambia, Malawi, Botswana and adjacent territories; Zimbabwe directory including Botswana & Malawi; Braby's commercial directory of Zimbabwe** (1984/85); **Boldad's commercial directory of Zimbabwe** (1986-). Includes Botswana, Mozambique. Detailed lists of officials, residents, and commercial directory. Certain sections also published separately, e.g. **Salisbury** (later **Harare) directory** (1962-); **Bulawayo directory** (1962-); **Zambia directory** (1963-).

660

Year book and guide of the Rhodesias and Nyasaland. Salisbury, Rhodesian Pubns., 1937-?1962. Annual (irreg.)

Issues for 1937, 1938/39, 1940/41, 1942/43, 1943/44, 1944/45, 1946/47, 1948/49, 1950/51, 1962. In addition to topographical, historical and economic information contains a gazetteer (150/200 locations), and a biography section (400/600 entries).

661

Central African classified directory: business and trades. Salisbury, Morris Publishing Co., 1953-1961. 8 issues.

Principal coverage of Northern and Southern Rhodesia and Nyasaland; more summary coverage of Kenya, Tanganyika and Uganda; Mozambique; Madagascar; Belgian Congo, and in 7th and 8th eds., Ghana and Nigeria. Over 1,000pp. per issue. An exclusively commercial directory, with no information other than names and addresses.

662

Braby's Central and East African directory. Durban, A.C. Braby (*later* Ndola/Bulawayo, B & T Directories), 1954- . Annual. 30th ed. 1984/85.

Title varies: **Directory of Central Africa/Central Africa business directory/Braby's commercial directory of Central Africa/Zimbabwe &**

Rhodesia business directory (1981-). Coverage varies: principal coverage of Rhodesia/Zimbabwe with details of government and commercial directory; Angola, Botswana, Lesotho, Malawi, Mauritius, Mozambique, Swaziland, Zambia have commercial directory only. From 1981 includes Kenya, Réunion, Seychelles, Namibia, excludes Angola, Mozambique.

See also 544, 903, 1439, 1445-1447, 1462, 1463.

STATISTICS

663
Federation of Rhodesia & Nyasaland. Central African Statistical Office. **Monthly digest of statistics of the Federation of Rhodesia and Nyasaland.** Salisbury, 1954-1964.

DIRECTORIES OF ORGANIZATIONS

664
University College of Rhodesia and Nyasaland. Library. **Directory of libraries in the Federation of Rhodesia and Nyasaland.** Salisbury, 1960. 42pp.

103 entries.

See also 551, 1480, 1482.

BIOGRAPHICAL SOURCES

665
Central and East African who's who for 1953 [etc.]. Salisbury, Central Africa Who's Who Ltd., 1953-56. 3 issues.

Issues for 1953, 1955, 1956. Covers Northern and Southern Rhodesia, Nyasaland, Kenya, Uganda, Tanganyika, Mozambique, Belgian Congo. Includes about 3,300 entries per issue.

incorporated into :

Who's who of the Federation of Rhodesia and Nyasaland, Central and East Africa. Johannesburg, Ken Donaldson, 1957-59. 3 issues.

continued by:

Who's who of Rhodesia, Mauritius, Central and East Africa. Johannesburg, Combined Publishers [etc.], 1960- . Annual.

Published separately, and also as a section within **Who's who of Southern Africa** (1959- *see* 1494). Includes Rhodesia/Zimbabwe, Zambia, Malawi, Botswana, Mauritius, Mozambique.

ATLASES & GAZETTEERS

Atlases

666
Federation of Rhodesia and Nyasaland. Department of the Surveyor General. **Federal Atlas, Federation of Rhodesia and Nyasaland.** Salisbury, 1960-1964. 24 maps. 69 x 69cm.

24 topographic and thematic sheets, mostly at 1:2,500,000.

See also 1536.

Gazetteers

667
U.S. Board on Geographic Names. **Rhodesia & Nyasaland: official standard names approved by the U.S.B.G.N.** Washington, DC, 1956. 214pp.

Pp. 1-101, Northern Rhodesia; pp. 102-178, Southern Rhodesia; pp. 179-214, Nyasaland. Includes c.17,000 names. Later eds. pub. in separate vols. for **Malawi** (*see* 687), **Zambia** (*see* 715), **Southern Rhodesia** (*see* 751).

See also 656.

MALAWI

HANDBOOKS

668
G.B. War Office. Intelligence Department. **Précis of information concerning the British Central African Protectorate**, with notes on adjoining territories. London, 1899. 53pp. maps.

Comp. C.B. Vyvyan "from official sources, Sir Harry Johnston's works etc.". General survey of topography, history, communications, administration, industries, missions.

669
British Central African Protectorate. **British Central African Protectorate: Diary 1905; with official handbook on the Protectorate completed in the Secretariat.** Zomba, 1906. 108pp.

Covers topography, natural history, mining, population, history and communications, with a commercial directory.

670
Handbook of Nyasaland, comprising historical, statistical and general information concerning the Nyasaland Protectorate. Zomba, Government Printer, 1908. vi, 292pp. illus. map.

- - 2nd ed. London, Wyman & Sons, 1910. xi, 288pp. illus. map.

- - 3rd ed. London, Crown Agents for the Government of Nyasaland, 1922. v, 314pp. illus.

- - 4th ed. London, Crown Agents for the Government of Nyasaland, 1932, 432pp. illus.

3rd & 4th eds. compiled by S.S. Murray. "This handbook, though in part compiled from official records, is not an official publication" (title page of 1st & 2nd eds.). Detailed accounts of each province. Covers history, administration, the economy. Includes lists of societies, missions, European residents. Numerous photos.

671
G.B. War Office. General Staff. **Military report and general information**

concerning Nyasaland. London, 1909. (B. 87). 342pp. map in pocket.

Comp. Capt. St.G. McRae. Similar coverage and structure to the **Précis ...** (*see* 668) though with much greater detail.

672
G.B. Foreign Office. Historical Section. **Nyasaland**. London, 1920. 90pp. (F.O. Handbook, 95).
Also pub. in F.O. **Peace handbooks**, vol. 15. London, 1920.

673
G.B. War Office. Military Operations Directorate. **Military report on Nyasaland**. London, 1939. (B. 532). v, 100pp.

Covers history, administration, topography, ethnography, communications. Detailed coverage of Blantyre, Lilongwe, Limbe, Zomba.

674
Schimmelfennig, E. **Malawi**. Bonn, Schroeder for Deutsche Afrika-Gesellschaft, 1965. (Die Länder Afrikas, 30). 95pp. illus. maps.

Expanded revision of the relevant sections of 657.

675
Area handbook for Malawi; comp. H.D. Nelson, *et al.* Washington, DC, U.S. Department of Defense, 1975. xiv, 353pp. illus. maps.

Review, *IJAHS*, 16, 1983, 148-149.

676
Crosby, C.A. **Historical dictionary of Malawi**. Metuchen, NJ, Scarecrow Press, 1980. (African historical dictionaries, 25). 169pp.

See also 524, 525, 527.

YEARBOOKS

677
G.B. Colonial Office. **[Annual reports]: Nyasaland, 1891-1962**. London, 1894-1964.

As **Report ... on the first three years administration of the Eastern portion** of British Central Africa, 1894, Report ... on the trade and general condition of British Central African Protectorate, 1895/96-1896/97, Annual report on the British Central African Protectorate, 1897/98 (not pub. 1898-1902), Report on the trade and general conditions of the British Central African Protectorate, 1902-03, British Central Africa Protectorate report, 1903/04-1906/07, Nyasaland Protectorate report, 1907/08-1908/09, Nyasaland Report, 1909/10-1918/19, (all as Command papers); Colonial Office annual report [title varies], 1919/20-62 (not pub. 1926, 1939-45). 1962 report issued by Commonwealth Relations Office. *For fuller details see Appendix.*

678
Malawi. Department of Information. **Malawi.** Blantyre, 1968- . Annual.

Title varies: **Malawi: an official handbook** (1970-72); **Malawi yearbook** (1973-75, 1978-). Not published 1976-77, when replaced by much briefer (24pp.) **Malawi: the year in review.**

679
Malawi directory. Blantyre, A.C. Braby (Blantyre), 1966- . Annual.

See also 539, 541.

STATISTICS

680
Southern Rhodesia. Central African Statistical Office. **Statistical handbook of Nyasaland.** Salisbury, 1950-1952. 2 issues.

Issues for 1950, 1952.

681
Malawi. Ministry of Finance [etc.]. **Quarterly digest of statistics.** Zomba, 1964-1970.

continued by:

Malawi. National Statistical Office. **Monthly statistical bulletin.** Zomba, 1971- .

682
Malawi. Ministry of Development Planning [etc.]. **Compendium of statistics.** Zomba, 1965-1970. Irreg. 3 vols.

Issues for 1965, 1966, 1970.

continued by:

Malawi. National Statistical Office [etc.]. **Malawi statistical yearbook**. Zomba, 1972- . Annual.

Abbreviated version published as **Malawi in figures**. Zomba, 1981-. Annual.

683
Statistik des Auslandes: Länderberichte: Malawi. Wiesbaden, Statistisches Bundesamt, 1967- . Irreg.

Issues for 1967, 1984, 1986, 1988.

DIRECTORIES OF ORGANIZATIONS

684
University of Malawi. **Directory of Malawi libraries**. Zomba, 1976. vii, 111pp.

- - 2nd ed. Zomba, 1990. ii, 47pp. (University of Malawi publication, 6).

1st ed. comp. S.M. Made, includes 91 entries; 2nd ed. comp. J.J. Uta, lists 168.

ATLASES & GAZETTEERS

Atlases

685
Agnew, S. & Stubbs, M. **Malawi in maps**. London, University of London Press, 1972. 144pp.

47 black and white maps with accompanying text.

686
Malawi. Department of Surveys. **National atlas of Malawi**. Blantyre, 1985. 85pp. loose-leaf in ring-binder. 45 x 48cm.

70 maps, including 20 general topographic maps mostly at 1:250,000 and 41 thematic maps, mostly at 1:1M or 1:2M. Transparent overlay at 1:2M showing population distribution. Includes gazetteer.

Gazetteers

687

U.S. Board on Geographic Names. **Malawi: official standard names approved by the U.S.B.G.N.** Washington, DC, 1970. (Gazetteer, 113). iii, 161pp.

Includes 10,200 names from 1:50,000 (for central and southern areas), 1:250,000 (for northern areas) map series. A revision of the section for Nyasaland in **Rhodesia & Nyasaland ...** (*see* 667).

- - **Gazetteer supplement: Africa and South-West Asia**. Washington, DC, 1972. (pp. 103-104, Malawi).

ZAMBIA

HANDBOOKS

688

G.B. War Office. Intelligence Division. **Précis of information concerning Barotseland.** London, 1898. (A. 541). 35pp. map in pocket.

Comp. Maj. C.T. Dawkins. Standard coverage of topography, history, communications, administration and peoples.

689

G.B. War Office. General Staff. **Précis of information concerning North-Eastern Rhodesia.** London, 1904. (A. 878). iv, 48pp. map in pocket.

Topography, history, communications, peoples, and the administration. Map at 1:2M.

690

G.B. War Office. Military Operations Directorate. **Military report on Northern Rhodesia, 1939.** London, 1939. (B. 531). iv, 139pp.

Covers history, administration, ethnography and communications.

691

Northern Rhodesia. Information Department. **Northern Rhodesia handbook.** Lusaka, 1939. 144pp.

692

Northern Rhodesia. Department of Information. **Northern Rhodesia official handbook.** Lusaka, 1947. 92pp. 1 folding map.

- - 2nd ed. 1948. 98pp.

continued by:

Northern Rhodesia. Department of Information. **Northern Rhodesia handbook.** Lusaka, 1950. 232pp.

- - rev. ed. Lusaka, 1952.

- - rev. ed. Lusaka, 1953. 263pp.

A more substantial work with greater factual detail than the 1947 and 1948 issues.

693

Zambia. Information Services. **A handbook to the Republic of Zambia.** Lusaka, 1964. vi, 153pp.

Cover title: **Zambia today**. General topographical and historical information.

694

Schmidt, W. **Zambia**. Bonn, Schroeder for Deutsche Afrika-Gesellschaft, 1965. (Die Länder Afrikas, 31). 176pp. illus. maps.

Expanded revision of the appropriate sections of 657.

695

Area handbook for Zambia, comp. H.D. Nelson, *et al.* Washington, DC, U.S. Department of Defense, 1969. xvi, 482pp. maps.

- - 2nd ed. comp. I. Kaplan, *et al.* Washington, DC, 1974. lxxxvi, 484pp. maps.

- - 3rd ed. **Zambia: a country study**. Washington, DC, 1979. 308pp. illus. maps.

696

Grotpeter, J.J. **An historical dictionary of Zambia**. Metuchen, NJ, Scarecrow Press, 1979. (African historical dictionaries, 19). 429pp.

697

Zambia. Central Statistical Office. **Country profile: Zambia**. Lusaka, 1984.

- - 2nd ed. Lusaka, 1986.

See also 527.

YEARBOOKS

698

G.B. Colonial Office. **[Annual reports]: Northern Rhodesia, 1924/25-1962.** London, 1926-1964.

As **Colonial Office annual report**, 1924-62 (not pub. 1939-45). Pub. for

1924/25 and 1925/26, then annually, commencing 1926. One report pub. for 1961 & 1962. *For fuller details see Appendix.*

See also 539, 659.

STATISTICS

699

Southern Rhodesia. Central African Statistical Office. **Economic and statistical bulletin of Northern Rhodesia.** Salisbury, 1948-1954.

Continued by **Monthly digest of statistics of the Federation of Rhodesia & Nyasaland** (*see* 663).

700

Zambia. Central Statistical Office. **Monthly digest of statistics.** Lusaka, 1965-

701

Zambia. Central Statistical Office. **Statistical yearbook.** Lusaka, 1967-1971. Annual. 5 issues.

702

Statistik des Auslandes: Länderberichte: Sambia. Wiesbaden, Statistisches Bundesamt, 1979- . Irreg.

Issues for 1979, 1983, 1985, 1987.

703

Zambia. Central Statistical Office. **Zambia in figures.** Lusaka, 1980- . Annual.

DIRECTORIES OF ORGANIZATIONS

704

Zambia Library Association. **A directory of libraries in Zambia.** Lusaka, 1975. iii, 15pp.

- - 2nd ed. comp. E. Lumande. Lusaka, 1979. ii, 6pp.

1st ed. gives brief details of 75 libraries, 2nd ed. of 83.

705
Zambia. National Council for Scientific Research. **Directory of scientific research organizations in Zambia.** Lusaka, 1975. 78pp.

BIOGRAPHICAL SOURCES

706
Sampson, R. **They came to Northern Rhodesia:** being a record of persons who had entered what is now the territory of Northern Rhodesia by 31st Dec. 1902. Lusaka, Commission for the Preservation of Natural & Historical Monuments & Relics, 1956. xiv, 49pp.

Lists 874 names of those who had arrived before the large influx following the South African War. Very brief biographical information and a reference to sources.

707
Who is who in Zambia 1967/68. Lusaka, Kingstons (Zambia) Ltd., 1967. 107pp.

- - rev. ed. **... 1979.** Ndola, Roan Consolidated Mines Ltd., 1979. 39pp.

1979 vol. ed. K.G. Mlenga, includes 168 entries.

ATLASES & GAZETTEERS

Atlases

708
Zambia. Survey Department. **Republic of Zambia Atlas.** Lusaka, 1966- ? .

Thematic atlas issued in separate sheets, mostly 45 x 54cm, some 74 x 90cm. Covers climate, soils, minerals, tribes and languages, education, medical facilities and agriculture.

709
Hywel Davies, D. **Zambia in maps.** London, University of London Press, 1971. 128pp.

Includes 55 thematic black and white maps with accompanying text.

710

Atlas for Zambia. Glasgow & Lusaka, Collins-Longman, 1973. 49pp.

Includes 7 maps of Zambia, 3 of Central Africa, 8 of the rest of Africa, 16 of the rest of the world.

711

Zambia. National Council for Scientific Research. **Atlas of the population of Zambia**. Lusaka, 1977. 15 sheets. 56 x 65cm.

- - rev. ed. Lusaka, 1987- .

Comp. M.E. Jackman & D. Hywel Davies. Includes brief explanatory text.

712

Zambia. Survey Department. **The Republic of Zambia atlas**. Lusaka, 1986-1988.

14 thematic sheets, 11 at 1:3M, showing administration, soils, climate, education, communications, natural resources, history.

See also 753.

Gazetteers

713

Zambia. Ministry of Land and Natural Resources. **Gazetteer of geographical names in the Barotse Protectorate**. Lusaka, 1959. iii, 156pp.

Now the Western Province of Zambia.

714

Zambia. Ministry of Lands and Mines. **Gazetteer of geographical names in the Republic of Zambia**. Lusaka, Government Printer, 1966. 319pp.

Includes c.35,000 entries arranged by province.

715

U.S. Board on Geographic Names. **Zambia: official standard names approved by the U.S.B.G.N.** Washington, DC, 1972. iv, 585pp.

A revision of the section for Northern Rhodesia in **Rhodesia and Nyasaland** ... (*see* 667).

- - 2nd ed. **Gazetteer of Zambia**. Washington, DC, 1983. 2 vols.

Includes 38,500 names.

ZIMBABWE

HANDBOOKS

716

Handbook for Mashonaland: the country and how to reach it. London, Eglington, 1892. 94pp.

717

G.B. War Office. Intelligence Division. **Précis of information concerning Southern Rhodesia.** London, 1899. 55pp.

Comp. Maj. C.T. Dawkins "from official documents, reports of well-known travellers" (preface). Standard "précis" format covering topography, communications, natural resources, administration and peoples.

718

British South Africa Company. **Rhodesia: general handbook.** London, 1907. 64pp.

719

G.B. War Office. General Staff. **Military report on Rhodesia.** London, 1913. (A. 1756). 128pp.

Includes coverage of geography, ethnology, history, communications, natural resources and finance. Appendices include a list of mission stations.

720

Beira and Mashonaland and Rhodesian Railways. **Guide to Rhodesia for the use of tourists and settlers.** Bulawayo, 1914. xvi, 395pp. maps.

- - 2nd ed. Bulawayo, 1924. xvi, 432pp. illus. maps.

Includes detailed background information on topography, peoples and natural resources.

721

Southern Rhodesia. Publicity Bureau. **Southern Rhodesia: an illustrated handbook for the use of tourists and settlers.** Bulawayo, 1930. 130pp. illus.

Numerous short chapters on land settlement, education, industries, agriculture, communications etc. Many photos.

722

Willson, F.M.G., *et al.* **Source book of Parliamentary elections and referenda in Southern Rhodesia, 1898-1962**. Salisbury, University College of Rhodesia, Department of Government, 1963. (Source book series, 1). 255pp.

Provides chronological tables of parliamentary sessions, and detailed results of all general and by-elections.

723

Willson, F.M.G., *et al.* **Southern Rhodesia: holders of administrative and ministerial office, 1894-1964, and members of the Legislative Council, 1899-1923, and the Legislative Assembly, 1924-1964**. Salisbury, University College of Rhodesia, Department of Government, 1966. (Source book series, 3). 77, 10pp.

724

Schmidt, W. **Rhodesien**. Bonn, Schroeder for Deutsche Afrika-Gesellschaft, 1970. (Die Länder Afrikas, 40). 231pp. illus. maps.

Expanded revision of the appropriate sections of 657.

725

Encyclopedia Rhodesia. Salisbury, College Press, 1973. 445pp. 10 maps.

General ed. M. Akers. Short entries with particular emphasis on flora and fauna. Numerous line-drawings. Appendices with statistics, chronology, lists of office-holders, texts of treaties.

726

Area handbook for Southern Rhodesia, comp. H.D. Nelson, *et al.* Washington, DC, U.S. Department of Defense, 1975. xiv, 394pp.

- - 2nd ed. **Zimbabwe: a country study**, comp. H.D. Nelson, *et al.* Washington, DC, 1983. 360pp.

727

Rasmussen, R.K. **Historical dictionary of Rhodesia/Zimbabwe**. Metuchen, NJ, Scarecrow Press, 1979. (African historical dictionaries, 18). 479pp.

Reviews, *JAH*, 23, 1982, 139; *IJAHS*, 15, 1982, 371-372.

- - 2nd ed. **Historical dictionary of Zimbabwe**, comp. R.K. Rasmussen & S.L. Roberts. Metuchen, NJ, 1990. (African historical dictionaries, 46). xxxviii,

502pp.

"This work now stands as the best reference on Zimbabwean history as well as a challenge for most other volumes in the series to meet", *ARBA*, 23, 1992, 40.

728
House, J. & House, M. **Zimbabwe: a handbook**. Harare, Mercury Press, 1983. 164pp. illus.

Popular approach, but useful detail.

729
Tabex encyclopedia Zimbabwe. Harare, Quest Publishing, 1987. xv, 431pp. illus. maps.

Ed. K. Sayce. 44 col. plates. Sponsored by Tabex, a local tobacco company. Alphabetical format with 'subject index' re-arranging entries under some 20 broad subject headings. Emphasis on botanical and zoological entries. Extremely detailed and critical review in *Moto magazine* (Harare) 66, 1988, 22-24, emphasizes uneveness of topic selection and level of entry. Very selective coverage of politicians of the colonial period "whose role was essentially negative" (preface). **Svinga: a Zimbabwe encyclopedia**, comp. T. Mechin, *et al*. Harare, Media Technology, 1990 is a CD-ROM "multimedia journal through Zimbabwe incorporating the **Tabex encyclopedia Zimbabwe**" (*Africana libraries newsletter*, 70, 1992, 11).

730
A concise encyclopedia of Zimbabwe. Gweru, Mambo Press, 1988. viii, 444pp.

Ed. D. Berens, *et al*. Mostly short entries, including biographies, with long articles on churches, education, international relations, law, literature, publishing, sports and trade unions. "Quick and concise answers for the person in a hurry" (preface).

See also 1405, 1413.

YEARBOOKS

731
The directory of Bulawayo and handbook to Matabeleland 1895/96 [-1899].

Bulawayo, Alexander Davis, 1895-1899. 3 issues. (1895/96 ed. reprinted in facsimile with new introduction by L.W.Bolze, Bulawayo, Books of Zimbabwe, 1981).

Issued 1895/96, 1898, 1899. Compiled "under the auspices and patronage of the British South Africa Company". Davis was founding ed. of *Bulawayo sketch*. Includes coverage of history and topography with residential and commercial directories and a civil list.

732
"Free Press" directory and handbook of Matabeleland. Bulawayo, F. Norris, 1901-?. Issues for 1901, 1902.

Includes a chronology of events in Rhodesia, and general historical and topographical information, with residential and commercial directories.

733
Official year book of the colony of Southern Rhodesia. Salisbury, Government Printer, 1924-1952. Irreg. 4 issues.

No. 1, 1924. xvi, 329pp; no. 2, 1930. xx, 862pp., "covering mainly the period 1924-1928"; no. 3, 1932. xiv, 804pp., "covering mainly the period 1926-1930"; no. 4, **Official year book of Southern Rhodesia.** 1952. xvi, 792pp., "with statistics mainly up to 1950". Nos. 2 and 3 compiled by Government Statistical Bureau (created 1928), no. 4 by Central African Statistical Bureau. A major source of detailed information, especially nos. 2-4. Includes gazetteer (300/450 entries).

See also 1437, 1442, 1444.

STATISTICS

Bulletins

734
Southern Rhodesia. Central African Statistical Office [etc.]. **Economic and statistical bulletin of Southern Rhodesia 1933/34 [-1954].** Salisbury, 1934-1955. Semi-monthly. 21 vols.

Continued by **Monthly digest of statistics of the Federation of Rhodesia & Nyasaland** (*see* 663).

735

Rhodesia/Zimbabwe. Central Statistical Office [etc.] **Monthly digest of statistics**, Salisbury/Harare, 1964- . n.s. 1980- .

Not issued March 1966-September 1968.

Annuals

736

Southern Rhodesia. Department of Statistics [etc.]. **Statistical yearbook of Southern Rhodesia: official annual of the social and economic conditions of the colony**. Salisbury, 1938. xiv, 156pp.

- - 2nd issue. Salisbury, 1947. xiv, 256pp.

Preface to 1938 issue : "Decided that the **Year book** [i.e. **Official year book ...** *see* 733] should now be re-issued, but ... composed almost entirely of statistical tables".

737

Southern Rhodesia. Department of Statistics. **Statistical handbook of Southern Rhodesia**. Salisbury, 1939. 29pp.

- - 2nd issue, Salisbury, 1945. 33pp.

Compact abbreviated versions of the **Statistical yearbook** (*see* 736).

738

Rhodesia/Zimbabwe. Central Statistical Office [etc.]. **Statistical yearbook of Rhodesia [later Zimbabwe]**. Salisbury/Harare, 1975- . Annual. n.s. 1985- .

739

Statistik des Auslandes: Länderberichte: Simbabwe. Wiesbaden, Statistisches Bundesamt, 1985- . Irreg.

Issues for 1985, 1987, 1990.

DIRECTORIES OF ORGANIZATIONS

740

Southern Rhodesia [etc.]. Scientific Council of Rhodesia. **Directory of organizations concerned with scientific research and technical services in**

Rhodesia. Salisbury, 1959-1979. Irreg. (eds. approximately every 3 years).

741
Rhodesia. National Archives of Rhodesia. **Directory of Rhodesian libraries;** comp. A. McHarg & S. Phillips. Salisbury, 1969. vii, 29pp.

- - 2nd ed. comp. D. Hartridge & T. Roberts. Salisbury, 1975. iv, 24pp.

- - 3rd ed. comp. B.L. Mushonga & R.G.S. Douglas. Salisbury, 1981. 25pp.

- - rev. ed. **Directory of libraries in Zimbabwe**, comp. S.R. Dube & R.G.S. Douglas. Harare, National Archives of Zimbabwe, 1987. 28pp.

1st ed contains 123 entries, 2nd ed. 237, 3rd ed. 240, 1987 ed. 243.

See also 1485.

BIOGRAPHICAL SOURCES

742
Hickman, A.S. **Men who made Rhodesia: a register of those who served in the British South Africa Company's Police.** Salisbury, British South Africa Company, 1960. 462pp. illus. maps.

An historical survey of the Police, followed by a list of 879 names of those who served 1889-1892, arranged by date of enrolment with an index of names.

743
Tabler, E.C. **Pioneers of Rhodesia.** Cape Town, Struik, 1966. viii, 185pp.

Includes "adult male foreigners (including coloureds and a few Africans) who arrived in the defined area [Southern Rhodesia, the Caprivi Strip, Barotse Valley, Victoria Falls Region, the Tati Concession and part of Bechuanaland] 1836-1880".

744
Cary, R. & Mitchell, D. **African nationalist leaders in Rhodesia who's who.** Johannesburg, Africana Book Society/Bulawayo, Books of Rhodesia, 1977. 310 pp.

- - [rev ed.]. Mitchell, D. **African nationalist leaders in Zimbabwe who's who 1980.** Salisbury, author, 1980. x, 106pp.

- - [rev. ed.] Mitchell, D. **Makers of history: who's who 1981-82: nationalist leaders in Zimbabwe**. Salisbury, author, 1981. 170pp. - - **Supplement 1982/83**. Harare, 1983. 21pp.

Earliest ed. includes 78 biographies.

745
Prominent African personalities of Rhodesia. Salisbury, Cover Publicity Services, [1977?]. xi, 196pp.

Includes about 500 entries, many with portraits.

See also 723.

ATLASES & GAZETTEERS

Atlases

746
Rhodesia: its natural resources and economic development. Salisbury, M.O. Collins, 1965. ii, 51pp. 43 x 38cm.

22 maps accompanied by text written by government officials. 4 topographical sheets at 1:1M, 18 thematic at 1:2,500,000 or 1:5M, covering climate, agriculture, natural resources and the economy. Gazetteer index to 1:1M maps.

747
Atlas for Zimbabwe. Salisbury, Collins-Longman Atlases, 1978. 49pp.

Comp. H.A.B. Simons.

Gazetteers

748
Southern Rhodesia. Division of Native Affairs. Information Services Branch. **Lore and legend of Southern Rhodesian place names**. Salisbury, 1960. 36pp.

749
Southern Rhodesia. Ministry of Lands and Natural Resources. Department of the Surveyor General. **Gazetteer of geographical place names in Southern Rhodesia**. Salisbury, 1963. 97pp.

750

Smith, R.C. **Avondale to Zimbabwe: a collection of cameos of Rhodesian towns and villages.** Borrowdale, author, 197-. 314pp. map.

Lists 130 towns and villages with geographical co-ordinates and a brief account of each.

751

U.S. Board on Geographic Names. **Southern Rhodesia: official standard names approved by the U.S.B.G.N.** Washington, DC, 1973. iv, 362pp.

Includes 22,500 names from 1:250,000 map series. Revision of the appropriate section of **Rhodesia and Nyasaland ...** (*see* 667).

See also 1559.

FRANCOPHONE CENTRAL AFRICA

DIRECTORIES OF ORGANIZATIONS

752
École pratique des hautes études, CARDAN. **Bibliothèques et organismes de documentation: inventaire des bibliothèques et centres de documentation en Afrique centrale.** Paris, 1974. (*Bulletin d'information et de liaison*, 6(4) 1974). xxi, 154pp.

Comp. F. Mbot. Covers 272 institutions in Cameroon, Central African Republic, Chad, Congo, Gabon, Zaire.

ATLASES & GAZETTEERS

753
Institut national pour l'étude agronomique du Congo (INEAC). **Atlas climatique du bassin congolais.** Brussels, 1971-1977. 4 vols. 32 x 33cm.

Vol. 4 entitled **... du bassin zaïrois.** Covers Zaire, Burundi, Rwanda, Congo, Central African Republic, northern Angola, northern Zambia, western Tanzania. Maps with accompanying statistics and tables.

FORMER FRENCH EQUATORIAL AFRICA

HANDBOOKS

754
G.B. War Office. Intelligence Department. **Military report on French Congo.** London, 1903. (A. 792). 42pp. maps.

Comp. Maj. A.L. Lynden Bell. Covers topography, communications, resources, administration. Maps at 1:3M from **Livre-atlas des colonies françaises** (*see* 376).

755
Bruel, G. **L'Afrique équatoriale française: le pays, les habitants, la colonisation, les pouvoirs publics.** Paris, Larose, 1918. xii, 558pp. 33 diagrs. 7 maps.

- - rev. ed. **La France équatoriale africaine.** Paris, 1935. xvi, 558pp. 190 photos. 26 diagrs. 6 col. maps.

Detailed treatment of topography, climate, flora and fauna, peoples, natural resources, agriculture, industry, administration, trade and finance. 2nd ed. adds coverage of Cameroon, and updates statistics, but is otherwise little changed.

756
G.B. Foreign Office. Historical Section. **French Equatorial Africa.** London, 1920. 71pp. (F.O. Handbook, 108). 71pp.
Also pub. in F.O. **Peace handbooks,** vol. 17. London, 1920.

757
Bruel, G. **L'Afrique équatoriale française.** Paris, Larose, 1930. (Collection "France d'outre-mer"). 256pp. illus. maps.

Brief handbook, essentially a summary of his 1918 work (*see* 755).

758
G.B. Admiralty. Naval Intelligence Division. **French Equatorial Africa and Cameroons.** London, 1942. (Geographical handbook series, B.R. 515). xi, 524pp. 59 illus. 2 maps in pocket. 113 maps & figs. in text.

Detailed topographical description, plus information on natural resources, peoples, administration, history (separate section for the Cameroons), agriculture and trade. Descriptive gazetteer of some 70 settlements.

759
La France équatoriale. Paris, Sociéte d'éditions géographiques, maritimes et coloniales, 1947. (Terres lointaines, 1). ix, 150pp. illus. maps.

Includes pp. 3-122, "L'Afrique équatoriale française" by E. Trézenem; pp. 123-246, "Le Cameroun" by B. Lembezat.

- - 2nd ed. Paris, 1950. 286pp. illus. maps.

- - 3rd ed. **L'Afrique équatoriale française,** by E. Trezénem. Paris, 1955. (Terres lointaines, 1^1). 208pp.

3rd ed. of section for Cameroon published separately as **Le Cameroun** (1954, *see* 1164).

760

Afrique équatoriale française: l'encyclopédie coloniale et maritime (encyclopédie de l'Union française). Paris, Encyclopédie coloniale et maritime, 1950. x, 590, viipp. 348 photos, 44 maps, 36 diagrs.

"Sous la direction d'Eugène Guernier". Detailed treatment of history, geography, politics and administration, communications, the economy and the arts. For the encyclopedia as a whole, *see* 35.

761

Hänel, K. **Französisch-Äquatorial-Afrika**. Bonn, Schroeder for Deutsche Afrika-Gesellschaft, 1958. (Die Länder Afrikas, 1). 78pp. illus. maps.

762

Afrique centrale: les républiques d'expression française. Paris, Hachette, 1962. (Les guides bleus). clxxxviii, 533pp. folding maps.

Series of introductory essays on topics such as geography, economics, followed by separate sections for Congo, Gabon, Central African Republic, Chad and Cameroon.

See also 897.

YEARBOOKS

763

Annuaire officiel illustré de la colonie du Congo. Paris, R. Chapelot, 1906. 230pp. map.

G. Bruel, *Bibliographie de l'Afrique équatoriale française*, Paris, 1914, records this as a single vol. Gregory and Library of Congress, *Guide to official publications of French speaking central Africa*, Washington, 1973, suggest it was the first in a series continued by the following titles.

764

Annuaire du gouvernement générale de l'Afrique équatoriale française. Paris, 1912-1922?

continued by:

A.E.F. **Afrique équatoriale Française**. Paris, 1922-1958. Annual.

Annual report on the administration, with extensive statistics.

765

Annuaire de la fédération des territoires de l'Afrique équatoriale française. Paris, Compagnie française de propagande et publicité, 1951-1953. 2 issues.

Issues for 1951, 1953/54. Covers government and administration with a commercial directory and statistics.

766

Guid'Afrique équatoriale 1960/61 [etc.]. Paris, Diloutremer, 1960- . Annual.

Title varies: **Guid'Afrique centrale** (1970-). Covers Central African Republic, Chad, Congo, Gabon. From 1964 includes Cameroon, previously covered by **Guid'Cameroun** (*see* 1175) from the same publisher. Includes general information on topography, the economy, and the administration, with directories of institutions and commercial enterprises.

767

Union douanière et économique de l'Afrique centrale (UDEAC). **Annuaire officiel.** Douala, 1972-1976. 5 issues.

Covers Cameroon, Central African Republic, Chad, Congo, Gabon. For each country provides brief topographical, historical and demographic data, with details on communications, agriculture, industry, trade and finance. Amount of general information steadily declines: issue 2, 1973, 563pp; issue 5, 1976, 266pp.

See also 544.

STATISTICS

768

A.E.F. Service de la statistique générale [etc.]. **Bulletin d'informations économiques et sociales.** Brazzaville, 1947-1959. Monthly. Issues 1-134.

Title varies: **Bulletin mensuel de statistique** (1957-1959).

continued by:

Union douanière équatoriale [etc.]. **Bulletin des statistiques générales.** Brazzaville, 1963-1965. Quarterly. Issues 1-12.

769

A.E.F. Haut Commissariat. **Annuaire statistique de l'Afrique équatoriale française**. Brazzaville, 1950-1956. 2 issues.

Issues for 1936/1950 (1950), 1951/55 (1956).

770

L'économie des pays de l'Afrique centrale. Paris, Ediafric-La documentation africaine, 1971- . Irreg.

Covers Chad, Central African Republic, Congo, Gabon. Largely statistical in content.

BIOGRAPHICAL SOURCES

771

Personnalités publiques de l'Afrique centrale 1968 [etc.]. Paris, Ediafric-La documentation africaine, 1969. 373pp.

- - 2nd ed. Paris, 1972. 314pp.

Special issues of *Bulletin de l'Afrique noire*. Covers Cameroon, Chad, Congo, Central African Republic, Gabon. Includes some 2,000 entries.

ATLASES & GAZETTEERS

Atlases

772

France. Sous-sécretariat d'état des colonies. Service géographique. **Atlas des côtes du Congo français**. Paris, 1893. 22 plates of maps. 37 x 57cm.

Maps at scale of 1:80,000. Index map annotated "Reconnaissance faite en suivant le visage par Henri Pobegui, chef de station, février & août 1890, 25 jan-27 juin 1891".

Gazetteers

773

U.S. Board on Geographic Names. **Preliminary N.I.S gazetteer, Equatorial**

1952. iv, 636pp.

Pp. 1-447, French Equatorial Africa; pp. 449-574, French Cameroons; pp. 575-613, Spanish Guinea; pp. 615-636, São Tomé e Principe.

CENTRAL AFRICAN REPUBLIC

HANDBOOKS

774

France. Direction de la documentation. **La République centrafricaine**. Paris, 1960. (*Notes et études documentaires*, 2733, 19 Dec. 1960). 49pp.

- - [rev. ed.]. Paris, 1971. (*Notes et études documentaires*, 3833/3834, 10 Nov. 1971). 82pp.

775

Kalck, P. **Historical dictionary of the Central African Republic**. Metuchen, NJ, Scarecrow Press, 1980. (African historical dictionaries, 27). xlii, 152pp.

Critical review in *JAH* 23, 1982, 143.

STATISTICS

776

Ubangui-Shari/Central African Republic. Direction de la statistique générale et des études économiques [etc.]. **Bulletin d'informations statistiques**. Bangui, 1952-68. Monthly/quarterly. Issues 1-17.

Title varies : **Bulletin mensuel/Bulletin trimestrial de statistique** (1956-).

777

Ubangui-Shari. Direction de la statistique générale et des études économiques. **Annuaire statistique de l'Oubangui-Shari 1940/1955**. Bangui, 1956. 206pp.illus.

continued by:

Central African Republic. Direction de la statistique générale et des études économiques. **Annuaire statistique de la république centrafricaine 1952/62** [etc.]. Bangui, 1962- . Irreg.

Issues for 1952/62 (1962), 1963/70 (1975), 1971/77 (1978).

778

Statistik des Auslandes: Länderberichte: Zentralafrikanische Republik.

Wiesbaden, Statistisches Bundesamt, 1986- . Irreg.

Issues for 1986, 1988.

ATLASES & GAZETTEERS

Atlases

779
Central African Republic. Ministère de l'éducation nationale & Institut géographique nationale, Paris. **Atlas de la République centrafricaine**. Paris, 1973. 21pp.

Colour maps. No notes.

780
Atlas de la République centrafricaine. Paris, "Jeune Afrique", 1984. 64pp.

Comp. P. Vennetier. 19 thematic maps with text.

Gazetteers

781
U.S. Board on Geographic Names. **Central African Republic: official standard names approved by the U.S.B.G.N.** Washington, DC, 1962. (Gazetteer, 64). iii, 220pp.

Includes 15,700 names from maps at 1:200,000. Revision of the appropriate sections of **Equatorial Africa ...** (*see* 773).

 - - **Gazetteer supplement: Africa and South-West Asia**, Washington, DC, 1972. (pp. 37-38, Central African Republic).

782
Mangold, M. **A Central African pronouncing gazetteer**. Saarbrücken, Universität des Saarlandes, Institut für Phonetik, 1985. (Africana Saraviensia linguistica, 10). 98pp.

Over 2,000 entries with official and phonetic spelling.

CHAD

HANDBOOKS

783

France. Direction de la documentation. **La République du Tchad**. Paris, 1960. (*Notes et études documentaires*, 1696, 31 Aug. 1960). 67pp.

784

Fuchs, P. **Tschad**. Bonn, Schroeder for Deutsche Afrika-Gesellschaft, 1966. (Die Länder Afrikas, 33). 101pp. illus. maps.

785

Area handbook for Chad, comp. H.D. Nelson, *et al*. Washington, DC, U.S. Department of Defense, 1972. xiv, 261pp. maps.

- - 2nd ed. **Chad: a country study**, comp. T. Collelo. Washington, DC, 1990. xxiv, 254pp. illus. maps.

786

Malval, J. **Essai de chronologie tchadienne (1707-1940)**. Paris, Centre national de recherche scientifique, 1974. 156pp.

Concerned principally with French colonial activities. Review, *Africa* 46, 1976, 108-109.

787

Decalo, S. **Historical dictionary of Chad**. Metuchen, NJ, Scarecrow Press, 1977. (African historical dictionaries, 13). 437pp.

Detailed critical review, *IJAHS* 11, 1978, 376-379.

- - 2nd ed. Metuchen, NJ, 1987. xxxvi, 532pp.

Bibliography, pp. 339-532. Review, *IJAHS* 21, 1988, 709.

YEARBOOKS

788

Chad. Service de l'information Tchadien. **Annuaire du Tchad 1950/51** [etc.]. Lille, 1950- . Irreg.

2nd issue, 1958. Broad coverage of geography, history, archaeology and administration.

789

Chad. Direction de l'information Tchadien. **Annuaire officiel du Tchad**. Paris, Diloutremer, 1970- . Annual.

STATISTICS

790

Chad. Direction de la statistique, des études économique et démographique [etc.]. **Bulletin statistique**. N'Djamena, 1951-1977. Monthly/quarterly.

Title varies: **Bulletin mensuel de statistique** (1958-68); **Bulletin de statistique** (1969-). Not pub. August-November 1958, January-April, June-September 1959.

791

Statistik des Auslandes: Länderberichte: Tschad. Wiesbaden, Statistisches Bundesamt, 1964- . Irreg.

Issues for 1964, 1984, 1990.

792

Chad. Sous-direction de la statistique [etc.]. **Annuaire statistique du Tchad**. N'Djamena, 1966-1975. Annual (irreg.)

Not published 1971, 1973.

continued by:

Chad. Direction de la statistique. **Tchad: relance économique en chiffres**. N'Djamena, 1984- . Annual.

DIRECTORIES OF ORGANIZATIONS

793

Chad. Centre nationale d'appui à la recherche. **Annuaire des chercheurs de la république du Tchad**. N'Djamena, 1992- .

1st issue lists 244 researchers under 30 subject fields.

BIOGRAPHICAL SOURCES

794

Le Rouvreur, A. **Eléments pour un dictionnaire biographique du Tchad et du Niger (Téda et Daja)**. Paris, Editions du Centre nationale de recherche scientifique, 1978. 48pp. (Contributions à la connaissance des élites africaines, fasc. 1).

ATLASES & GAZETTEERS

Atlases

795

Chad. Institut national tchadien pour les sciences humaines & Institut géographique nationale, Paris. **Atlas pratique du Tchad**. Fort Lamy & Paris, 1972. 78pp. 38 x 29cm.

Comp. J. Cabot. 34 plates of thematic maps with accompanying text. Basic scale 1:5M. Includes archaeological and language maps. 4 town plans at 1:25,000.

Gazetteers

796

U.S. Board on Geographic Names. **Chad: official standard names approved by the U.S.B.G.N.** Washington, DC, 1962. (Gazetteer, 65). v, 232pp.

Includes 16,000 names from 1:200,000 series maps. Revision of appropriate section of **Equatorial Africa ...** (*see* 773).

- - **Gazetteer supplement: Africa and South-west Asia**. Washington, D.C., 1972. (p. 39, Chad).

- - 2nd ed. **Gazetteer of Chad**. Washington, DC, 1989. xvi, 529pp.

Includes 20,000 names from maps at 1:250,000

CONGO

HANDBOOKS

797
France. Direction de la documentation. **La République du Congo.** Paris, 1960, (*Notes et études documentaires*, 2732, 17 Dec. 1960). 38pp.

- - [rev. ed.]. **La République démocratique du Congo.** Paris, 1971. (*Notes et études documentaires*, 3765/3766, 20 Feb. 1971). 63p.

798
Area handbook for People's Republic of the Congo (Congo Brazzaville), comp. G.C. McDonald, *et al.* Washington, DC, U.S. Department of Defense, 1971. xiii, 256pp. maps.

799
Thompson, V.M. & Adloff, R. **Historical dictionary of the People's Republic of the Congo (Congo-Brazzaville).** Metuchen, NJ, Scarecrow Press, 1974. (African historical dictionaries, 2). 139pp.

- - 2nd ed. **Historical dictionary of the People's Republic of the Congo.** Metuchen, NJ, 1984. 239pp.

2nd ed. contains bibliog. of only 10pp., very brief compared with most volumes in this series. Review, *IJAHS* 19, 1986, 167-168.

STATISTICS

800
Congo. Direction de la statistique [etc.]. **Bulletin mensuel de statistique.** Brazzaville, 1957-1962; n.s. 1963- . Monthly.

801
Congo. Direction de la statistique [etc.]. **Annuaire statistique 1958/63** [etc.]. Brazzaville, 1966- . Irreg.

Issues for 1966, 1969, 1974, 1982.

802
Statistik des Auslandes: Länderberichte: Kongo. Wiesbaden, Statistisches

802
Statistik des Auslandes: Länderberichte: Kongo. Wiesbaden, Statistisches Bundesamt, 1986- . Irreg.

Issues for 1986, 1988.

BIOGRAPHICAL SOURCES

803
Mamonsono, L.P. & Bemba, S. **Bio-bibliographie des écrivains congolais (belles lettres-littérature).** Brazzaville, Éditions littéraires congolaises for Ministère de la culture et des arts de la République populaire du Congo, 1979. 32pp.

Covers 76 authors.

ATLASES & GAZETTEERS

Atlases

804
ORSTOM. **Atlas du Congo.** Paris, 1969. 10 sheets. 15pp. text. 50 x 62cm.

Coverage is principally of climate and geology.

805
ORSTOM. **Atlas de Brazzaville;** comp. Roland Devauges. Paris, 1984. (Collection travaux et documents, 180). x, 100 maps with transparent overlay.

"Cartes réalisés par traîtment informatique des données urbaines" (title page). Maps 1:20,000, mostly computer printed dots to show density of topic illustrated. Topics are largely demographic and include age, length of residence, literacy and education, occupation, size of households, type of buildings and services available.

806
Atlas de la République populaire du Congo. Paris, "Jeune Afrique", 1977. 64pp. col. maps.

Comp. J. Vennetier. 18 thematic maps with text.

Gazetteers

807
U.S. Board on Geographic Names. **Republic of the Congo (Brazzaville): official standard names approved by the U.S.B.G.N.** Washington, DC, 1962. (Gazetteer, 61). iii, 109pp.

Includes 7,700 names. Revision of the appropriate sections of **Equatorial Africa ...** (*see* 773).

- - **Gazetteer supplement: Africa and South-West Asia.** Washington, DC, 1972. (pp. 45-46, Congo).

GABON

HANDBOOKS

808

Walker, A.R. **Notes d'histoire du Gabon**. Montpellier, Impr. Charité, 1960. (Mémoires de l'Institut d'études centrafricaines, Brazzaville, 9). 158pp. illus. maps.

Introduction and additional material by M. Soret. A miscellaneous collection of information including biographies of 19th century African chiefs, a classified list of ethnic groups, and a chronology of Gabonese history, 1300-1929.

809

France. Direction de la documentation. **La République Gabonaise**. Paris, 1961. (*Notes et études documentaires*, 2795, 10 July 1961). 56pp.

- - [rev. ed.]. Paris, 1970. (*Notes et études documentaires*, 3703, 27 June 1970). 36pp.

810

Le Gabon, 1960-1980. Libreville, "L'Union", 1981. 150pp. illus.

Survey of political, economic and social conditions with statistics by the staff of the *L'Union* daily newspaper.

811

Gardinier, D.E. **Historical dictionary of Gabon**. Metuchen, NJ, Scarecrow Press, 1981. (African historical dictionaries, 30). xxviii, 254pp.

"A reference work which is authoritative, internally consistent and easy to use" (*JAH* 24, 1983, 142-143).

YEARBOOKS

812

Annuaire Gabonaise. Libreville, Éditions Gabon communité, 1966- . Annual.

Includes civil list, commercial directory.

813
Gabon. Ministère de l'information et du tourisme du Gabon. **Annuaire national**. Paris & Libreville, Éditions des quatre points cardinaux, 1966- . Annual (irreg.) Issue for 1974.

Title varies: **Annuaire national officiel de la République Gabonaise**. Directory of the administration with biographies of ministers and leading officials, general economic information and statistics.

STATISTICS

814
Gabon. Direction de la statistique et des études économiques [etc.]. **Bulletin mensuel de statistique**. Libreville, 1959- . Monthly.

815
Gabon. Direction générale de la statistique. **Annuaire statistique du Gabon 1957/64** [etc.]. Libreville, 1969- . Irreg.

Issues for 1957/64, 1964, 1968, 1970/75, 1976/80.

816
L'économie Gabonaise. Paris, Ediafric-La documentation africaine, 1976- . Irreg.

Issues for 1976, 1977, 1982.

817
Statistik des Auslandes: Länderberichte: Gabon. Wiesbaden, Statistisches Bundesamt, 1978- . Irreg.

Issues for 1978, 1985, 1987.

BIOGRAPHICAL SOURCES

818
Les élites gabonaises: qui est qui au Gabon. Paris, Ediafric-La documentation africaine, 1977. xxi, 217pp.

- - 2nd ed. Paris, 1983. 209pp.

ATLASES & GAZETTEERS

Atlases

819

Lafont, P. **Petit atlas du Gabon**. [Paris, Éditions Alain, 1958]. 48pp. incl. col. maps. 28 x 31cm.

Compiled for the Chambre de commerce, d'agriculture et d'industrie du Gabon. Thematic, covering geology, climate, population, ethnography, education, missions, agriculture, and natural resources.

820

Gabon. Ministère de l'éducation nationale du Gabon. Institut pedagogique national. **Géographie et cartographie du Gabon: atlas illustré**. Paris, EDICEF, 1983. 135pp. 27 x 35cm.

30 thematic chapters of text with coloured maps at 1:3M, photographs and statistics.

Gazetteers

821

U.S. Board on Geographic Names. **Gabon: official standard names approved by the U.S.B.G.N.** Washington, DC, 1962. (Gazetteer, 59). iv, 113pp.

Includes 8,000 names from 1:200,000 map series. Revision of the appropriate sections of **Equatorial Africa ...** (*see* 773).

- - **Gazetteer supplement: Africa and South-West Asia**. Washington, DC, 1972. (p. 69, Gabon).

FORMER BELGIAN AFRICA

In addition to the works listed in this general sections, it is likely that many of the titles noted below under Zaire will also contain some reference to Burundi and Rwanda.

HANDBOOKS

822
Franck, L. **Le Congo belge**. Brussels, La Renaissance du livre, 1928. 2 vols. (379pp; 489pp). illus. maps.

Large-scale encyclopaedic compilation.

823
Congo-nil: ouvrage de documentation. Brussels, Van Assche for Société des chemins de fer vicinaux du Congo, et Touring Club du Congo belge. Brussels, [1934]. 491pp. illus. maps.

- - 2nd ed. Brussels, 1936. 545pp. illus. maps.

- - 3rd ed. Brussels, 1937. 693pp. illus. maps.

- - 4th ed. **Congo-nil: guide du Congo belge et du Ruanda-Urundi, 1938/39**. Brussels, 1938. 663pp. illus. maps.

- - 6th ed. **... 1948/49**. Brussels, 1949.

- - 7th ed. Brussels, 1950. 871pp. illus. maps.

A wide-ranging guidebook that includes detailed information on the history of the region, communications, administration, peoples, art, language, and commercial activities.

824
Guide du voyageur au Congo belge et au Ruanda-Urundi. Brussels, Office du Tourisme du Congo belge et du Ruanda-Urundi, 1949. xxxix, 757pp. illus. maps.

- - 2nd ed. Brussels, 1951. xxxix, 828pp. illus. maps.

- - 3rd ed. Brussels, 1954. xxxix, 796pp. illus. maps.

- - **Renseignements pratiques et itinéraires; extraits de la 3ième éd. du** *Guide* ... Brussels, [1954]. 745pp.

- - 4th ed. **Congo belge et Ruanda-Urundi, guide du voyageur.** Brussels, Office de l'information et des relations publiques pour le Congo Belge et le Ruanda-Urundi, 1958. xvi, 798pp. illus. maps.

- - English trans. pub. as **Traveler's guide to the Belgian Congo and Ruanda-Urundi.** Brussels, Tourist Bureau for the Belgian Congo & Ruanda-Urundi, 1951. 757pp. illus. maps.

- - 2nd ed. Brussels, 1956. 790pp.

An emphasis on communications and topography, but includes much more detailed information on history, geography, administration and ethnography than the normal tourist guide. Also published in Flemish as **Reisgids voor Belgisch Congo en Ruanda-Urundi** (editions in 1950 and 1952).

825
Bevel, M.L. **Le dictionnaire colonial (encyclopédie): explication de plus de 7,000 noms et expressions se rapportant aux diverses activités coloniales, depuis l'époque héroïque jusqu'aux temps présents.** Brussels, E. Guyot, 1950-1951. 2 vols. illus. maps.

- - 2nd ed. Brussels, 1952. 202pp.

- - 3rd ed. **Le dictionnaire colonial (encyclopédie): explication de plus de 8,000 noms ...** Brussels, 1955. 202pp.

- - [1st Suppl.] 26pp. bound with & apparently issued as part of 3rd ed; - - 2nd Suppl. Brussels, 1957. 20pp; - - 3rd Suppl. Brussels, 1959. 20pp.

Author was former Administrator in the Belgian Congo. Includes Ruanda-Urundi. Numerous brief entries (c.50 to a page, double column) for flora and fauna, diseases, crops, ethnic groups, and settlements. Includes one-line biographies. Folding map at 1:4M.

826
Encyclopédie du Congo Belge. Brussels, Bieleweld, [1950-1953]. 3 vols. (iv, 722pp; iv, 668pp; iv, 862pp.). illus. maps.

Includes Ruanda-Urundi. Thematic arrangement. Vol. 1 covers prehistory, history, peoples, geology, climate, soils, botany and agriculture; vol. 2, forestry, fauna, fisheries, livestock and minerals; vol. 3, public health, the economy, industry, administration, public finance, mining and tourism. Statistics include information up to 1948. Signed articles by over 50 specialist contributors, but no sources given. Numerous photographs and line drawings, and over 70 maps. Detailed contents lists for each vol. and general index in vol. 3.

827

Ethnographic survey of Africa: BelgianCongo/Congo/Zaire. London, International African Institute/Tervuren, Musée Royale du Congo Belge (*later* de l'Afrique Centrale), 1954-1960. (Monographies ethnographiques). 5 vols. illus. maps.

Sub-series of the **Ethnographic survey** (*see* 54). Vol.1, 'Les tribus Ba-Kuba et les peuplades apparentées', by J. Vansina. 1954. ix, 64pp; vol. 2, 'Les Bira et les peuplades limitrophes', by H. Van Geluwe. 1957. xii, 165pp; vol. 3, 'Les Mamvu-Mangutu et Balese-Mvubu', by H. Van Geluwe. 1953. xv, 195pp; vol. 4, 'Les peuplades de l'entre Congo-Ubangui', by H. Burssens. 1959. xi, 219pp; vol. 5, 'Les Bali et les peuplades apparentées', by H. Van Geluwe. 1960. ix,130pp.

828

Meyer, R. de. **Introducing the Belgian Congo.** Brussels, Office de publicité, 1958. 137pp.

829

Belgium. Office de l'information et des relations publiques du Congo belge et du Ruanda-Urundi (INFORCONGO). **Le Congo belge.** Brussels, 1958-1959. 2 vols. illus. maps.

Vol. 1, 1958. 535pp. Covers topography, peoples, history, administration and the economy. Vol. 2, 1959. xx, 189pp. 12 folding maps. Extensive statistical data to illustrate the narrative of vol. 1.

- - English trans. **Belgian Congo.** Brussels, 1959-1960. 2 vols. (547pp; 187pp).

830

Kauffmann, H. **Belgisch-Kongo und Ruanda-Urundi.** Bonn, Schroeder for Deutsche Afrika-Gesellschaft, 1959. (Die Länder Afrikas, 18). 144pp. illus. maps.

STATISTICS

831

Belgian Congo. Direction de la statistique [etc.]. **Bulletin mensuel des statistiques du Congo belge et du Ruanda-Urundi**. Léopoldville, 1950-1954. Vols. 1-5. Monthly.

continued by:

Bulletin mensuel des statistiques générales du Congo belge et du Ruanda-Urundi (from 1960 ... **de la République du Congo**). Léopoldville, 1955-1961. Monthly.

Trade statistics were covered by a separate series, **Bulletin mensuel du commerce extérieur du Congo belge et du Ruanda-Urundi**. Léopoldville, Direction de la statistique, 1955-1961. Monthly.

832

Belgium. Ministère des affaires africaines. Direction des études économiques. **La situation économique du Congo belge et du Ruanda-Urundi**. Brussels, 1950-1959. Annual. 10 issues.

Covers Belgian Congo only from 1950 to 1954, includes Ruanda-Urundi from 1955. Detailed tabulated statistics of the economy.

BIOGRAPHICAL SOURCES

833

Biographie coloniale belge. Brussels, Institut royal coloniale belge (*later* Académie royale des sciences d'outre-mer), 1948- . Vols. 1-6, 7, fascs. a & b. (Vols. 1-6 pub. 1948-1968; vol. 7, fasc. a, 1973; fasc. b, 1977).

Vols. 6 and 7 are entitled **Biographie belge d'outre-mer**. Over 2,000 substantial and well documented biographies of deceased figures who contributed to the history and development of the Belgian Congo. Includes non-Belgians (e.g. Livingstone, Stanley). Each vol. has a complete alphabetical sequence, together with addenda and corrigenda and a cumulative index to earlier vols.

ATLASES & GAZETTEERS

Atlases

834
Institut royal colonial belge (*later* Académie royale des sciences d'outre-mer). **Atlas générale du Congo et du Ruanda-Urundi.** Brussels, 1948-1963. 39 x 39cm.

Large-scale thematic work issued as 34 separate plates with accompanying text in French and Flemish. Seven sections: history, geodesy, physical geography, biology, anthropology and culture, politics, administration and society, economics. 2nd ed. of "avant-propos" issued 1954. Most maps at 1:5M. Index of c.5,000 names. Reviews, JAH 3, 1962, 167-168; *Geographical review*, 41, 1951, 483; 47, 1957, 575. Revised version issued as **Atlas générale de la République du Zaire** (1976- *see* 892).

835
Atlas géographique et historique du Congo belge et des térritoires sous mandat du Ruanda-Urundi. Brussels, Éditions René de Rouck, 1938. 14pp. 12 plates col. maps. 36 x 27cm.

- - 2nd ed. Brussels, 1945. 12pp. 12 plates col. maps.

- - 3rd ed. Brussels, 1947. 12pp. 12 plates col. maps;

- - 4th ed. Brussels, 1954. 12pp. 13 plates col. maps.

- - 5th ed. Brussels, 1951. 12pp. 13 plates col. maps.

Comp. R. de Rouck. Eds. largely unchanged. Each includes 45 maps and plans of seven cities. Index of 5,972 names.

836
Institut national pour l'étude agronomique du Congo belge. **Carte des sols et de la végétation du Congo belge et du Ruanda-Urundi.** Brussels, 1954-1960. 75 maps. 29 x 24cm.

- - 2nd ed. Brussels, 1960-1970.

Issued in 26 parts, each with maps and text.

837
Derkinderen, G. **Atlas du Congo belge et du Ruanda-Urundi**. Paris & Brussels, Elsevier, 1955. viii, 204pp. illus.

Popular work with profusely illustrated text and 15 coloured maps.

Gazetteers

838
Devroey, E.-J. 'Note concernant l'orthographie des noms géographiques du Congo belge et du Ruanda-Urundi', *Bulletin de séances d'Institut royale coloniale belge*, 24, 1953, 1464-1478.

BURUNDI & RWANDA

*Note that in addition to works listed under **Former Belgian Africa** (above), a number of the titles recorded under **Zaire** (below) may also have passing reference to these countries.*

HANDBOOKS

839
Belgium. Office de l'information et des rélations publiques du Congo belge et du Ruanda-Urundi (INFORCONGO). **Le Ruanda-Urundi**. Brussels, 1959. 377pp. illus. 18 col. maps (6 in pocket).

Sections for geography, history, administration, economics and social life.

- - English trans. by G. Blankoff-Scarr. **Ruanda-Urundi**. Brussels, 1960. 4 pts.

840
Hausner, K.-H. & Jezic, B. **Rwanda-Burundi**. Bonn, Schroeder for Deutsche Afrika-Gesellschaft, 1968. (Die Länder Afrikas, 36). 121pp.

Rev. ed. of appropriate sections of 830.

See also 527, 585, 592.

YEARBOOKS

841
Belgium. Ministère des Colonies. **Rapport sur l'administration belge des térritoires occupés de l'est-africain allemand et spécialement du Ruanda et de l'Urundi, 1917/21**. Brussels, 1921.

continued by:

Belgium. Ministère des Colonies [etc.]. **Rapport sur l'administration belge du Ruanda-Urundi**. Brussels, 1921-1960. Annual.

Title varies slightly. Reports for 1939/44, 1945/46 issued as combined vols. Post 1946 vols. also issued with separate title-page as 'Rapport soumis par le Gouvernement belge à l'Assemblée Générale des Nations Unies au sujet de l'administration du Ruanda-Urundi'

STATISTICS

842

Statistik des Auslandes: Länderberichte: Ruanda-Urundi. Wiesbaden, Statistisches Bundesamt, 1962.

ATLASES & GAZETTEERS

843

Atlas du Ruanda-Urundi. Brussels, De Visscher, [1952]. iipp, 21 maps. 22 x 30cm.

Thematic maps at 1:1M, covering geology, climate, population, health, education, trade, communications.

BURUNDI

HANDBOOKS

844
Area handbook for Burundi, comp. G.C. McDonald, *et al.* Washington, DC, U.S. Department of Defense, 1969. xiv, 203pp. maps.

845
Weinstein, W. **Historical dictionary of Burundi**. Metuchen, NJ, Scarecrow Press, 1976. (African historical dictionaries, 8). 368pp.

STATISTICS

846
Burundi. Département de statistiques [etc.]. **Bulletin de statistique**. Bujumbura, 1966- . Quarterly/bi-monthly.

Title varies : **Bulletin statistique trimestriel**.

847
Burundi. Département de statistiques [etc.]. **Annuaire statistique 1962/65** [etc.]. Bujumbura, 1966- . Annual.

From 1988 issued by Institut de statistique et d'études économiques du Burundi (ISTEEBU).

848
Statistik des Auslandes: Länderberichte: Burundi. Wiesbaden, Statistisches Bundesamt, 1967- . Irreg.

Issues for 1967, 1984, 1986, 1988, 1990. Also covered in vol. for Ruanda-Urundi, 1962 (*see* 842)

ATLASES & GAZETTEERS

Atlases

849
France. Ministère de la co-opération française, Centre d'études de géographie

tropicale, Bordeaux, & Université de Burundi, Bujumbura. **Atlas du Burundi.** Paris & Bujumbura, 1979. viiipp. 30 col. plates. 68pp. text interleaved with unnumbered pp. of black & white maps, charts, illus., & statistics. 32 x 42cm.

Maps compiled at the Université de Bordeaux III, under auspices of Centre nationale de recherche scientifique. Countrywide thematic maps at 1:750,000. 4 thematic maps of Bujumbura at 1:36,000. 1 map of Gitega at 1:13,000. No index or gazetteer.

Gazetteers

850
U.S. Board on Geographic Names. **Burundi: official standard names approved by the U.S.B.G.N.** Washington, DC, 1964. (Gazetteer, 84) ii, 44pp.

Revision of appropriate sections of **Belgian Congo ...** (*see* 894).

 - - **Gazetteer supplement: Africa and South-West Asia.** Washington, DC, 1972. (p. 29, Burundi).

RWANDA

HANDBOOKS

851
Area handbook of Rwanda, comp. R.F. Nyrop, *et al.* Washington, DC, U.S. Department of Defense, 1969. xiv, 212pp. maps.

Reissued 1982 as **Rwanda: a country study**.

STATISTICS

852
Rwanda. Direction de la statistique [etc.]. **Bulletin de statistique**. Kigali, 1964- . Quarterly.

Limited to economic and financial statistics.

853
Rwanda. Direction de la statistique [etc.]. **Bulletin de statistique: supplément annuel**. Kigali, 1974- . Annual.

Wider coverage of topics than the **Bulletin** itself.

854
Statistik des Auslandes: Länderberichte: Ruanda. Wiesbaden, Statistisches Bundesamt, 1985- . Irreg.

Issues for 1985, 1987. Also covered in vol. for Ruanda-Urundi, 1962 (*see* 842).

ATLASES & GAZETTEERS

Atlases

855
France. Ministère de la co-opération de la République française & Université du Rwanda, Kigali. **Atlas du Rwanda**. Paris & Kigali, 1981. ix, 67pp. 45 x 32cm.

Eds. C. Prioul & P. Sirven. 32 coloured thematic maps, most at 1:800,000, with accompanying text and transparent overlay showing political divisions. Covers physical features, vegetation, population, with 4 historical maps (pre 1896, 1896-1916, 1916-1962, Roman Catholic Church, 1900-1976).

856
Rwanda. Ministère des travaux publics et de l'équipment. Cellule des aménagements urbaines et ruraux. **Atlas rural du Rwanda**. Kigali, [1982]. 66pp.

26 coloured maps with commentary, covering administration, peoples, public services, mining, and agriculture.

Gazetteers

857
U.S. Board on Geographic Names. **Rwanda: official standard names approved by the U.S.B.G.N.** Washington, DC, 1964. (Gazetteer, 85). iii, 44pp.

Includes 3,000 names from 1:500,000 map series. Revision of the appropriate sections of **Belgian Congo ...** (*see* 894).

ZAIRE

HANDBOOKS

858
Goffart, F.J.L. **Traité methodique géographie du Congo.** Antwerp, C. Thibaut, 1897. 218pp. illus.

- - 2nd ed. **Le Congo: géographie physique, politique et économique;** rev. et mise à jour par G. Morissens. Brussels, Misch & Thron, 1908. viii, 502pp. maps.

A detailed account of geology, ethnography, natural resources, government and administration, agriculture, industry and communications.

859
G.B. War Office. General Staff. **Military report on the Congo Free State.** London, 1904. (A. 915). xiii, 245pp. illus. maps.

Comp. Lt. Col. G.F. Milne & Lt. H. de Watteville. A particularly detailed example of the War Office military report. In addition to the usual coverage of history, geography, administration, and ethnography, includes appendix listing 73 trading companies, missionary societies and other organizations. 5 maps.

860
G.B. Admiralty. Naval Intelligence Division. Geographical Section. **A manual of Belgian Congo.** London, 1919. 332pp.

Detailed coverage of topography, peoples, administration, agriculture, mining and trade. Lacks gazetteer element usually present in this series. Some statistical data commence in 1887, others in 1903.

861
G.B. Foreign Office. Historical Section. **Belgian Congo.** London, 1920. (F.O. Handbook, 99). 135pp.
Also pub. in F.O. **Peace handbooks,** vol.16, London, 1920.

862
G.B. Admiralty. Naval Intelligence Division. **The Belgian Congo.** London, 1944. (Geographical handbook series, B.R. 522). xiii, 558pp. 105 illus, 91 maps and figs.

Comp. H.S.L. Winterbotham, E. Gardiner Smith & F. Longland. The usual detailed coverage of topography, history, peoples and economic data provided by this series, with a descriptive gazetteer of 145 settlements, and a list of tribes with a map of their distribution.

863
Area handbook for the Republic of the Congo (Léopoldville). Washington, DC, U.S. Department of Defense, 1962. xii, 657pp. maps,

- - 2nd ed. **Area handbook for the Democratic Republic of the Congo (Congo-Kinshasa),** comp. G.C. McDonald, *et al.* Washington, DC, 1971. xviii, 587pp. maps.

- - 3rd ed. **Zaire: a country study,** comp. I. Kaplan, *et al.* Washington, DC, 1979. xxi, 332pp. illus. maps.

864
Centre de recherche et d'information socio-politiques (CRISP). **Les partis politiques congolais.** Brussels, 1964. (Travaux africains: dossier documentaire). 156pp.

Comp. J.C. Willame. Alphabetical list of parties with details of their history, activities, and leading figures.

865
Dictionnaire des rites. Bandudu, Centre d'études ethnologiques du Bandudu (CEEBA), 1984- .

Ed. H. Hochegger. Multi-volume encyclopaedia arranged alphabetically, which describes individual Zaïrois rites (those of daily life, religious ceremonies etc.) with reference to relevant sections of the same publisher's **La langage des gestes rituels.**

866
Bobb, F.S. **Historical dictionary of Zaire.** Metuchen, NJ, Scarecrow Press, 1988. (African historical dictionaries, 43). 349pp.

Review, *Africa* 60, 1990, 465.

867
Mwanyimi-Mbomba, M. **Chronologie générale de l'histoire du Zaïre (des origines à 1988).** 2nd ed. Kinshasa, Centre de recherches pédagogiques, 1989.

Post independence section is divided by subject, then province.

See also 527, 655, 1368.

YEARBOOKS

868
Annuaire du Congo belge: administratif, commercial, industriel, agricole 1897 [-1958/59]. Brussels, Bodden & Dechy, 1897-1960? Annual (irreg. 7th ed. 1913, 10th ed. 1921, 41st ed. 1951).

Includes civil list, list of towns and principal villages with addresses of local administration and missions, lists of professional organizations and a commercial directory.

869
Belgium. Ministère des Colonies. **Annuaire de l'État indépendant du Congo.** Brussels, 1903-1906. Annual. 4 issues.

continued by:

Annuaire colonial belge. Brussels, 1908-1960. Annual (irreg).

Includes civil list for the Congo and relevant Belgian ministries and a commercial directory.

870
Belgium. Ministère des Colonies [etc.]. **Annuaire officiel/Officieel jaarboek.** Brussels, 1908-1960. Annual (irreg.) 36 issues.

Not pub. 1915-1920, 1949. 1940/41 issued as 1 vol. Vols. for 1910-1939 in French, thereafter in French & Flemish. Includes texts of documents, civil lists, information on commercial companies.

871
Belgium. Ministère des Colonies. **Congo belge: rapport annuel.** Brussels, 1909-1958. Annual.

Title varies: **Rapport sur l'administration du Congo belge** (1919-1960). 1939/44, 1945/46 issued as combined vols.

872

Belgian Congo and U.S.A. directory, 1943. New York, Moretus Press, 1943. 206pp.

"Information presented for the citizens of the U.S. on possessions of our allies". Includes texts of "Charter of the Belgian Congo" and similar documents including war-time decrees; general topographical and statistical information, civil and military lists, commercial directory, and extensive descriptive gazetteer (c. 2,500 entries).

873

Annuaire colonial. Ghent, Foire internationale, 1951-55. Annual.

874

Centre de recherche et d'information socio-politiques (CRISP). **Congo 1959** [etc.]. Brussels, 1959-1966. Annual. 8 issues.

Annual documentary surveys of the Congo, basically concerned with political life.

875

Congo (Congo-Kinshasa). Agence nationale de publicité congolaise. **Annuaire de la République démocratique du Congo.** Kinshasa, 1969- . Annual.

Includes political, administrative and economic data and commercial directory.

See also 541, 544, 1445, 1446

STATISTICS

876

Belgium. Ministère de l'Intérieur [etc.]. **Annuaire statistique de la Belgique et du Congo belge.** Brussels, 1911-1959. Annual.

An expanded version of the former **Annuaire statistique de la Belgique** (1870-1910) to include the Belgian Congo.

877

Belgian Congo. Direction de la statistique du Congo belge. **Discours de statistiques du Congo belge.** Léopoldville, 1947-1959. Annual.

Title varies: **Bulletin annuel des statistiques du Congo belge** (1957-1959).

878
Congo (Congo-Kinshasa)/Zaire. Institut national de la statistique. **Bulletin trimestriel des statistiques générales.** Kinshasa, 1962- . Quarterly.

879
Statistik des Auslandes: Länderberichte: Zaire. Wiesbaden, Statistisches Bundesamt, 1962- . Irreg.

Issues for 1962, 1970, 1978, 1985, 1987, 1990.

880
Zaire. Institut national de la statistique. **Annuaire statistique du Zaïre.** Kinshasa, 1971- . Annual.

Abridged ed. published annually as **Le Zaïre en chiffres**.

DIRECTORIES OF ORGANIZATIONS

881
Fleischle-Jaudas, W. **Répertoire de développement, Zaïre 1985.** Kinshasa, Centre d'études pour l'action sociale, 1985. 428pp.

A list of some 3,500 organizations in Zaire.

See also 864

BIOGRAPHICAL SOURCES

882
Janssens, E. & Cateaux, A. 'Les belges au Congo: notices biographiques', *Bulletin de la société royale de géographie d'Anvers*, 33, 1909, 747-906; 34, 1910, 39-214, 411-574; 35, 1911, 29-550.

883
Artigue, P. **Qui sont les leaders congolais?** Brussels, Éditions Europe-Afrique, 1960. (Collection 'Carrefours africains'). 139pp.

- - 2nd ed. Brussels, 1961. 375pp.

1st ed. includes some 200, 2nd ed. over 800 biographies of living figures.

884

Diana, P. **Lavoratori italiani nel Congo Belge: elenco biografico**. Rome, Istituto Italiano per l'Africa, 1961. (Collana di studi di storia e politica Africana, 4). 483pp.

Over 3,000 biographical entries for Italian nationals active at any period in the Belgian Congo. Modelled on **Biographie coloniale belge** (*see* 833).

885 (*also entered at* 1079)

Encyclopedia Africana Dictionary of African biography. Vol. 2, Sierra Leone and Zaire. Algonac, MI, Reference Publications, 1979. 372pp.

Zaire, pp. 178-372, ed. J.C. Yoder. Includes 102 biographies, most with portraits and bibliogs. For the planned encyclopaedia, *see* 31; for the dictionary of biography *see* 299.

886

Malumba, M. & Makombo, M. **Cadres et dirigeants au Zaïre, qui sont-ils? Dictionnaire biographique**. Kinshasa, Éditions du Centre de recherches pédagogiques, 1986. 541pp.

830 biographies, mostly of those involved in politics and administration since independence.

See also 665, 864.

ATLASES & GAZETTEERS

Atlases

887

De Boeck, A. **Petit atlas du Congo belge**. Brussels, De Boeck, [1911?]. 68pp.

Includes 26 maps.

888

Atlas du Katanga. Brussels, A. Bieleveld for Comité spécial du Katanga, 1929-1952. 6 vols. in 5. cxvii, 405pp. 36 x 46cm.

Originally ed. H. Droogmans, M. Robert, & G. Maury. Compiled by Service géographique et géologique. Issued as loose sheets in portfolios, including maps, photographs and text, each portfolio covering a number of provinces. Scales vary between 1:200,000 and 1:1M. A massively detailed work.

889
Libot, M. **Oefenatlas: Belgisch Congo**. Lier, J. van In, [1940]. 32pp. incl. maps.

Thematic.

890
Institut géographique du Congo Belge. **[Provincial atlas of the Belgian Congo]**. Léopoldville, 1956. 6 parts.

Issued as 6 separate vols. : **Province de l'Equateur: cartes des térritoires, éd. provisoire**, 22 maps; **Province du Kasai ...**, 22 maps; **Province du Katanga ...**, 24 maps; **Province du Kivu ...**, 19 maps; **Province du Léopoldville ...**, 25 maps; **Province Orientale ...**, 25 maps.

891
Atlas des collectivités du Zaïre. Kinshasa, Presses Universitaires du Zaïre, 1976. 65pp.

Comp. L. de Saint Moulin. 14 black and white maps showing administrative sub-divisions, together with population statistics for each.

892
Académie royale des sciences d'outre-mer. **Atlas générale de la République du Zaïre**. Brussels, 1976- .

Issued as sheets with explanatory pamphlets in 3 languages (English, French, Flemish). A revision of **Atlas générale du Congo et du Ruanda-Urundi** (1948-63, *see* 834).

893
Atlas de la République du Zaïre. Paris, "Jeune Afrique", 1978. 72pp.

Comp. G. Laclavère.

Gazetteers

894
U.S. Board on Geographic Names. **Preliminary N.I.S gazetteer, Belgian Congo: official standard names approved by the U.S.B.G.N.** Washington,

DC, 1953. ii, 349pp.

Pp. 1-322, Belgian Congo; pp. 323-349, Ruanda-Urundi.

895
U.S. Board on Geographic Names. **Republic of the Congo (Léopoldville): official standard names approved by the U.S.B.G.N.** Washington, DC, 1964. (Gazetteer, 80). iv, 426pp.

Includes 30,400 names from maps at 1:1M. Revision of the appropriate sections of 894.

- - **Gazetteer supplement: Africa and South-West Asia.** Washington, DC, 1972. (p. 41, Zaire).

See also 872.

WEST AFRICA

Anglophone West Africa
    Gambia
    Ghana
    Nigeria
    Sierra Leone

    Liberia
    St. Helena

Francophone West Africa
    Benin
    Burkina Faso
    Cameroon
    Côte d'Ivoire
    Guinea
    Mali
    Mauritania
    Niger
    Senegal
    Togo

    Lusophone West Africa
        Cape Verde Islands
        Guinea Bissau
        São Tomé e Principe

    Former Spanish Africa
        Equatorial Guinea
        Western Sahara

HANDBOOKS

896
Newland, H.O. **West Africa: a handbook of practical information for the official, planter, miner, financier and trader.** Ed. with an introduction by E. Lewin. London, Daniel O'Connor, 1922. 441pp. 32 photos. map.

The author died before publication, and the work was completed by Lewin who contributed a chapter on the Gambia. Intended as a source to cover both Anglophone and Francophone regions. Includes three sections on "geology and history", "ethnology and psychology" and "commercial exploitation" which consider the whole region, and a section "administration, trade and transport" arranged by state: Cameroons, French West Africa, Gambia, Gold Coast, Liberia, Nigeria, Portuguese West Africa, Sierra Leone, Spanish West Africa, Togoland. No index.

897
Ethnographic survey of Africa: Western Africa: English series. London, International African Institute, 1950-1960. 15 vols.

Sub-series of **Ethnographic survey** (*see* 54). Vol. 1, 'The Akan and Ga-Adangme peoples of the Gold Coast', by M. Manoukian. 1950. 112pp; vol.2, 'The peoples of Sierra Leone Protectorate', by M. McCulloch. 1950. 102pp; vol. 3, 'The Ibo and Ibibio-speaking peoples of south-eastern Nigeria', by D. Forde & G.I. Jones. 1950. 80pp; vol.4, 'The Yoruba-speaking peoples of south-western Nigeria', by D. Forde. 1951. 102pp; vol. 5, 'Tribes of the northern territories of the Gold Coast', by M. Manoukian. 1951. 102pp; vol. 6, 'The Ewe-speaking people of Togoland and the Gold Coast', by M. Manoukian. 1952. 63pp; vol. 7, 'The peoples of the plateau area of Northern Nigeria', by H.D. Gunn. 1953. 111pp; vol.8, 'The Tiv of central Nigeria', by L. & P. Bohannan. 1953. 100pp; vol. 9, 'Peoples of the central Cameroons' by M. McCulloch & M. Littlewood. 1954. 174pp; vol. 10, 'Peoples of the Niger-Benue confluence', by D. Forde *et al.* 1955. 160pp; vol. 11, 'Coastal Bantu of the Cameroons', by E. Ardener. 1956. 116pp; vol.12, 'Pagan peoples of the central area of Northern Nigeria', by H.D. Gunn. 1956. 146pp; vol. 13, 'The Benin kingdom and the Edo-speaking peoples of south-western Nigeria', by R.E. Bradbury. 1957. 212pp; vol. 14, 'The Wolof of Senegambia, together with notes on the Lebu and the Serer', by D.P. Gamble. 1957. 110pp; vol. 15, 'Peoples of the middle Niger region of Northern Nigeria', by H.D.Gunn & F.P. Conant. 1960. 136pp.

- - **French series: Monographies ethnologiques africaines.** Paris, Presses universitaires de France for International African Institute, 1954-1963. 10 vols.

Vol.1, 'Les Bambara', by V. Paques. 1954. xiii, 131pp; 'Les Songhay', by J. Rouch. 1954. 100pp; vol. 3, 'Les Coniagui et les Bassari (Guinée française)', by M. de Lestrange. 1955. 86pp; vol. 4, 'Les Dogon', by M. Palkau-Marti. 1957. xii, 122pp; vol. 5, 'Les Sénoufo (y compris les Minainka)', by B. Holas. 1957. 183pp; vol. 6, 'Le groupe dit Pahouin', by P. Alexandre. 1958. vi, 152pp; vol. 7, 'Les Kongo Nord-Occidentaux' by M. Soret. 1959. viii, 144pp; vol. 8, 'Les populations du Tchad' by A. M.-D. Lebeuf. 1959. viii, 130pp; vol. 9, 'Les populations païennes du Nord Cameroun', by B. Lembezat. 1962. 252pp; vol. 10, 'Les populations du Nord-Togo', by J.-C. Froelich, *et al.* 1963. 195pp.

898

Westermann, D. & Bryan, M.A. **Languages of West Africa**. London, Oxford University Press for International African Institute, 1952. (Handbook of African languages, pt. 2). 215pp. map in pocket.

- - rev. ed. Folkestone, Dawsons for International African Institute, 1970. 277pp.

Classified listing with estimates of numbers of speakers and their topographical distribution. Review, *Africa*, 23, 1953, 163-166. Rev. ed. includes supplementary bibliography comp. by D.W. Arnott. For a note on the **Handbook**, *see* 66.

899

Mauny, R. **Tableau géographique de l'Ouest Africain au moyen age d'après les sources écrites, la tradition et l'archéologie**. Dakar, Institut français d'Afrique noire, 1961. (Mémoires de l'IFAN, 61). 587pp. illus. maps.

Detailed analysis of sources, followed by sections on economic and human geography for the period 622-1434 A.D. "Likely to remain a standard work of reference for many years" (*JAH* 5, 1964, 319-321).

900

Centre des hautes études administratives sur l'Afrique et l'Asie modernes (CHEAM). **Carte des religions de l'Afrique de l'Ouest: notice et statistiques**. Paris, 1966. 135pp.

YEARBOOKS

901

West Africa annual. Lagos, John West Publications, 1962- . Annual (irreg.). 12th ed. 1987.

Ed. by L.K. Jakande (issues 1-10), B.A. Salau (issue 11-). Covers Dahomey/Benin, Upper Volta/Burkina Faso, Cameroon, Cape Verde Is., Côte d'Ivoire, Equatorial Guinea, Ghana, Guinea, Guinea-Bissau, Liberia, Mali, Mauritania, Niger, Nigeria, Senegal, Sierra Leone, Togo. Basic information on each country with history, topography, economy.

902

West African directory 1962 [-1967/68]. London, Thomas Skinner, 1962-1967. Annual. 6 issues.

Covers Cameroon, Dahomey, Gambia, Guinea, Ivory Coast, Liberia, Mali, Niger, Nigeria, Portuguese Guinea, São Tomé e Principe, Senegal, Sierra Leone, Spanish Guinea, Togo, Upper Volta. General information on topography, the economy and public and social services, with a commercial directory.

903

New African yearbook: West and Central Africa, 1983/84 [-1985/86]. London, I.C. Magazines Ltd., 1983-1985. 2 issues.

Issued as vol. [2] of **New African yearbook**, 5th and 6th eds. (*see* 121).

DIRECTORIES OF ORGANIZATIONS

904

Banjo, A.O. **Social science libraries in West Africa: a directory**. Lagos, Nigerian Institute of International Affairs, 1987. (N.I.I.A. monograph series, 13). 63pp.

BIOGRAPHICAL SOURCES

905

Fung, K. 'Index to "portraits" in *West Africa*, 1948-1966', *African studies bulletin* 9, 1966, 103-120.

"Portraits" were short biographies.

906

Kirk-Greene, A.H.M. *ed*. *West Africa* **portraits: a biographical dictionary of West African personalities, 1947-1977**. London, Cass, 1987.

Some 300 biographical sketches reprinted from *West Africa*.

ATLASES & GAZETTEERS

Atlases

907

West African secondary school atlas. London, Nelson, 1963. 76pp. illus.

- - 2nd ed. London, 1966. 80pp.

Ed. T. Wreford Watson & A.K. Wareham. Topographic and thematic maps. West Africa in general (pp.6-10); individual countries of West Africa (pp. 11-23); Africa as a whole (pp. 24-33); rest of the world (pp. 34-64).

908
Wheaton West African atlas. rev. ed. Exeter, Wheaton, 1967. 51pp.

- - 3rd ed. **New West African atlas.** Abure, Olaiya Fegbemigbe, 1977. 51pp.

Topographic and thematic maps. Maps 2-9, Africa; 10-15, West Africa; 16-25, Anglophone countries of West Africa; 26-41, rest of the world.

909
International atlas of West Africa. Dakar, IFAN for OAU, Scientific, Technical & Research Commission, 1968-1978. 44 sheets. 53 x 76cm.

Thematic atlas issued loose-leaf, with a portfolio. Scale 1:5M. Legend in English and French. Initial proposals were made at a Dakar conference in 1945, working parties were established in 1955/56, a detailed schedule was announced in 1963, first 8 sheets were published in 1968. Covers Benin, Burkina Faso, Gambia, Ghana, Mali, Mauritania, Niger, Nigeria, Senegal, Togo. A most detailed source.

910
Economic atlas of West Africa: maps, facts, figures and notes. Ibadan, Adébárá Publishing, 1978. 160pp.

Comp. D. Adébárá. Black and white thematic sketch maps accompanied by statistics. Section on West Africa in general followed by country sections, covering both Anglophone and Francophone areas.

911
Senior secondary atlas. London, Collins-Longman, 1983. 155pp. col. maps. 20 x 27cm.

Prepared for Nigerian schools. Includes 13 maps of West Africa in general, 37 maps of Nigeria, 49 of other West African countries, 64 of the rest of Africa, 64 of the rest of the world.

Gazetteers

912

Teixeira da Moto, A. **Topónimos de origem portuguesa na costa occidental de África: desde o Cabo Bojador as Cabo de Santa Caterina.** Bissau, Centro de Estudos da Guiné Portuguesa, 1950. 411pp. 5 maps.

Based upon 117 original and 26 secondary sources dating from the 14th to the 20th century. Lists 442 names with co-ordinates and citations to the sources for topographical features from Western Sahara round the coast to Fernando Po.

913

U.S. Central Intelligence Agency. **N.I.S gazetteer, West Africa.** [Washington, D.C.], 1954. 2 vols, 1,645pp.

Vol. 1, pp. 1-49, British Cameroons; pp. 51-103, Gambia; pp. 105-224, Gold Coast; pp. 225-583, Nigeria; pp. 585-636, Portuguese Guinea; pp. 637-688, Sierra Leone; pp. 689-741, Spanish Sahara; pp. 743-764, Togo; pp. 765-792, Togoland. Vol. 2, pp. 795-1645, French West Africa (Senegal, Mauritania, Niger, Upper Volta, Ivory Coast).

ANGLOPHONE WEST AFRICA

HANDBOOKS

914
Tremearne, A.J.N. **The Niger and West Sudan; or, the West African's notebook**. London, Hodder & Stoughton, 1910. vii, 151pp.

Pp. 1-79 cover history, topography, statistics and local peoples. Although emphasis is on Nigeria, the other British colonies are also covered. Remainder of the text is basically concerned with hints for travellers.

915
G.B.Foreign Office. Historical Section. **British West Africa (general)**. London, 1920. (F.O. Handbook, 90). 16pp.
Also pub. in F.O. **Peace handbooks**, vol. 15. London, 1920.

Extremely brief treatment, intended only as an introduction to the more detailed accounts of individual territories (*see below*) and included here only for bibliographical completeness of the series.

916
Macmillan, A. **The red book of West Africa: historical and descriptive, commercial and industrial facts, figures and resources**. London, W.H. & L. Collingridge, 1920. 312pp. illus. maps. (Reprinted London, Cass, 1968).

"Claims the distinction of being the first of its kind ever issued on West Africa, also the most profusely illustrated" (preface). Pp. 19-138, Nigeria; pp. 139-228, Gold Coast; pp. 229-272, Sierra Leone; pp. 273-294, Gambia; pp. 295-312, General. For each country covers topography, climate, history, commerce and industry (giving statistics for exports, 1900-1918), agriculture, railways, towns, the constitution, law, religion, education, conditions of life. Provides lists of governors and a commercial directory. Biographical section with some 160 entries (including Africans). Much biographical information is also included under entries for commercial firms. No maps. Profusely illustrated with over 450 photographs including many portraits, scenes and buildings.

YEARBOOKS

917
Payne's Lagos and West Africa almanack and diary. London, J.S. Phillips,

1875-1894. Annual. 17 issues (not published 1888-1892).

Ed. J.A. Otombo Payne, High Sheriff of Lagos. 16th issue (1893) contains separate sections for Lagos, Gold Coast Settlements, and Sierra Leone, with much briefer treatment for the Gambia, Niger Territories, Oil Rivers Protectorate and Liberia. Includes much miscellaneous information on history (including a 20pp. chronology), religion, and administration, with civil lists, texts of ordinances and statistics.

918
The West African yearbook. London, West African Publishing Syndicate, 1901-1902. 3 issues.

1901 issued in 2 editions: 1st ed. 306pp; 2nd ed. 484pp. "Although it is only just over four months since the first issue, there have been such important developments that no excuse need be offered for presentation of a second" (preface to 2nd ed.). Covers British territories and includes general information on natural resources, communications and topography with specific notes on each colony. Brief coverage for non-Anglophone areas which is increased in the 1902 issue.

919
The West African directory and yearbook, 1920/21. London, "African and Orient Review", [1920]. 253pp.

Ed. Dusé Mohamed Ali & W.F. Hutchison. Includes Liberia, Sierra Leone, Gold Coast, Nigeria and the Gambia. For each covers history, geography and topography, population, administration, finance, trade, agriculture, education, law, communications, and a general review of events of 1917 with a brief civil list and professional directory. Statistics up to 1916.

GAMBIA

HANDBOOKS

920
G.B. War Office. Intelligence Branch. **Précis of information concerning British possessions and native states in the valley of the Gambia.** London, 1887. 52pp.

Comp. Capt. L. Darwin. Standard "précis" format. No maps.

921
G.B. War Office. General Staff. **Précis of information concerning the Colony and Protectorate of the Gambia.** London, 1905. (A. 968). vii, 147pp. map in pocket.

In addition to the standard "précis" format, appendices include a more lengthy bibliography than that contained in many volumes in this series, and a detailed list of districts with notes on their boundaries, resident tribes, and major settlements. Map at 1:1M.

922
G.B. War Office. General Staff. **Route book for the Colony and Protectorate of the Gambia.** London, 1905. iii, 126pp.

Presumably meant to accompany the **Précis** ... (*see* 921) although this is not referred to. Gives details of 51 land and 2 river routes.

923
Archer, F.B. **The Gambia Colony and Protectorate: an official handbook.** London, Nelson, 1906. xix, 364pp. illus. maps. (Reprinted, London, Cass, 1967 with introduction by J.M. Gray and a few corrections to the early historical chapters).

Author was Assistant Colonial Secretary in Lagos when writing **Lagos official handbook** (*see* 995) and Colonial Treasurer when writing the present work. Covers history, administration and communications, arranged district by district and includes records of service for the colonial administration.

924
G.B. War Office. General Staff. **Military report on the Colony & Protectorate of the Gambia.** London, 1915. 108pp. map in pocket.

Covers topography, ethnography, history and administration, resources and trade. Includes list of districts, similar in structure to but less detailed than that in the **Précis ...** of 1905 (*see* 922). Map at 1:500,000.

925
G.B. Foreign Office. Historical Section. **Gambia**. London, 1920. (F.O. Handbook, 91). 37pp.
Also pub. in F.O. **Peace handbooks**, vol. 15. London, 1920.

926
G.B. War Office. General Staff. **Military report on the Colony & Protectorate of the Gambia**. London, 1926. (B. 65-1, B. 65-2). 2 vols. maps.

Vol. 1, General. 98pp. Covers history, geography, politics, resources, communications. Maps at 1:250,000. Vol. 2, Routes. 107pp. Describes 45 land and 2 river routes, which are indicated on the accompanying maps at 1:250,000.

927
Schramm, J. **Gambia**, Bonn, Schroeder for Deutsche Afrika-Gesellschaft, 1965. (Die Länder Afrikas, 32). 52pp. illus. maps.

Revised version of the appropriate section of K.H. Pfeffer, **Sierra Leone und Gambia** (*see* 1067).

928
Gailey, H.A. **Historical dictionary of the Gambia**. Metuchen, NJ, Scarecrow Press, 1975. (African historical dictionaries, 4). 180pp.

- - 2nd ed. 1987. xxi, 176pp.

325 entries in 2nd ed. (largely unchanged from the first). Weighted towards entries concerned with the 19th century. Critical reviews in *Africa* 59, 1989, 540-541 and *IJAHS* 21, 1988, 720-721.

See also 1067.

YEARBOOKS

929
G.B. Colonial Office. **[Annual reports]: Gambia, 1848-1964/65**. London, etc., 1849-1966.

As **Reports: the past and present state of H.M. colonial possessions**, 1848-1885, (not issued 1874), **Report on the Blue Book for the Gambia**, 1886-1889, **Annual report on the Gambia**, 1890-1919, (all as Command papers); **Colonial Office annual report**, 1920-63 (not issued 1939-45). 1950/51 to 1962/63 issued biennially. Report for 1964/18.2.1965 issued by the Government of Gambia. *For fuller details see Appendix.*

930
Gambia. Ministry of Finance and Trade. **Gambia trade directory**. Banjul, 1983. 91pp.

Commercial directory with extensive statistics.

STATISTICS

931
Gambia. Statistics Office. **Statistical summary 1964 [-1967/68]**. Bathurst, 1965-1969. Irreg.

Issued as Sessional Papers of the Gambia House of Representatives: issues for 1964 (paper 7 of 1965); 1965 (paper 6 of 1966); 1966/67 (paper 9 of 1967); 1967/68 (paper 5 of 1969).

932
Statistik des Auslandes: Länderberichte: Gambia. Wiesbaden, Statistisches Bundesamt, 1985- . irreg.

Issues for 1985, 1987.

933
Gambia. Ministry of Finance & Economic Affairs. Central Statistics Department. **Statistical abstract of the Gambia**. Banjul, 1990- . Annual.

See also 930.

DIRECTORIES OF ORGANIZATIONS

934
Gamble, D.P. **Abbreviations and acronyms used in the Gambia**. San Francisco, CA, San Francisco State University, Department of Anthropology, 1981. ii, 28pp.

Basically a list of Gambian organizations.

BIOGRAPHICAL SOURCES

935
Who's who in the Gambia. Banjul, Book Production & Material Resources Unit, 1978.

ATLASES & GAZETTEERS

Gazetteers

936
U.S. Board on Geographic Names. **Gambia: official standard names approved by the U.S.B.G.N.** Washington, DC, 1968. (Gazetteer, 107). ii, 35pp.

Includes 2,400 names from 1:50,000 map series. Revision of appropriate section of **West Africa** (*see* 913).

- - **Gazetteer supplement: Africa and South-West Asia**. Washington, DC, 1972. (p. 71, Gambia).

GHANA

HANDBOOKS

937

G.B. War Office. Intelligence Branch. **Précis of information concerning the Gold Coast Colony.** London, 1887. 221pp.

Comp. Capt. L. Darwin. Standard "précis" format. Preface refers to the compilation being based upon the "précis compiled by Major J.R. Oliver in 1877 and Lt. Mitchell in 1880" but these have not been traced as published works. Appendix (pp. 125-221) describes 36 road routes. Map at 1:506,880.

938

G.B. War Office. Intelligence Division. **Report on the Northern Territories of the Gold Coast** (provisional issue). London, 1899. 160pp. maps in pocket.

Comp. Lt.Col. H.P. Northcott. Covers topography, history and administration, religion and languages, natural resources and trade. Appendices include a seven language vocabulary (pp. 79-150).

939

G.B. War Office. Intelligence Division. **Précis of information concerning the Colony of the Gold Coast and Ashanti, March 1904.** London, 1904. (A. 871). iv, 254pp.

Comp. Maj. V.C. Climo. A particularly detailed example of the War Office "précis", with many statistics, a list of some 150 settlements, a chronology and bibliography.

940

G.B. War Office. General Staff. **Route book of the Gold Coast Colony, Ashanti and the Northern Territories.** London, 1906. 2 vols. maps in pocket.

Essentially a companion to the **Précis ...** (*see* 939). Vol. 1. xiv, 371pp. Lists routes 1-143 for Gold Coast Colony; vol. 2. xiv, 277pp. Lists routes 201-352 in separate sequences for Ashanti and for Northern Territories.

941

G.B. War Office. General Staff. **Military report on the Gold Coast, Ashanti and Northern Territories.** London, 1912. (A. 1530). 2 vols.

Vol. 1, [Report]. vi, 257pp. Covers topography, ethnography, history, administration, communications, with statistical appendices. Vol. 2, Routes. vi, 357pp. Includes 139 routes arranged by region.

942
G.B. Foreign Office. Historical Section. **Gold Coast**. London, 1920. (F.O. Handbook, 93). 66pp.
Also pub. in F.O. **Peace handbooks**, vol. 15. London, 1920.

943
Rattray, R.S. **A short manual of the Gold Coast**. London, British Empire Exhibition, 1924. 88pp. illus. maps.

Basic data, compiled for the 1924 Exhibition at Wembley.

944
Danquah, J.B. **The Akim Abuakwa handbook**. London, Forster Groom, 1928. 128pp.

"Compiled at the request of the Paramount chief of the State". Covers history, topography, natural resources, the administration and the economy.

945
Cardinall, A.W. **The Gold Coast 1931**: a review of conditions ... as compared with those of 1921, based on figures and facts collected by the Chief Census Officer ... together with an historical, ethnographical and sociological survey of the people. Accra, Census Office, 1931. vii, 265pp.

Author was Chief Census Officer, and author of *A bibliography of the Gold Coast* (1932). Sections for geography, history, ethnography, economics, the 1931 census, social conditions, non-African peoples. No index.

946
G.B. War Office. General Staff. **Military report on the Gold Coast, Ashanti, the Northern Territories and mandated Togoland**. London, 1931. (B. 70-1). 2 vols?

Vol. 1. General, 1931. 224pp. maps in pocket. Covers history, administration, geography, communications, and natural resources. Includes town plans of Takoradi, Accra, Sekondi, Kumasi. Vol. 2, Routes, *never published*?

947
Ghana. Ministry of Information and Broadcasting. **A brief guide to Ghana**.

Accra, 1958.

- - rev. ed. Accra, 1960. 60pp.

Brief details, arranged by region, principally covering history, agriculture and recent political developments.

948
Pfeffer, K.H. **Ghana**. Bonn, Schroeder for Deutsche Afrika-Gesellschaft, 1958. (Die Länder Afrikas, 5). 104pp. illus. map.

- - 2nd ed. Bonn, 1964. 152pp.

949
Special warfare area handbook for Ghana, comp. D.M. Bouton, *et al.* Washington, DC, U.S. Department of Defense, 1962. xii, 533pp. maps.

- - 2nd ed. **Area handbook for Ghana**. comp. I. Kaplan, *et al.* Washington, DC, 1971. xiv, 449pp. maps.

950
McFarland, D. M. **Historical dictionary of Ghana**. Metuchen, NJ, Scarecrow Press, 1985. (African historical dictionaries, 39). lxxx, 296pp.

Extensive bibliography, pp. 199-289 (1000+ items). Reviews, *IJAHS*, 19, 1986, 558-559; *JAH*, 27, 1986, 410-411.

951
Kropp Dakubu, M.E. *ed*. **The languages of Ghana**. London, Kegan Paul for International African Institute, 1988. 181pp.

"To provide an easily accessible handbook of current knowledge about the languages of Ghana, their geographical distribution, their relationships" (preface).

YEARBOOKS

952
Gold Coast almanack for the year of Our Lord 1842. Cape Coast Castle, 1841. 61pp. (incl. some blank).

In addition to astronomical data includes lists of the British, Dutch and

Danish establishments, and the Wesleyan Mission.

953

Anaman, J.B. **The Gold Coast guide for the year 1895/96**. London, "Christian Herald", 1894. 112pp.

- - 2nd ed. London, 1902. ix, 175pp.

"But the **Gold Coast almanack** enlarged and improved". (There are other references to this earlier work, but no copy has been traced). Historical, topographical, economic and social information. Lists of government officials, missions, schools. 2nd ed. adds a chronology.

954

Wood, S.R. (i.e. Kofi Esemotoo). **Handbook of the Gold Coast for 1907 and 1908**. Manchester & London, John Heywood, 1907. xx, 306pp.

Offered as a successor to the author's earlier **Gold Coast almanack** (no copies traced). "To be issued annually". Includes historical background, details of administration, civil list and records of service, commercial directory.

955

The Gold Coast Colony, Ashanti and Northern Territories manual, 1916/17. Accra, Government Printer, 1918. 320pp.

Covers history, administration, the economy, communications, and includes (pp. 177-320) texts of treaties and significant ordinances.

956

Gold Coast handbook: containing general and statistical information reflecting the Colony, Ashanti, Northern Territories and mandated territory of Togoland. Accra, Government Press, 1923-1928. 3 issues.

1st issue, 1923. xiii, 632, xvipp. 2nd issue, 1924. xiii, 635, xxxiiipp. 3rd issue, 1928. xvi, 525pp. Comp. by J. Maxwell, Secretary for Native Affairs. "This handbook is not an official publication but is issued with the approval of the Gold Coast Government" (preface to 1923 issue). Very detailed coverage of history, topography, natural resources, communications, and the economy. Includes civil list and commercial directory. Numerous photographs.

957

Gold Coast handbook. London, West African Publicity for the Government of the Gold Coast, 1937. xiv, 442pp.

Wide ranging general coverage, including civil list, commercial directory, and particularly detailed statistics. Apparently an attempt to revive item 956 as a regular publication.

958
Gold Coast. Ministry of Commerce, Industry and Mines. **Gold Coast: handbook of trade and commerce.** Accra, 1951-?1955. Irreg.

General economic information and statistics, with commercial directory.

959
Gold Coast year book. Accra, "Daily Graphic", 1953-?1966. Annual.

Title varies: **Ghana year book** (1957-?1966). Includes civil list. statistics, commercial directory, biographical section.

960
Ghana. Ministry of Commerce and Industry. **Ghana handbook of commerce and industry.** Accra, 1957- . Irreg.

"1st issue", 1957, but basically a continuation of **Gold Coast: handbook of trade and commerce** (*see* 958). Issue for 1967, xix, 321pp.

961
Directory of Ghana. London, Diplomatic Press & Publishing Co. (Diprepu Co.) Ltd., 1959-1967. Irreg. 5 issues.

Issues for 1959, 1960, 1961/62, 1964, 1967. Title varies: **Directory of the Republic of Ghana** (1960-1961/62); **Trade directory of the Republic of Ghana** (1964); **Ghana trade directory** (1965-1967). Includes civil list, statistics, commercial directory, and in the issues for 1960 and 1961/62 a "who's who" section of about 200 names per issue.

962
Ghana. Ministry of Information [etc.]. **Ghana: an official handbook.** Accra, 1961- . Irreg.

Issues for 1961, 1969, 1971, 1974, 1975. Title varies: **Ghana 1974, a review of 1973** (1974); **Ghana 1975: an official handbook** (1975). A substantial compilation (1975 ed., 363pp.) of social, economic, topographic and administrative information.

963

Ghana 1966. Accra, Anowuo Educational Publications, 1967. 152, 7pp.

"An objective summary ... on current affairs" (cover). A day by day chronology of events.

964

Ghana year book. Accra, Graphic Corporation, ?1975- . Annual.

Issues for 1975-1977. 1977 issue provides a general survey of the country's history, topography, legal system etc. Directories of lawyers, doctors, schools and colleges. Who's who section of some 125 individuals. A resurrection of item 959?

See also 661.

Colonial reports

965

G.B. Colonial Office. **[Annual reports]: Gold Coast, 1846-1954**. London, 1847-1956.

As **Reports: the past and present state of H.M. colonial possessions**, 1846-1886 (not issued 1862-66, 1872-74, 1880, 1883, 1887), **Report on the Blue Book for the Gold Coast**, 1888, (not issued 1889-91), **Annual report on the Gold Coast**, 1892-1919 (all as Command papers); **Colonial Office annual report**, 1920-54, (not issued 1939-45). No full report for 1857, 1861. Report for 1885 includes Lagos. Report for 1886 includes districts. *For fuller details see Appendix.*

966

G.B. Colonial Office. **[Annual reports]: Gold Coast (Northern Territories) 1901-1925/26**. London, 1902-1927.

As **Annual report on the Gold Coast (Northern Territories)**, 1901-18, (as Command papers); **Colonial Office annual report**, 1919-1925/26. Subsequently continued in **[Colonial reports]: Gold Coast** (*see* 965). *For fuller details see Appendix.*

967

G.B. Colonial Office. **[Annual reports]: Ashanti, 1905-1925/26**. London, 1906-1927.

As **Annual report on Ashanti**, 1905-1919 (in Command series); **Colonial**

Office annual report, 1920-21, 1922/23-1925/26. Subsequently continued in [Colonial reports]: Gold Coast (*see* 965). *For fuller details see Appendix.*

STATISTICS

968
Hay, G.B. & Hamer, S. **The political economy of colonialism in Ghana: a collection of documents and statistics, 1900-1960.** Cambridge, Cambridge University Press, 1972. 431pp.

Statistics drawn mostly from the Blue books and covering population, wages, trade, finance, communications, and education.

969
Ewusi, K. **Statistical tables on the economy of Ghana, 1950-1985.** Accra, University of Ghana, Institute of Statistical, Social and Economic Research, 1986. 11pp. 135 tables.

Bulletins

970
Gold Coast. Central Bureau of Statistics. **Monthly statistical bulletin of the Gold Coast.** Accra, 1948-1951. Issues 1-36.

continued by:

Economic and statistical bulletin. Accra, 1952-1953. vols. 1(1)-2(1).

continued by:

Gold Coast/Ghana. Central Bureau of Statistics. **Digest of statistics.** Accra, 1953-1980. Monthly/quarterly.

continued by:

Ghana. Central Bureau of Statistics. **Quarterly digest of statistics.** Accra, 1981- .

Yearbooks

971
Ghana. Central Bureau of Statistics. **Statistical yearbook.** Accra, 1961-1973.

Annual. 7 issues.

Issues for 1961-64, 1965/66, 1967/68, 1969/70. Abridged version issued as **Statistical handbook**. Accra, 1966-1970. Annual. 4 issues.

972
Statistik des Auslandes: Länderberichte: Ghana. Wiesbaden, Statistisches Bundesamt, 1961- . irreg.

Issues for 1961, 1967, 1985, 1987, 1989.

DIRECTORIES OF ORGANIZATIONS

973
Ghana. Council for Scientific and Industrial Research. Central Reference & Research Library. **Directory of special libraries in Ghana.** Accra, 1974. v, 71pp.

- - rev ed. **Directory of special and research libraries in Ghana.** Accra, 1977. 81pp.

Comp. L. Agyei-Gyane.

974
University of Ghana. Department of Library and Archival Studies. **Directory of libraries in Ghana,** Legon, 1974. (Occasional papers, 11). 62pp.

Comp. A. Nitecki.

BIOGRAPHICAL SOURCES

975
Sampson, M.J. **Gold Coast men of affairs (past and present).** London, Stockwell, 1937. 224pp. (Reprinted, London, Dawsons, 1969).

976
Furley, J.T. 'Provisional list of some Portuguese governors of the Captaincy da Mina', *Transactions of the Gold Coast and Togo Historical Society*, 2, 1956, 53-62.

See also his 'Notes on some Portuguese Governors of the Captaincy da Mina', ibid. 3, 1958, 194-214.

977
Ephson, I.S. **Gallery of Gold Coast celebrities 1632-1958**. Accra, Ilem Publishing Co., 1969. 3 vols.

Covers 116 individuals, most with portraits.

978
Ghana who's who 1972/73 [etc]. Accra, Bartels, 1973-   . Irreg.

Title varies: **Who's who in Ghana 1974/76** (1978). Vol. for 1972/73 includes much miscellaneous information, such as membership of all assemblies since 1954.

979 (*also entered at* 459)
Encyclopedia Africana Dictionary of African Biography. Vol. 1, Ethiopia & Ghana. Algonac, MI, Reference Publications, 1977. 367pp.

Ghana section, pp. 167-342, ed. I. Wilks, with contributions from 39 scholars. Includes 138 biographies of Africans and Europeans, many with portraits, and list of sources. "Concise guide to Ghana names and terms", pp. 330-338. Reviews, *IJAHS*, 11, 1978, 546-550; *ASA review of books* 6, 1980, 285-287 which is critical of "outdated and erroneous information". For the encyclopedia, *see* 31; for the dictionary of biography, *see* 299.

See also 959, 961, 964.

ATLASES & GAZETTEERS

Atlases

980
Gold Coast. Survey Department. **Atlas of the Gold Coast**. Accra, [1927-1928]. 26 pp. incl. 24 col. maps. 43 x 30cm.

- - 2nd ed. Accra, 1935. 3pp. 20 col. maps. 36 x 29cm.

- - 3rd ed. Accra, 1939. 5pp. 21 col. maps.

- - 4th ed. Accra, 1945. 5pp. 21 col. maps.

- - 5th ed. Accra, 1949. 9pp. 21 col. maps.

Thematic atlas at basic scale of 1:1.5M. Includes administrative areas, tribes, topography, geology, minerals, climate, forestry, agriculture and communications. 2nd to 5th eds. have town plans of Kumasi (1:12,500), Takoradi (1:18,000) and Accra (1:25,000).

981
Gold Coast. Survey Department. **Modified atlas of the Gold Coast.** Accra, 1947. 8pp. incl. 6 col. maps. 28 x 30cm.

Maps at 1:3M.

982
Hilton, T.E., *comp.* **Ghana population atlas.** Edinburgh, Nelson for University College of Ghana, 1960. 40pp. 30 x 41cm.

16 maps, 3 in colour. 1:1.5M/1:3M. Tables in text. Based upon author's 1955 Ph.D thesis submitted to University of London, "The distribution and density of population in the Gold Coast and Togoland". Maps show population density, distribution and change based on 1931 and 1948 census reports.

983
Ghana. Survey of Ghana & Census Office. **Atlas of population characteristics.** Accra, 1964. (1960 Population Census of Ghana). ii, 29pp.

26 maps (2 col.) with transparent overlay showing administrative areas. Scale 1:2M. Shows current and former distribution, education, occupations.

984
Ghana. Survey of Ghana. **Portfolio of Ghana maps.** Accra, 1967-1969. 13 loose sheets in titled folder.

Thematic maps showing administrative divisions, physical features, vegetation, soil, geology, agriculture, minerals, and climate, all at 1:2M. Plans of Accra (1:25,000), Kumasi (1:4,000) and Sekondi-Takoradi (1:4,000).

985
Usshar, A.K.L. **Climatic maps of Ghana for agriculture.** Legon, Ghana Meteorological Services, 1969. 36pp.

29 maps at 1:1.5M showing rainfall, temperature, solar radiation, winds.

986

Ghana. Council for Scientific & Industrial Research. National Atlas Project. **Ghana national atlas.** Accra, 1973- . 60 x 45cm.

200 sheets planned at 1:1.5M in 5 sections: topography, economics, population, transport, trade. Only 35 completed by 1986, mostly covering agriculture and population. Virtually no accompanying text, or details on basis of compilation.

Gazetteers

987

Gold Coast. Postmaster General. **Post Office handbook.** Accra, 1924. 138pp.

988

Berry, J. **The place names of Ghana (problems of standardization).** London, 1958. 2 vols. (iii, 19, 11; 28, 4, 25, 7pp.)

989

Ghana. Census Office. **1960 population census of Ghana. Vol. 1. The gazetteer.** Accra, 1962. 405pp.

990

U.S. Board of Geographic Names. **Ghana: official standard names approved by the U.S.B.G.N.** Washington, DC, 1967. (Gazetteer, 102). iii, 282pp.

Includes 20,000 names from 1:250,000 map series. revision of appropriate sections of **West Africa** (*see* 913).

- - **Gazetteer supplement: Africa and South-West Asia.** Washington, DC, 1972. (p. 173, Ghana).

991

Ghana. Census Office. **1970 population census of Ghana. Vol. 1. The gazetteer.** Accra, 1971. 662pp.

NIGERIA

Bibliographies of reference works

992
Asomugha, C.N.C. **A brief guide to Nigerian reference books**. Onitsha, ABIC Publishers, 1978. 47pp.

Lists 85 titles.

HANDBOOKS

993
G.B. War Office. Intelligence Branch. **Précis of information concerning the Colony of Lagos, together with notes on the neighbouring native territories.** London, 1888. 95pp. map.

Comp. Capt. L. Darwin. Standard format with appendix describing 22 route itineraries. Map at 1:506,880. Only very brief coverage of "neighbouring territories".

994
G.B. War Office. Intelligence Division. **Précis of information concerning the Niger Protectorates**. London, 1890. 71pp.

Comp. Maj. L. Darwin. Covers Oil Rivers, Lower Niger, Sokoto, Gandu, and Benuel districts. Emphasis on topographical description. Map at 1:506,880.

995
Archer, F.B. **The Lagos official handbook, 1897/1898**: showing the civil establishments, names and descriptions of the civil servants of government. London, printed Waterlow & Sons, 1898. 149pp.

Author was Assistant Colonial Secretary. Includes a variety of miscellaneous historical and administrative information, with histories of service for some 100 officers on the civil list.

996
G.B. War Office. Intelligence Division. **Précis of information concerning Nigeria**. London, 1900. 179pp.

Comp. Maj. T.H.B. Forster. Standard "précis" format. Unusually long and detailed "books of reference" section for this series, including lists of Parliamentary papers. No maps.

997
G.B. War Office. General Staff. **Précis of information concerning Nigeria and the Colony and Protectorate of Lagos.** London, 1902. 193pp. map in pocket.

Covers topography, history, administration, and peoples in standard "précis" format.

998
G.B. War Office. General Staff. **Military report on Southern Nigeria.** London, 1908-1909. 2 vols.

Comp. by Capt. W.H. Beverley, and drawing upon **Précis ...** (*see* 996). Vol. 1, 1908. General. viii, 147pp. Covers geography, history, administration, communications. Vol. 2, 1909. Communications. vi, 336pp. Detailed description of 106 routes.

999
G.B. War Office. General Staff. **Military report on Northern Nigeria.** London, 1908. 2 vols.

"Based on the **Précis ...** [*see* 996] rev. by Capt. H.N. Kempthorne". Vol. 1, General. vii, 164pp; vol. 2, Routes (A. 1278). viii, 468pp. Details of 168 routes.

1000
G.B. War Office. General Staff. **Military report on Northern Nigeria.** London, 1912. 2 vols.

Vol.1 *not traced.* Vol. 2, Routes. vi, 312pp. Includes 72 itineraries selected by Capt. G. Howell.

1001
G.B. Foreign Office. Historical Section. **Nigeria.** London, 1920 (F.O. Handbook, 94). 82pp.
Also pub. in F.O. **Peace handbooks**, vol. 15. London, 1920.

1002
Nigeria. **Gazetteers of the Northern Provinces.** Lagos [etc.], 1921-1934. 12 vols.

Series of volumes compiled for each province and containing a wide range of background information for the benefit of colonial officers. Reprinted as **Gazetteers of the Northern Provinces of Nigeria**, London, Cass, 1972. 4 vols. with valuable notes on the series, the background to its compilation and each individual title by A.H.M. Kirk-Greene. The reprint includes : vol. 1, 'The Hausa Emirates: Bauchi', comp. F.B. Gall, (orig. pub. 1920), 32pp; 'Sokoto', comp. E.J. Arnett, (orig. pub. 1920), 72pp; 'Zaria', comp. E.J. Arnett, (orig. pub. 1920), 40pp; 'Kano', comp. W.F. Gowers, (orig. pub. 1920), 56pp; vol. 2, 'The Eastern Kingdoms: Muri', comp. J.M. Fremantle, (orig. pub. 1922), 77pp; 'Yola', comp. C.O. Migeod, (orig. pub. 1927), 47pp; 'Bornu', comp. H.R. Palmer, rev. J.B. Welman, (orig. pub. 1929), 112pp; vol. 3, 'The Central Kingdoms: Kontagora', comp. E.C. Duff, rev. W. Hamilton-Browne, (orig. pub. 1920), 72pp; 'Nassarawa', comp. J.C. Sciortino, (orig. pub. 1920), 32pp; 'Nupe', comp. E.G.M. Dupigny, (orig. pub. 1920), 84pp; 'Ilorin', comp. K.V. Elphinstone, (orig. pub. 1921), 67pp; vol. 4, 'The Highland Chieftaincies: Plateau', comp. C.G. Ames, (orig. pub. 1934), 358pp.

1003
G.B. War Office. General Staff. **Military report on Nigeria**. London, 1929. 2 vols?

Vol. 1, 1929. 373pp. + Amendments, June 1932. London, 1932. 32pp. One of the most detailed examples of the War Office handbooks. Pt. 1, History; pt. 2, Geography (with gazetteer details of 74 settlements); pt. 3, Communications; pt. 4, Material & Economic resources; pt. 5, Military & other forces. 16 maps, incl. town plans of Lagos and Port Harcourt. Vol. 2 *not published?*

1004
Kauffman, H. **Nigeria**. Bonn, Schroeder for Deutsche Afrika-Gesellschaft, 1958. (Die Länder Afrikas, 2). 83pp.

- - 2nd ed. Bonn, 1962. 304pp.

1005
Nigeria. Ministry of Information. **Nigeria 1960**. Lagos, 1961. 63pp.

1006
Nigeria. Ministry of Information. **Facts about Nigeria**. Lagos, 1961. 9 parts.

A series of self contained pamphlets covering topics such as topography, commerce, industry, and public utilities.

1007

Area handbook for Nigeria. Washington, DC, U.S. Department of Defense, 1961. viii, 579pp. maps.

- - 2nd ed. comp. J.A. Cookson, *et al*. Washington, DC, 1964. xvii, 579pp. illus. maps.

- - 3rd ed. comp. H.D. Nelson, *et al*. Washington, DC, 1972. xvi, 485pp. illus. maps.

- - 4th ed. **Nigeria: a country study**, comp. H.D. Nelson, *et al*, Washington, DC, 1982. xxviii, 358pp. illus. maps.

1008

Nitecki, A. **Nigerian tribes: preliminary list of headings for use in libraries**. Legon, University of Ghana, Department of Library Studies, 1972. vi, 106pp.

1009

Hansford, K. *et al*. **An index of Nigerian languages**. Accra, Summer Institute of Linguistics, 1976. (Study in Nigerian languages, 5).

1010

Nwafor Orizu, A.A. **Insight into Nigeria: the Shehu Shagari era; a reference book focusing on the statistical data of Nigerian States ...** Ibadan, Evans Bros. (Nigerian Publications), 1983. xv, 324pp.

Author was formerly President of the Senate. Individual chapters for each of the 19 states and the federal government. Written in discursive style but with a wide range of data.

1011

Wente-Lukas, R. **Handbook of ethnic units in Nigeria**. Wiesbaden, Franz Steiner, 1985. (Studien zur Kulturkunde Frobenius Institute, Universität der Frankfurt, 74). 466pp.

Comp. "with the assistance of Adam Jones". Alphabetical list of all known ethnic groups (some 550), with variant names, details of sub-groups, present and previous geographical locations, population estimates and language affiliations. Bibliography pp. 365-401. Review, *Africa* 57, 1987, 391-396.

1012

Oyewole, A. **Historical dictionary of Nigeria**. Metuchen, NJ, Scarecrow Press, 1987. (African historical dictionaries, 40). xvii, 391pp.

Particularly strong on biographical entries. Much shorter bibliography than in many volumes in this series. Review *JAH*, 30, 1989, 341-342.

1013
Nigeria: the first 25 years. Lagos, Infodata and Heinemann Educational Books (Nigeria), 1988. xviii, 582pp.

General ed. U. Eleazu with some 30 contributors. To provide need for "an authorative handbook of information on Nigeria" (preface). Pt. 1 provides a survey of political, legal and administrative developments since independence; pts. 2 and 3 cover the economy; pt. 4 gives a state by state survey, giving for each an account of its history and topography, economic and social developments and tourist attractions. Statistical appendix, pp. 545-569.

1014
Oyenchi, N.N. **Nigeria's book of firsts: a handbook on pioneer Nigerian citizens, institutions and events**. Owerri, Nigeriana Publications, 1989. 277pp.

Some 1,000 entries under 19 thematic headings such as "politics", "religion" etc.

YEARBOOKS

1015
A Bornu almanac for the year 1916. London, Oxford University Press, 1916. 119pp.

"The idea of this almanac and some of the information contained therein is adapted from the **Sudan almanac** [*see* 505]" (prefatory note, signed P.A. Benton). A wide range of miscellaneous information on the Muslim calendar, festivals, plants, medical terms, administrative districts, Muslim sects, "notes on the saints" (pp. 24-52), routes, weights and measures, etc.

1016
Nigerian handbook; containing statistical and general information respecting the Colony and Protectorate. Lagos, Government Printer/London, West African Publishing Ltd., 1917-1936. Irreg. 11 issues.

Issues for 1917, 1919, 1921, 1922/23, 1924, 1925, 1926, 1927, 1929, 1933, 1936. Issues 1 to 3 (1917-21), "not an official publication, but issued with the approval of the Nigerian Government" and compiled by A.C. (later Sir A.)

Burns. Subsequent eds. "published by authority". Includes coverage of history, topography, and the economy, with statistics and a commercial directory.

1017
Nigeria. Department of Commerce and Industries. **Handbook of commerce and industry in Nigeria**. Lagos, 1952- . Irreg.

Issues for 1952, 1954, 1957, 1960, 1962. Despite title includes much general social and topographic information.

1018
Nigeria year book. Lagos, "Daily Times", 1952- . Annual. (38th ed. 1992).

Includes civil list, commercial directory, statistics, state by state surveys. Amount of data steadily increases: 1952 issue, 128pp; 1989 issue, 392pp.

1019
Nigeria handbook. London, Crown Agents for Government of Nigeria, 1953-1954. Annual. 2 issues.

Issues for 1953 (339pp), 1954 (354pp).

continued by:

Nigeria. Ministry of Information [etc.]. **Nigeria handbook**. Lagos, 1970-. Annual (irreg.)

Issues for 1970-74, 1975/76, 1977, 1978/79, 1982, 1991. Wide ranging general information including statistics, lists of members of government.

1020
National directory of Nigeria. London, Unimex, 1959- . Annual (irreg.)

3rd ed. 1963.

1021
Directory of the Federation of Nigeria. London, Diplomatic Press & Publishing Co. (Diprepu Co.) Ltd., 1960-1965. Irreg. 4 issues.

Issues for 1960, 1962, 1963/64, 1965/66. Title varies: **Trade directory of the Federation/Federal Republic of Nigeria** (1962-1965/66). Includes civil list, statistics, commercial directory, and in issues 1 to 3, "Biographical section" (c.200 entries).

1022

"Times" trade and industrial directory. Apapa, "Daily Times" Press, ?1979-

6th ed. 1984.

1023

The Guardian Nigerian handbook, 1982/83 [etc.]. London, Collins, 1982- . Annual.

Covers politics, the economy, social life, and includes commercial directory.

1024

Nigeria handbook. Lagos, Patike Communications Ltd., 1985- .

Magazine format with essays, commercial directory, and "who's who" (120+ entries). 1985 ed. is subtitled "25 years of progress: a silver jubilee review".

See also 661.

Colonial reports

1025

G.B. Foreign Office. **[Annual reports]: Niger Coast Protectorate, 1891-99**. London, 1895-1900.

As **Report on the administration of the Niger Coast Protectorate**, 1891/94-1894/95 (not issued 1895/96), **Annual report for Niger Coast Protectorate, 1896/97-1898/99**, (all as Command papers). Subsequently pub. as **Annual report on Southern Nigeria** (*see* 1027). *For fuller details see Appendix.*

1026

G.B. Colonial Office. **[Annual reports]: Northern Nigeria, 1900/01-1913**. London, 1902-1916.

As **Report on Northern Nigeria**, 1900/01-1913, (as Command papers). Report for 1900/01 covers Jan. 1 1900 to March 31 1901. *For fuller details see Appendix.*

1027

G.B. Colonial Office. **[Annual reports]: Southern Nigeria 1899/1900-1913**. London, 1901-1916.

As **Report on Southern Nigeria**, 1899/1900, 1900-1913, (as Command papers). Previously pub. as **Report for Niger Coast Protectorate**. (*see* 1025). *For fuller* *details see Appendix.*

1028
G.B. Colonial Office. [Annual reports]: Southern Nigeria (Lagos), 1862-1905. London, 1864-1906.

As **Reports: the present and past state of HM colonial possessions,** 1862-1887, (not pub. 1870, 1883-84), **Report on the Blue Book,** for 1887-88, **Annual report on Lagos,** 1889-1905, (all as Command papers). No full report for 1862, 1865, 1866. Two reports issued for 1885, one C.4071 for Lagos and Gold Coast, the other C. 5239 for Lagos only). 1900-1901 covered in one report. *For fuller details see Appendix.*

1029
G.B. Colonial Office. [Annual reports]: Nigeria, 1914-57. London, 1916-1961.

As **Annual report on Nigeria,** 1914-19, (as Command papers); **Colonial Office annual report,** 1920-55, (not pub. 1939-45), no report pub. for 1956, **Annual report for Federal Nigeria, 1957.** *For fuller details see Appendix.*

STATISTICS

Bibliography

1030
Moses, S.C. 'Nigerian State statistical yearbooks', *ARD*, 8/9, 1975, 57-59.

1031
Adamu, S.O. **The Nigerian statistical system: retrospect and prospect.** Ibadan, Ibadan University Press, 1978. 221pp.

Author was member of Nigerian Department of Statistics. Describes activities as of 1975, with a list of statistical publications current in 1975 in Appendix III, pp. 178-210.

Bulletins & yearbooks

1032
Nigeria. Department of Statistics [etc.]. **Digest of statistics.** Lagos, 1951- . Quarterly.

1033
Nigeria. Department of Statistics [etc.]. **Annual abstract of statistics**. Lagos, 1960- . Annual.

1034
Statistik des Auslandes: Länderberichte: Nigeria. Wiesbaden, Statistisches Bundesamt, 1961- . Irreg.

Issues for 1961, 1967, 1977, 1985, 1987.

DIRECTORIES OF ORGANIZATIONS

1035
National Library of Nigeria. **Libraries in Nigeria: a directory, 1966/67**. Lagos, 1970. 17pp.

- - rev. ed. **...**, **1967/68**. Lagos, 1970. 21pp.

Both eds. comp. I.O. Oarhe.

- - rev. ed. **Libraries in Nigeria, 1971**. Lagos, 1973.

Lists 52 collections.

1036
Directory of law libraries in Nigeria. 2nd ed. Lagos, Government Printer, 1970. 110pp.

Comp. A. Adefidiya.

1037
Ahmadu Bello University. Kashim Ibrahim Library. **A directory of Nigerian libraries and documentation centres**. Zaria, 1983. 132pp.

Comp. M.A. Omoniwa and M.O. Salaam. Lists 124 collections (51 academic, 31 special, 25 public, 17 judicial).

1038
Dictionary of professional bodies in Nigeria. Lagos, K.O. Associates, 1990. 67pp.

Covers some 50 organizations arranged by subject.

BIOGRAPHICAL SOURCES

Bibliographies

1039
National Library of Nigeria. **A bibliography of biographies and memoirs on Nigeria**. Lagos, 1968. (National Library publications, 9). 11pp.

General

1040
Who's who in Nigeria. Ibadan, Advent Press, 1949. 59pp.

Comp. "Amicus" (*pseud.* i.e. A.T. Odusanya).

1041
Who's who in Nigeria: a biographical dictionary. Lagos, "Daily Times", 1956. 278pp.

Contains some 1,500 entries.

- - 2nd ed. Apapa, "Daily Times", 1971. 232pp.

Includes about 750 entries.

- - 3rd ed. **Who's who in Nigeria, 1978: biographies of some eminent Nigerian citizens**. Apapa, 1978. 173pp.

About 500 entries, much fuller than those in previous editions.

1042
Orimoloye, S.A. **Biographiana Nigeriana: a biographical dictionary of eminent Nigerians**. Boston, MA, G.K. Hall, 1977. 368pp.

Includes 1,007 entries for living and recently deceased figures, based on questionnaires.

1043
Nigeria who's who, 1981-82. Lagos, Biographical Centre of Nigeria Ltd., 1981. 95pp.

Some 300 entries.

- - 3rd ed. **Who's who in Nigeria**. Lagos, 1985. 144pp.

Ed. H.U. Ukegbu. Biographees are arranged in categories, e.g. politicians, businessmen, traditional rulers, religious leaders with no overall index.

1044
Who's who in Nigeria: including the Executive and Legislature, 1983. Lagos, "Daily Times", 1983. 558pp.

1045
Who's who in Nigeria. Lagos, Newswatch, 1990- . Annual. (issues for 1990, 1991).

Comp. N. Osso. Each issue contains over 800pp. and 2,500 entries; the largest compilation of its kind for Nigeria. "Splendid resource" (*ABPR* 17, 1991, 294).

See also 1011, 1021, 1024.

Special categories

1046
Nigeria who is who in the Legislature (The House of Representatives), 1979-1983. Lagos, Nigerian Federal Department of Information, Research Section, 1983. 227pp.

Lists 445 members with brief biographies of nearly 300 arranged by state.

1047
The Nigerian Legislature: who is who in the Senate, 1979-1983. [Lagos, Nigerian Federal Department of Information], 1983. 144pp.

93 short biographies with portraits.

1048
Osuji, C. **His Royal Highness: a historical data and reference book on traditional rulers in Anambra, Cross River, Imo and River States.** Owerri, Opinion Research and Communications Consultants, 1984. viii, [158pp].

Separate sections for each State. Lists some 900 contemporary rulers, but less than 150 have full biographical entries, usually with a portrait.

1049
Who's who of Nigerian women. Lagos, Nigerian Association of University

Women, 1985. 281pp.

Ed. C. Osinulu and O. Jegede. 257 entries. Index by profession.

1050
Nigerian artists: a who's who and bibliography. Oxford, Hans Zell, forthcoming 1993. 622pp. col. illus.

Comp. B.M. Kelly, ed. J.L. Stanley. Covers more than 350 artists active between 1920 and 1990 giving date of birth, address, details of exhibitions, awards, commissions. Based on collections at the National Museum of African Art Branch Library, Smithsonian Institution Libraries. Includes a bibliography of modern Nigerian art.

ATLASES & GAZETTEERS

Atlases

1051
Oxford atlas for Nigeria. rev. ed. London & Ibadan, Oxford University Press, 1968. 66, 12pp.

- - rev. ed. London & Ibadan, 1978. 66, 12pp.

Comp. by the Cartographic Department of the Clarendon Press, with the advice of F.C.A. McBain. Pp.ii-vii, 1-21 cover Nigeria and west Africa.

1052
Ofomata, G.E.K. *ed.* **Nigeria in maps: eastern states.** Benin City, Ethiope, 1975. 146pp.

18 contributors discuss 51 themes with accompanying maps. Intended as first in a series to cover all Nigeria.

1053
Nigeria. Federal Surveys. **National atlas of the Federal Republic of Nigeria.** Lagos, 1978. 136pp. 45 x 58cm.

Coloured thematic maps compiled 1968-1977. Basic scale 1:3M. 12 town plans at 1:50,000. Preceded by a series of 1:3M sheets published 1949-56 without text and known as the "Atlas series".

1054

Agboola, S.A. **An agricultural atlas of Nigeria**. London, Oxford University Press, 1979. xiv, 248pp. maps.

1055

Barbour, K.M. *et al.* **Nigeria in maps**. London, Hodder & Stoughton/New York, Holmes & Meier, 1982. vii, 148pp.

60 thematic maps with accompanying text. Very favourable review in *GJ*, 149, 1983, 390-391.

Gazetteers

1056

Nigeria. Surveyor General's Dept. **Gazetteer of place names on the map of Nigeria**. Lagos, 1932. 91pp.

Based on the 15 sheets of the 1:500,000 series. Over 20,000 entries.

1057

Nigeria. Director of Surveys. **Colony and Protectorate of Nigeria: gazetteer of place names on map of Nigeria 1:500,000**. Zaria, Gaskiya Corporation, 1949. 167pp.

Arranged in 5 sections: towns, villages and hamlets; rivers and creeks; lakes; mountains and hills; forest and game reserves.

1058

U.S. Board on Geographic Names. **Nigeria: official standard names approved by the U.S.B.G.N.** Washington, DC, 1971. (Gazetteer, 117). iv, 641pp.

Includes 42,000 names from 1:250,000 map series. Revision of appropriate sections of **West Africa** (*see* 913).

- - **Gazetteer supplement: Africa and South-West Asia**, Washington, DC, 1972. (p. 127, Nigeria).

1059

Nigeria. Director of Federal Surveys. **Gazetteer of place-names: Federal Republic of Nigeria**. Lagos, 1965. 2 vols.

Vol. 1. 172pp. Northern Nigeria; vol. 2. 176pp. Western Nigeria and Municipality of Lagos, Eastern Nigeria.

- - 3rd ed. **Gazetteer of place-names.** Lagos, 1973. ii, 836pp.

1060

Nigeria. National Population Bureau. Demographic Division. **National gazetteer of place names.** Lagos, 1985. 20 vols.

One vol. for each state. Anambra (iv, 133pp.); Bauchi (iv, 108pp.); Bendel (iv, 123pp.); Benue (iv, 133pp.); Borno (iv, 164pp.); Cross River (iv, 93pp.); Federal Capital Territory, Abuja (iv, 32pp.); Gongola (iv, 56pp.); Imo (iv, 151pp.); Kaduna (iv, 48pp.); Kano (iv, 28pp.); Kwara (iv, 47pp.); Lagos (iv, 32pp.); Niger (iv, 14pp.); Ogu (iv, 140pp.); Ondo (iv, 58pp.); Oyo (iv, 78pp.); Plateau (iv, 81pp.); Rivers (iv, 71pp.); Sokoto (iv, 30pp.)

SIERRA LEONE

HANDBOOKS

1061

G.B. War Office. Intelligence Division. **Précis of information concerning the Colony of Sierra Leone**. London, 1887. 66pp. map.

Comp. Capt. L. Darwin. Standard "précis" format. Notes on 7 routes and very detailed diagram of trans-Saharan caravan routes. Map at 1:506,880.

1062

G.B. War Office. Intelligence Division. **Précis of information concerning the Colony and Protectorate of Sierra Leone**. London, 1901. 210pp. map in pocket.

Comp. A.R. Stuart. Extensively rev. ed. of 1887 volume (*see* 1061). Covers topography, history, local peoples, descriptions of administrative districts, trade and agriculture. 42 routes listed and described.

1063

G.B. War Office. Intelligence Division. **Military report on the Colony and Protectorate of Sierra Leone**. London, 1908-1910. 2 vols.

Comp. W. Gillman. Based upon **Précis ...** (*see* 1002). [Vol. 1], 1908. vi, 150pp. Contains general description, history, administration, agriculture. Vol. 2, 1910. Routes. 420pp. 2 maps in pocket. Detailed descriptions of 39 itineraries.

1064

G.B. Foreign Office. Historical Section. **Sierra Leone**. London, 1920. (F.O. Handbook, 92). 58pp.
Also pub. in F.O. **Peace handbooks**, vol. 15. London, 1920.

1065

Goddard, T.N. **Handbook of Sierra Leone**. London, Grant Richards, 1925. xvi, 335pp. illus. maps.

Author was Assistant Colonial Secretary. Six sections on geography, history, population, administration, finance and general information followed by numerous appendices with lists of office holders, a civil list, texts of significant documents and statistics.

1066

G.B. War Office. General Staff. **Military report on the Colony and Protectorate of Sierra Leone**. London, 1933. 2 vols.?

Vol. 1, General (B. 73-1). 287pp. 4 maps in pocket. "A revised ed. to replace ed. pub. in 1908" (*see* 1063). Detailed information on history, civil administration, geography, population, climate, sports and recreation, and communications. Appendices include summarized census data, and a brief district gazetteer. Vol. 2 *never published*?

1067

Pfeffer, K.H. **Sierra Leone und Gambia**. Bonn, Schroeder for Deutsche Afrika-Gesellschaft, 1958. (Die Länder Afrikas, 11). 88pp.

Sierra Leone, pp. 9-64; Gambia, pp. 65-80. Rev. ed. of section on Gambia later pub. as **Gambia** (*see* 927).

1068

Area handbook for Sierra Leone, comp. I. Kaplan, *et al*. Washington, DC, U.S. Department of Defense, 1976. xiv, 400pp.

1069

Foray, C.P. **Historical dictionary of Sierra Leone**. Metuchen, NJ, Scarecrow Press, 1977. (African historical dictionaries, 12). 336pp.

Critical review in *ASA review of books* 4, 1978, 109-110, which makes detailed corrections and suggestions for topics that might be included in a new edition.

1070

Sierra Leone. Office of the President. **Background to Sierra Leone**. Freetown, 1980. 240pp.

Illustrated handbook prepared for 17th Summit Conference of the Organization of African Unity.

YEARBOOKS

1071

Sierra Leone almanac for the year of our Lord 1822. Freetown, Government & Council, 1822. 69pp.

Includes historical chronology, civil list, statistics.

1072
G.B. Colonial Office. **[Annual reports]: Sierra Leone, 1846-1958.** London, 1847-1960.

As **Reports: the past and present state of HM Colonial possessions,** 1846-1882 (not pub. 1849, 1865, 1874, 1877-79, 1883-86), **Report on the Blue Book,** 1887-1889, **Annual report on Sierra Leone,** 1890-1919 (all as Command papers); **Colonial Office annual report,** 1920-1958 (not pub. 1939-45). Corrigendum added to report for 1956. 1881-82 pub. as one report. No full report for 1858-59, 1862, 1864, 1866, 1869, 1872, 1875. *For fuller details see Appendix.*

1073
Merriman-Labor, A.B.C. **Handbook of Sierra Leone for 1901/02 [-1904/05].** Manchester, John Heywood, 1902-1905. 2 issues.

Issues for 1901/02, 1904/05. "Though not a government publication it has been prepared under the patronage of the Governor ... and mainly from official records". Includes historical chronology, topographical and economic information, civil list, statistics and a commercial directory. First issue includes a biographical section (62 entries).

1074
Sierra Leone year book. Freetown, "Daily Mail", 1956-?1978 Annual (irreg.). Not pub. 1973-77.

Includes civil list, basic economic statistics, "who's who" (50/75 entries)

STATISTICS

1075
Sierra Leone. Central Statistics Office. **Annual digest of statistics.** Freetown, 1962- . Annual. (irreg.) 16th ed. 1989.

Title varies: **Annual statistical digest.**

1076
Sierra Leone. Central Statistics Office. **Quarterly statistical bulletin.** Freetown, 1963- .

Title varies: **Statistical bulletin** (1967-).

1077
Statistik des Auslandes: Länderberichte: Sierra Leone. Wiesbaden, Statistisches Bundesamt, 1962- . irreg.

Issues for 1962, 1984, 1986, 1989.

DIRECTORIES OF ORGANIZATIONS

1078
Sierra Leone Library Association. **Directory of libraries and information services.** Freetown, 1971. 22pp.

- - 2nd ed. Freetown, 1976. ii, 31pp.

Both comp. J.S.T. Thompson. 1st ed. lists 23 libraries, 2nd ed. lists 22, but omits Fourah Bay College which was one of five libraries not returning the questionnaire.

BIOGRAPHICAL SOURCES

1079 (*also entered at* 885)
Encyclopedia Africana Dictionary of African Biography. Vol. 2, Sierra Leone and Zaire. Algonac, MI, Reference Publications, 1979. 372pp.

Sierra Leone section pp. 35-178, ed. by U. Flett. 137 biographies of Africans and Europeans, many with portraits and lists of sources; also "concise guide to Sierra Leone names and terms" and 4 maps. For the encyclopedia, *see* 31; for the dictionary of biography, *see* 299.

1080
Who's who in Sierra Leone. [Freetown, Lyns Publicity, 1980]. 56pp.

Ed. M.R. Johnson. Some 180 entries.

See also 1073, 1074.

ATLASES & GAZETTEERS

Atlases

1081
Sierra Leone. Survey and Lands Department. **Atlas of Sierra Leone.** Freetown, 1953. 6pp. text. 16pp. col. maps. 40 x 27cm.

- - 2nd ed. Freetown, 1966. iv, 16pp.

Includes 16 coloured thematic maps. at 1:1M/1:3M, and 4 plans of Freetown, Bonthe, Magburaka and Bo at 1:15,000. Index gazetteer.

1082
Clarke, J.I. **Sierra Leone in maps.** London, University of London Press, 1966. 120pp.

- - 2nd ed. London, 1969. 120pp.

Includes 51 black and white maps, mostly at 1:30M with facing text. Compiled by 14 past and present members of the staff at Fourah Bay College, with maps drawn in the Geography Department of the College. The first volume in what later became a significant series covering several African countries. Review of 1st ed., *GJ*, 132, 1966, 583.

Gazetteers

1083
Gazetteer of place names in and adjacent to the Colony of Sierra Leone. London, Waterlow & Sons, 1889. 51pp.

1084
U.S. Board on Geographic Names. **Sierra Leone: official standard names approved by the U.S.B.G.N.** Washington, DC, 1966. (Gazetteer, 101). ii, 125pp.

Includes 8,800 names from 1:250,000 map series. Revision of appropriate sections of **West Africa** (*see* 913).

- - **Gazetteer supplement: Africa and South-West Asia.** Washington, DC, 1972. (p. 133, Sierra Leone).

LIBERIA

HANDBOOKS

1085
G.B. War Office. General Staff. **Military report on the Republic of Liberia**. London, 1905. (A. 1025). viii, 43pp. map in pocket.

Comp. C.C. Bigham and Sir E. Grogan. Standard War Office survey.

1086
Johnston, *Sir* H.H. **Liberia**. London, Hutchinson, 1906. 2 vols. 454 illus. 22 maps.

Vol. 1 covers history and geography, vol. 2, flora and fauna, anthropology and languages. Massively detailed account.

1087
G.B. Foreign Office. Historical Section. **Liberia**. London, 1920. (F.O. Handbook, 130). 65pp.
Also pub. in. F.O. **Peace handbooks**, vol. 20. London, 1920.

1088
Querengaesser, F.A. **Liberia**. Bonn, Schroeder for Deutsche Afrika-Gesellschaft, 1965. (Die Länder Afrikas, 24). 162pp. illus. maps.

1089
Area handbook for Liberia, comp. T.D. Roberts, *et al*. Washington, DC, U.S. Department of Defense, 1964. xiii, 419pp. maps.

- - 2nd ed. comp. T.D. Roberts, *et al*. Washington, DC, 1972. xlviii, 388pp. maps.

- - 3rd ed. **Liberia: a country study**, comp. H.D. Nelson, *et al*. Washington, DC, 1984, 340pp. illus. maps.

1090
Liberia. Ministry of Information, Cultural Affairs and Tourism. Overseas Press Bureau. **Facts about Liberia**. Monrovia, 1964.

- - rev. ed. Monrovia, 1973. vi, 110pp.

"Aim ... is to supply basic information on contemporary Liberia for the benefit of the general public" (preface). Brief data arranged under some 60 headings.

1091

Holsoe, S.E. **A standardization of Liberian ethnic nomenclature.** Philadelphia, Institute for Liberian Studies, 1979. ii, 28pp.

List agreed upon by a group of American scholars meeting at the Peabody Museum. Includes lists of alternative names.

1092

Dunn, D.E. & Holsoe, S.E. **Historical dictionary of Liberia.** Metuchen, NJ, Scarecrow Press, 1985. (African historical dictionaries, 38). 274pp.

Includes bibliography of 782 titles. All dictionary entries include refs. to sources. Reviews, *IJAHS*, 19, 1986, 573-575; *JAH* 28, 1987, 468-469 ("far more scholarly than most of the other Scarecrow volumes").

See also 1102.

YEARBOOKS

1093

Twentieth century calendar and handbook of Liberia 1904/05 [etc.]. Liverpool, J.A. Thompson, 1903-?. Annual. (5th issue 1908/09).

1094

The Liberian yearbook. London/Monrovia, "Liberian review", 1956-1962. 2 issues.

Ed. H.B. Cole. "Not officially pub. ... but the contributions are confirmed by government officials as being accurate". Includes historical background and details on contemporary politics, commerce and industry. Numerous statistics. A particularly detailed and well set out example of its kind.

1095

Handbook and directory of Liberia. Monrovia, Chamber of Commerce, 1963. 132pp.

1096

Directory with who's who in Liberia, 1970/71. Monrovia, A & A Enterprises, 1971. 340pp.

Ed. J. Adighibe. Cover title : "A & A directory and who's who".

1097
Liberia. Ministry of Commerce, Industry & Transportation. **Liberian trade directory.** Monrovia, ?1974- . Irreg.

Issues for 1974, 1975/76, 1979/80.

STATISTICS

1098
Statistik des Auslandes: Länderberichte: Liberia. Wiesbaden, Statistisches Bundesamt, 1961- .

Issues for 1961, 1973, 1985, 1987.

1099
Liberia. Bureau of Statistics. **Economic survey of Liberia.** Monrovia, 1967- . Annual.

Pt. 1, "General survey of the economy"; pt. 2, "Statistical abstract".

1100
Liberia. Bureau of Statistics. **Quarterly statistical bulletin of Liberia.** Monrovia, 1970- .

Title varies : **Statistical bulletin of Liberia** (1986- . 2 issues p.a.)

BIOGRAPHICAL SOURCES

See 1096.

ATLASES & GAZETTEERS

Atlases

1101
Gnielinski, S. van. **Liberia in maps.** London, University of London Press, 1972. 112pp.

50 black and white maps with text on facing page.

1102
Liberia. Ministry of Planning and Economic Affairs & Deutsche Gesellschaft für Technische Zusammenarbeit. **Republic of Liberia planning and development atlas.** Monrovia, 1983. 74, 67pp.

First section contains 37 maps at 1:1M with facing text including notes on utilization of the information, and three transparent overlays (2 showing population density, 1 for transport). Second section is a "Handbook" of 67pp. with detailed information and statistics on a wide range of themes: natural resources, the economy, administration, agriculture, trade, etc; a virtual encyclopedia.

Gazetteers

1103
U.S. Board on Geographic Names. **Liberia: official standard names approved by the U.S.B.G.N.** Washington, DC, 1968. (Gazetteer, 106). iii, 61pp.

Revision of appropriate sections of **West Africa** (*see* 913).

 - - 2nd ed. Washington, DC, 1976. 167pp.

2nd ed. includes 10,600 names from maps at 1:250,000.

St. HELENA

HANDBOOKS

1104
G.B. War Office. General Staff. **Military report and general information concerning the Colony of St. Helena.** London, 1904. (A. 925). vi, 36pp. map.

Covers topography, inhabitants, climate, communications, history, trade and administration. Map at 1:25,000. There are references to an earlier War Office **Précis ...** relating to St. Helena pub. 1877, but no copy has been traced.

YEARBOOKS

1105
G.B. Colonial Office. **[Annual reports]: St Helena, 1845-1973.** London, 1846-1976.

As **Reports: the past and present state of HM colonial possessions,** 1845-1886 (not pub. 1852, 1874, 1883), **Report on the Blue Book, St Helena,** 1887-1889, **Annual report for St Helena,** 1890-1919 (all as Command papers); **Colonial Office annual report,** 1920-73 (not pub. 1939-46). From 1950-1951 pub. biennially, with 1970-73 covered in one report. No full report for 1861, 1863-68. Report for 1964 & 1965 issued by Commonwealth Office. From 1966 issued by Foreign and Commonwealth Office. *For fuller details see Appendix.*

1106
St. Helena almanac and annual register. St. Helena, 1847. (Gregory).

ATLASES & GAZETTEERS

Gazetteers

1107
U.S. Board on Geographic Names. **South Atlantic: official names approved by the U.S.B.G.N.** Washington, DC, 1957. (Gazetteer, 31). 53pp.

Includes St. Helena (650 names), Ascension Island, Tristan da Cunha, the Falklands and Antarctic Islands.

FRANCOPHONE WEST AFRICA

HANDBOOKS

1108

G.B. War Office. Intelligence Department. **Military report on the French West African colonies of Senegal, Guinea, Ivory Coast and Dahome.** London, 1903. (A. 831). xv, 181pp. 2 maps in pocket.

Separate sections for each territory covering topography, communications, resources and peoples.

- - **Addenda.** London, 1904 (A 937). iv, 118pp.

Comp. A. Lynden Bell. Covers 15 land routes, the Senegal-Niger railway and Niger navigation.

1109

G.B. Foreign Office. Historical Section. **French West Africa.** London, 1920. (F.O. Handbook, 100). 21pp.
Also pub. in F.O. **Peace handbooks,** vol. 17. London, 1920.

Very brief generalised information covering only developments post 1895, intended as an introduction to the more detailed regional vols. (for which *see below*).

1110

Guy, C. **L'Afrique occidentale française.** Paris, Larose, 1929. (Collections "France d'outre-mer"). xii, 208pp.

Author was "Gouverneur honoraire des colonies". Sections for geography, ethnography, history, communications and the economy.

1111

Chazelas, V. **Térritoires africains sous mandat de la France: Cameroun et Togo.** Paris, Société d'éditions géographiques, maritimes et coloniales, 1931. (Exposition coloniale internationale de Paris). 240pp. illus. maps.

Covers history, peoples, administration, natural resources, agriculture, trade, and communications. Cameroon, pp. 17-82 and 126-182; Togo, pp. 83-124 and 183-240.

1112
Delavignette, R. **Afrique occidentale française**. Paris, Société d'éditions géographiques, maritimes et coloniales, 1931. (Exposition coloniale internationale de Paris). vi, 244pp. illus. maps.

A general overview with emphasis on topography, history and ethnography. Less factual and statistical than the companion volume by Chazelas (*see* 1111), since this approach was provided for by the individual volumes for each country of French West Africa compiled for the exposition (*see below* under each country).

1113
G.B. Admiralty. Naval Intelligence Division. **French West Africa**. London, 1943-1944. (Geographical handbook series, B.R. 512, B.R. 512ª). 2 vols. 211 illus. 141 maps.

Vol. 1, The federation; vol. 2, The colonies with separate treatment for each, including Togo. Detailed, wide-ranging coverage.

1114
Spitz, G. **L'Ouest africain français: A.O.F. et Togo**. Paris, Société d'éditions géographiques, maritimes et coloniales, 1947. (Terres lointaines, 2). 508pp.

Author was a colonial governor in West Africa. Pp. 17-422, A.O.F.; pp. 423-484, Togo. Detailed accounts of topography, peoples, history, administration, natural resources, agriculture, industry and commerce. Bibliography and 5 page list of maps.

1115
Afrique occidentale française: l'encyclopédie coloniale et maritime (Encyclopédie de l'empire français). Paris, Encyclopédie coloniale et maritime, 1949. 2 vols.

"Sous la direction d'Eugène Guernier" with over 50 named contributors.. Vol. 1, ix, 390, iiipp. 178 photos. 34 maps. 34 diagrs. "L'histoire et la géographie; la structure politique et administrative; économique"; vol. 2, ii, 400, xpp. 244 photos. 24 maps. 17 diagrs. "Économique (contd.); l'équipment; tourisme et chasse; les arts et les lettres". Index to whole work. Detailed scholarly coverage. For information on the encyclopaedia as a whole, *see* 35.

1116
Richard-Molard, J. **Afrique occidentale française**. Paris, Berger-Levrault, 1949. (L'Union française). xiv, 239pp. illus.

- - 3rd ed. Paris, 1956. 252pp. illus.

Author was head of Section géographique at IFAN. A general survey with sections for geography, peoples, history and the economy.

1117
Cameroun, Togo: encyclopédie de l'afrique française (Encyclopédie coloniale et maritime). Paris, Éditions de l'Union française, 1951. iii, 572, ixpp. 420 photos. 48 maps. 44 diagrs.

"Sous la direction d'Eugène Guernier, avec la participation de René Briat". Pp. 1-388, Cameroun; pp. 389-572, Togo, each following the same sequence of "Le cadre naturel, historique et humain; la structure politique et administrative; le progrès social; le progrès economique; l'équipment; tourisme, chasse, folklore; l'oeuvre des missions". The detailed coverage provided by all vols. of this encyclopaedia (*see* 35).

1118
De Lavergne de Tressan, M. **Inventaire linguistique de l'Afrique occidentale française et du Togo.** Dakar, Institut français de l'Afrique noire, 1953. (Mémoires de l'IFAN, 30). 241pp. map.

Classification of languages together with estimates of numbers of speakers and their locations. Includes some account of neighbouring Anglophone and Lusophone areas. Review, *Africa*, 25, 1955, 190-191.

1119
Afrique occidentale francaise [et le] Togo. Paris, Hachette, 1958. (Les guides bleus). ccxliv, 542pp. illus. maps.

Includes detailed essays on geography, economy, history etc. by scholars under the direction of Professor Monod of IFAN, followed by sections on each country and settlement.

- - Paris, 1968. Reprint of the 1958 edition with a 32pp. supplement of updated information.

1120
Reichhold, W. **Französisch-Westafrika.** Bonn, Schroeder for Deutsche Afrika-Gesellschaft, 1958. (Die Länder Afrikas, 7). 80pp.

Provides a general survey to complement the various volumes in the series which cover individual countries.

YEARBOOKS

1121
Annuaire du Sénégal et dépendances, St. Louis, 1858-1902. Annual.

continued by:

A.O.F. **Annuaire du gouvernement général de l'Afrique occidentale française**. St. Louis/Dakar, 1903-1922. Annual (irreg.)

Covers general colonial agencies, then colony by colony account with notes on history, administration, communications, and including statistics and a civil list

1122
Guid'Afrique occidental français. Dakar, Agence Havas & Agence distribution de Presse/Paris, Diloutremer, 1948- . Annual.

Title varies; **Guid'Ouest africain** (1958/59-). 26th ed. 1971/72. Excludes Cameroon for which see **Guid' Cameroun** (1175). Separate sections for each country. Includes political, historical and administrative information, together with lists of societies and universities and a commercial directory. Numerous maps and town plans.

1123
Annuaire des républiques de l'Ouest africain. Paris, Diloutremer, 1960- . Annual.

Excludes Cameroon and Togo.

STATISTICS

1124
A.O.F. **Situation générale**. Dakar, 1907-1910. Annual.

Title varies: **Statistiques générales** (1910).

1125
A.O.F. Service de la statistique générale. **Annuaire statistique de l'Afrique occidentale française, 1933/34 [etc.]**. Dakar, 1936-1957. 6 issues.

Issue 1, 1936; 2, 1937; 3, 1939; 4, 1949-51; 5, 1955; 6, 1957.

1126

A.O.F. Haut Commission pour l'A.O.F. **Bulletin de la statistique générale de l'Afrique occidentale française**. Dakar, 1946-1956. 6 p.a.

From 1956 merged with 1127 (*see below*).

1127

A.O.F. Service de la statistique générale [etc.]. **Bulletin mensuel de statistiques**. Dakar, 1949-1960.

Title and name of issuing agency vary: **Bulletin économique mensuel** (August 1949-April 1954); **Bulletin statistique et économique mensuel** (May 1954-June 1960). Issues for July 1959-June 1960 pub. by Service fédéral de la statistique, Fédération du Mali. Continued by **Bulletin statistique et économique mensuel** issued by Service de la statistique, Sénégal (*see* 1272).

1128

A.O.F. Service de la statistique générale [etc.]. **Bulletin statistique trimestriel/bimestriel**. St. Louis, 1953-1960. Quarterly/6 p.a.

Vol. for 1959 issued by Service fédéral de la statistique générale, Fédération du Mali et République du Sénégal. Vol. for 1960 issued by Ministère du Développement, Sénégal. After 1960 merged into **Bulletin statistique et économique mensuel** issued by Service de la Statistique, Sénégal (*see* 1272).

1129

Banque centrale des états de l'Afrique de l'ouest. **Notes d'information et statistiques**. Dakar, 1956- . Monthly.

Each issue highlights two member countries and includes detailed economic statistics.

1130

L'économie des pays du Sahel. Paris, Ediafric-La documentation africaine, 1976- . Irreg.

Covers Chad, Mali, Mauritania, Niger, Senegal, Upper Volta.

DIRECTORIES OF ORGANIZATIONS

1131

Conseil de l'Entente. Programme d'assistance aux entreprises africaines.

Répertoire des centres de documentation et bibliothèques: Bénin, Côte d'Ivoire, Haute-Volta, Niger, Togo. Abidjan, 1980. 257pp.

BIOGRAPHICAL SOURCES

1132
Personnalités publiques de l'Afrique de l'ouest 1968. Paris, Ediafric-La documentation africaine, 1969. 299pp.

- - 2nd ed. ... **1969.** Paris, 1970. 428pp.

- - 3rd ed. ... **1971.** Paris, 1971. 428pp.

Issued as special numbers of *Bulletin de l'Afrique noire*. Each ed. contains some 2,500/3,000 brief biographies covering Francophone countries (excluding Cameroon).

ATLASES & GAZETTEERS

Atlases

1133
A.O.F. Service géographique. **Atlas des cartes ethnographiques et administratives des différentes colonies du gouvernement général.** Paris, E. Larose, 1911. 2pp. 7 col. maps. 38 x 28 cm.

- - 2nd ed. **Atlas des cartes administratives et ethnographiques des colonies de l'A.O.F.** Paris, M. Forest, 1922. 4pp. 9 col. maps. 38 x 28 cm.

- - 3rd ed. **Petit atlas administratif, ethnographique et économique de l'A.O.F.** Paris, Girard, 1928. 10pp. 17 col. maps. 38 x 28 cm.

3rd ed. compiled at Dakar under direction of E. de Martonne.

1134
A.O.F. Service géographique. **Atlas des cercles de l'Afrique occidentale française.** Paris, M. Forest, 1924-1926. 8 parts in 1 vol. col. maps. 50 x 36 cm.

Compiled at Dakar under the direction of E. de Martonne. 114 maps numbered 1-49, 51-115, at 1:1M or 1:500,000. Part 1, Côte d'Ivoire, maps 1-19; part 2, Dahomey, maps 20-31; part 3, Guinée française, maps 32-49; part 4,

Haute-Volte, maps 51-61; part 5, Mauretanie, maps 62-69; part 6, Niger, maps 70-79; part 7, Sénégal, maps 80-94; part 8, Soudan français, maps 95-115.

Gazetteers

1135

Flutre, L.-F. **Pour une étude de la toponymie de l'A.O.F.** Dakar, Institut français de l'Afrique noire, 1957. (Publications de la section de langues et littéraires, 1). 188pp.

Discusses general problems of the region's toponymy, examines sources available and looks at the characteristics of place-names of European, Arab, Berber and African origin.

See also 913.

BENIN

HANDBOOKS

1136
G.B. Foreign Office. Historical Section. **Dahomey**. London, 1920. (F.O. Handbook, 105). 42pp.
Also pub. in F.O. **Peace handbooks**, vol. 17. London, 1920.

1137
Le Dahomey. Paris, Société d'éditions géographiques, maritimes et coloniales, 1931. (Exposition coloniale internationale de Paris). iii, 151pp. illus. maps.

Prepared by the Government of A.O.F. Covers history, geography, peoples, politics and administration, the economy and communications.

1138
Akindele, A. & Aguessy, C. **Le Dahomey**. Paris, Société d'éditions géographiques, maritimes et coloniales, 1955. (Pays africain, 6). 126pp. illus. maps.

1139
France. Direction de la documentation. **La République du Dahomey**. Paris, 1966. (*Notes et études documentaires*, 3307, 8 July 1966). 41pp.

1140
Zimmer, B. **Dahomey**. Bonn, Schroeder for Deutsche Afrika-Gesellschaft, 1969. (Die Länder Afrikas, 39). 94pp.

1141
Decalo, S. **Historical dictionary of Dahomey (People's Republic of Benin)**. Metuchen, NJ, Scarecrow Press, 1976. (African historical dictionaries, 7). 201pp.

- - 2nd ed. **Historical dictionary of Benin**. Metuchen, NJ, 1987. xxix, 349pp.

2nd ed. contains extensive bibliography (pp. 229-349).

1142
Ceccaldi, P. **Essai de nomenclature des populations, langues et dialectes de la République populaire du Bénin**. Paris, École des hautes études en sciences sociales, Centre d'études africaines, CARDAN, 1979. 2 vols. (328pp.)

Reproduces the card file of peoples and languages maintained at CARDAN, including details of relationships of each group or language to others, references from alternative name forms, geographical locations and numbers of population/speakers, and bibliographical sources.

STATISTICS

1143
Dahomey. Service de la statistique générale. **Bulletin statistique du Dahomey.** Cotonou, 1953-1960. Monthly (irreg.)

continued by:

Dahomey. Direction des affaires économiques. **Bulletin économique et statistique.** Cotonou, 1960-1965. Irreg.

continued by:

Dahomey/Benin. Institut national de la statistique et de l'analyse économique [etc.]. **Bulletin de statistique.** Cotonou, 1966- . Irreg.

1144
Dahomey/Benin. Institut national de la statistique et de l'analyse économique [etc.]. **Annuaire statistique.** Cotonou, 1965- . Annual (irreg.)

Issue 7, 1987.

1145
Statistik des Auslandes: Länderberichte: Benin. Wiesbaden, Statistisches Bundesamt, 1984- . irreg.

Issues for 1984, 1986, 1988, 1990.

BIOGRAPHICAL SOURCES

1146
Institut de recherche appliqué du Dahomey (IRAD). **Dictionnaire bio-bibliographique du Dahomey.** Porto-Novo, 1969. 183pp.

ATLASES & GAZETTEERS

Gazetteers

1147
U.S. Board on Geographic Names. **Dahomey: official standard names approved by the U.S.B.G.N.** Washington, DC, 1965. (Gazetteer, 91). iv, 89pp.

Includes 6,250 names from 1:200,000 map series. Revision of appropriate sections of **West Africa** (*see* 913).

- - **Gazetteer supplement: Africa and South-West Asia.** Washington, DC, 1972. (pp. 47-48, Dahomey).

BURKINA FASO

HANDBOOKS

1148

La Haute-Volta. Paris, Société d'éditions géographiques, maritimes et coloniales, 1931. (Exposition coloniale internationale de Paris). iv, 170pp. illus. maps.

Prepared by the Government of A.O.F. Covers history, geography, ethnography, the economy, communications, administration.

1149

France. Direction de la documentation. **La République de Haute-Volta**. Paris, 1960. (*Notes et études documentaires*, 2693, 19 Aug. 1960). 64pp.

1150

Fischer, W. **Ober-Volta**. Bonn, Schroeder for Deutsche Afrika-Gesellschaft, 1962. (Die Länder Afrikas, 26). 142pp. illus. map.

1151

McFarland, D.M. **Historical dictionary of Upper Volta**. Metuchen, NJ, Scarecrow Press, 1978. (African historical dictionaries, 14). 239pp.

Review, *IJAHS*, 11, 1978, 560-561 ("only reference work currently available in English").

1152

Tiendrebeogo, G. **Langues et groupes ethniques de Haute-Volta**. Abidjan, Agence de co-operation culturelle et technique (ACCT) & Institut de linguistique appliqué, 1983. (Atlas et études sociolinguistiques des états du conseil de l'entente). iii, 64pp.

Lists peoples and languages with references to their associated groups, and notes on location and numbers of speakers.

YEARBOOKS

1153
Répertoire national de Haute Volta. Paris, Marcomer, 1963- .

Includes lists of the administration, of major official and private organizations and biographical section (1963 ed. has some 350 brief biogs.)

STATISTICS

1154
Upper Volta. Institut national de la statistique et de la démographie [etc.]. **Bulletin mensuel de statistique** [etc.]. Ouagadougou, 1960- . Monthly (irreg.).

Not pub. 1965-1968. Recommences n.s. vol. 9, 1969- as **Bulletin mensuel d'information statistique et économique**. N.s., 1985- .

1155
Upper Volta. Institut national de la statistique et de la démographie [etc.]. **Bulletin annuaire d'information statistique et économique** [etc.]. Ouagadougou, 1959-1983. Annual.

Pub. as supplement to **Bulletin mensuel** (*above*), sometimes separately, sometimes in last monthly issue for the year. Title varies frequently: **Bulletin annuaire statistique et économique/ Bulletin mensuel ... ; supplément/ Bulletin annuaire de statistique**.

continued by:

Burkina Faso. Institut national de la statistique et de la démographie. **Annuaire statistique du Burkina Faso**. Ouagadougou, 1984- . Annual.

1156
L'économie voltaïque. Paris, Ediafric-La documentation africaine, 1971- . Annual.

Issue for 1971. Largely statistical tables.

1157
Statistik des Auslandes: Länderberichte: Upper Volta/Burkina Faso. Wiesbaden, Statistisches Bundesamt, 1962- . Irreg.

Issues for 1962, 1984, 1988.

BIOGRAPHICAL SOURCES

See 1153.

ATLASES & GAZETTEERS

Atlases

1158
Upper Volta. Centre nationale de la recherche scientifique et technologie (*later* Centre voltaïque de la recherche scientifique). **Atlas de Haute Volta.** Ouagadougou, 1968- .

Issued in parts, text plus maps. "Very incomplete" (Barry & Perkins).

1159
Atlas de la Haute-Volta. Paris, "Jeune Afrique", 1975. 48pp. col. maps.

Comp. Y. Péron and V. Zalacain. 15 thematic maps with text.

Gazetteers

1160
U.S. Board on Geographic Names. **Upper Volta: official standard names approved by the U.S.B.G.N.** Washington, DC, 1965. (Gazetteer, 87). iii, 168pp.

Includes 11,900 names from 1:200,000 map series. Revision of appropriate sections of **West Africa** (*see* 913).

- - **Gazetteer supplement: Africa and South-West Asia.** Washington, DC, 1972. (pp. 181-182, Upper Volta).

CAMEROON

See also sections relating to Former German Africa in the section for Africa in general above, and note that many French language reference sources choose to treat Cameroon as a part of Central Africa, and will be listed above under Central Africa : Francophone.

HANDBOOKS

1161
G.B. War Office. Intelligence Division. **Military report on the Kameruns and Togo**. London, 1903. (A. 835). viii, 79pp. map in pocket.

Comp. by D.J.M. Fasson. Pp. 1-30, Kameruns; pp. 33-79, Togo.

1162
G.B. War Office. **Military report on the Cameroons (Kamerun)**. London, 1908. (A. 1256). vii, 123pp. 3 maps in pocket.

Comp. Maj. D'A. Legand. Rev. ed. of relevant section of 1903 vol. above. Maps include one at 1:15,840 of Douala.

1163
G.B. Foreign Office. Historical Section. **Cameroon**. London, 1920. (F.O. Handbook, 111). 83pp.
Also pub. in F.O. **Peace Handbooks**, vol. 17. London, 1920.

1164
Lembezat, B. **Le Cameroun**. 3rd ed. Paris, Éditions maritimes et coloniales, 1954. (Terres lointaines, 1²). 208pp. illus. map.

Eds. 1 and 2 published as **La France équatoriale** (*see* 759).

1165
Weiler, C. **Kamerun**. Bonn, Schroeder for Deutsche Afrika-Gesellschaft, 1958. (Die Länder Afrikas, 9). 120pp.

- - 2nd ed. Schramm, J. **Kamerun**. Bonn, 1964. 132pp.

- - 3rd ed. Bonn, 1970. 174pp.

1166

France. Direction de la documentation. **La République du Cameroun**. Paris, 1961. (*Notes et études documentaires*, 2741, 16 Jan 1961). 56pp.

1167

Cameroon. Ministry of Information & Tourism. **Cameroon**. Yaoundé, The Ministry/ Paris, Presse Africaine Associée, 1970. 189pp.

A general popular survey.

1168

Area handbook for the United Republic of Cameroon, comp. H.D. Nelson *et al.* Washington, DC, U.S. Department of Defense, 1974. xiv, 335pp. maps.

1169

LeVine, V.T. & Nye, R.P. **Historical dictionary of Cameroon**. Metuchen, NJ, Scarecrow Press, 1974. (African historical dictionaries, 1). 210pp.

- - 2nd ed. **Historical dictionary of the Republic of the Cameroon**, comp. M.W. DeLancey & N.M. Mokeba. Metuchen, NJ, 1990. (African historical dictionaries, 48). xxii, 297pp.

1170

L'encyclopédie de la République unie du Cameroun. Abidjan, etc., Nouvelles éditions africaines, 1981. 4 vols.

Vol. 1 covers topography and ethnography; vol. 2, history and administration; vol. 3, the economy; vol.4, social life.

1171

Fonkoué, J. **Essai de nomenclature des populations et de langues du Cameroun**. Paris, École de hautes études en sciences sociales & Centre d'études africaines, CARDAN, 1981. 2 vols. (viii, 243pp). maps.

Reproduces card files maintained at CARDAN arranged by preferred name of ethnic group or language, with references from other forms, and notes on location and numbers.

See also 755, 758, 762, 1111, 1117.

YEARBOOKS

1172
G.B. Colonial Office. **[Annual reports]: Cameroons, c.1917/21-1959.** London, 1922-1961.

As **Reports to the Council of the League of Nations on the British sphere,** c.1917/21, (Cmd.1647); **Reports on the British sphere, 1922, Report on the administration of the British Cameroons ...to the Council of the League of Nations,** [title varies], 1923-38, (not issued 1939-46), **Report ... to the Trusteeship Council of the UN, 1947; Report to the General Assembly of the UN, 1948-59,** (in Colonial series). *For fuller details see Appendix.*

1173
France. **Rapport du gouvernement français ... sur l'administration du Cameroun placé sous la tutelle de la France, 1920/21 [etc.].** Paris, 1922-1957. Annual.

Not pub. 1938-46. Presented initially to the League of Nations, then post 1946 to the Trusteeship Council of the United Nations. Detailed and well illustrated. Includes "Annexe statistique".

1174
Annuaire du Cameroun. Douala, Agence africaine de publicité, 1952- . Annual.

Very detailed (large format, double column) compendium of historical, topographical, administrative and economic information, including commercial directory.

1175
Guid' Cameroun. Paris, Diloutremer, 1959-1964. Irreg. 3 issues.

Issues for 1959, 1961, 1964; coverage of Cameroon then moves to the same publisher's **Guid' Afrique équatoriale** (*see* 766). Lists of government departments and other institutions and a commercial directory.

1176
Cameroon. Ministère de l'Information. **Annuaire national/National year book.** Douala, 1963- . Annual (irreg.)

Directory of the administration and of commercial organizations, with some historical background.

1177

Cameroon year book, Limbe, Gwellem Publications, 1973- . Annual.

1985/86 ed. 270pp. Largely biographical: c. 250 lengthy biogs.

See also 767.

STATISTICS

1178

Morel, Y. **Tables économiques du Cameroun**. Douala, Collège Libermann, 1978. 232pp.

147 tables of statistics, covering human resources, trade, communications, finance etc.

Bulletins

1179

French Cameroon. Service de la statistique générale. **Bulletin de la statistique générale**. Yaoundé, 1950-1962. Monthly. Vols. 1-12.

continued by:

Cameroon. Direction de la statistique. **Résumé des statistiques du Cameroun oriental**. Yaoundé, 1963-1967. Monthly. Vols. 1-5

continued by:

Bulletin mensuel de statistique. Yaoundé, 1968- . Monthly.

1180

Cameroon. Direction de la Statistique [etc.]. **Note trimestrielle sur la situation économique du Cameroun**. Yaoundé, 1964-1973. Quarterly.

Title varies: **Note trimestrielle de statistique**.

1181

West Cameroon. Department of Statistics. **Monthly digest of statistics: West Cameroon**. Buea, 1965-?1972.

During the existence of the Cameroon Federal Republic (1961-1972), separate statistical series were issued for West Cameroon (the former Southern Cameroons of the British mandate): *see also* 1182.

Yearbooks

1182
France. Service coloniale des statistiques/Cameroon. Service de la statistique générale. **Annuaire statistique du Cameroun.** Paris/Yaoundé, 1947-1959. 2 issues.

Issues for 1938/45 (1947), 1946/57 (1959).

1183
Statistik des Auslandes: Länderberichte: Kamerun. Wiesbaden, Statistisches Bundesamt, 1961- . irreg.

Issues for 1961, 1968, 1977, 1982, 1985, 1987.

1184
West Cameroon. Department of Statistics. **West Cameroon digest of statistics/Résumé des statistiques du Cameroun occidental.** Buea, 1962-1965. Annual.

Issues for 1955/62-1964/65.

continued by:

Statistics annual report of West Cameroon/Annuaire statistique du Cameroun occidental, 1965/66 [-1968/69]. Buea, 1967-1969. Annual. 2 issues.

Issues for 1965/66-1966/67 (1967), 1968/69 (1969).

1185
Cameroon. Direction de la statistique [etc.]. **Note annuelle de statistique.** Yaoundé, 1964- . Annual.

Abridged version published as **Le Cameroun en chiffres.**

1186
L'économie camerounaise. Paris, Ediafric-La documentation africaine, 1971- . Irreg.

Issues for 1971, 1977, 1984 (5th ed). Largely statistical.

See also 1174.

DIRECTORIES OF ORGANIZATIONS

1187
Chateh, P. **Guide des bibliothèques et centres de documentation de Yaoundé.** Yaoundé, Université de Yaoundé, Service centrale de bibliothèques, 1973. (Collection études et recherches en bibliothéconomie, 1). 26pp.

See also 752.

BIOGRAPHICAL SOURCES

1188
Les élites camerounaises. Paris, Ediafric-La documentation africaine, 1976. xxxi, 233pp.

- - 2nd ed. Paris, 1980. iv, 254pp.

Over 1,700 brief biographies.

1189
Baratte-eno Belinga, T. **Écrivains, cinéastes et artistes camerounais: bio-bibliographie.** Yaoundé, Cameroun, Ministère de l'information et de la culture, 1978. 217pp.

93 entries.

See also 771, 1177.

ATLASES & GAZETTEERS

Atlases

1190
Cameroon. Haut Commissaire de la République française au Cameroun. **Atlas du Cameroun.** Paris, Editions SELPA, [1946-1948]. 20pp. text + 8 folding col. maps. 33 x 25cm.

Maps comp. J.H. Calsat. Most at 1:3M.

1191
Cameroon. Institut de recherches scientifiques. **Atlas du Cameroun**. Yaoundé, 1956-1975?

Issued as separate plates, 72 x 94cm or 72 x 47cm with accompanying text, and a slip-case (36 x 47cm). Plate 1, 1956. Géologie, 2 sheets, 10pp.; plate 2 (? *not published*); plates 3 & 4, n.d. Climatologie, 4 pp; plate 5, n.d. Fleuves et rivières, 7pp; plate 6, 1957. Les sols, 6pp; plate 7, 1958. Phytogéographie, 6pp; plate 8, 1969. Éléments de Géophysique, 3pp; plate 9, n.d. Faits d'intêret medical, 3pp; plate 10 (? *not published*); plates 11 & 12, 1971-73. Demographie, 3 sheets, 10pp; plate 13, 1973. Activités de production etc., 6pp; plate 14, 1972. Les industries, 2 sheets; plate 15, 1975. Énergie électrique etc.; plate 16, 1975. Les exploitations forestières, 3pp. text. Scales vary: majority at 1:2M.

1192
Office de la recherche scientifique et technique outre-mer (ORSTOM) de Yaoundé. **Atlas régional de la République Cameroun**. Yaoundé/Paris, 1965-1974. 5 vols.

Atlas régional sud ouest, 2 vols; ... Mandara-Lozore, 1 vol; ... Région ouest, 2 vols.

1193
Atlas de la République Unie du Cameroun. Paris, "Jeune Afrique", 1979. 72pp. col. maps.

- - English. trans. **Atlas of the United Republic of Cameroon**. Paris, 1980. 72pp.

Comp. G. Laclavère. 20 thematic maps with text.

Gazetteers

1194
U.S. Board on Geographic Names. **Cameroon: official standard names approved by the U.S.B.G.N.** Washington, DC, 1962. (Gazetteer, 60). 255pp.

Includes 18,000 names from maps at 1:200,000. Revision of sections for "French Cameroons" in **Equatorial Africa ...** (*see* 773) and for "British Cameroons" in **West Africa** (*see* 913).

1195
Office de la recherche scientifique et technique (ORSTOM) de Yaoundé.

Répertoire géographique du Cameroun. Yaoundé, 1965- .

Issued in numbered fascs., 1-19, 1965-1970, thereafter un-numbered. Each fasc. is a "Dictionnaire des villages" of an administrative district. Based on 1:200,000 series. Each entry contains co-ordinates and brief descriptions: population totals, major ethnic groups, existence of churches, schools.

CÔTE D'IVOIRE

HANDBOOKS

1196
G.B. Foreign Office. Historical Section. **Ivory Coast**. London, 1920. (F.O. Handbook, 104). 39pp.
Also pub. in F.O. **Peace handbooks**, vol. 17. London, 1920.

1197
La Côte d'Ivoire. Paris, Société d'éditions géographiques, maritimes et coloniales, 1931. (Exposition coloniale internationale de Paris). iv, 134pp.

Prepared by government of A.O.F. Covers history, geography, ethnography, administration, the economy and communications.

1198
Avice, E. **La Côte d'Ivoire**. Paris, Société d'éditions géographiques, maritimes et coloniales, 1951. (Pays africains, 1). 96pp. illus. maps.

1199
Area handbook for the Ivory Coast. Washington, DC, U.S. Department of Defense, 1962. xii, 485pp.

- - 2nd ed. comp. T.D. Roberts *et al*. Washington, DC, 1973. lx, 449pp.

2nd ed. is a reprint of the 1st with addition of a 50 pp. "Survey of events, January 1963-December 1972" and a supplementary bibliography.

1200
Rayneaud, F. **Elfenbeinküste**. Bonn, Schroeder for Deutsche Afrika-Gesellschaft, 1962. (Die Länder Afrikas, 25). 164pp. illus. maps.

1201
France. Direction de la documentation. **La République de Côte d'Ivoire**. Paris, 1965. (*Notes et études documentaires*, 3308, 12 July 1966). 51pp.

- - [rev. ed.] Paris, 1973. (*Notes et études documentaires*, 3989/3990, 21 May 1973). 56pp.

1202
Côte d'Ivoire. Ministère d'Information. **Ivory Coast: facts and figures, 1966**.

Abidjan, 1966. 131pp.

Covers geography, history and economic and social life.

1203
Dictionnaire économique et politique de la Côte d'Ivoire. Paris, Ediafric-La documentation africaine, 1973. vii, 201pp.

Includes entries for persons, institutions, products, and services.

1204
Ceccaldi, P. **Essai de nomenclature des populations, langues et dialectes de Côte d'Ivoire**. Paris, École pratique des hauts études & Centre d'études africaines, CARDAN, 1974. 2 vols. (v, 145, 135, 34pp.)

Reproduces card file maintained at CARDAN of names with references from alternative forms, geographical location and population of each group and bibliographical sources.

1205
Le grand dictionnaire encyclopédique de la Côte d'Ivoire. Abidjan, Nouvelles éditions africaines, 1986- .

4 vols. pub. by 1991 (vol. 4, I-M, 1988). Ed. R. Borremans; title on spine "Dictionnaire Borremans". Large scale, lavish production with numerous illus. (many in colour) and maps. Mostly short entries for places, people, flora and fauna, including bibliographical references.

1206
Mundt, R.J. **Historical dictionary of the Ivory Coast (Côte d'Ivoire)**. Metuchen, NJ, Scarecrow Press, 1988. (African historical dictionaries, 41). xxvii, 246pp.

Concentrates on post 1945 period. The particularly detailed entries for ethnic groups and the bibliography of over 1,300 items are praised by *JAH* 30, 1989, 541, although *IJAHS* 22, 1989, 347-348 finds the bibliography lacking in balance.

YEARBOOKS

1207
Annuaire national de la Côte d'Ivoire. Abidjan, Annuaire National, 1964- .

Annual. Issue for 1973.

Includes civil list and professional and commercial directories.

STATISTICS

1208
Côte d'Ivoire. Direction de la statistique et des études économiques et démographiques. **Inventaire économique et social de la Côte d'Ivoire, 1947 à 1958**. Abidjan, 1960. 283pp.

Detailed statistical compilation.

Bulletins and yearbooks

1209
Côte d'Ivoire. Direction de la statistique [etc.]. **Bulletin statistique de la Côte d'Ivoire** [etc.]. Abidjan, 1948- . Monthly.

Title varies: **Bulletin statistique mensuel/Bulletin mensuel de statistique**.

1210
Côte d'Ivoire. Direction de la statistique et des études économiques. **Situation économique de la Côte d'Ivoire**. Abidjan, 1960-?1963. Annual.

1211
Statistik des Auslandes: Länderberichte: Côte d'Ivoire. Wiesbaden, Statistisches Bundesamt, 1962- . Irreg.

Issues for 1962, 1969, 1984, 1986, 1988.

1212
L'économie ivoirienne. Paris, Ediafric-La documentation africaine, 1970- irreg.

Issues for 1970, 1971, 1973, 1975, 1976, 1977. Largely statistical.

1213
Côte d'Ivoire. Direction de la statistique. **La Côte d'Ivoire en chiffres: annuaire statistique**. Abidjan, 1975- . Annual/ biennial.

Title varies: **Mémento chiffre de la Côte d'Ivoire** (1982/83-).

BIOGRAPHICAL SOURCES

1214
Les élites ivoiriennes. Paris, Ediafric-La documentation africaine, 1976. xv, 178pp.

- - 2nd ed. Paris, 1978. xxvi, 235pp.

- - 3rd ed. Paris, 1982. 209pp.

Each issue contains between 1,500 and 1,800 brief biographies.

1215
Bonneau, R. **Écrivains, cinéastes et artistes ivoiriens: aperçu bio-bibliographique.** Abidjan, Nouvelles éditions africaines, 1973. 176p.

Covers 71 living figures. Entries based upon interviews.

ATLASES & GAZETTEERS

Atlases

1216
ORSTOM, Ministère du Plans de Côte d'Ivoire & Université d'Abidjan. **Atlas de Côte d'Ivoire.** Bondy & Abidjan, 1971-1979. [141pp]. 57 x 42cm.

45 col. plates of thematic maps mostly at 1:2M, originally issued in 14 sections with accompanying text. Includes useful series of maps showing development of administrative sub-divisions, 1893-1976.

1217
Atlas de la Côte d'Ivoire. Paris, "Jeune Afrique", 1978. 72pp. col. maps.

- - 2nd ed. Paris, 1983. 72pp.

Comp. P. Vennetier & G. Laclavère. 20 thematic maps with text.

Gazetteers

1218
Côte d'Ivoire. Service de la statistique et de la mécanographie. **Répertoire des villages de la Côte d'Ivoire.** Abidjan, 1955. 2 vols. (477pp; 273pp.)

villages de la Côte d'Ivoire. Abidjan, 1955. 2 vols. (477pp; 273pp.)

1219
U.S. Board on Geographic Names. **Ivory Coast: official standard names approved by the U.S.B.G.N.** Washington, DC, 1965. (Gazetteer, 89). iv, 250pp.

Includes 17,700 names from maps at 1:200,000. Revision of appropriate sections of **West Africa** (*see* 913).

- - **Gazetteer supplement: Africa and South-West Asia.** Washington, DC, 1972. (pp. 93-99, Ivory Coast).

GUINEA

HANDBOOKS

1220

G.B. Foreign Office. Historical Section. **French Guinea**. London, 1920. (F.O. Handbook, 103). 65pp.

Also pub. in F.O. **Peace handbooks**, vol. 17. London, 1920.

1221

La Guinée. Paris, Société d'éditions géographiques, maritimes et coloniales, 1931. (Exposition coloniale internationale de Paris). iv, 143pp.

Prepared by government of A.O.F. Includes coverage of history, geography, ethnography, the economy, administration and communications.

1222

Houis, M. **La Guinée Française**. Paris, Société d'éditions géographiques, maritimes et coloniales, 1953. (Pays africain, 3). 94pp.

1223

Area handbook for Guinea, comp. G.L. Harris, *et al*. Washington, DC, U.S. Department of Defense, 1961. xii, 534pp. maps.

- - 2nd ed. comp. H.D. Nelson, *et al*. Washington, DC, 1975. xii, 386pp. maps.

1224

France. Direction de la documentation. **La République du Guinée**. Paris, 1965. (*Notes et études documentaires*, 3202, 21 June 1965). 42pp.

1225

Voss, J. **Guinea**. Bonn, Schroeder for Deutsche Afrika-Gesellschaft, 1968. (Die Länder Afrikas, 37). 252pp.

1226

O'Toole, T.E. **Historical dictionary of Guinea**. Metuchen, NJ, Scarecrow Press, 1978. (African historical dictionaries, 16). 183pp.

Review, *IJAHS*, 12, 1979, 728-729 ("a model for this series").

- - 2nd ed. **Historical dictionary of Guinea (Republic of Guinea/Conakry)**. Metuchen, NJ, 1987. xxv, 204pp.

Bibliography, pp. 125-204. Review, *IJAHS* 21, 1988, 722-724.

STATISTICS

1227
Guinea. Service de la statistique générale. **Bulletin statistique de la Guinée.** Conakry, 1955-1962. Monthly (irreg.)

Title varies: **Bulletin mensuel de la statistique** (1957-58).

continued by:

Bulletin spéciale de statistique. Conakry, 1962- . Quarterly.

1228
Statistik des Auslandes: Länderberichte: Guinea. Wiesbaden, Statistisches Bundesamt, 1961- . Irreg.

Issues for 1961, 1967, 1985, 1987, 1989.

ATLASES & GAZETTEERS

Gazetteers

1229
U.S. Board on Geographic Names. **Guinea: official standard names approved by the U.S.B.G.N.** Washington, DC, 1965. (Gazetteer, 90). iv, 175pp.

Includes 12,400 names from maps at 1:200,000. Revision of appropriate sections of **West Africa** (*see* 913).

- - **Gazetteer supplement: Africa and South-West Asia.** Washington, DC, 1972. (pp. 75-77, Guinea).

MALI

HANDBOOKS

1230

Le Soudan. Paris, Société d'éditions géographiques, maritimes et coloniales, 1931. (Exposition coloniale internationale de Paris). iii, 166pp. illus. maps.

Prepared by government of A.O.F. Covers history, geography, peoples, administration, the economy, communications.

1231

Spitz, G. **Le Soudan français**. Paris, Société d'éditions géographiques, maritimes et coloniales, 1955. (Pays africains, 5). 111pp. illus. maps.

1232

France. Direction de la documentation. **La République du Mali**. Paris, 1961. (*Notes et études documentaires*, 2739, 13 Jan 1961). 65pp.

1233

Beuchelt, E. **Mali**. Bonn, Schroeder for Deutsche Afrika-Gesellschaft, 1966. (Die Länder Afrikas, 34). 153pp. illus. maps.

1234

Imperato, P.J. **Historical dictionary of Mali**. Metuchen, NJ, Scarecrow Press, 1977. (African historical dictionaries, 11). 235pp.

- - 2nd ed. Metuchen, NJ, 1986. 359pp.

Lengthy critical review in *IJAHS*, 20, 1987, 565-569.

STATISTICS

1235

Imperato, P.J. & E.M. **Mali: a handbook of historical statistics**. Boston, MA, G.K. Hall, 1982. xxv, 339pp.

Detailed comparative statistics covering 1935 to 1975.

Bulletins & yearbooks

1236
French Sudan. Service statistique. **Bulletin statistique du Soudan français.** Koulouba, 1952-1956. Monthly/quarterly.

continued by:

Mali. Direction nationale de la statistique. **Bulletin mensuel de statistique.** Bamako, 1959- . Monthly.

1237
Mali. Direction nationale de la statistique [etc.]. **Annuaire statistique du Mali [etc.].** Bamako, 1960- . Annual.

1238
Statistik des Auslandes: Länderberichte: Mali. Wiesbaden, Statistisches Bundesamt, 1966- . irreg.

Issues for 1966, 1984, 1986, 1988, 1990.

ATLASES & GAZETTEERS

Atlases

1239
Urvoy, Y. **Petit atlas ethno-démographique du Soudan.** Paris, Larose, 1942.

1240
Atlas du Mali. Paris, "Jeune Afrique", 1981. 64pp.

Comp. M. Traoré and Y. Monnier. 20 thematic maps with accompanying text.

Gazetteers

1241
U.S. Board on Geographic Names. **Mali: official standard names approved by the U.S.B.G.N.** Washington, DC, 1965. (Gazetteer, 93). v, 263pp.

Includes 17,800 names from maps mostly at 1:500,000 (some at 1:200,000).

- - **Gazetteer supplement: Africa and South-West Asia.** Washington, DC, 1972. (p.15, Mali).

MAURITANIA

HANDBOOKS

1242

G.B. Foreign Office. Historical Section. **Mauritania**. London, 1920. (F.O. Handbook, 106). 32pp.
Also pub. in F.O. **Peace handbooks**, vol. 17. London, 1920.

1243

France. Direction de la documentation. **La République islamique de Mauritaine**. Paris, 1960. (*Notes et études documentaires*, 2687, 29 July 1960). 50pp.

1244

Reichhold, W. **Islamische Republik Mauretania**. Bonn, Schroeder for Deutsche Afrika-Gesellschaft, 1964. (Die Länder Afrikas, 28). 96pp. illus. maps.

1245

Area handbook for Mauritania, comp. B.D. Curran & J. Schrock. Washington, DC, U.S. Department of Defense, 1972. 185pp. maps.

- - 2nd ed. **Mauritania: a country study**, comp. R.E. Handloff. Washington, DC, 1990. xxv, 218pp. illus. maps.

1246

Gerteny, A.G. **Historical dictionary of Mauritania**. Metuchen, NJ, Scarecrow Press, 1981. (African historical dictionaries, 31). 116pp.

STATISTICS

1247

Mauritania. Direction de la statistique et des études économiques. **Bulletin mensuel statistique**. Nouakchott, 1960- . Monthly/quarterly.

Title varies: **Bulletin statistique et économique/Bulletin trimestriel statistique**.

1248

Mauritania. Direction de la statistique et des études économiques. [etc.] **Annuaire statistique**. Nouakchott, 1968- . Annual.

1249
L'économie mauritanienne. Paris, Ediafric-La documentation africaine, 1977- . Irreg.

Issue for 1977. Largely statistical.

1250
Statistik des Auslandes: Länderberichte: Mauretania. Wiesbaden, Statistisches Bundesamt, 1983- . irreg.

Issues for 1983, 1985, 1987.

ATLASES & GAZETTEERS

Atlases

1251
Atlas de la République islamique de Mauritanie. Paris, "Jeune Afrique", 1977. 64pp. col. maps.

Comp. C. Toupet and G. Laclavère. 19 thematic maps with text.

Gazetteers

1252
U.S. Board on Geographic Names. **Mauritania: official standard names approved by the U.S.B.G.N.** Washington, DC, 1966. (Gazetteer, 100). vii, 149pp.

Includes 10,000 names from maps at 1:200,000 (for south & west), 1:500,000 (rest of country). Revision of appropriate sections of **West Africa** (*see* 913).

- - **Gazetteer supplement: Africa and South-west Asia**. Washington, DC, 1972. (pp. 417-418, Mauritania).

NIGER

HANDBOOKS

1253

G.B. Foreign Office. Historical Section. **Upper Senegal and Niger.** London, 1920. (F.O. Handbook, 107). 60pp.
Also pub. in F.O. **Peace handbooks,** vol. 17. London, 1920.

1254

Le Niger. Paris, Société d'éditions géographiques, maritimes et coloniales, 1931. (Exposition coloniale internationale de Paris). iv, 88pp. illus. maps.

One of a series ompiled by the government of A.O.F. Includes data on history, topography, ethnography, administration, the economy and communications.

1255

Séré de Rivières, E. **Le Niger.** Paris, Société d'éditions géographiques, maritimes et coloniales, 1952. (Pays africains, 2). 96pp. illus. maps.

1256

France. Direction de la documentation. **La République du Niger.** Paris, 1960. (*Notes et études documentaires,* 2638, 26 Feb. 1960). 50pp.

- - [rev. ed.] Paris, 1973. (*Notes et études documentaires,* 3994/3995, 12 June 1973). 54pp.

1257

Beuchelt, E. **Niger.** Bonn, Schroeder for Deutsche Afrika-Gesellschaft, 1968. (Die Länder Afrikas, 38). 147pp. illus. maps.

1258

Decalo, S. **Historical dictionary of Niger.** Metuchen, NJ, Scarecrow Press, 1979. (African historical dictionaries, 20). 376pp.

- - 2nd ed. Metuchen, NJ, 1989. xxvi, 408pp.

2nd ed. includes detailed bibliography of 171pp.

STATISTICS

1259
Niger. Direction de la statistique et des comptes nationaux [etc.]. **Bulletin trimestriel de statistique**. Niamey, 1959- . Quarterly.

Title varies: **Bulletin de statistique** (1960-).

1260
Niger. Direction de la statistique et des comptes nationaux [etc.]. **Annuaire statistique**. Niamey, 1962- . Annual (irreg.)

1261
Statistik des Auslandes: Länderberichte: Niger. Wiesbaden, Statistisches Bundesamt, 1966- . irreg.

Issues for 1966, 1985, 1987.

BIOGRAPHICAL SOURCES

See 794.

ATLASES & GAZETTEERS

Atlases

1262
Atlas du Niger. Paris, "Jeune Afrique", 1980. 64pp. col, maps.

Comp. E. Bernus & S.A. Hamidou. 19 thematic maps with text.

Gazetteers

1263
U.S. Board on Geographic Names. **Niger: official standard names approved by the U.S.B.G.N.** Washington, DC, 1966. (Gazetteer, 99). iv, 207pp.

Includes 14,700 names from maps at 1:200,000 (for south), 1:500,000 (rest of country). Revision of appropriate sections of **West Africa** (*see* 913).

- - **Gazetteer supplement: Africa and South-West Asia**. Washington, DC, 1972. (p. 125, Niger).

SENEGAL

HANDBOOKS

1264

G.B. Foreign Office. Historical Section. **Senegal**. London, 1920. (F.O. Handbook, 102). 49pp.
Also pub. in F.O. **Peace handbooks**, vol. 17. London, 1920.

1265

Le Sénégal. Paris, Société d'éditions géographiques, maritimes et coloniales, 1931. (Exposition coloniale internationale de Paris). iv, 274pp. illus. maps.

1266

La circonscription de Dakar et dépendances. Paris, Société d'éditions géographiques, maritimes et coloniales, 1931. (Exposition coloniale internationale de Paris). iv, 174pp. illus. maps.

This and item 1265 were companion vols. prepared by the government of A.O.F. for the Paris exposition. Each covers history, geography, peoples, economic and social life and administration.

1267

Séré de Rivières, E. **Le Sénégal-Dakar**. Paris, Société d'éditions géographiques, maritimes et coloniales, 1953. (Pays africains, 4). 127pp. illus. maps.

1268

France. Direction de la documentation. **La République du Sénégal**. Paris, 1961. (*Notes et études documentaires*, 2754, 22 Feb. 1961). 48pp.

1269

Ernst, H. **Senegal**. Bonn, Schroeder for Deutsche Afrika-Gesellschaft, 1965. (Die Länder Afrikas, 29). 112pp. illus. maps.

1270

Area handbook for Senegal. Washington, DC, U.S. Department of Defense, 1963. xiv, 489pp. maps.

- - 2nd ed. comp. H.D. Nelson, *et al*. Washington, DC, 1974. xiv, 410pp. illus. maps.

1271
Colvin, L.G. **Historical dictionary of Senegal**. Metuchen, NJ, Scarecrow Press, 1981. (African historical dictionaries, 23). 355pp.

Reviews, *Africa*, 54, 1984, 113-115; *JAH* 24, 1983, 426 ("one of the better ones in the series").

STATISTICS

1272
Senegal. Direction de la statistique [etc.]. **Bulletin statistique et économique mensuel**. St. Louis/Dakar, 1960-   . Monthly.

Succeeds **Bulletin de la statistique générale** and **Bulletin statistique trimestriel/bimestriel** previously issued by government of A.O.F. (*see* 1126).

1273
Senegal. Direction de la statistique [etc.]. **Situation économique du Sénégal**. Dakar, 1962- . Annual.

1274
L'économie Sénégalaise. Paris, Ediafric-La documentation africaine, 1970- . Irreg.

Issues for 1970, 1973, 1975, 1977, 1983.

1275
Senegal. Ministère des Finances et des affaires économiques. **Le Sénégal en chiffres**. Dakar, 1976- . Irreg.

1276
Statistik des Auslandes: Länderberichte: Senegal. Wiesbaden, Statistisches Bundesamt, 1985- . Irreg.

Issues for 1985, 1987, 1990.

DIRECTORIES OF ORGANIZATIONS

1277
Université de Dakar. École des bibliothécaires, archivistes et documentalistes. **Répertoire des bibliothèques et organismes de documentation au Sénégal**.

Senegal

Dakar, 1973. vi, 131pp.

Comp. D.H. Zidouemba.

1278
Senegal. Centre nationale de documentation scientifique et technique. **Répertoire des organismes de documentation et d'information scientifiques et techniques.** Dakar, 1978. 184pp.

- - 2nd ed. Dakar, 1981.

- - 3rd ed. Dakar, 1984.

BIOGRAPHICAL SOURCES

1279
Les élites sénégalaises. Paris, Ediafric-La documentation africaine, 1984. 169pp.

About 1,000 brief biographies, mostly of government officials.

ATLASES & GAZETTEERS

Atlases

1280
Senegal. Ministère du plan et du développement. **Cartes pour servir à l'aménagement du térritoire.** Dakar, 1965. 40 maps. 28 x 39cm.

Atlas of 40 thematic maps at 1:5M.

1281
IFAN. **Atlas national du Sénégal.** Dakar, 1977. 147pp. including 65 plates. 54 x 40cm.

Produced with help of Institut geographique nationale, Paris, and ORSTOM. Ed. by R. Van Chi-Bonnardel. Thematic maps, the majority at 1:1,500,000. Includes a series on history showing archaeological sites, ancient kingdoms, colonization etc. Text includes diagrams and photographs.

1282
Atlas du Sénégal. Paris, "Jeune Afrique", 1980. 72pp. col. maps.

- - 2nd ed. Paris, 1983. 72pp.

Comp. P. Pelissier and G. Laclavère. 19 thematic maps with text.

Gazetteers

1283
Senegal. Ministère du plan et du développement. Service de la statistique. **Répertoire des villages.** Dakar, 1964.

- - 2nd ed. Ministère des Finances et des affaires économiques. Direction de la statistique. **Répertoire des villages.** Dakar, 1972. 233pp.

Lists villages firstly by their location in administration divisions, with population figures, secondly alphabetically. Does not provide geographical co-ordinates.

1284
U.S. Board on Geographic Names. **Senegal: official standard names approved by the U.S.B.G.N.** Washington, DC, 1965. (Gazetteer, 88). iv, 194pp.

Includes 13,600 names from maps at 1:200,000. Revision of appropriate sections of **West Africa** (*see* 913).

- - **Gazetteer supplement: Africa and South-West Asia.** Washington, DC, 1972. (pp. 131-132, Senegal).

1285
Mangold, M. **A Senegalese pronouncing gazetteer.** Saarbrücken, Universität des Saarlandes, Institut für Phonetik, 1984. (Africana Saraviensia Linguistica, 7). 75pp.

1,100 entries, with Wolof pronunciation for 300.

TOGO

See also sections for **Former German Africa.**

HANDBOOKS

1286
G.B. War Office. Intelligence Division. **Military report on Togoland**. London, 1909. (A. 1337). iv, 54pp.

Comp. Maj. A.V.F. Russell. Rev. ed. of relevant sections of **Military report on the Kameruns & Togo** (*see* 1160).

1287
G.B. Foreign Office. Historical Section. **Togoland**. London, 1920. (F.O. Handbook, 110). 55pp.
Also pub. in F.O. **Peace handbooks**, vol. 18. London, 1920.

1288
Schramm, J. **Togo**. Bonn, Schroeder for Deutsche Afrika-Gesellschaft, 1959. (Die Länder Afrikas, 19). 86pp.

- - 2nd ed. Bonn, 1962. 92pp.

1289
Banque centrale des états de l'Afrique de l'ouest. **Togo 1960; faits et chiffres**. Lomé, 1960. vi, 217pp.

Compact and very detailed compilation of data, compiled with the help of government departments. Covers economic and social life, with sections on history, topography and peoples. Numerous statistics and bibliography.

1290
France. Direction de la documentation. **Le Togo**. Paris, 1968. (*Notes et études documentaires* 3531, 31 Oct 1968). 26pp.

1291
Decalo, S. **Historical dictionary of Togo**. Metuchen, NJ, Scarecrow Press, 1976. (African historical dictionaries, 9). 261pp.

- - 2nd ed. Metuchen, NJ, 1987. xxix, 331pp.

"An abundance of interesting and pertinent information", *IJAHS* 22, 1989, 340-341 reviewing 2nd ed.

See also 946, 1111, 1114, 1117.

YEARBOOKS

1292
G.B. Colonial Office. [**Annual reports**]: **Togoland, 1920-1955**. London, 1922-1956.

As **Report to the Council of the League of Nations on the British Mandated sphere of Togoland**, 1920/21 (Cmd.1698); **Report of administration under mandate**, [title varies], 1922-38 (not pub. 1939-46), **Report ... to the Trusteeship Council of the UN**, 1947, **Report ... to the General Assembly of the UN**, 1948-55 (in Colonial series). *For fuller details see Appendix.*

1293
France. **Rapport du gouvernement français ... sur l'administration du Togo placé sous la tutelle de France**. Paris, 1921-1957. Annual.

Presented initially to the League of Nations, then, post 1946, to the Trusteeship Council of the United Nations. Particularly detailed series (many vols. of over 300pp.) with extensive statistics and numerous maps.

1294
Annuaire du Togo. Paris, Diloutremer/Lomé, Service de l'information du Togo, 1962- . Annual.

Historical, administrative and economic data.

1295
Togo. Service de l'information. **Annuaire économique officiel de la république togolaise**. Lomé, 1983- . Annual.

Covers, history, administration, resources and includes commercial directory.

STATISTICS

1296
Togo. Direction de la statistique [etc.]. **Bulletin mensuel de statistique**. Lomé,

Togo

1952- . Monthly.

1297
Statistik des Auslandes: Länderberichte: Togo. Wiesbaden, Statistisches Bundesamt, 1961- . irreg.

Issues for 1961, 1969, 1978, 1984, 1986, 1988, 1991.

1298
Togo. Direction de la statistique. **Annuaire statistique du Togo.** Lomé, 1966- . Annual.

See also 1292, 1293

ATLASES & GAZETTEERS

Atlases

1299
Atlas du Togo. Paris, "Jeune Afrique", 1981. 64pp.

Comp. Y.E. Gù-Konu & G. Laclavère. 25 thematic maps with accompanying text.

See also 982.

Gazetteers

1300
U.S. Board on Geographic Names. **Togo: official standard names approved by the U.S.B.G.N.** Washington, DC, 1966. (Gazetteer, 98). iii, 100pp.

Includes some 7,000 names from maps at 1:200,000. Revision of appropriate sections of **West Africa** (*see* 913).

 - - **Gazetteer supplement: Africa and South-West Asia.** Washington, DC, 1972. (p.161, Togo).

LUSOPHONE WEST AFRICA

CAPE VERDE ISLANDS

HANDBOOKS

1301
G.B. Foreign Office. Historical Section. **Cape Verde Islands**. London, 1920.
(F.O. Handbook, 117). 42pp.
Also pub. in F.O. **Peace handbooks**, vol. 19. London, 1920.

1302
Mendes Corrêa, A.M. **Ultramar Português II: ilhas de Cabo Verde**. Lisbon,
Agência-Geral do Ultramar, 1954. 262pp. illus. 9 maps.

Detailed handbook covering topography, geology, climate, natural resources,
peoples, culture, administration and the economy. Each chapter has an
English summary.

1303
Portugal. Agência-Geral do Ultramar. **Cabo Verde: pequena monografia**.
Lisbon, 1961. 53pp.

- - 2nd ed. Lisbon, 1966. 81pp.

Handbook format, covering history, geography, natural resources, and
administration. List of governors, 1587-1962.

1304
Lobban, R. **Historical dictionary of the Republics of Guinea-Bissau and
Cape Verde**. Metuchen, NJ, Scarecrow Press, 1979. (African historical
dictionaries, 22). 209pp.

- - 2nd ed. Lobban, R. & Halter, M. **Historical dictionary of the Republic of
Cape Verde**. Metuchen, NJ, 1988. (African historical dictionaries, 42). xix,
171pp.

2nd ed. provides much more detailed coverage (*see also* 1316).

1305
República de Cabo Verde: 5 anos de independência, 1975-1980. Lisbon,

Comissão do V Aniversário da Independência Nacional, 1980. 94pp.

General handbook covering geography, history, politics and the economy.

STATISTICS

1306
'Alguns dados estatísticos sobre Cabo Verde', *Boletim da Agência- Geral das coloniás* 45, 1929, 221-226

1307
Cape Verde. Serviço Naçional de Estatística [etc.]. **Anuário estatístico, Colónia de Cabo Verde.** Praia, 1933-1952. Irreg. Issues 1-20.

1308
Cape Verde. Serviço Nacional de Estatística [etc.]. **Boletim trimestral de estatística.** Praia, 1949- . Quarterly.

1309
Cape Verde. Direcção Geral de Estatística. **Boletim anual de estatística.** Praia, 1987- . Annual.

1310
Länderbericht: Kap Verde. Wiesbaden, Statistisches Bundesamt, 1990- . Irreg.

Issue for 1990. Collection of statistical data.

ATLASES & GAZETTEERS

Gazetteers

1311
Lereno, A. **Dicionário corográfico do arquipélago de Cabo Verde.** Lisbon, Agência-Geral do Ultramar. 1952. 568pp.

Alphabetical list of place names, linking each to its administrative district, and including many alternative forms.

1312
U.S. Board on Geographic Names. **Portugal and the Cape Verde Islands: official standard names approved by the U.S.B.G.N.** Washington, DC, 1961.

(Gazetteer, 50). v, 321pp.

Pp.309-321, Cape Verde Islands. Includes c.1,000 names from maps at 1:150,000.

GUINEA-BISSAU

HANDBOOKS

1313
G.B. Foreign Office. Historical Section. **Portuguese Guinea**. London, 1920.
(F.O. Handbook, 118). 39pp.
Also pub. in F.O. **Peace handbooks**, vol. 19. London, 1920.

1314
Teixeira da Moto, A. **Guiné Portuguesa**. Lisbon, Agência-Geral do Ultramar,
1954. (Monografias dos territórios do Ultramar). 2 vols. illus. maps.

Includes coverage of São Tomé e Principe. Vol. 1, xxv, 394pp. Topography,
vegetation, fauna, peoples and languages with English summary pp. 361-383;
vol. 2, 297pp. History, administration, health, economy, education, production
and trade, with English summary pp. 233-248.

1315
Portugal. Agência-Geral do Ultramar. **Guiné: pequena monografia**. Lisbon,
1961. 53pp.

 - - 2nd ed. Lisbon, 1967. 80pp.

Brief handbook covering history, administration, natural resources.

1316
Lobban, R. & Forrest, J. **Historical dictionary of the Republic of Guinea-
Bissau**. Metuchen, NJ, 1988. xx, 211pp.

A 2nd ed. of the appropriate sections of R. Lobban. **Historical dictionary of
the Republics of Guinea Bissau and Cape Verde** (1980, *see* 1304). Review in
IJAHS 24, 1991, 446 comments favourably on the revised eds. of the Cape
Verde and Guinea Bissau volumes, and sees them as "valuable reference
works ... because of the dearth of information available on these two
countries".

YEARBOOKS

1317
Portugal. Ministério das Colonias. **Anuário da Provincia da Guiné do ano de**

1925. Lisbon, 1925. 218pp.

Comp. A.A. Gonçalves de Morais e Castro.

1318
Anuário da Guiné Portuguesa. Lisbon, Governo da Colónia, 1946-1948. 2 issues.

Ed. F. Duarte. 1946. xxvii, 692pp; 1948. xxvii, 875pp. One of the most detailed examples of its kind. Historical, topographical and economic data, civil list and commercial directory.

STATISTICS

1319
Portuguese Guinea/Guinea-Bissau. Direcção Geral de Estatística [etc.]. **Boletim trimestral de estatística** [etc.]. Bissau, 1938- . Quarterly.

1320
Portuguese Guinea/Guinea-Bissau. Direcção Geral de Estatística [etc.]. **Anuário estatístico** [etc.]. Bissau, 1947- . [n.s.] 1974- Annual.

1321
Länderbericht: Guinea-Bissau. Wiesbaden, Statistisches Bundesamt, 1990- . Irreg.

Issue for 1990. Collection of statistical data.

ATLASES & GAZETTEERS

Gazetteers

1322
Primeira relação da nomes geográfico da Guiné Portuguesa. Lisbon, Imprensa Nacional, 1948. 75pp.

1323
U.S. Board on Geographic Names. **Portuguese Guinea: official standard names approved by the U.S.B.G.N.** Washington, DC, 1968. (Gazetteer, 105). iii, 122pp.

Includes 8,700 names from maps at 1:50,000. Revision of appropriate sections of **West Africa** (*see* 913).

- - **Gazetteer supplement: Africa and South-West Asia**. Washington, DC, 1972. (p. 129, Guinea-Bissau).

SÃO TOMÉ & PRINCIPE

HANDBOOKS

1324
G.B. Foreign Office. Historical Section. **San Thomé and Principe**. London, 1920. 41pp. (F.O. Handbook, 119).
Also pub. in F.O. **Peace handbooks**, vol. 19. London, 1920.

1325
Unzueta y Yuste, A. de. **Islas de Golfo de Guinea (Elobeyes, Corisco, Annobon, Principe y Santo Tomé)**. Madrid, Instituto de Estudios Políticos, 1945. 386pp.

Covers topography, resources, history, administration, ethnology.

1326
Portugal. Agência-Geral do Ultramar. **São Tomé e Principe: pequena monografia**. Lisbon, 1964. 110pp.

Standard handbook, covering topography, natural resources, peoples, history, administration, the economy. Chronological list of governors, 1586-1963.

See also 1314.

YEARBOOKS

1327
Anuário da ilha de S. Tomé (ilustrado) relativo ao ano de 1902. Marinha Grande, 1902. 189pp.

1328
Anuário comercial industrial e agricola da provincia de S. Tomé e Principe. Lisbon, 1928- ?. (NUC)

STATISTICS

1329
'Alguns dados estatísticos sôbre S. Tomé e Principe', *Boletim de Agência-Geral das coloniás* 43, 1929, 159-170.

1330
São Tomé e Principe. Repartição dos Serviços de Estatística. **Boletim trimestral de estatística.** São Tomé, 1939- . Monthly/quarterly.

Text in French and Portuguese.

ATLASES & GAZETTEERS

Gazetteers

1331 (*also entered at* 1347)
U.S. Board on Geographic Names. **Rio Muni, Fernando Po and São Tomé e Principe: official standard names approved by the U.S.B.G.N.** Washington, DC, 1962. (Gazetteer, 63). iv, 95pp.

Pp. 83-95, São Tomé e Principe. Includes 800 names from 1:150,000 (for São Tomé), 1:75,000 (for Principe) map series. Revision of appropriate sections of **Equatorial Africa ...** (*see* 773).

1332
Portugal. Junta de Investigações do Ultramar, Centro de Geografia do Ultramar. **Relação dos names geograficos de São Tomé e Principe.** Lisbon, 1968. 82pp.

Includes 38,000 names from 1:250,000 map series.

FORMER SPANISH AFRICA

HANDBOOKS

1333
Pélissier, R. **Les térritoires espagnols d'Afrique**. Paris, La documentation française, 1963. (*Notes et études documentaires* 2951, 3 Jan 1963). 40pp.

- - Spanish trans. **Los territorios espanoles de Africa**. Madrid, Consejo Superior de Investigaçiónes Científicas e Instituto de Estudios Africanos, 1964. 94pp.

For each colony gives basic data on geography, history, demography, the economy, trade and communications.

YEARBOOKS

1334
Anuario de Canarias. Las Palmas, 1944- . Annual.

Title varies: **Anuario de Canarias, Africa Occidental, Guinea Española** (1951-) when scope was enlarged to accommodate Spanish Sahara and Guinea. For a detailed account of coverage of this work see Berman, S. *Spanish Guinea: an annotated bibliography* (MLS, Catholic University of America, 1961) pp. 123-124.

STATISTICS

1335
Spain. Dirección General de Plazas y Provincias Africanas e Instituto de Estudios Africanos. **Resumen estadístico de Africa española [1947/52-1965/66]**. Madrid, 1954-1966. Irreg.

Issues for 1947/52, 1953/55, 1956/58, 1959/60, 1961/62, 1963/64, 1965/66.

ATLASES & GAZETTEERS

1336
Spain. Dirección General de Marruecos y Colonías e Instituto de Estudios

Africanos. **Atlas histórico y geográfico de Africa Española.** Madrid, 1955. 204pp. 47 col. maps. 43 x 31cm.

'Atlas historico', pp. 13-67, covers 23 topics, each with accompanying maps, including six historical maps covering peoples, prehistory, early and recent history, exploration and voyages. 'Atlas geografico', pp. 69-165, contains physical and geological maps for Ifni (1:200,000), Spanish Sahara (1:3M), Spanish Guinea (1:600,000), Fernando Po (1:250,000), Annobon (1:50,000). Text includes statistics and diagrams. Detailed index of place names.

EQUATORIAL GUINEA

HANDBOOKS

1337
G.B. Foreign Office. Historical Section. **Spanish Guinea**. London, 1920. 58pp. (F.O. Handbook, 125).
Also pub. in F.O. **Peace handbooks**, vol. 20. London, 1920.

1338
Unzueta y Yuste, A. de. **Guinea continental española**. Madrid, Instituto de Estudios Políticos, 1944. 394pp.

Encyclopaedic survey of history, politics, administration, topography and ethnology.

1339
Baguena Corella, L. **Guinea**. Madrid, Consejo Superior de Investigaçiónes Científicas e Instituto de Estudios Africanos, 1950. 160pp. (Manuales del Africa española, 1).

Covers geography and geology, climate, natural resources, peoples, history and administration, communications.

1340
Aulet, M.L. **Spanish territories of the Gulf of Guinea: a guide book to Fernando Poo/Territorios Españoles del Golfo de Guinea: guia de Fernando Poo**. Fernando Po, Import Colonial, 1951. 48, 46pp. 1 map. 1 plan.

English and Spanish text in 1 vol. Includes brief commercial directory, plans of Fernando Po and Santa Isabel.

1341
Liniger-Goumaz, M. **La Guinée équatoriale: un pays méconnu**. Paris, L'Harmattan, 1979. 511pp. maps.

Historical dictionary. Very similar in overall structure and choice of entry terms to his **Historical dictionary ...** (*see* 1342) but somewhat fuller in content.

1342
Liniger-Goumaz, M. **Historical dictionary of Equatorial Guinea**. Metuchen, NJ, Scarecrow Press, 1979. (African historical dictionaries, 21). 246pp.

- - 2nd ed. Metuchen, NJ, 1988. xxx, 238pp.

See also 1325.

STATISTICS

1343
Spain. Dirección General de Plazas y Provincias Africanos e Instituto de Estudios Africanos. **Resumenes estadísticos del Gobierno General de los Territorios Españoles del Golfo de Guinea.** Madrid, 1941- . Irreg.

Title varies : **Negoçiado de estadística: resumenes del año/Anuario estadístico de los territorios ...** Issues for 1941, 1942/43, 1944/45, 1946/47, 1948/49, 1950/51, 1952/53, 1954/55, 1956/57, 1958/59, 1959/60.

1344
Equatorial Guinea. Dirección General de Estadística. **Boletín estadístico anual.** Malabo, 1981- . Annual (irreg.)

Summary version pub. as **Resena estadística de la República de Guinea Ecuatorial** (Malabo, 1981-).

1345
Statistik des Auslandes: Länderberichte: Äquatorialguinea. Wiesbaden, Statistisches Bundesamt, 1984- . Irreg.

Issues for 1984, 1986.

ATLASES & GAZETTEERS

Gazetteers

1346
Baguena Corella, L. **Toponomia de la Guinea Continental Española.** Madrid, Instituto de Estudios Africanos, 1947. 497pp.

Lists 3,477 names and features with notes on their etymology.

1347 (*also entered at* 1331)
U.S. Board on Geographic Names. **Rio Muni, Fernando Po and São Tomé e Príncipe: official standard names approved by the U.S.B.G.N.** Washington,

DC, 1962. (Gazetteer, 63). iv, 95pp.

Pp. 1-82, Rio Muni and Fernando Po. 5,700 names from 1:100,000 map series. Revision of appropriate sections of **Equatorial Africa ...** (*see* 773).

WESTERN SAHARA (SAHARAN ARAB DEMOCRATIC REPUBLIC)

HANDBOOKS

1348

G.B. Foreign Office. Historical Section. **Spanish Sahara**. London, 1920. (F.O. Handbook, 124). 35pp.
Also pub. in F.O. **Peace handbooks**, vol. 19. London, 1920.

1349

Hodges, T. **Historical dictionary of Western Sahara**. Metuchen, NJ, Scarecrow Press, 1982. (African historical dictionaries, 35). 431pp.

Produced as a by-product of the research for the author's *Western Sahara: the roots of a desert war*, Beckenham, Croom Helm, 1984.

STATISTICS

1350

Spanish West Africa. Gobierno del Africa Occidental Española, Secretaría General. **Sahara español, anuario estadístico 1946 [-1950]**. Sidi Ifni, 1949-1953. Annual. 5 vols.

1351

Spain. Instituto Nacional de Estadística. **Anuario estadístico de España**. Madrid, 1858- . Annual.

Vols. for 1959-1968 include Spanish Sahara under section "Provincias africanos"; 1969-75 has separate section for "Provincia africana del Sahara español/Sahara español".

1352

Spain. Consejo Superior de Investigaçiónes Científica. **Resumen estadistíco del Sahara español 1969**. Madrid, 1970. 31pp.

No more published? (L.F.Sipe, *Western Sahara: a comprehensive bibliography*, New York, 1984).

ATLASES & GAZETTEERS

Gazetteers

1353
Ruiz, I.C. **Vocabulario geografico-Saharico**. Madrid, Consejo Superior de Investigaçiónes Científicas e Instituto de Estudios Africanos, 1955. 287pp.

Descriptive gazetteer of Ifni and Spanish Sahara.

1354
U.S. Board on Geographic Names. **Spanish Sahara: official standard names approved by the U.S.B.G.N.** Washington, DC, 1969. v, 52pp.

Includes c.3,000 names from maps at 1:500,000. Revison of appropriate sections of **West Africa** (*see* 913).

SOUTHERN AFRICA

South Africa
    Cape
    Natal
    Orange Free State
    Transvaal
Namibia

Botswana
Lesotho
Swaziland

Indian   Ocean   Islands   (Francophone
               Southern Africa)
    Comoro Islands
    Madagascar
    Mauritius
    Réunion
    Seychelles

Lusophone Southern Africa
    Angola
    Mozambique

*Most sources which are principally concerned with the region represented by modern political **South Africa** are also at least partly concerned with one or more neighbouring countries, especially Namibia, Botswana, Lesotho and Swaziland, and Mozambique. No attempt has been made therefore to distinguish between sources relating to **Southern Africa** in general and those relating only to **South Africa** and all have been placed under the latter heading.*

SOUTH AFRICA

Bibliographies of reference sources

1355

Musiker, R. **Guide to South African reference books.** Cape Town, University of Cape Town, School of Librarianship, 1955. ix, 43pp.

  - - 2nd ed. Cape Town, 1958. vii, 43pp.

- - 3rd ed. Grahamstown, Rhodes University, 1963. ix, 161pp.

- - 4th ed. Cape Town, Balkema, 1965. x, 110pp.

- - 5th ed. Cape Town, 1971. 138pp.

- - **Cumulative supplement to 5th ed. covering 1970-76.** Johannesburg, University of the Witwatersrand Library, 1977. iv, 112pp.

1356
Musiker, R. **South Africa**. Oxford, Clio Press, 1979. (World bibliographical series, 7). 220pp.

"This work succeeds the author's **Guide to South African reference books** [*see* 1355] and all its supplements" (preface). Some 1,200 items.

1357
Musiker, R. 'Significant South African reference books of the 1970s', *South African libraries* 47, 1980, 139-145.

Narrative survey covering 182 items.

1358
Musiker, R. **South African reference books and bibliographies of 1979-80.** Johannesburg, University of the Witwatersrand Library, 1981. ix, 58pp.

- - **...** **of 1979-83**. Johannesburg, 1983. vi, 100pp.

Detailed critical review in *ARD* 36, 1984, 39-41.

HANDBOOKS

Bibliographies

1359
Inskip, C.A. **List of guide books and handbooks dating from 1800 to the present day dealing with South Africa and the Western Province.** Cape Town, University of Cape Town, School of Librarianship 1949. 31pp.

Includes some directories and almanacks but concentrates on travel guides and emigration handbooks. No annotations.

General

1360
Glanville, T.B. **The guide to South Africa, or, the Cape Colony, Griqualand West, the diamond fields, gold fields, Transvaal and the Free State as they are**. London, Richards, Glanville & Co., 1875. 112pp.

11 eds. pub. to 1890, with very little change and no expansion of contents. Title varies: **Glanville's guide to South Africa ...** (4th-8th eds., 1877-1885); **The Union Steam Ship Co.'s ed. of 'The guide to South Africa'** (9th-11th eds., 1888-1890)

1361
Handbook for South Africa. London, S.W. Silver & Co., 1875. viii, 487pp.

An earlier work from the same publisher, **Handbook to South Africa ... physical geography, climate and resources of the Cape of Good Hope and Natal**, London, 1872. ii, 61pp, was, despite its title, concerned mainly with the diamond fields. This ed. provides detailed wide-ranging coverage in a standard format for each administrative unit covering history, geography, industry, peoples, administration, education, and trade. Descriptive gazetteer of some 300 places.

- - 2nd ed. **Handbook to South Africa**. London, 1879. x, 567pp.

Includes "the Cape Colony, Natal, the Diamond Fields, the Transvaal, Orange Free State etc." (sub-title). Claims many important additions to text because of recent large annexations of territory to the Cape. Also includes Delagoa Bay.

- - 3rd ed. London, 1880. xii, 576pp.

- - 4th ed. London, 1891. xviii, 793pp.

4th ed. incorporates major revisions to include British Bechuanaland, Bechuanaland Protectorate, Zambesia, German South West Africa, Zululand, Swaziland and Tongaland.

1362
Noble, J. *ed.* **Illustrated official handbook of the Cape and South Africa**. Cape Town, Juta/London, Edward Stanford, 1893. xvi, 568pp. illus.

- - 2nd ed. Cape Town, 1896. xvi, 568pp.

An expanded version of the 1886 volume compiled by Noble (*see* 1378) covering newly acquired territories, each with a separate section. 2nd ed. is a reprint with a 10pp. summary of developments 1893-1896.

1363
Die Afrikaanse Kinderensiklopedie. Cape Town, NASOU, 1943-1954. 10 vols. illus.

- - 2nd ed. Cape Town, 1963-1964. 10 vols. illus.

- - 3rd ed. Cape Town, 1976. 10 vols. illus.

- - **Nuwe Afrikaanse Kinderensiklopedie.** Goodwood, NASOU, 1980-1982. 12 vols. illus.

- - 2nd ed. Goodwood, 1986. 12 vols. illus.

Original ed. C.F. Albertyn. Although intended primarily as a general encyclopedia for the juvenile market the thematically arranged volumes contain much useful data on South African topics, especially history, literature, and biography.

1364
Mockford, J. *ed.* **Overseas reference book of the Union of South Africa;** including South-West Africa, Basutoland, Bechuanaland Protectorate and Swaziland. London, Todd, 1945. 567pp. illus. maps.

Ed. was Public Relations Officer at South Africa House, London. General articles, followed by detailed chapters on industry and agriculture, population, trade and commerce. "City and town guide" gives details of some 230 settlements. Civil list, and classified lists of major commercial institutions, the press, societies and libraries. Detailed atlas section of 55 black and white maps. Valuable compilation of data from official sources on the region at the end of World War II.

1365
Schmidt, W. **Südafrikanische Union.** Bonn, Schroeder for Deutsche Afrika-Gesellschaft, 1958. (Die Länder Afrikas, 4). 105pp.

- - 2nd ed. Bonn, 1963. 256pp.

1st ed. includes coverage of South-West Africa and Botswana, Lesotho and Swaziland in 4pp.; 2nd ed. expands this coverage to 50pp.

1366
Rosenthal, E. ed. **Encyclopedia of Southern Africa.** London, Warne, 1961. viii, 600pp. illus.

- - 2nd ed. London, 1964. viii, 604pp. illus.

- - 3rd ed. London, 1965. viii, 628pp. illus.

- - 4th ed. London, 1967. viii, 638pp. illus.

- - 5th ed. London, 1970. xii, 653pp. illus.

- - 6th ed. London, 1973. xii, 662pp. illus.

- - 7th ed. Cape Town, Juta, 1978. 577pp. illus.

Approximately 5,000 brief entries, including biographies, together with some 20 much longer articles which have their own contents list. Coverage is of Republic of South Africa and Namibia; Botswana, Lesotho and Swaziland; Malawi, Zambia and Zimbabwe; Angola and Mozambique (the last omitted from 7th ed.) 7th ed. also pub. in Afrikaans as **Ensiklopedie van Suidelike Afrika.**

1367
Kennis: die eerste Afrikaanse ensiklopedie in kleur. Cape Town, Kennis-uitgewers, 1969. 17 vols. illus.

- - 2nd ed. Cape Town, 1978-1980. 17 vols. illus.

- - 3rd ed. Cape Town, 1983. 17 vols. illus.

- - 4th ed. Cape Town, Human & Rousseau, 1987. 17 vols. illus.

Compiled with the help of Fabbri Editori, Milan.

1368
Standard encyclopedia of Southern Africa. Cape Town, NASOU, 1970-1976. 12 vols. illus. maps.

Vols. 1 to 11, main text; vol. 12, supplement and general index. Ed. in chief D.J. Potgeiter, with some 1,400 contributors, many of them civil servants drawing on non-public information. Over 5,000 illustrations, many taken from newspaper libraries. "Emphasis on the Republic of South Africa ... and its immediate neighbours" but also lengthy treatment for Angola, Zaire, Kenya, Uganda and Tanzania. Over 10,000 articles ranging from many short entries for biographies, plants, and animals to lengthy surveys (e.g. "Anglo-Boer War", 19pp). Useful articles on documentary & institutional sources (e.g. "Almanacs and yearbooks", "Academies", "Biography, dictionaries of").

1369
Area handbook for the Republic of South Africa, comp. I. Kaplan, *et al.* Washington, DC, U.S. Department of Defense, 1971. xvi, 845pp. maps.

- - 2nd ed. **South Africa: a country study**. Washington, DC, 1981. 464pp. illus. maps.

1370
Ensiklopedie van die wêreld. Stellenbosch, C.F. Albertyn, 1971-1978. 11 vols. illus.

- - **Supplements** [1-3]. Stellenbosch, 1983. 376pp; 1987. 389pp; 1989. 354pp.

Afrikaans language work based upon the Dutch **Winkler Prins** encyclopedia. Covers the world, but has particularly detailed articles on Southern African topics.

1371
Holcroft's South African calendar: facts, figures, dates. Pretoria, Vergne, 1975. 128pp. illus.

- - 2nd ed. Pretoria, 1976. 126pp.

Quick reference source with brief entries on fauna and flora, climate, education, government, population, and sport.

1372
Total book of Southern Africa records. Johannesburg, Total South Africa, 1975. 160pp. illus.

- - 2nd ed. Johannesburg, 1982. 160pp. illus.

Comp. E. Rosenthal. Includes a wide range of records relating to the natural world, sport, and the administration, also lists of honours and awards.

1373
Wêreldvisie. Johannesburg, Ensiklopedie Afrikana, 1977. 10 vols. illus.

- - 2nd ed. Johannesburg, 1981. 10 vols. illus.

Arranged thematically. Vol. 4, "Lande en volke: Africa".

Wêreldfokus: 'n geillustreerde ensiklopedie van Suid-Afrika en die wêreld. Johannesburg, Ensiklopledie Afrikana, 1978. 16 vols. illus.

- - 2nd ed. Johannesburg, 1981. 16 vols. illus.

Wêreldspektrum. Johannesburg, Ensiklopedie Afrikana, 1982. 30 vols. illus.

Three linked reference sources based on titles originally published in Barcelona. Supplemented by yearbook, **Boek van die jaar: die wêreld in 1985** [etc.] (1985-).

1374
Concise illustrated South African encyclopedia. Johannesburg, Central News Agency, 1980. 206pp. illus.

Comp. P. Schirmer. Popular work with some 1,500 entries and over 400 illus. Also pub. in Afrikaans as **Die beknopte geïllustreerde ensiklopedie van Suid-Afrika.** Johannesburg, 1981. 218pp.

1375
Saunders, C. **Historical dictionary of South Africa.** Metuchen, NJ, Scarecrow Press, 1983. (African historical dictionaries, 37). xxviii, 241pp.

Reviews, *IJAHS*, 17, 1984, 709-710, and *JAH*, 27, 1986, 408-409 ("well above the standard of many others in this series")

Cape

1376
Noble, J. *ed.* **Descriptive handbook of the Cape Colony: its condition and resources.** Cape Town, Juta/London, Edward Stanford, 1875. v, 315pp. illus. maps.

Sections for "physical features", "past history", "present aspect and conditions" (mostly topography and natural resources). Includes summarized statistics from 1875 census.

1377
G.B. War Office. Intelligence Branch. **Précis of information concerning South**

Africa: the Eastern Frontier of the Cape Colony, Kafraria and Basutoland, with special reference to the native tribes. London, 1877. 84pp. map in pocket.

Separate sections for each of the three administrations, sub-arranged by districts with a standardised treatment of topics: boundaries, topography, roads, towns and villages, inhabitants, and the administration.

1378
Noble, J. *ed.* **Official handbook: history, productions and resources of the Cape of Good Hope.** Cape Town, Government Printers, 1886. viii, 328pp.

Cover-title : **Cape of Good Hope official handbook.** Author was Clerk of House of Assembly. "Prepared at the request of the Committee appointed ... for the representation of the Colony at the Colonial and India Exhibition, London, 1886". A detailed, well-structured collection of information on history, topography and the economy.

1379
Macmillan, A. **The Eastern Province of the Cape Colony: an illustrated commercial & general review.** East London, Standard Printing Co., 1902. 160pp.

One of a series of "illustrated commercial and general reviews" produced by the author (*see* 525, 916, 1678) which also included several for specific South African cities, e.g. **The city of Bloemfontein** (1902); **The city of Grahamstown** (1902); **The city of Pretoria** (1903).

1380
G.B. War Office. General Staff. **Military report on Cape Colony.** London, 1908-09. 2 vols. maps in pocket.

Vol. 1, 1909. General. viii, 162pp. Standard War Office handbook covering topography, history, administration. Vol. 2, 1908. Routes. (A. 1249). 696pp. Includes section of general statistics broken down by district, followed by 117 very detailed itineraries.

1381
Official guide to the Province of the Cape of Good Hope. Cape Town, Beerman, 1953. 261pp. illus.

Arranged by regions, with entries for major towns and topics under each region.

Natal

1382

Algar, F. **Handbook to the colony of Natal, 1865.** London, Colonial Newspaper Agency, [1866]. 60pp.

One of a series of guides compiled by Algar for the colonies. Intended for prospective settlers, and emphasizes information on crop production but also contains sections on commerce, climate, education and local institutions.

1383

G.B. War Office. Intelligence Branch. **Précis of information concerning the Colony of Natal.** London, Feb. 1875. 92pp. map in pocket.

- - [rev. ed.] London, June 1875. 101pp.

- - ... **corrected to June 1879.** London, 1879. ii, 163pp. map in pocket.

Standard War Office "précis" coverage. Appendix to 1879 ed. includes 16 itineraries.

1384

G.B. War Office. Intelligence Branch. **Précis of information concerning the Zulu Country.** London, 1878. 34pp. map.

- - **Addendum.** London, 1878. 18pp.

- - ... **corrected to Jan. 1879.** London, 1879. 53pp. maps.

- - ... **corrected to July 1879.** London, 1879. 63pp. maps.

Standard "précis" coverage.

1385

G.B. War Office. Intelligence Division. **Précis of information concerning Zululand corrected to Oct. 1885.** London, 1885. 146pp. maps.

- - ... **corrected to Dec. 1894.** London, 1895. 175pp. map in pocket.

Comp. Capt. Wemyss. Standard War Office "précis". 15 routes are described in detail. 1885 ed. includes map at 1:253,440 (2 sheets); 1895 ed. has map at 1:380,160.

1386
Colonial & Indian Exhibition. **Natal, official handbook;** compiled under the directions of the Natal Commissioners. London, William Clowes, 1886. 108pp.

A wide range of information on history, geography, peoples, administration, local institutions and the economy with financial statistics from 1868 and trade statistics from 1846.

1387
Ingram, J.F. **Colony of Natal: an official illustrated handbook and railway guide.** London, Agent General for Natal, 1895. 273pp. 143 photos.

General section covering geography, peoples, the administration, natural resources and communications, followed by 15 chapters on particular districts.

1388
Harrison, C.W.F. **Natal: an illustrated official railway guide and handbook of general information.** London, Payne Jennings, 1903. xiii, 300pp. illus.

"Published by authority". Cover-title : **Natal: illustrated official railway guide and general handbook.** 'Book 1' is arranged by district, 'book 2' gives general information. Over 250 photographs. Sections of this work were revised and pub. as **Port Natal: illustrated handbook of general information relating to Durban Port Natal & railways in connection.** London, Payne Jennings, 1905. x, 82pp.

1389
G.B. War Office. General Staff. **South Africa: military report on Zululand.** London, 1906. (A. 1061). viii, 458pp. 3 maps in pocket.

Comp. Lt. F.A. Fynney. Pp. 1-179 cover topography, settlements, peoples, history and the administration; pp. 180-405 give details of 42 itineraries.

1390
G.B. War Office. General Staff. **Natal route book.** London, 1906. 2 vols. (vol. 2, B. 141). x, 364pp; x, 714pp. illus. Separate portfolio with 12 maps.

Outlines 42 itineraries with a wealth of detail on the topography, resources and peoples of the region.

1391
G.B. War Office. General Staff. **South Africa: military report on Natal.** London, 1909. vi, 163pp. maps in pocket.

General description, with sections on history, administration, native tribes and communications.

1392
South African Railways. **Natal Province: descriptive guide and official handbook**. Durban, 1911. xii, 574pp. illus. maps.

Ed. A.H. Tatlow with numerous contributors. Detailed information on history, topography, agriculture, industry, natural resources.

1393
Natal official guide. Cape Town, R.Beerman/Durban, Selected Publications, 1959. 397pp. illus.

Introductory sections on history, topography and public services followed by descriptive sections for each major town and city.

See also 1621.

Orange Free State

1394
G.B. War Office. General Staff. **Précis of information concerning South Africa: Orange River Free State and Griqualand West**. London, 1878. 101pp. map.

Pp. 1-66, Orange River State; pp. 67-101, Griqualand West. Standard War Office "précis". Maps at 1:100,000 (Orange Free State), 1:633,600 (Griqualand West).

- - **Appendix to Précis on Griqualand West**. London, 1879. 31pp. Includes 20 itineraries.

1395
G.B. War Office. Intelligence Branch. **Précis of information concerning South Africa: District of Griqualand West, 1884**. London, 1885. 71pp. map.

Includes some 25 brief itineraries.

1396
Orange Free State official guide. Cape Town, R. Beerman, 1956. 401pp.

General data and descriptive gazetteer of individual towns. Over 400 illus.

Transvaal

1397
Handbook to the Transvaal. London, S.W. Silver & Co., 1877. viii, 125pp.

Topography and natural resources; administrative divisions; industries and agriculture; trade & finance; history. Appendices of texts of documents relevant to the annexation of Transvaal.

1398
Becker, C.J. **Guide to the Transvaal.** Dublin, J. Dollard, 1878. 214pp. (Reprinted, Pretoria, State Library, 1976).

Information, especially on agriculture and local institutions aimed principally at the prospective immigrant. Less factual detail than in the 1877 **Handbook to the Transvaal** (*see* 1397).

1399
G.B. War Office. Intelligence Branch. **Précis of information concerning South Africa: the Transvaal Territory.** London, 1878. 89pp. map.

Standard précis. Map at 1:1,850,000.

- - **Appendix ...** London, 1879. 47pp.

Gives details of 15 itineraries.

- - [rev. ed.] **Précis ... corrected to Nov. 1880.** London, 1881. 178pp.

1400
National guide to the Transvaal. London, Simpkin Marshall for Diamond & Co., 1902. vii, 190pp. map.

1401
Bell, H.T.M. & Lane, C.A. **A guide to the Transvaal.** Johannesburg, South African Association for the Advancement of Science, 1905. xvi, 288pp. illus. maps.

1402
G.B. War Office. General Staff. **Military report on the Transvaal.** London, 1906-1907. 2 vols. maps in pocket.

Vol. 1, 1906. General (A. 1076). vi, 77pp. Includes geography, history, administration, natural resources, lists of tribes distributed by district. Vol. 2, 1907. Communications (A. 1132). v, 502pp. A particularly expansive example of the War Office "Routes" volumes with much ancillary detail on the local areas and peoples included under each itinerary.

1403
Transvaal official guide. Cape Town, Beerman, 1960.

Special topics

Ethnography

1404
Van Warmelo, N.J. **A preliminary survey of the Bantu tribes of South Africa,** Pretoria, South African Department of Native Affairs, 1935. (Ethnological publications, 5). 123, ixpp. 23 maps.

Includes alphabetical list of ethnic groups, statistics on their distribution by geographical district, and a classified account under five main divisions, noting distribution, approximate numbers and rulers of each group.

1405
Ethnographic survey of Africa: Southern Africa. London, International African Institute, 1953-1954. 4 vols. illus. maps.

Sub-series of **Ethnographic survey** (*see* 54). Vol. 1, 'The Swazi', by H. Kuper. 1952. 89pp; vol. 2, 'The southern Sotho', by V.G.J. Sheddick. 1953. 86pp; vol. 3, 'The Tswana', by I. Schapera. 1953. 77pp; vol. 4, 'The Shona and Ndebele of Southern Rhodesia', by H. Kuper, *et al.* 1954. 131pp.

Language and literature

1406
Pettman, C. **Africanderisms: a glossary of South African colloquial words and phrases, and of place and other names.** London, Longmans, 1913. xviii, 579pp. (Reprinted, Detroit, MI, Gale, 1969).

- - Swart, C.P. **Africanderisms: a supplement to the Rev. Charles Pettman's glossary.** M.A. thesis, University of South Africa, Pretoria, 1934.

- - Jeffreys, M.D.W. 'Africanderisms [not in Pettman]', *Africana notes and news* 16, 1964, 43-95; 17, 1967, 216-220; 19, 1970, 29-41.

Includes quotations to illustrate use.

1407
Grove, A.P. **Letterkundige sakwoordeboek vir Afrikaans.** [Cape Town, NASOU, 1964]. 104pp.

Dictionary of literary terminology. Includes bio-bibliographies of selected Afrikaans authors.

1408
Beeton, D.R. & Dorner, H.H.T. **A dictionary of English usage in Southern Africa.** Cape Town, Oxford University Press, 1975. xix, 196pp.

Includes glossary of local vocabulary and idiom, and a record of "mistakes and problems" in local usage.

1409
Branford, J. **A dictionary of South Africanisms in English.** Cape Town, Oxford University Press, 1978. 352pp.

- - rev. ed. **A dictionary of South African English.** Cape Town, 1980. xxxi, 361pp.

- - 3rd ed. Cape Town, 1987. xxxi, 444pp.

Some 4,000 entries ranging from historical terms to modern slang, with definitions, etymology, and illustrations of use in context.

1410
Adey, D. *et al.* **Companion to South African literature.** Johannesburg, Donker, 1986. 220pp.

Contains 450 author entries, 39 articles on literary genres, and entries for major titles or topics. Includes authors born or resident in South Africa, Botswana, Lesotho and Swaziland, together with those who made the region a major theme in their work.

1411
Grobler, E. *et al.* **Language atlas of South Africa: language and literacy patterns.** Pretoria, Human Sciences Research Council, 1990. 74pp.

23 language maps with accompanying analysis.

See also 1524.

Music

1412
South African music encyclopedia (SAME). Cape Town, Oxford University Press for Human Sciences Research Council, 1979-1986. 4 vols.

Ed. in chief, J.P. Malan. Project for compilation commenced 1962, under auspices of National Bureau for Educational and Social Research. Covers history of music in South Africa 1652-1960, both European and indigenous. Entries for musicians and composers, musical instruments, histories of music in particular cities, theatres and concert halls. Detailed sources given. Lengthy introduction to vol. 1 discusses the problems of compilation and gaps in coverage. No general index. Review, *ABPR* 14, 1988, 108-109.

Politics

1413
Südafrika Handbuch: Südafrika, Namibia und Zimbabwe Politisches Lexikon. Wuppertal, Jugenddienst-Verlag, 1982. (Handbucher für die entwicklungspolitische Aktion und Bildungsarbeit, 4). 436pp. illus. maps.

Comp. by AKAFRIK (Aktionskomitee Afrika). Pt. 1 (pp. 21-168) is the "lexikon" with alphabetically arranged entries for current political leaders, parties and other groups and for regions of Southern Africa. Pt. 2 has general articles on broad themes, pt. 3 is bibliographical.

1414
Davies, R.H., *et al.* **The struggle for South Africa: a reference guide to movements, organizations and institutions.** London, Zed Books for Centre of African Studies, Eduardo Mondlane University, 1984. 2 vols.

- - rev. ed. London, 1988. 2 vols.

Accounts of specific political, religious, social and economic organizations. Detailed coverage of activities from 1984. Rev. ed. retains text of the original and adds an "Update" chapter at the end of each vol. covering events 1983-1987. Review, *IJAHS*, 23, 1990, 688-690.

1415
Williams, G. & Hackland, B. **Dictionary of contemporary politics of Southern Africa**. London, Routledge; New York, Macmillan, 1988. 339pp.

Covers South Africa; Botswana, Lesotho and Swaziland; Angola and Mozambique; Namibia; Malawi, Zambia and Zimbabwe; Tanzania. Entries for political figures, organizations, and terms.

1416
Kotzé, H. & Greyling, A. **Political organizations in South Africa**. Cape Town, Tafelberg, 1991. vi, 255pp. map.

"Published in conjunction with the Centre for South African Politics at the University of Stellenbosch". Lists some 150 organizations alphabetically with information on their membership, policies and activities. Includes general entries for e.g. "churches", "business organizations", "media", "sport". Biographical section covers 38 "political opinion leaders".

1417
Riley, E. **Major political events in South Africa, 1948-1990**. New York, Facts on File, 1991. 250pp. maps.

A detailed account of events year by year, accompanied by some 30 brief biographies.

YEARBOOKS

Bibliographies

1418
Bosman, F.C.L. 'Almanacs and year-books', *Standard encyclopedia of Southern Africa*, 1, 1970, 307-311.

Usefully selective list of major titles, arranged by date of publication.

1419
De Kock, C.I. **A guide to directories, year books and buyer's guides in the Republic of South Africa**. Durban, Bureau of Market Research, 1978. (Research reports, 63). 60pp.

See also 1359.

General

1420

The African court calendar and directory/De Afrikaansche Staatsalmanak.
Cape Town, Government Printing Office, 1801-1826. Annual.

Issue for 1801 preserved in manuscript only. No copy of issue for 1803 known
to survive (*SAB*). Published "under government approval". Includes civil and
military list, and from 1810, list of principal residents.

continued by:

The South African almanack and directory. Cape Town, George Greig [etc.],
1827-1897. Annual.

Title and publisher vary; principal variants include: **Cape of Good Hope
annual register/Cape calendar and annual register/Cape of Good Hope
almanac and annual register**, Cape Town, B.J. van de Sandt/ B.J. Van de
Sandt Villiers/John Noble (1837-1863); not published 1836, 1864; **Cape Town
directory**, Cape Town, C. Goode (1865-1867); **Cape of Good Hope commercial
directory and general business guide/General directory and guide book to
the Cape of Good Hope and its dependencies**, Cape Town, Saul Solomon &
Co. (1868-1887); **Argus annual and Cape of Good Hope directory/Argus
annual and South African directory/Argus annual and South African
gazetteer**, Cape Town, Argus Printing & Publishing (1888-1897). Contents
vary: issues for 1845 and 1846 are particularly detailed. Many issues contain
special articles. By the 1890s contains detailed statistics and commercial
directory. *SAB* vol. 1, pp. 25-26 gives a volume by volume account of this
work for 1801-1897. *Mendelssohn*, 1, pp.23-35 under the heading "Almanacs"
gives a very detailed account of many of the issues between 1805 and 1897,
listing individual features contained in each volume. *See also* Ogilvie, J.H.
'Cape almanacs,' in Smith, A.H. *ed.* **Africana curiosities**, Johannesburg,
Donker, 1973. The South African Library, Cape Town have a programme of
reprinting all vols. in the earliest series of almanacks in facsimile (including
the manuscript of the 1801 vol.).

1421
The Cape of Good Hope calendar and agriculturists guide. London, T. & J.
Allman, 1819. xxxii, 132pp.

Comp. G. Ross. Includes topographical, historical and economic data, with
lists of civil and military officials.

1422
The Cape of Good Hope almanack for 1826. Cape Town, W. Brideskerk, 1826. 68pp.

1423
Cape of Good Hope annual register, directory and almanack for the year 1829. Cape Town, W. Brideskerk, [1828?]. 44pp.

1424
South African almanack for ... 1829. Cape Town, W. Brideskerk, [1828?]. 104pp.

English and Dutch. Includes "Directory for Cape Town and its environs", pp. 73-100.

1425
De Kaapsche almanak en naamboek/Cape calendar and directory. Cape Town, J.S. de Lima [etc.], 1832-1851. Irreg.

Title varies: **Kaapsche almanak en naamlyst/Cape[of Good Hope] almanac and directory** (1837-1851). Issues for 1832-39, 1841-43, 1848, 1851 (*SAB*). Comp. and pub. by J. Suasso de Lima. Correspondence in the Cape Archives suggests that the series commenced in 1830 and continued to 1854 but copies for 1830-31 and 1852-54 have not been traced (*QBSAL*, 3, 1948-49, 12). De Lima also compiled the much abbreviated **Kaapsche zak almanak/Cape pocket almanac** (1844, 1851, 1857-59)

1426
G.B. Colonial Office. **[Annual reports]: Cape of Good Hope, 1846-1882.** London, 1847-1883.

As **Reports: the past and present state of HM colonial possessions**, 1846-82, (not issued 1847, 1850-52, 1856, 1876-78, 1880-81), (as Command papers). No full report for 1853, 1857-60, 1864, 1867; "no report received" for 1869. *For fuller details see Appendix.*

1427
Eastern Province directory & almanac. Grahamstown, Godlonton and White, 1848-1849. 2 issues.

Title varies: **Eastern Province annual directory ...** (1849). Comp. R. Godlonton. Includes civil and military lists, surveys of each division of the Province, and a list of European inhabitants of Grahamstown.

1428

Eastern Province year book & annual register. Grahamstown, Godlonton & Richards [etc.], 1861-1884. Irreg.

Issues for 1861-1862, 1872-1873, 1875, 1878-1884 (*SAB*). Title varies: **Eastern Province year book [&] diary [& commercial directory]** (1872-1879); **Commercial directory & guide to the Eastern Province** (1880-1881); **Eastern Province year book & commercial directory** (1882-1884).

1429

Port Elizabeth directory and guide to the Eastern Province. Port Elizabeth, J.W.C. Mackay, 1872-85. Annual (irreg.) 12 issues.

Issues for 1872-1882, 1885.

1430

G.B. Colonial Office. **[Annual reports]: Griqualand West, 1873-75.** London, 1875-1877.

As **Reports: the past and present state of HM colonial possessions**, 1873-75, (as Command papers). *For fuller details see Appendix.*

1431

The general directory of South Africa. Cape Town etc., Dennis Edwards, 1888- . Annual.

Title varies; **Business directory of South Africa** (1919-). Regional coverage varies over the years, but basically includes South Africa, South-West Africa/Namibia, Botswana, Lesotho and Swaziland, Mozambique, with more summary coverage for central and eastern African countries. Up to the change of name in 1919 much non-commercial information was included: lists of civil, military, naval, religious, legal and medical personnel, a press directory, lists of graduates from Cape Town University etc. After 1919, emphasis is on a commercial directory.

1432

Brown's South Africa. London, Sampson Low, Marston & Co. for Union Castle Mail Steamship Co., 1893-1940, 1947-1949.

Title varies: **Guide to South Africa** (1894-1910/11); **Guide to South and East Africa** (1911/12-1918); **South and East African year book and guide** (1918-1949). Initially ed. A.S. & G.G. Brown. From 1911/12 adds information on eastern Africa, reflecting extension of Union Castle's sailings, and from 1913 has separate "East Africa" section, including British East Africa, Uganda, German East Africa, Nyasaland, Portuguese East Africa, Zambesia. From 1921 includes 64pp. atlas, also coverage of Mauritius. A major long-running source of primarily topographic, social and economic information. Continued by **Year book and guide to East Africa** (1950-65, *see* 541) and **Year book and guide to Southern Africa** (1950-71, *see* 1448).

1433
The Cape Town directory. Cape Town, Dennis Edwards, 1893-1899. Irreg. 3 issues.

Issues for 1893 (xliv, 223pp), 1897/98 (vi, 306pp), 1899 (xcvii, 427pp). Title varies: **The South Africa year book and directory of Cape Town** (1899). 1899 issue includes increased statistical coverage, and clerical, legal and medical directories.

1434
Donaldson & Hill's Eastern Province (Cape Colony) directory. Johannesburg, Donaldson & Hill, 1900-1905. Annual. 4 issues.

Issues for 1900, 1902/03, 1904, 1905.

1435
Longlands' Cape Town & district [peninsular] directory. Cape Town, Longlands, 1901-1904. 4 issues.

Comp. H. Longlands.

1436
Donaldson & Hill's Western Province (Cape Colony) directory. Johannesburg, Donaldson & Hill, 1902-1905.

Issues for 1902/03, 1904, 1905.

1437
South African year-book 1902/03 [etc.]. London, W. & A.K. Johnston [etc.]/ Cape Town, Darter Bros, & Walton [etc.], 1902-1903. 2 issues.

Issues for 1902/03 (xiii, 1056pp.) and 1903/04 (xxxiii, 888pp.). Comp. & ed. S.M. Gluckstein. A detailed work with particular emphasis on the Anglo-Boer War. Separate sections for each colony and for Rhodesia, Bechuanaland, Basutoland, Portuguese East Africa, German South-West Africa.

1438

The Imperial trades directory of South Africa, 1904. London & Cape Town, n.p., 1903. 816pp.

The bulk of the work comprises a directory of mining companies (alphabetical by name), and one of commercial organizations, by city, but there is also general information, history and statistics for each state, and a list of all South African railway stations.

1439

Official South African municipal year book. Cape Town/Pretoria, South African Association of Municipal Employees, 1909- . Annual.

Gives brief description, administrative structure, lists of officials, and statistics for municipalities of each province. Includes South-West Africa. Early issues also include Rhodesia.

1440

The South African almanack and reference book, 1911/12; the national South African chronicle, gazetteer and year book. Cape Town, Argus Printing & Publishing, 1911. 864pp.

Comp. E. Glanville. "Continues, with regard to South Africa, the service performed formerly by the **Argus annual**" (*see* 1420). Biographical section, pp. 149-182.

1441

South African year book. London, George Routledge, 1914. iv, 680pp.

Comp. W.H. Hosking. "First issue of an annual ... based largely on ... information supplied by the Union Government, the several provincial governments etc." (preface). Wide ranging treatment of topography, natural resources, flora and fauna, races and languages, communications, finance, administration, and the press. Major emphasis on trade (pp. 192-456). Biographical section with some 90 entries.

1442

Laite's commercial blue book for South Africa. Cape Town, South Africa Publishers Ltd., 1914-1916. 3 issues.

Comp. W.J. Laite. Large scale work (1916 ed. 727pp.) combining general topographical information with a very detailed civil service list, summaries of the census, statistics for production and trade, commercial directory etc. In 1916 ed., pp. 678-727 cover Southern Rhodesia (principally statistics and civil list).

1443
South Africa. **Official year book of the Union of South Africa**. Pretoria, Board of Census and Statistics, 1917-1960. Annual (irreg.) 30 vols.

Issues for 1917-1919, 1921-1925, 1926/27-1934/35, 1937-1941, 1946, 1948-1950, 1952/53, 1954-55, 1956-57, 1960. Title varies: from issue 3 (1919) **... and of Basutoland, Bechuanaland Protectorate and Swaziland**. Issues 1-7 (1917-1924) also issued in Dutch; from issue 8 (1925) onwards also issued in Afrikaans. Each issue contains comparative statistics since 1910; issues 1 to 8 include an indication of this on the volume's spine (e.g. issue 5, 1922, has "1910-21") which has led some sources to catalogue the series as commencing publication in 1910. Very detailed information on every aspect, with excellent detailed table of contents. Many issues contain special articles whose existence can be traced from the indexes to later volumes. Coverage was eventually continued by **South Africa: official yearbook of the Republic of South Africa** (*see* 1450) for general factual data, and **South African statistics** (*see* 1473) for statistical tables.

1444
Harrison, C.W.F. **The trade, industries, productions and resources of British South Africa and adjacent territories, 1923/24 [etc.]: a handbook of commercial information**. Woodchester [etc.], Arthur's Press, 1923-1927. Irreg. 4 issues.

Issues for 1923, 1924, 1926, 1927. Title varies: **Harrison's business and general year-book of South Africa and adjacent territories, 1927/28** (1927). First issue "an extension of the reviews issued in 1921 and 1922" (preface), i.e. **Report[s] on the trade conditions ... in British South Africa**, compiled for the Federation of British Industries. Includes coverage of Rhodesia and Portuguese East Africa.

1445
Braby's commercial directory of south, east & central Africa 1924/25 [etc.]. Durban, A.C. Braby, 1924- . Annual.

Title varies: **Braby's commercial directory of south and central/ ... of southern Africa**. Regional coverage varies, but basically includes modern South Africa and Namibia, Botswana, Lesotho and Swaziland, Angola and Mozambique, Malawi, Zambia and Zimbabwe, Réunion, Mauritius and

Seychelles. At times, e.g. in late 1940s, also included some coverage of Kenya, Uganda, Tanzania and Belgian Congo. 1926 ed. 996pp; 1949 ed. 2,718pp; 1985 ed. 3 vols. Braby's also publish a series of derived and expanded local directories for South African provinces and major cities (*see below* for the major provincial directories).

1446
Cape Times South African directory [etc.]. Cape Town, "Cape Times" [etc.], 1933- . Annual.

Title varies : **Cape Times directory of southern Africa; Directory of southern Africa** (1964-). 38th ed. 1971, xliii, 36, 1434pp. 1987 ed. 4 vols. Regional coverage varies but basically includes the modern South Africa and Namibia; Botswana, Lesotho and Swaziland; Mozambique; Malawi, Zambia and Zimbabwe. Earlier vols. also covered the Belgian Congo. Contains civil list, detailed commercial directory by country and province. A competitor to **Braby** (*see* 1445).

1447
The national business directory of South Africa. Cape Town, National Publishing Co., 1928- . Annual.

Title varies: **The 1955** [etc.] **national trade index and directory of southern Africa** (1955-68); **The business blue-books national trade-index of South Africa and Rhodesia** (1969-).

1448
Year book and guide to southern Africa. London, Sampson Low, Marston/ Hale for Union-Castle Mail Steamship Co., 1950-1971.

Not published 1968, 1970. Title varies: **Guide to southern Africa** (1969, 1971). A continuation for Southern Africa of **Brown's South Africa** later **South & East Africa yearbook and guide** (1893-1949, *see* 1432). Includes modern South Africa and Namibia; Botswana, Lesotho and Swaziland; Malawi, Zambia and Zimbabwe.

1449
State of the Union of South Africa: economic, financial and statistical yearbook for the Union of South Africa. Johannesburg, Da Gama Publications, 1957- . Annual.

Title varies: **State of South Africa: economic, financial and statistical yearbook for the Republic of South Africa ...** (1963-). Sub-title varies.

resources, industry, agricultural and trade.

1450
South Africa. Department of Foreign Affairs and Information. **South Africa: official yearbook of the Republic of South Africa**. Pretoria, 1974- . Annual.

A continuation of the general reference data formerly contained in **Official yearbook of the Union of South Africa** (1917-1960, *see* 1443). From 1991/92 (1991) appears in a much shortened version (c.200 rather than 800pp).

Cape

> *Only titles which continued, or commenced publication after the formation of the Union of South Africa in 1910 are listed here. Earlier titles covering "Cape of Good Hope", "Cape Colony" etc. are listed in the main sequence above.*

1451
Juta's directory of Cape Town. Cape Town, Juta, 1897- . Annual.

Title varies: **Juta's directory of the Cape peninsula** (1928-32); **Cape Times Cape peninsula directory** (1933-1963/64); **Cape Times peninsula directory** (1964/65-).

1452
Donaldson & Braby's Cape Province directory 1912/13 [etc]. Cape Town, 1912- . Annual.

Title varies: **Donaldson's Cape Province directory** (1925-55); **Braby's Cape Province directory** (1956-). At various times included coverage of Eastern Griqualand, Tembuland, Bechuanaland, South-West Africa.

Natal

1453
Port Natal almanac. Durban, J. Cullingworth etc., 1851-1903. Annual (irreg.)

Title varies: **Cullingworth's Port Natal almanac** (1858-1863); **Cullingworth's Natal almanac and Durban directory** (1851-1903). Issues for 1851-1853, 1858, 1860-61, 1863-65, 1869-72, 1874, 1877, 1882, 1886-90, 1899, 1903 (*SAB*).

1454
G.B. Colonial Office. **[Annual reports]: Natal, 1853-92**. London, 1854-1894.

As **Reports: the past and present state of HM colonial possessions,** 1853-80 (not issued 1872-79, 1881-86), **Report on the Blue Book for Natal,** 1887-89 (not issued 1890), **Annual report for Natal,** 1891-92, (as Command papers). *For fuller details see Appendix.*

1455
Natal almanac and yearly register. Pietermaritzburg, P. Davis & Sons, 1863-1910. Annual.

Title varies: **Natal almanac, directory & yearly register** (1871-1906); **Natal directory** (1907-1910).
- - Vietzen, C. **The "Natal almanac & yearly register", 1863-1906: a bibliographical index.** Cape Town, University of Cape Town, School of Librarianship, 1963. vii, 38pp.

1456
G.B. Colonial Office. **[Annual reports]: Zululand, 1889-1896.** London, 1890-1897.

As **Report on the Blue Book for Zululand,** 1889, **Annual report on Zululand,** 1890-1896 (all as Command papers). *For fuller details see Appendix.*

1457
Donaldson & Hill's Natal directory, 1901/02 [etc.]. Johannesburg, Donaldson & Hill/ Durban, A.C. Braby, 1901- . Annual (irreg.)

Title varies: **Braby's Natal directory including Zululand, Griqualand East and Pondoland** (1908-09); **Braby's Natal directory** (1910-). Lists of administration, residents and commercial directory.

Orange Free State

1458
Donaldson & Hill's Orange Free State directory, 1899/1900 [etc.] Johannesburg, Donaldson & Hill/ Durban, etc. A.C. Braby, 1899- . Annual (irreg).

Title varies: issues 2-4, **... Orange River Colony directory** (1903-05); **Braby's Orange River Colony directory,** n.s. issues 1-4 (1907-1910); **Braby's Orange Free State and Northern Cape directory,** issue 5 (1911-).

Transvaal

1459
Transvaal book almanac & directory. Pietermaritzburg [etc.], P. Davis [etc.],
1877-1889. Irreg. 5 issues.

Comp. F. Jeppe. Issues for 1877, 1879, 1881, 1887, 1889. Title varies: **Jeppe's
Transvaal almanac and directory** (1889). Includes statistics and civil list.

1460
G.B. Colonial Office. **[Annual reports]: Transvaal, 1878.** London, 1880.

As **Papers relating to colonial possessions**, 1878. (C.2598). One report only
issued. *For fuller details see Appendix.*

1461
Barnes's Transvaal almanac and directory. Pretoria, Flavell, Brown & Co.,
1888-1889. 2 issues.

Comp. H. Cornforth & A. Barnes. General information and business directory.

1462
Longland's Johannesburg & suburban directory. Johannesburg, Longlands
Directory & Advertising Co., 1892-1905. 12 issues.

Title varies: **Longland's Johannesburg & district directory** (1893-1896);
Longland's Johannesburg & South African Republic [& Rhodesia] directory
(1897-1899); **Longland's Transvaal [& Rhodesian] directory** (1902-1905).

1463
Donaldson & Hill's Transvaal & Rhodesia directory. Johannesburg,
Donaldson & Hill, etc., 1898- . Annual (irreg.)

Issues for 1898, 1899, 1903, 1904, 1905; then title varies: **Donaldson & Braby's
Transvaal and Rhodesia directory** (1910-1914); **Braby's Transvaal [&
Rhodesia] directory** (15th ed. 1970).

1464
Holmden's directory of the Transvaal. London, etc., F.H. Clarke & Co., 1904.
xxviii, 2199pp.

Johannesburg (pp. 1-1518); Pretoria (pp. 1524-1826). Very detailed commercial
and residential directory.

1465
The United Transvaal directory. Johannesburg, United Transvaal Directory
Co., 1908- ?. Irreg.

Issues traced for 1910, 1911, 1913, 1914, 1917, 1918, 1928. Includes Lourenço
Marques.

STATISTICS

Bibliographies

1466
Geertsma, G. & Klerck, J.R. **A guide to statistical sources in the Republic of
South Africa**. Pretoria, University of South Africa, Bureau of Market Research,
1962. 2 vols.

- - 2nd ed. comp. M.H. Naudé. Pretoria, 1972. (Research report, 30). 214pp.

- - rev. ed. comp. E.M. Steenkamp. Pretoria, 1979. (Research report, 70).
177pp.

1979 ed. lists some 600 different sources.

1467
South Africa. Department of Cultural Affairs, Division of Library Services.
**Bibliography of South African government publications: Department of
Statistics, 1910-1968**. Pretoria, 1969. v, 123pp.

- - **Supplement, 1969-1977**. Pretoria, 1978. microfiche.

1468
Horner, D., *et al.* **A short list of South African statistical sources**, Cape Town,
University of Cape Town, School of Economics, Division of Research, 1980.
23pp.

Features 31 major official sources, with many more "other sources".

General

1469
South Africa. Bureau of Census and Statistics. **Union statistics for fifty years**.
Pretoria, 1960. [vi, 448pp].

A major compilation of comparative statistical data for 1910-1960.

1470
Southern Africa Data. Pretoria, Africa Institute of Southern Africa, 1969-1973.

Statistics issued as collections of loose-leaf sheets in 11 topical groups: population, health, education, labour, field and animal husbandry, forestry and fishing, mining, water and electricity, transport, postal services, housing and judicial.

Bulletins

1471
South Africa. Office of Census and Statistics. **Half-Yearly abstract of Union statistics 1919/20**. Pretoria, 1919. 1 issue + supplement.

continued by:

Quarterly abstract of Union statistics. Pretoria, 1920-1922. 12 issues.

continued by:

South Africa. Central Statistical Services [etc.]. **Monthly bulletin of Union statistics**. Pretoria, 1922- . Monthly/quarterly.

Title and frequency vary: **Monthly bulletin of statistics** (1961-67); **Bulletin of statistics** (1967- Quarterly).

Yearbooks

1472
South Africa. Bureau of Census and Statistics [etc.]. **Statistical yearbook of the Union of South Africa 1912/13 [- 1915/16]**. Pretoria, 1913-1916. Nos. 1-4, with supplements to no. 3, 1914/15 and no. 4, 1915/16.

No. 1 in English, nos. 2-4 in English and Dutch. Continued by statistical sections in **Official yearbook of the Union of South Africa** (*see* 1443).

1473
South Africa. Bureau of Census and Statistics. **Statistical yearbook**. Pretoria, 1964- . Annual, 1964-1966, then every 2 years.

Title varies : **South African statistics** (1968-). A continuation of the statistical section of the **Official yearbook of the Union of South Africa** (*see* 1443). First issue, 1964, has lengthy section of comparative statistics for the period 1945-1963, not repeated in later issues.

1474
Statistik des Auslandes: Länderberichte: South Africa. Wiesbaden, Statistisches Bundesamt, 1985- . Irreg.

Issues for 1985, 1987.

Regional

1475
Cape Colony. **Cape Colony statistical register.** Cape Town, 1873-1909. 37 issues.

1476
Transvaal. **Statistics of the Transvaal Colony.** Pretoria, 1907-1909. 3 vols.

Coverage is of 1902/07, 1903/08, 1904/09.

1477
Statistical abstracts on self-governing territories in South Africa. Sandton, Institute for Development Research, Development Branch of South Africa in collaboration with the governments of the territories, 1987- . Annual.

DIRECTORIES OF ORGANIZATIONS

1478
South Africa. Council for Scientific and Industrial Research. **Directory of scientific research organizations.** Pretoria, 1950.

continued by :

South Africa. Council for Scientific and Industrial Research. **Directory of scientific resources in South Africa.** Pretoria, 1961. looseleaf in continuation.

Updated until 1966, in 5 sections : research organizations; sources of scientific information in South African libraries; scientific societies; scientific & technical periodicals; list of acronyms.

continued by:

South Africa. Council for Scientific and Industrial Research. **Directory of scientific research organizations in South Africa**. Pretoria, 1967- . Annual.

and:

South Africa. Council for Scientific and Industrial Research. **Directory of scientific and learned societies in South Africa**. Pretoria, 1967- . Annual.

1479
Musiker, R. **Guide to sources of information in the humanities**. Potchefstroom, Potchefstroom University & South African Library Association, 1962. iv, 100pp.

- - **Supplement**. Potchefstroom, 1965. ii, 25pp.

Directory of libraries and special collections. Original vol. lists 84 institutions, supplement adds 13 new entries and gives revised information for 22.

1480
State Library, Pretoria. **Directory of South African libraries: part 1, Scientific & research libraries**. Pretoria, 1965. 576pp.

336 entries for South Africa & South-West Africa; Malawi, Rhodesia and Zambia.

continued by:

Handbook of Southern African libraries. Pretoria, 1970. cxiv, 939pp.

Essentially a 2nd ed. of **Directory of South African libraries** (1965) *above*. 833 entries. Includes Rhodesia.

continued by:

Directory of Southern African libraries, 1975. Pretoria, 1976. ix, 301pp.

3rd ed. of the directory. 941 entries for South Africa and South-West Africa; Botswana, Lesotho and Swaziland; Malawi and Zambia. Rhodesia omitted since now covered by **Directory of Rhodesian libraries** (1969, *see* 741).

- - 4th ed. Pretoria, 1983. 533pp.

Contains 1,348 entries.

- - 5th ed. Pretoria, 1990. xiii, 463pp.

1,377 entries for South Africa, the "homelands", Botswana, Lesotho and Swaziland; Malawi, Zambia, Zimbabwe.

1481
Educational institutions in South Africa. Johannesburg, Erudite Publications, 1967. xii, 425pp.

1482
Fransen, H. **Guide to the museums of Southern Africa.** Cape Town, South African Museums' Association, 1969. 147pp.

- - 2nd ed. Cape Town, 1978. 231pp.

Arranged by country: covers South Africa, Namibia and Transkei; Botswana, Lesotho and Swaziland; Malawi, Rhodesia and Zambia; Angola and Mozambique.

1483
South Africa. Human Sciences Research Council. **Directory of research organizations in the human sciences in South Africa.** Pretoria, 1970. 159pp.

- - 2nd ed. Pretoria, 1972. vi, 227pp.

Includes central state and local governments, university departments and private organizations.

1484
Bridge 1987: an index of organizations at work in South Africa. Grant Park, Human Awareness Programme, 1987. 2 vols. (550pp.)

Lists institutions alphabetically and by province with an emphasis on the fields of education, health and welfare, religion, legal aid and social assistance.

1485
Kontak 1989. Randburg, Thomson Publications, [1989?]. 264pp.

Ed. D. Fiansky. Lists provincial and local government bodies, also a variety of institutions including museums and universities in South Africa, Botswana, Lesotho, Swaziland, the "homelands" and Zimbabwe.

1486
South Africa. Council for Scientific and Industrial Research. **Directory of South African associations, 1991.** Pretoria, 1990. 209pp.

See also 1414-1416.

BIOGRAPHICAL SOURCES

Bibliographies

1487
Ushpol, R. **A select bibliography of South African autobiographies.** Cape Town, University of Cape Town, School of Librarianship, 1958. iv, 48pp.

Lists 143 titles.

1488
Johannesburg Public Library. **Alphabetical index to the biographical notices in "South Africa", 1892-1928.** Johannesburg, 1963. 114pp.

Comp. E. Rosenthal. A continuation covering 1929-1970 was noted as "in progress" (*ARD*, 21, 1979, 17).

1489
Olivier, Le R. **Versamelde Suid-Afrikaanse biografië: 'n bibliografie.** Cape Town, University of Cape Town, School of Librarianship, 1963. v, 71pp.

A guide to collected biography.

1490
Van Oordt, L.C. 'Biography, Dictionaries of', *Standard encyclopedia of Southern Africa*, 2, 1970, pp. 329-334.

Brief list of major titles arranged chronologically. Provides only sketchy bibliographical details.

1491
Stern, M.J. **South African Jewish biography 1900-1966: a bibliography.** Cape Town, University of Cape Town Library, 1972. 28pp.

General

1492

Anglo-African who's who and biographical sketch book. London, L. Upcott Gil/Walter Judd, 1905-1910. 3 issues.

Issues for 1905, 1907, (ed. W.H. Wills), and 1910 (ed. L. Weinthal). 2nd and 3rd issues include portraits. 1907 issue includes some 2,000 entries, varying from 2 lines to 3 pages; 1910 issue contains shorter and fewer entries (about 1,600), with a separate section on the "South African Press" including biographies of 91 editors of South African newspapers. Overall coverage basically confined to South Africa.

1493

Men of the times. Johannesburg, Transvaal Publishing Co., 1905-1906. 2 vols.

Vol. 1, 1905. viii, 390pp. "Pioneers of the Transvaal and glimpses of South Africa"; vol. 2, 1906. ix, 645pp. "Old colonists of the Cape Colony and Orange River Colony".

- - **Index to "Men of the times" vol. 2.** Cape Town, University of Cape Town Libraries, 1960 (Libraries Varia, 3.) i, 22pp.

Extensive biographies, with many portraits, of some 2,000 individuals.

1494

Natal who's who: an illustrated biographical sketch book of Natalians. Durban, Natal Who's Who Publishing Co., 1906-1907. Annual. 2 issues.

Includes some 1,500 biographies per issue, many with portraits.

continued by:

South African who's who 1907 [etc.]. Johannesburg, Combined Publishers/ Ken Donaldson [etc.], 1908- . Annual (irreg.)

Title varies: **Who's who of Southern Africa** (1959-) with expanded coverage of neighbouring countries. The major continuing biographical source for the region. Sections for Central Africa are also published separately as **Who's who of Rhodesia, Mauritius, Central and East Africa** (1960-) *see* 665. Includes portraits.

1495

Die Afrikaner-personenregister. Johannesburg, Afrikaner se Koop Gids, 1942. 373pp.

Some 2,250 short biographies of Afrikaners, living and dead, with portraits.

1496
Nienaber, P.J. **Afrikaanse biografiese woordeboek. Vol. 1.** Johannesburg, L. & S. Boek en Kunssentrum, 1947. 290pp. *No more published.*

Just over 200 entries with references to sources, principally items in newspapers.

1497
Wie is wie in Suid-Afrika. Johannesburg, Vitae Uitgewers, 1958-1967. Annual.

Some text in Anglish, some in Afrikaans. Includes South-West Africa.

1498
South African dictionary of national biography. London, Warne, 1966, xxxix, 430pp.

Comp. E. Rosenthal. About 2,000 brief entries for prominent personalities from 1460 to the present.

1499
Dictionary of South African biography (DSAB). Pretoria, Human Sciences Research Council [etc.], 1968- .

Vol. 1, 1968; vol. 2, 1972; vol. 3, 1977, vol. 4, 1981, vol. 5, 1987. A major work of co-operative scholarship. Founder and editor-in-chief until 1970, W.J. De Kock; editors-in-chief, D.W. Krüger (1970-72), C.J. Beyers (1973-). Each volume has a self-contained alphabetical sequence, together with an index to all entries in previous volumes. Articles are signed and have detailed references. Most entries are at least a page, and some considerably longer (e.g. "Smuts", 21pp). Over 4,500 entries in vols. 1 to 5. Also pub. in Afrikaans as **Suid-Afrikaanse biografiese woordeboek.** A description of the extensive planning involved is in : W.J. De Kock, 'Launching the **Dictionary of South African biography**', *QBSAL*, 17, 1962/63, 127-132.

1500
De Beer, M. **Who did what in South Africa.** Craighill, Donker, 1988. 196pp.

Popular biographical dictionary with some 1,200 entries for the living and the dead.

Genealogy, heraldry & works on early settlers

Bibliography

1501
Lombard R.T.J. **Handbook for genealogical research in South Africa.** Pretoria, Human Sciences Research Council for Institute for Historical Research, 1977. (I.H.R. Genealogy Publication, 6) 147pp. illus.

- - 2nd ed. Pretoria, 1984. xii, 164pp. illus.

- - 3rd ed. Pretoria, 1990. 146pp. illus.

A history of genealogy in South Africa, a discussion of methodology, and a descriptive guide to institutional sources, with a select bibliography of works of collective biography and a very extensive list of individual family histories.

General

1502
De Villiers, C.C. **Geslacht-Register der oude Kaapsche familiën.** Cape Town, de Sandt de Villiers, 1893-94. 3 vols.

Vol. 1, A-J; vol. 2, K-O; vol. 3, P-Z. Supplemented by Hoge, J. **Bydraes tot die genealogie van ou Afrikaanse families.** Cape Town, Balkema, 1958. 224pp., whose corrections and additions are incorporated into :

De Villiers, C.C. **Genealogies of old South African families**; completely rev. ed. augmented and rewritten by C. Pama. Cape Town, Balkema, 1966. 3 vols.

- - 2nd ed. Cape Town, 1981. 2 vols.

De Villiers' work, seen through the press after his death by G. M. Theal, is the classic guide to South African genealogy that all later work has built upon. Most genealogies in the original edition end in 1806, while Pama's revision covers from 1652 to 1850, and includes some 1,500 families, mostly Dutch and German with some French and English. For a discussion of De Villiers' work and the reasons why a revision was thought necessary, *see* C.Pama, 'Genealogy in South Africa', *QBSAL* 10, 1955/56, 128-132. Explanations and origins of the Dutch and German names in De Villiers are given in : Krige, J.D.A. **Oorsprong en beteknis van Nederlandse en Duitse familiename in die "Geslacht-register ...".** Pretoria, van Schaik, 1934. 109pp. The whole of De Villiers/Pama is eventually to be incorporated into Heese (*see* 1517).

1503

Kannemeyer, A.J. **Hugenote-familieboek**. Cape Town, Unie-Volkspers, 1940. vi, 282pp.

Covers original French emigrants to the Cape with brief notes on their subsequent family history.

1504

Hoge, J. 'Personalia of the Germans at the Cape, 1652-1806', *Archives yearbook for South African history*, 9, 1946, 1-495.

Identifies 4,000 names.

1505

Nienaber, G.S. **Afrikaanse familiename: 'n geselsie vir belangstellende leke oor die beteknis van oor Afrikaanse Vanne**. Cape Town, Balkema, 1955. 108pp.

The origins and development of Afrikaans family names.

1506

Malherbe, D.F. du T. **Driehonderd jaar nasiebou-stamouers van die Afrikanervolk**. Stellenbosch, Tegniek, 1959. xxv, 267pp.

- - 2nd ed. Stellenbosch, 1959.

- - 3rd ed. **Family register of the South African nation**. Stellenbosch, 1966. xxvii, 1208pp.

3rd ed has text in Afrikaans and English. Details of families not included in De Villiers (*see* 1502), covering 1652 to 1961.

1507

Rosenthal, E. **South African surnames**. Cape Town, Timmins, 1965. 262pp.

Gives origins and meanings of some 2,500 names of English, Afrikaans, Jewish and African origin.

1508

Raven-Hart, R. **Before Van Riebeck: callers at South Africa from 1488-1652**. Cape Town, Struik, 1967. 216pp.

Some 100 biographies.

1509

Jones, E. M. **Roll of the British settlers in South Africa.** Part 1 : Up to 1826. Cape Town, Balkema, 1969. ix, 174pp. *No more published?*

- - 2nd ed. Cape Town, 1971. xi, 174pp. A reprint of 1st ed. with 2pp. of additions and corrections.

Produced under the auspices of the 1820 Settlers' Monument Committee. Gives short biographies of some 100, and minimal detail on an additional 500 settlers in three sequences according to whether they arrived prior to 1820, actually in 1820 or between 1821 and 1826.

1510

Pama, C. **Heraldry of South African families: coats of arms, crests, ancestry.** Cape Town, Balkema, 1972. x, 365pp. illus.

Describes more than 1,100 coats of arms, almost all illustrated.

1511

Tabler, E.C. **Pioneers of Natal and south eastern Africa, 1552-1878.** Cape Town, Balkema, 1977. (South African biographical and historical studies, 21). 117pp.

Brief biographies of 244 individuals active in the area of modern Natal, Transvaal Low Veld, Swaziland and Southern Mozambique.

1512

Spencer, S.O'B. **British settlers in Natal, 1824-1857: a biographical register.** Pietermaritzburg, University of Natal Press, 1981-   .

5 vols. pub. to 1992, covering A-Dykes. Estimated that complete work will contain some 2,600 names. Most entries are very detailed, except for those individuals already covered in the **Dictionary of South African biography** (*see* 1499). Very full list of archival, manuscript and printed sources.

1513

Pama, C. **Die groot Afrikaanse familienaamboek.** Cape Town, Human & Rousseau, 1983. 380pp. illus.

Lists some 3,000 family names with notes on their origin, and of the earliest known settlers bearing them. Numerous coloured illustrations of coats of arms.

1514

Philip, P. **British residents at the Cape, 1795-1819: biographical records of 4,800 pioneers.** Cape Town, David Philip, 1983. xxiii, 484pp.

Covers the period before the first large scale British settlement which began in 1820. Based on the Cape Archives, the works of G.M. Theal and printed sources. Only brief entries for those who also have entries in the **Dictionary of South African Biography** (see 1499). Review, ABPR, 8, 1982, 59-60.

1515

Zöllner, L. & Heese, J.A. **The Berlin missionaries in South Africa and their descendants.** Pretoria, Human Sciences Research Council, Institute for Historical Research, 1984. (Genealogy publications, 19). viii, 586pp.

Traces descendants of 130 German immigrants who came to South Africa as members of the Berlin Missionary Society, together with biographical details on another 65 who left no descendants.

1516

Alexander, E.G.M., et al. **South African orders, decorations and medals.** Cape Town, Human & Rousseau, 1986. 160pp. illus.

1517

Heese, J.A. comp. **Suid-Afrikaanse geslagregisters/South African genealogies;** ed. R.T.J. Lombard. Pretoria, Human Sciences Research Council, 1986- .

Vol. 1, 1986. A-C. viii, 698pp; vol. 2, 1989. D-G. viii, 602pp. When complete will be the single major source in its field, and will include all data currently in de Villiers/Pama (see 1502) estimated to be some 13% of the entries envisaged. To contain complete family registers of all Afrikaans families from 1652 to about 1830; those of new progenitors of Afrikaans families up to 1867, and a number of English and coloured families. Vol. 1 includes some 75,000 names.

Special categories

Art

1518

Gordon-Brown, A. **Pictorial art in South Africa during three centuries to 1875, with notes on over four hundred artists.** London, Sawyer, 1952. 172pp. illus.

Short biographies, and a chronological list of lithographers and engravers. Addenda in *Africana notes and news*, 12, 1957, 229-269.

1519
Gordon-Brown, A. **Pictorial Africana: a survey of old South African paintings, drawings and prints to the end of the 19th century, with a biographical dictionary of one thousand artists.** Cape Town, Balkema, 1975. x, 254pp.

Essentially a revised and considerably expanded version of his **Pictorial art** ... (*see* 1518).

1520
Jeppe, H. **South African artists, 1900-1962.** Johannesburg, Afrikaanse Pers Boekhandel, 1963. 172pp.

- - **Index.** comp. F. Goldman. Johannesburg, Johannesburg Public Library, 1966. 6pp.

Brief biographies.

1521
Register of South African and South West African artists, 1900-1968. Pretoria, South African Association of Arts, 1969. 83pp.

Brief biographies.

1522
Berman, E. **Art and artists of South Africa: an illustrated biographical dictionary and historical survey of painters and graphic artists since 1875.** Cape Town, Balkema, 1970. xvi, 368pp.

Covers over 300 artists.

- - rev. ed. Cape Town, 1983. 545pp.

1523
Ogilvie, G. **The dictionary of South African painters and sculptors.** Johannesburg, Everard Read, 1988. 799pp.

Over 1,800 living artists.

Literature

1524
Nienaber, P.J. **Hier is ons skryvers: biografiese sketse van Afrikaanse syryvers**. Johannesburg, Afrikaanse Pers Boekhandel, 1949. 475pp.

Biographies of Afrikaans writers.

See also 1407.

Politics

1525
Gale, F.H. *ed*. **Who's who in the Union Parliament**: portraits and biographies of the two Houses of the first Parliament of the Union of South Africa. Cape Town, "Cape Times", 1911. 96pp.

1526
Karis, T. & Carter, G.M. *eds*. **From protest to challenge: a documentary history of African politics in South Africa, 1882-1964. Vol. 4. Political profiles**. Stanford, Hoover Institution, 1977. xv, 178pp. illus.

333 entries, including 48 whites. About half the entries are for living figures. 60 portrait and 8 group photographs.

1527
International Defence and Aid fund. **Prisoners of apartheid: a biographical list of political prisoners and banned persons in South Africa**. London, 1978. v, 180pp.

Brief biographies of 317 South African and 54 Namibian political prisoners, and of 175 banned persons.

1528
Gastrow, S. **Who's who in South African politics**. Johannesburg, Ravan Press, 1985. xiv, 347pp.

- - 2nd ed. Johannesburg, 1987. 365pp.

- - 3rd ed. Oxford, Hans Zell, 1990. vii, 368pp.

Lists parliamentary office-bearers, and officers of political organizations and provides detailed accounts of significant current politicians. 1st ed. covers 112 individuals; 2nd ed. covers 123, with 54 new entries; 3rd ed. covers 132, and notes another 92 covered in earlier eds. Entries often based on interviews, or on newspaper items. Review of 2nd ed., *IJAHS*, 21, 1988, 371-372. 4th ed. announced for 1993.

Ethnic & social groups: *Blacks*

1529
The African yearly register: being an illustrated national biographical dictionary (who's who) of black folks in Africa. Johannesburg, R.L. Esson, 1930.

- - 2nd ed. Johannesburg, 1932. xvii, 450pp.

- - 3rd ed. **African who's who**: an illustrated classified register and national biographical dictionary of the Africans in the Transvaal. Johannesburg, Central News Agency, 1963. 373pp.

All eds. comp. T.D. Mweli Skota. The first major biographical source for blacks only. 1st and 2nd eds. give coverage to all Africa although emphasis is very much on Southern Africa. 3rd ed. includes a wide range of miscellaneous information in addition to biographical entries, e.g. lists of black graduates from University of the Witwatersrand, lists of black schools and hospitals, notes on churches and clergy.

1530
Dee, S.D. **Black South Africans: 57 profiles of Natal's leading blacks: a whos who**. Cape Town, Oxford University Press, 1978. xxiii, 210pp. illus. map.

Based largely on interviews. Review, *ABPR*, 5, 1979, 94.

1531
The Black who's who of Southern Africa today. Johannesburg, African Business Publications, 1979- . Irreg.

Issues for 1979, 1982. Ed. S. Keeble. Includes introductory section on membership of black organizations, universities, etc., followed by brief biographical entries for individuals.

Indians

1532
The South African Indian who's who & commercial directory 1936/37. Pietermaritzburg, "Natal Witness", 1936.

Ed. D. Bramdaw.

Jews

1533
South African Jewry: a survey of the Jewish community, its contribution to South Africa, directory of commercial institutions, and who's who of leading personalities. Johannesburg, Fieldhill Publishing Co., 1965-1976. 3 issues.

Issues for 1965, 1968, 1976/77. Ed. L. Feldberg. "Incorporates **South African Jewish year book** and **Who's who in South African Jewry**" (preface).

See also 1491.

Women

1534
Lewis, T.H. *ed.* **Women of South Africa: a historical, educational and industrial encyclopedia and social directory of the women of the sub-continent.** Cape Town, Le Quesne & Hooton-Smith, 1912. various paging.

Brief biographies with portraits of some 1,500 women, followed by articles on women's organizations.

1535
South African woman's who's who. Johannesburg, Biographies (Pty) Ltd., 1938. 528pp.

ATLASES & GAZETTEERS

Atlases

1536
The Castle Line atlas of South Africa. London, Donald Currie, 1895. 47pp. 16 col. plates.

- - rev. ed. **The Union-Castle atlas of South Africa.** Capetown, Juta/London, Union Castle Mail Steamship Co., 1903. 48 pp. 21 col. plates.

30 topographic maps including 4 town plans. Covers South Africa and British Central Africa. Index of 6,000 names.

1537

Talbot, A.M. & Talbot, W.J. **Atlas of South Africa**: a selection of maps ... showing the distribution of crops, livestock etc. in 1946. Cape Town, University of Cape Town, Department of Geography, 1947. 48pp. maps. 25 x 41cm.

1538

Talbot, A.M. & Talbot, W.J. **Atlas of the Union of South Africa**. Pretoria, Govt. printer, 1960. [vii], lxiv, 177pp. 41 x 56cm.

Prepared in collaboration with the Trignometrical Survey Office and under the aegis of the National Council for Social Research. Text in English and Afrikaans. 592 black and white and 4 coloured thematic maps, chiefly 1:8M, in seven sections: physical geography, climate, population, agriculture, industry, transport, trade. Text contains descriptive data and very detailed statistical information. Includes Swaziland and Lesotho. "Material ... assembled, checked and mapped with meticulous care" (*GJ*, 129, 1963, 369-70).

1539

Road atlas and touring guide of Southern Africa. Johannesburg, Automobile Association of South Africa, 1960. 192pp.

- - 2nd ed. Johannesburg, 1963. 200pp.

- - 3rd ed. Johannesburg, 1968. 200pp.

- - 4th ed. Johannesburg, 1974. 232pp.

1540

South Africa. Department of Planning. **Development atlas**. Pretoria, 1966-1976. loose-leaf.

Issued in sections with text and maps, the majority at 1:3,500,000. Section 1, physical background (10 pp); 2, social aspects (30pp); 3, water (6pp); 4, minerals and mines (14pp); 5, agriculture (25pp); 6, communications (6pp); 7, industry (*not published?*); 8, commerce (6pp); 9, finance (*not published?*); 10, economic aspects (6pp); 11, possible development regions (*not published?*).

1541

RSA atlas. Cape Town, NASOU, 1970. 67pp.

- - 2nd ed. Cape Town, 67pp.

- - 3rd ed. **NASOU-atlas for the RSA.** Parow, 1981. iii, 75pp.

1542
Senior atlas for Southern Africa. Cape Town, Collins-Longman, 1976. 160pp.

Maps 1-9, South Africa; 10-43 other regions of Africa; 44-128 rest of the world.

1543
University of Stellenbosch. Institute for Cartographic Analysis. **Economic atlas of South Africa.** Stellenbosch, 1981. (Publication, 8). 160pp.

Ed. H.L. Zietsman & I.J. Van der Merwe. Includes 132 partially coloured maps. Also pub. in Afrikaans as **Ekonomie atlas van Suid-Afrika.**

1544
Reader's Digest atlas of Southern Africa. Cape Town, Reader's Digest Association, South Africa, 1984. 256pp.

Compiled in association with the Directorate of Surveys and Mapping. 213 maps, majority at 1:500,000. Index gazetteer of 30,000 names.

1545
Philip's atlas of Southern Africa and the world. London, Jonathan Ball with George Philip, 1986. 12, 48, 96, 64pp.

Maps 4-36, Africa; 37-97, rest of the world.

1546
University of Stellenbosch. Institute for Cartographic Analysis. **Population census atlas of South Africa.** Stellenbosch, 1986. (Publication, 15). 212pp. illus. 34 x 30cm.

Ed. H.L. Zeitsman & I.J. Van der Merwe.

See also 1364, 1411, 1432.

Historical atlases

1547
Walker, E.A. **Historical atlas of South Africa.** Cape Town, Oxford University Press, 1922. 26pp. text. 26 maps.

Detailed notes on sources used.

1548

Stockenström, E. **Historiese atlas van Suid-Afrika**. Stellenbosch, Pro-Ecclesia Drukkerj, 1928. 27pp. 67 maps.

Especially detailed for the history of the Cape.

1549

Boeseken, A.J., *et al.* **Geskiedenis atlas vir Suid-Afrika**. Cape Town, Nasional Boekhandel, 1948. x, 92pp.

 - - 2nd ed. Cape Town, Nasou, 1953. xii, 92pp.

World atlas with 80 black and white maps of which 32 cover South Africa. "Important for establishing the current spelling and form of geographical and historical names" (Musiker).

Gazetteers

Bibliographies

1550

Raper, P.E. & Möller, L.A. **Onomastic source guide**. Pretoria, Human Sciences Research Council, 1970-1981. 2 vols.

Vol. 2 is a supplement to vol. 1 covering literature pub. 1971-1978. Sources for both personal and place-names.

1551

Raper, P.E. **Source guide for toponomy and topology**. Pretoria, Human Sciences Research Council, 1975. (Onomastic series, 5). 478pp.

Detailed bibliography of books, articles, theses, and newspaper items concerned with the study of places and place-names.

1552

Raper, P.E., *et al.* **Manual for the giving of place names**. Pretoria, Human Sciences Research Council, 1979. 24pp.

Gazetteers

1553

G.B. Army. South African Field Force. Field Intelligence Division. **Districts, towns, villages, railway stations, sidings, post and telegraph offices in Cape**

Colony. Cape Town, 1901. xvii, 174pp.

- - [rev. ed.] **Directory of districts ...** . Cape Town, 1902. xv, 127pp.

Comp. by Capt. P.H. du P. Casgrain. Cover title of each ed. **Cape Colony directory.**

1554
Botha, C.G. **Place names in the Cape Province.** Cape Town, Juta, 1926. 186pp.

1555
Pettman, C. **South African place names past and present.** Queenstown, "Daily representative", 1931. 194pp. (Reprinted with a new foreword by P.E. Raper, Johannesburg, Lowry, 1985. xiv, 238pp).

Includes chapters on the origins of Bushman, Hottentot, Bantu, Portuguese, Dutch, French, English and German names. No index. Based on a series of articles published in *South African journal of science*, and in the *Bloemfontein friend*, 1915ff.

1556
South Africa. Department of the Interior. Departmental Committee on the Form and Spelling of Geographical Proper Names. 'Provisional list of geographical proper names in the Union of South Africa and in South West Africa,' *Union of South Africa Government Gazette*, 113 (2359) 24 August 1938, 567-639.

In Afrikaans and English. Lists 9,000 names. The first official attempt to standardize place names. Detailed comments on the list and the problems it raised include : H.G. Fourcade, 'Geographical names', *South African survey journal*, 5, 1939, 164-169; M. Aurousseau, 'Geographical names in South Africa', *GJ*, 94, 1939, 45-49. The South African Place Names Committee was appointed in 1940 to continue work on the list, and to be responsible for the approval of all proposed new or changed place names.

1557
Alphabetical classification of South African place names by Magisterial areas. Durban, Punched Card Services, 1949. 78pp.

- - 3rd ed. Johannesburg, Stability Typing & Copying Co., 1970. ii, 76pp.

- - rev. ed. Johannesburg, 1974. 101pp.

- - rev. ed. Johannesburg, 1984. 146pp.

In Afrikaans and English.

1558
South Africa. Post-master General. **Post offices in the Union of South Africa and neighbouring territories.** Pretoria, 1949. 151pp.

- - rev. ed. Pretoria, 1958. 192pp.

- - rev. ed. **List of post offices in the Republic of South Africa and neighbouring territories.** Pretoria, 1964. 183pp.

- - rev. ed. **List of post offices in the Republic of South Africa, in South-West Africa and other countries of the African Postal Union.** Cape Town, 1970. 179pp.

In Afrikaans and English.

1559
South Africa. Department of Education, Arts and Science. Place Names Committee. **Official place names in the Union and S.W. Africa approved to end 1948.** Pretoria, Government Printer, 1951. 376pp.

- - **Supplement, 1949-1952.** Pretoria, 1952. 54pp.

- - rev. ed. **Official place names in the Republic of South Africa and in South West Africa approved to 1 April 1977.** Pretoria, 1978. 329pp.

Includes names of townships, post offices, agricultural holdings and railway stations. Includes some names from Botswana, Lesotho, Swaziland and Zimbabwe. Supplement for 1978-1987 in preparation, with newly approved names pub. annually from 1988.

1560
U.S. Board on Geographic Names. **Preliminary N.I.S. gazetteer South Africa: offical standard names approved by the U.S.B.G.N.** Washington, DC, 1954. 2 vols. (iii, 1081pp).

Vol. 1. Union of South Africa, A-N; vol. 2. Union of South Africa, O-Z, Basutoland, Bechuanaland, South West Africa, Swaziland.

- - **Gazetteer supplement: Africa and South-West Asia.** Washington, DC,

1972. (pp. 138-140, Botswana; p. 137, Lesotho; pp. 141-142, South-West Africa; pp. 143-144, Swaziland)

1561
Holt, B.F. **Place names in the Transkeian Territories**. Johannesburg, African Museum, 1959. viii, 48pp.

1562
Nienaber, P.J. **Suid-Afrikaanse pleknaomwoordeboek: vol. 1**. Cape Town, Suid-Afrikaanse Boeksentrum, 1963.

- - 2nd ed. Cape Town, Tafelberg, 1972. 418pp.

Particularly concerned with the origins of Hottentot, Bantu, Portuguese and French names.

1563
Nienaber, P.J. **South African place names with special reference to Bushmen, Hottentot and Bantu place names**. Pp. 334-345 *in* Proceedings of the 8th International Congress of Onomastic Sciences, 1963. The Hague, 1966.

1564
Leistner, O.A. & Morris, J.W. **Southern African place names**. Grahamstown, Cape Provincial Museums, 1976. (Annals, 12). 565pp.

42,000 names for South Africa, Namibia, Botswana, Lesotho and Swaziland. Includes latitude and longitude and grid references.

1565
Merrett, C.E. **Index to the 1:50,000 maps series**. Pietermaritzburg, Natal Society Library, 1977. 2 vols.

Vol. 1. i, 37pp. Natal; vol. 2. i, 48pp. Cape, Orange Free State, Transkei and Transvaal. Covers features of human settlement (villages, towns, mission stations, historic sites, game parks). References to sheet number and name, but no actual co-ordinates.

1566
Nienaber, G.S. & Raper, P.E. **Toponymica hottentotica**. Pretoria, Human Sciences Research Council, 1977-82. 3 vols.

Series A, 2 vols. (Naamkundreeks 6, 7). vol. 1, A-G (1977). xx, 502pp.; vol. 2, H-Z (1979). xviii, 503-1126pp. Series B, 1 vol. (Naamkundreeks, 10). xviii,

822pp. Supplementary entries, with a cumulated index of all names covered by the 3 vols. Hottentot place names.

1567

Nienaber, G.S. & Raper, P.E. **Hottentot (Khoekhoen) place names**; trans. P.S. Rabie. Durban, Butterworths for Human Sciences Research Council, 1983. 243pp. illus. maps.

Based upon their Afrikaans work of 1977-82 (*see* 1566).

1568

Encyclopaedia of South African post offices and postal agencies. Tokai, Putzel, 1986-1990. 4 vols.

Comp. R.S. Putzel.

1569

Raper, P.E. **Dictionary of South African place names.** Johannesburg, Lowry, 1987. ix, 368pp.

- - 2nd ed. Johannesburg, Jonathan Ball, 1989. x, 608pp.

Covers the Republic of South Africa, Ciskei, Transkei and Venda; Namibia; Botswana, Lesotho and Swaziland. A descriptive gazetteer, with origins of names where known. Author was head of Onomastic Research Centre of the Human Sciences Research Council.

See also 1361, 1364, 1406.

NAMIBIA

*See also sections for **Former German Africa**. Many works published after 1920 and listed above under **South Africa** will also cover this region.*

HANDBOOKS

1570
G.B. War Office. General Staff. **Military report on German South-West Africa**. London, ?

- - 2nd ed. London, 1904. (A. 906) ?

- - 3rd ed. London, 1906. (A. 1131) vi, 208pp. 3 maps in pocket. - - **Addendum** I, London, 1908; - - **Addendum** II, London, 1910 (A. 1415). 213pp.

- - [4th ed] Pt. I. London, 1913. (A. 1723). 168pp. (All published? Copy of Pt. I in FCO Library contains original letter from War Office, dated 9 Feb 1915 stating "No part II has been issued").

Standard contents for War Office reports. Addenda follow same structure as the original volumes.

1571
Dove, K. **Deutsch Südwest-Afrika**. Berlin, W. Süsseroth, 1903. 208pp. illus. maps.

Detailed account of geography, history, natural resources and peoples.

1572
Dove, K. **Die deutschen Kolonien, 4: Südwestafrika**. Berlin & Leipzig, G.J. Göschen'sche Verlagsbuchhandlung, 1913. 96pp. illus. maps.

General handbook covering topography, ethnography, flora and fauna, administration. A shorter and updated version of his 1903 vol. (*see* 1571).

1573
Handbook of German South-West Africa. Johannesburg, "Transvaal Leader", 1914. vi, 52pp. illus. maps.

"Based upon ... work written by Prof. Dove [*see* 1572] but drawing on other official sources" (preface).

1574
G.B. Foreign Office. Historical Section. **South West Africa**. London, 1920. (F.O. Handbook, 112). 114pp.
Also pub. in F.O. **Peace handbooks**, vol. 18. London, 1920.

1575
SWA handbook 1964/65 [etc.]. Windhoek, South West Africa Agency, 1964.

- - 4th ed. **1967/68**. Windhoek, 1967. 110pp. illus. map.

- - 6th ed. **1971/72**. Windhoek, 1971. 127pp. illus. map.

Text in English/German/Afrikaans. Includes civil list, statistics, an historical chronology, and coverage of topography, natural resources and fauna.

1576
SWA/Namibia today. Windhoek, South West Africa/Namibia Information Service, 1979. 120pp. illus. map.

Ed. I. Van Rooyen. Also pub. in German and Afrikaans eds. Covers topography, peoples, history, administration, the economy, natural resources and tourism.

1577
Putz, J., *et al.* **Namibia handbook and political who's who**. Windhoek, Magus, 1989. 448pp.

A development of the earlier **Political who's who of Namibia** (*see* 1586). Lists active and inactive major and minor parties, and other political groups, giving details of their history, policies and manifestos, together with biographies of their leaders ranging from a line to a page. The detailed introduction claims that no political opinions are to be implied by inclusions or exclusions, and discusses the problems of compilation (e.g. all SWAPO data is from secondary sources).

- - 2nd "post election" ed. Windhoek, 1990. 446pp.

Covers events up to September 1989, with details on the new constitution and biographies of the anticipated Cabinet and National Assembly.

1578
Namibia 1990: an Africa Institute country survey. Pretoria, Africa Institute of South Africa, 1991. 240p. maps.

Comp. E. Leistner & P. Esterhuysen. Detailed collection of data, with emphasis on economic statistics. Appendices include brief biographies of members of the government and opposition parties.

See also 1413, 1415.

YEARBOOKS

1579
Taschenbuch für Südwestafrika. Leipzig, William Weisher/Berlin, Reimer, 1908-1914. Annual.

Eds. K. Schwabe, P. Kuhn, G. Fock.

1580
Adressbuch für Deutsch-Sudwestafrikanischesgebiet. Swakopmund, Verlag der Deutsch-Süd-Westafrika, ? . Issues for 1910, 1915/16 (*SAB*).

1581
South West Africa annual/jaarboek/jahrbuch. Windhoek, South West Africa Publications, 1945- . Annual.

A collection of individual contributions in each issue rather than a standardised presentation of data, but often contains useful statistical information.

1582
Braby's South West Africa directory. Durban, A.C. Braby, 1969- . Annual.

Title varies: **Braby's S.W.A./Namibia business directory** (1979-).

See also 662, 1431, 1437, 1452.

STATISTICS

1583
Statistik des Auslandes: Länderberichte: Namibia. Wiesbaden, Statistisches Bundesamt, 1986- . Irreg.

Issues for 1986, 1988.

DIRECTORIES OF ORGANIZATIONS

1584
South African Institute for Librarianship and Information Science, SWA/Namibia Branch. **Libraries in SWA/Namibia**. Windhoek, 1988. 58pp.

64 entries.

See also 1577.

BIOGRAPHICAL SOURCES

1585
Taylor, E.C. **Pioneers of South West Africa and Ngamiland, 1738-1880**. Cape Town, Balkema, 1973. (South African biographical and historical studies, 19). ix, 142pp.

Biographical notes on 333 adult male foreigners who travelled and settled in the region.

1586
Putz, J., *et al.* **Political who's who of Namibia**. Windhoek, Magus, 1987. 313pp.

Later revised and published with much additional non-biographical information as **Namibia handbook and political who's who** (*see* 1577).

See also 1527

ATLASES & GAZETTEERS

Atlases

1587
University of Stellenbosch. Institute for Cartographic Analysis & South West Africa/Namibia. Department of Civil Affairs and Manpower. **National atlas of South West Africa (Namibia)**. Cape Town, National Book Printers, 1983. 184pp. illus.

Ed. J.H. van der Merwe. 92 coloured maps, topographic and thematic, with detailed accompanying text, 29 tables, 50 diagrams and photographs.

Gazetteers

1588
Schumann, G. von & Rusch, W. **Index of names appearing on the 'Kriegskarte von Deutsch-Südwestafrika 1904'.** Windhoek, 1987. ii, 38pp. 1 map.

Lists, with grid references, some 4,000 names (including 200 translated into English) shown on the 8 sheets of the war maps, originally issued 1904, reprinted by Antiquariat am Klosterberg, Basle, 1987. The most detailed source for the region's early place names.

See also 1556, 1558-1560, 1564, 1569.

BOTSWANA, LESOTHO, SWAZILAND

*Many of the sources noted under **South Africa** (above) will also be relevant to these countries, especially for the period before independence.*

HANDBOOKS

1589

The guide to Botswana, Lesotho and Swaziland: a comprehensive companion for visitors and investors. Saxonwold, Winchester Press, 1983. 1212pp. illus. maps.

Pp. 7-441, Botswana, by A. Campbell; pp. 443-863, Lesotho, by D. Ambrose; pp. 865-1212, Swaziland, by D. Johnson. Detailed factual information on the countries, their peoples and the economy, with brief notes on sources.

See also 1361, 1364-1366, 1368, 1405, 1410, 1415.

BOTSWANA

HANDBOOKS

1590

G.B. War Office. General Staff. **Military report on the Bechuanaland Protectorate.** London, 1907. (A. 1136). 213pp. 3 maps in pocket.

Comp. by A.J.B. Wavell, based on an expedition undertaken in 1905. Standard War Office report treatment of topography, history and administration, natural resources, ethnography and communications.

1591

Stevens, R.P. **Historical dictionary of the Republic of Botswana.** Metuchen, NJ, Scarecrow Press, 1975. (African historical dictionaries, 44). 189pp.

- - 2nd ed. Morton, F., *et al.* **Historical dictionary of Botswana.** Metuchen, NJ, 1989. xxv, 216pp.

Although the 1st ed. was criticised by a number of reviewers for being largely based on readily available sources, the 2nd ed., re-written by former members so essential works of reference on Botswana" (*JAH*, 32, 1991, 174-175). Detailed bibliography of over 1,000 entries.

YEARBOOKS

1592
G.B. Colonial Office. **[Annual reports]: Bechuanaland, 1887/88-1965**. London, 1889-1966.

As **Annual report of the Administrator** 1887/88, 1888/89, **Annual report on British Bechuanaland**, 1889/90, **Report on Bechuanaland Protectorate**, 1890/92, 1892/93-1903/04 (not issued 1895/96, 1897/98-1901/02); **Annual report on British Bechuanaland 1904/05-1919/20,** (all as Command papers); **Colonial Office annual report**, 1920/21-65 (not issued 1939-45). 1902/03 & 1903/04 and 1961 & 1962 issued as one vol. 1947-62 issued by Commonwealth Relations Office; 1963-64 issued by Colonial Office; 1965 issued by Commonwealth Office. *For fuller details see Appendix.*

1593
Botswana directory. Gaborone, B. & T. Directories, 1977- . Annual.

1594
Botswana. Department of Information & Broadcasting. Publicity Section. **Botswana '83 [etc.]: an official handbook**. Gaborone, 1983- . Annual.

Ed. T. Obondo-Okoyo. 1986 ed. has cover title: "Botswana 1966-1986: twenty years of progress". Covers topography, peoples, government and administration, commerce and industry. Includes statistics.

See also 659, 662, 1431, 1437, 1442, 1445, 1446, 1452, 1480.

STATISTICS

1595
Botswana. Central Statistics Office. **Statistical abstract**. Gaborone, 1966-1979. Annual.

continued by:

Country profile. Gaborone, 1980- . Annual.

A general survey, with statistics. Abridged version pub. as **Botswana in figures** (1980-). Annual.

1596

Botswana. Central Statistics Office. **Statistical newsletter.** Gaborone, 1972-1975. Annual. Issues 1-4.

continued by:

Statistical bulletin. Gaborone, 1976- . Quarterly.

1597

Statistik des Auslandes: Länderberichte: Botsuana. Wiesbaden, Statistisches Bundesamt, 1985- . Irreg.

Issues for 1985, 1987.

DIRECTORIES OF ORGANIZATIONS

1598

Botswana. National Institute for Research in Development and African Studies. Documentation Unit. **Directory of libraries in Botswana.** Gaborone, 1977. (Working paper, 12). 55pp.

Comp. B.L.B. Mushonga.

1599

Botswana. National Institute of Development Research and Documentation. **Libraries and information centres in Botswana: a directory.** Gaborone, 1984. iv, 208, iiipp.

Comp. F. Inganji. Lists 103 libraries, including branch libraries of the Botswana Library Service and secondary school libraries.

1600

Norwegian Agency for International Development (NORAID). **A directory of non-governmental organizations in Botswana.** Oslo, 1985. 160pp.

- - 2nd ed. ..., **1989-1993.** Gaborone, 1989. 161pp.

See also 1480, 1482.

BIOGRAPHICAL SOURCES

See 665, 742.

ATLASES & GAZETTEERS

Atlases

1601
Atlas for Botswana. Johannesburg, Collins/Cape Town, Longman Southern Africa, 1973. 67pp.

6 pp. text, 61pp. maps.

1602
Atlas for Botswana. Gaborone, Longman Botswana, 1988. 49pp.

Cover title: 'Longman atlas for Botswana'. 14 maps of Botswana, 13 of Africa, 7 of the rest of the world.

1603
The Botswana Society social studies atlas. Gaborone, Botswana Society with Government of Botswana and Esselte Map Service, Stockholm, 1988. 49pp.

Pp. 6-17, Botswana, including 24 thematic maps; pp. 18-22, Southern Africa; pp. 25-31, Africa.

Gazetteers

1604
Botswana. Ministry of Local Government and Lands. Place Name Commission. **List of names and recommended or accepted spellings** [Gaborone, 1970]. 39pp.

- - rev. ed. Gaborone, 1981. 142pp.

1st ed. lists 1,043 names in a single sequence with a note on alternative spellings. Rev. ed. includes some 2,000 arranged by district.

1605
Botswana. Central Statistics Office. **Guide to the villages of Botswana.** Gaborone, 1973. 221pp.

Based on 1971 census. Details for each village on population, dwellings, communal establishments and access to government services.

See also 1558-1560, 1564, 1569.

LESOTHO

HANDBOOKS

1606
G.B. War Office. Intelligence Branch. **Précis of information concerning South Africa: Kafraria and Basutoland with special reference to native tribes.** London, 1877. 43pp. map in pocket.

Pp. 13-39, Kafraria (Transkei); pp. 40-43, Basutoland. Map at 1:1M.

1607
G.B. War Office. Intelligence Branch. **Précis of information concerning Basutoland.** London, 1880. 22pp. map.

- - **rev. to February 1898.** London, 1898. (A. 521). 54pp. map.

- - **rev. to 1905.** London, 1905. (A. 1034). 67pp. map.

1898 ed. rev. by F.A. Fortescue "based on report by Capt. Davis". Covers topography, communications, history, and the administration. Brief details of 40 routes. 1905 ed. omits routes in favour of increased narrative.

1608
G.B. War Office. Intelligence Division. **Military report and general information concerning Southern Basutoland,** London, 1905. (A. 1035). 198pp. maps.

Comp. S.W. Robinson, covering Quthing District, together with parts of Mohale's Hoek and Qacha's Nek Districts. Much of text comprises detailed itineraries.

1609
G.B. War Office. General Staff. **Military report on Basutoland.** London, 1910. 2 vols.

Comp. M.C. Dobson, based upon 1904-09 reconnaissance survey, and information previously included in **Précis ...** (*see* 1607) and **Military report and general information ...** (*see* 1608). Vol. 1, General (A. 1409). vi, 134pp. 2 maps in pocket; vol. 2, Routes (A. 1384). vi, 240pp. Wide ranging historical, topographical and administrative information. "Most complete description ever made of the country" (Willett & Ambrose).

1610

Ambrose, D.P. **The guide to Lesotho**. Johannesburg & Maseru, Winchester Press, 1974. 290pp. illus. map.

- - 2nd ed. Johannesburg & Maseru, 1976. 370pp. illus. map.

2nd ed. "expanded and completely revised" (preface). Aimed at the "tourist/visitor and resident" but with detailed historical, topographical and social information.

1611

Haliburton, G. **Historical dictionary of Lesotho**. Metuchen, NJ, Scarecrow Press, 1977. (African historical dictionaries, 10). xxxv, 223pp.

See also 1377.

YEARBOOKS

1612

G.B. Colonial Office. **[Annual reports] : Basutoland, 1883-1964**. London, 1886-1965.

As **Report of Resident Commissioner**, 1883/86, 1886/87-1889/90, **Annual report on Basutoland**, 1890/91-1919/20, (all as Command papers); **Colonial Office annual report**, 1920/21- 1964 (not issued 1939-45). Combined report pub. for 1934/35 as well as separate ones for 1934 and 1935; 1961 & 1962 issued as one vol. 1947-60 issued by Commonwealth Relations Office; 1961-63 issued by Colonial Office; 1964 issued by Govt. of Basutoland. *For fuller details see Appendix.*

1613

Basutoland Red Cross Society. **Year book and diary**. Maseru, The Society, 1958-1962. 4 issues.

Issues for 1958-1960, 1962. Willett & Ambrose, p. 3, give useful details of the significant contents of individual issues: "of the four years, the 1959 **Yearbook** is the most comprehensive". Issues for 1959 and 1960 contain genealogical tables of chiefs.

1614

Lesotho business directory. Maseru, A.C. Braby Lesotho, 1970- Annual. (18th issue, 1988).

See also 662, 1431, 1437, 1442, 1445, 1446.

STATISTICS

1615
Lesotho. Bureau of Statistics. **Annual statistical bulletin/review**. Maseru, 1964- . Annual.

Title varies: **Lesotho statistical yearbook/Statistical yearbook of the Kingdom of Lesotho** (1987-). No issue for 1974 (which is covered in vol. for 1975). Abridged version pub. as **Kingdom of Lesotho in figures** (1987- . Annual).

1616
Lesotho. Bureau of Statistics. **Quarterly statistical bulletin**. Maseru, 1976- .

1617
Statistik des Auslandes: Länderberichte: Lesotho. Wiesbaden, Statistisches Bundesamt, 1987- . Irreg.

Issue for 1987.

DIRECTORIES OF ORGANIZATIONS

See 1480, 1482.

ATLASES & GAZETTEERS

Atlases

1618
Atlas for Lesotho. Johannesburg, Collins/Cape Town, Longman Southern Africa, 1973. 67pp.

Comp. by D.P. Ambrose & J.W.B. Perry. World atlas with 3pp. maps of Lesotho.

Gazetteers

1619

Webb, R.S. **Gazetteer for Basutoland**: the first draft of a list of names, with special reference to the 1:250,000 maps G.S.G.S. no. 2567 of June 1911 ('Basutoland from a reconnaisance survey made in 1904-09, by Capt. M.C. Dobson, R.F.A.'). Paarl, Cape Province, the author, 1950. iii, 346, 66, 11pp.

Pt. 1 includes 5,600 place names derived from the Dobson map and other sources; pts. 2 and 3, 1,000 names from border and adjacent areas. Copies of this work with manuscript additions by the author are available in various libraries: a copy with especially detailed annotations is in the Natural History Museum Library, London.

See also 1558-1560, 1564, 1569.

SWAZILAND

HANDBOOKS

1620
G.B. War Office. General Staff. **Précis of information concerning Swaziland.**
London, 1898.

Comp. Maj. F.A. Fortescue.

1621
G.B. War Office. General Staff. **Précis of information concerning Swaziland,
Tongaland and North Zululand.** London, 1905. (A. 991). ii, 110pp. maps in
pocket.

Comp. T.A.M. Cunninghame & A.J.B. Wavell. Pp. 5-84, Swaziland; pp. 84-110,
North Zululand and Tongaland. Includes 27 route itineraries.

1622
Swaziland. Government Information Services. **A handbook to the Kingdom
of Swaziland.** Mbabane, 1968. 126pp. illus.

A general overview of the country, with statistics, compiled to mark
independence.

1623
Grotpeter, J.J. **Historical dictionary of Swaziland.** Metuchen, NJ, Scarecrow
Press, 1975. (African historical dictionaries, 3). 265pp.

YEARBOOKS

1624
G.B. Colonial Office. **[Annual reports]: Swaziland, 1906/07-1966.** London,
1908-1969.

As **Annual report on Swaziland,** 1906/07-1919/20 (as Command papers),
Colonial Office annual report, 1920-66 (not pub. 1939-45). Reports subsequent
to 1920/21, commencing with 1921, pub. for calendar year. 1947-62 issued by
Commonwealth Relations Office; 1963 issued by Colonial Office; 1964-65
issued by Commonwealth Office; 1966 issued by Foreign and Commonwealth
Office. *For fuller details see Appendix.*

1625
Swaziland annual and trade index 1966/67 [etc.]. Johannesburg, Norton, Glyn & Associates, 1966- . Annual.

Magazine style format with brief statistics.

See also 662, 1431, 1437, 1442, 1445, 1446, 1480.

STATISTICS

1626
Swaziland. Central Statistical Office [etc.]. **Annual statistical bulletin.** Mbabane, 1966- .

No issue for 1969.

1627
Swaziland. Central Statistical Office [etc.]. **Quarterly statistical bulletin.** Mbabane, 1967- .

Title varies: **Statistical news.**

1628
Statistik des Auslandes: Länderberichte: Swasiland. Wiesbaden, Statistisches Bundesamt, 1987- . Irreg.

Issue for 1987.

DIRECTORIES OF ORGANIZATIONS

1629
University College of Swaziland. **Directory of Swaziland libraries.** Kwaluseni, 1975. iv, 24pp.

Comp. A.W.Z. Kuzwayo & M. Ward.

- - 2nd ed. Kwaluseni, 1978. University of Botswana, Lesotho & Swaziland Libraries. (UBLS Libraries Publication, 1). 24pp.

See also 1480, 1482.

BIOGRAPHICAL SOURCES

1630
Ndwandwe, S.S. **Profiles of parliamentarians in the Kingdom of Swaziland: who's who in Parliament.** Mbabane, Swaziland Printing & Publishing Co., [?1968]. 44pp.

See also 1511.

ATLASES & GAZETTEERS

Atlases

1631
Atlas for Swaziland. Johannesburg, Collins/Cape Town, Longman Southern Africa, 1973. 67pp.

- - 2nd ed. Johannesburg/Cape Town, 1976. 67pp.

1632
Swaziland. National Trust Commission. **Atlas of Swaziland.** Lobamba, 1983. viii, 90pp.

Ed. A.S. Goudie & D.P. Williams. Cartography by Cartographic Unit, School of Geography, Oxford. 40 black and white thematic maps with accompanying text.

Gazetteers

See 1558-1560, 1564, 1569.

FRANCOPHONE SOUTHERN AFRICA

HANDBOOKS

1633
Madagascar et Réunion: l'encyclopédie coloniale et maritime. Paris, l'Encyclopédie de l'empire français, 1947. 2 vols. illus. maps.

Ed. M. de Coppet. Vol. 1, xi, 372, iiipp. 164 photos. 37 diagrs. 34 maps. Madagascar; vol. 2, iii, 368, xivpp. 184 photos. 23 diagrs. 28 maps. Pp. 1-232, Madagascar; pp. 233-264, Comoros; pp. 283-368, Réunion. Provides the detailed, wide-ranging treatment associated with the volumes of this encyclopaedia (*see* 35).

1634
Decary, R., *et al.* **La France de l'Océan indien: Madagascar, les Comores, la Réunion, la Côte française des Somalis, l'Inde Française.** Paris, Société d'éditions géographiques, maritimes et coloniales, 1952. (Terres lointaines, 2). 314pp. illus. maps.

Pp. 1-225, Madagascar and Antarctic dependencies by R. Decary; pp. 227-242, Comoros by P. Coudert; pp. 243-276, Réunion by H. Isnard; pp. 277-297, French Somaliland by R. Lemoyne. Covers topography, peoples, history, administration and the economic structure.

1635
Madagascar, Comores, Réunion, Île Maurice. Paris, Hachette, 1955. (Les guides bleus). 429pp. maps.

Detailed historical and topographical background in addition to itineraries.

1636
Hänel, J. **Madagaskar, Komoren, Reunion.** Bonn, Schroeder for Deutsche Afrika-Gesellschaft, 1958. (Die Länder Afrikas, 3). 121pp.

Pp. 101-105, Comoros; pp. 106-112, Réunion.

1637
Area handbook for the Indian Ocean territories, comp. F.L. Stoddard. Washington, DC, U.S. Department of Defense, 1971. xvi, 160pp. maps.

- - 2nd ed. **Indian Ocean: five island countries; area handbook series,** comp. F.M. Burge. Washington, DC, 1983. xxvii, 346pp. illus. maps.

2nd ed. pp. 1-126, Madagascar; pp. 127-166, Mauritius; pp. 167-194, Comoros; pp. 195-224, Seychelles. Also includes Maldive Islands.

1638
Marquardt, W. **Seychellen-Komoren-Maskarenen: Handbuch der Ost-afrikanischen Inselwelt.** Munich, Weltforum Verlag, 1976. (Afrika-Studien Sonderreihe Information und Dokumentation, 5). 344pp. 25 photos. 7 maps.

Contains separate sections for the Seychelles, Comoros, Mauritius and dependencies (Rodrigues, Diego Garcia), and Réunion. Includes an historical chronology, bibliography and a wide range of statistical tables.

YEARBOOKS

1639
Guide annuaire illustré des îles de l'Océan Indien, économique, commercial, touristique. Antananarivo, 1939. 347pp. illus.

Eds. U. Faurec & J. Bichelberger. Text in French and English. Covers Comoros, Madagascar, Mauritius, Réunion.

1640
Annuaire Noria: Océan Indien-Madagascar, La Réunion, Maurice 1960/61 [etc]. Limoges, Annuaires Noria, 1960-1961. 2 issues.

Issues for 1960/61, 1961/62. Incorporated into **Annuaire Noria: Afrique noire** from 1963 (*see above*). Includes section for Comoro Islands. Brief data on each country, followed by commercial directory.

DIRECTORIES OF ORGANIZATIONS

1641
Centre de documentation, de recherches et de formation indianocéaniques. **Directory: institutions/organisations and individuals in the South West Indian Ocean Islands and other French speaking countries/areas bordering the Indian Ocean.** Rose Hill, 1988. 261pp.

Lists 114 institutions arranged by island: covers Comoros, Madagascar,

Mauritius, Réunion, Seychelles.

ATLASES & GAZETTEERS

Atlases

1642
U.S. Central Intelligence Agency. **Indian Ocean atlas**. Washington, DC, 1976. 80pp.

Popular format, with accompanying photographs and text. Numerous general thematic maps and tables relating to the Ocean as a whole, with specific section (pp. 36-50) for islands on the African coast covering Zanzibar, Comoros, Madagascar, Réunion, Mauritius and Seychelles.

Gazetteers

1643
U.S. Board on Geographic Names. **Madagascar, Réunion and the Comoro Islands: official standard names approved by the U.S.B.G.N.** Washington, DC, 1955. (Gazetteer, 2). iii, 498pp.

Pp. 1-440, Madagascar (includes 20,000 names); pp. 441-478, Réunion (1,400 names); pp. 479-498, Comoros (700 names).

- - **Gazetteer supplement: Africa and South-West Asia**. Washington, DC, 1972. (p. 109, Madagascar).

COMOROS

YEARBOOKS

1644
France. Ministère de la Marine et des Colonies. **Annuaire de Mayotte et dépendances.** Paris, 1874, 1885. 2 issues.

See also 1659, 1661, 1662.

STATISTICS

1645
France. Institut national des études économiques. **Études sur les comptes économiques des territoires des Comores.** Paris, 1959- . Irreg.

1646
Statistik des Auslandes: Länderberichte: Komoren. Wiesbaden, Statistisches Bundesamt, 1985- . Irreg.

Issue for 1985.

MADAGASCAR

HANDBOOKS

1647

Oliver, S.P. **Madagascar: an historical and descriptive account of the island and its former dependencies**. London, Macmillan, 1886. 2 vols. (569pp; 562pp.). illus.

Large scale compilation covering history, topography, administration, economics and peoples produced the year following the assumption of French control of the island.

1648

G.B. War Office. Intelligence Division. **Military report on Madagascar and adjacent French islands**. London, 1902. (A. 753). 69pp. maps in pocket.

Comp. Maj. A.L. Lynden Bell. Includes brief treatment and maps (1:500,000) of Ste. Marie, Nossi Bé, Mayotte, Réunion, with map of Diego Suarez at 1:127,720 and of whole region at 1:2M.

1649

You, A. **Madagascar: histoire, organisation, colonisation**. Paris, Berger-Leuvrault, 1905. xvi, 636pp. illus. maps.

Encyclopaedic account of the island, its peoples and the early years of the French administration.

1650

You, A. **Madagascar, colonie française, 1896-1930**. Paris, Société d'éditions géographiques, maritimes et coloniales, 1931. xi, 556pp. illus. maps.

Complementary to his earlier survey of 1905 (*see* 1649) with emphasis on the 20th century. Sections for geography, ethnography, history, administration (both central and local), the legal system, religion, finance, trade, agriculture and the economy.

1651

Dictionnaire encyclopédique malgache/Firaketana ny Fiteny sy ny Zavatra Malagasay. Antananarivo, 1937-?1970. 9 vols. (272 fascs.)

Originally issued in fascs. as supplements to "Fiainana" and paged in vols.

Vol. 1 (fascs. 1-36, 1937-1939), A-And. 586pp; vol. 2 (fascs. 37-81, 1940-1944), And-Avy. 511pp; vol. 3 (fascs. 82-115, 1945-47), B-D. 615pp; vol. 4 (fascs. 116-157, 1947-1952), E-F. 744pp; vol. 5 (fascs. 158-182, 1952-1956), G-H. 362pp; vol. 6 (fascs. 183-205, 1956-1958), I. 368pp; vol. 7 (fascs. 206-244, 1958-1963), J-K. 408pp; vol. 8 (fascs. 245-271, 1963-1970). L-M. 420pp; vol. 9 (fasc. 272, 1970) Ma. 20pp. *No more published?* Text in Malagasay. Includes short entries for words, much longer entries for places, people, flora and fauna etc. Initial editor, E. Kruger.

1652
Ethnographic survey of Africa: Madagascar. Paris, Presses Universitaires de France for International African Institute, 1959. (Le peuple malgache: monographies ethnologiques). 1 vol. illus. maps.

Sub-series of the **Ethnographic survey** *(see* 54). Vol.1, 'Les Malgaches du sud-est', by H. Deschamps & S. Vianès. 1959. x, 118pp.

1653
France. Direction de la documentation. **La République Malgache**. Paris, 1960. (*Notes et études documentaires*, 2737, 23 Dec. 1960) 61pp.

1654
Rajemisa-Raolison, R. **Dictionnaire historique et géographique de Madagascar.** Fianarantsoa, Librairie Ambozontany, 1966. 383pp. illus. maps.

Includes biographical entries, and numerous maps and charts.

1655
Area handbook for the Malagasay Republic, comp. H.D. Nelson *et al.* Washington, DC, U.S. Department of Defense, 1973. xiv, 327pp. maps.

1656
Rajoelina, P. & Ramelet, A. **Madagascar, la grande île**. Paris, Harmattan, 1989. 329pp.

General handbook covering natural resources, history, topography, economic and social life.

YEARBOOKS

1657
France. Ministère de la Marine et des Colonies. **Annuaire de l'Île de Nossi-**

Bé. Paris, 1881-1887. 3 issues.

Issues for 1881, 1884, 1887.

1658
Annuaire de Madagascar. Antananarivo, 1894. 167pp. illus. maps.

G. Grandidier, *Bibliographie de Madagascar*, vol. 1, Paris, 1905 records this as a work distinct from the following titles.

1659
Madagascar. Gouvernement générale. **Annuaire de Madagascar et dépendances**. Antananarivo, 1898-?1926. Annual.

Title varies: **Guide-annuaire de Madagascar et dépendances** (1902-13); **Annuaire générale ...** (1914-   ). Includes Comoros. Large scale work with extensive civil lists for both central and provincial governments, statistics, numerous maps, and commercial directory in addition to historical and topographical data.

1660
Annuaire-guide de Madagascar et dépendances. Antananarivo, 1934-1938. Biannual. (Bibliothèque Nationale, Paris, *Périodiques malgaches*, Paris, 1970, records copies for 1934/35 to 1938/39)

1661
Annuaire du monde politique, diplomatique, administratif, et de la presse. Antananarivo, Madagascar Print & Press Co./Editions Madprint, 1959-   . Annual.

Not pub. 1974-78. Title varies: **Annuaire du monde politique, administratif et diplomatique de Madagascar** (1978-1981); **Annuaire de Madagascar** (1982-). Sub-title "Guide permanent de l'administration des pays de l'Océan Indien". By 1980s issued in 3 vols: vol. 1, "Politique et administratif"; vol. 2, "Diplomatique et international"; vol. 3, "Économique et financier".

1662
Madagascar. Directeur de l'Information. **Repoblika Malagasay: annuaire national, 1961/62** [etc.]. Antananarivo, 1961-1977. Annual.

Title varies: **Annuaire national de l'industrie et du commerce** (1970-1971); **L'économie malgache** (1972). From 1973 to 1976 called **L'économie: ...** with sub-title changing annually to reflect changing coverage: 1973 covers

Madagascar, Mauritius, Réunion, Seychelles, Comoros; 1974 adds Djibouti; 1975 adds Australia and France; **L'Économie au service des investisseurs** (1976-77). Principal contents are the civil list, information on the economy and a commercial directory.

See also 1691.

STATISTICS

1663
Madagascar. Service de statistique générale. **Bulletin de statistique générale de Madagascar.** Antananarivo, 1949- . Monthly.

Title varies: **Bulletin mensuel de statistique** (1955-).

1664
Madagascar. Service de statistique générale. **Annuaire statistique de Madagascar 1938/51** [etc.]. Antananarivo, 1953- ? . Annual. Ceased pub. by 1979.

1665
Statistik des Auslandes: Ländberichte: Madagascar. Wiesbaden, Statistisches Bundesamt, 1962- . Irreg.

Issues for 1962, 1973, 1984, 1986, 1988.

DIRECTORIES OF ORGANIZATIONS

1666
Madagascar. Ministère de la Recherche scientifique et technologique pour le développement. **Répertoire des bibliothèques et organismes de documentation de Madagascar.** Antananarivo, 1985. 32pp.

86 entries.

1667
Madagascar. Bibliothèque Nationale. **Répertoire des organismes de documentation, des maisons d'éditions, des imprimeries et des librairies de Madagascar.** Antananarivo, 1986. n.p.

772 entries.

ATLASES & GAZETTEERS

Atlases

1668

Grandidier, A. **Histoire de la géographie**. Paris, Imprimerie nationale, 1875-1892. (Histoire physique, naturelle et politique de Madagascar, vol. 1). 2 vols.

Vol. 2, 1892. Atlas. 47 plates on 62 sheets. Includes reproductions of maps from those of Idrisi (1153 A.D.) up to the 19th century. Library of Congress, *A list of geographical atlases in the Library of Congress*, vol. 3, Washington, DC, 1914, pp. 689-691, lists titles of all plates.

1669

Guide de l'immigrant à Madagascar: atlas. Paris, Colin, 1899. 24 plates.

Supervised by A. Grandidier. Thematic atlas covering physical geography, geology, ethnography, administration and communications. Includes large folding maps at 1:2,500,000 and 11 town plans (e.g. Antananarivo at 1:20,000).

1670

Madagascar. Service météorologique de Madagascar. **Atlas climatologique de Madagascar**. Antananarivo, 1948. 6pp.text. 95pp. maps. 29 x 22cm.

Comp. J. Ravet.

1671

Madagascar. Bureau pour le développement de la production agricole, Association de géographes de Madagascar, & Centre de l'Institut géographique nationale à Madagascar. **Atlas de Madagascar**. Antananarivo, 1969-1972. x, 140pp. text. 62 plates. 32 x 40cm.

'Préparé par l'Association des géographes de Madagascar sous la direction de F. et P. Le Bourdiec & R. Battastini'. 62 thematic maps at 1:4M with transparent overlay showing administrative divisions. Town plans at 1:50,000 of Antananarivo, Majunga, Antsirabe, Tulgar. Substantial notes on sources. 'Histoire de la géographie' shows exploration routes and text lists 138 travellers' journeys together with a detailed list of points touched by voyages. Review, *Africa* 42, 1972, 261.

1672

Ramiandrasoa, F. **Atlas historique du peuplement de Madagascar**. Antananarivo, Université de Madagascar, 1975. 31pp.

11 maps with accompanying French and Malagasay text, keyed to 181 sources listed in bibliography. Covers from prehistory to early 20th century.

Gazetteers

1673 *(also entered at* 419, 560)
G.B. Army. G.H.Q. Middle East. Survey Directorate. **East Africa: index gazetteer showing place-names in 1: 500,000 map series.** Cairo, 1946-1948. 3 vols. in 4.

Vol. 3, 1948. iii, 257pp. "Madagascar, Portuguese East Africa, Northern Rhodesia, Nyasaland and Southern Rhodesia". Coverage is basically of Madagascar and Portuguese East Africa, with parts of other countries as covered on edges of map sheets.

1674
Mangold, M. **A pronouncing dictionary of Malagasay place names.** Hamburg, Helmut Bucke, 1982. (Forum phoneticum, 25). vi, 176pp.

MAURITIUS

HANDBOOKS

1675

G.B. War Office. Intelligence Branch. **Précis of information concerning the island of Mauritius with papers on Rodrigues and the Seychelles Islands.** London/Port Louis, 1877. 190pp. maps.

"Prepared in Mauritius for the Intelligence Branch" (preface). 12 contributors cited. Detailed accounts of topography, communications, history, administration and the economy. Statistics from 1866. Map at 1:168,960 and 4 plans. 'Paper' on Seychelles reprinted from *Bolton's Mauritius almanac*, 1858. One of the most substantial of the early War Office "précis".

1676

D'Unienville, M.C.A.M. **Statistique de l'Île Maurice, et ses dépendences ...** Port Louis, Éditions Georges Houët, 1885-1886. 3 vols. in 1.

Originally compiled by the author, the colonial archivist, between 1819 and 1831. A general historical handbook.

1677

G.B. War Office. General Staff. **Military report and general information concerning the colony of Mauritius.** London, 1905. (A. 976). vii, 123pp. maps in pocket.

Standard War Office survey, with additional information on Rodrigues and Diego Garcia. 6 maps at 1:63,360.

1678

Macmillan, A. *ed*. **Mauritius illustrated: history and description, commercial and industrial factors, figures and resources.** London, W.H. & L. Collingridge, 1914. 456pp. illus.

Much miscellaneous information in a rather haphazard arrangement. Numerous illus. including portraits. Includes lengthy commercial directory, and a biographical section covering some 100 living personalities.

1679

Mauritius guide, 1968/69. Port Louis, Mauritius Chamber of Commerce, 1968. 87pp.

1680
Rivière, L. **Historical dictionary of Mauritius**. Metuchen, NJ, Scarecrow Press, 1982. (African historical dictionaries, 34). xxiv, 172pp.

Review, *IJAHS* 17, 1984, 527-528.

- - 2nd ed. comp. S. Selvon. Metuchen, NJ, 1991. (African historical dictionaries, 49). xxix, 253pp. illus. map.

Both authors were eds. of the daily *Le Mauricien*.

YEARBOOKS

Bibliographies

1681
M.T.S(auzier),'Notice bibliographique sur les calendriers almanacks publiés à l'Ile Maurice de l'origine à ce jour', *Mauritius almanach*, 1889, 308-314.

1682
Rae, A. 'List of almanacks and calendars published in Mauritius since 1769', *Mauritius almanac*, 1917, Section A, 95-97; ibid. 1921, Section A, 35-37.

> *Details given below of the works published before 1850 are based largely on these three articles, supplemented by the examination of sample issues of some titles.*

Yearbooks

1683
Calendrier des isles de France et de Bourbon. Isle de France, Imprimerie Royale, 1769-1794. Irreg.

Issues for 1769-72, 1775, 1778-91 (ed. L. Masson-Abraham); 1791-94 (ed. F.N. Bolle). Title varies: **Calendrier astronomique, politique et historique des colonies...** (1789); **Calendrier royal ...** (1790) ; **Calendrier ...** (1791); **Calendrier de l'Isle de France** (1792-93); **Calendrier républicain** (1794).

1684
Calendrier des isles de France et de la Réunion, 1802/03. Port Louis, Comp. & pub. by P.N. Lambert & C.F. Boudret, 1802.

1685
The Mauritius almanack and colonial directory for A.D. 1814. Port Louis, Government Printer, 1814. 35, 18pp.

Comp. D.F. Rodrigues. Text in English and French.

1686
The Mauritius calendar/Calendrier de l'Île Maurice. Port Louis, Imp. Baron & Souvigne, 1815-1822. Irreg. 4 issues.

Issues for 1815, 1816 (ed. C.A. Diabbadie); 1820, 1822 (ed. J.P.T. Souvignée)

1687
Almanach de l'Île Maurice. Port Louis, Imp. Tristan Mallac etc., 1828, 1837. 2 issues.

1688
Mauritius. **Bolton's Mauritius almanac and official directory.** Port Louis, 1851-1858. Annual (irreg.) 6 issues.

Issues for 1851-54, 1855/1856, 1857-58. Issue for 1854 also issued in French as **L'Almanach de Maurice pour l'année commune 1854** with abridged "Histoire de Maurice" not present in English edition. Comp. W.D. Bolton of the Colonial Secretariat.

1689
The Mauritius register: historical, official and commercial. Port Louis, L. Channel printer, 1859. 293pp.

Comp. T.E. Palmer & G.T. Bradshaw.

1690
The Mauritius civil service almanach. Port Louis, E. Dupuy & P. Dubois, 1862-1868. Annual. 6 issues.

Issues for 1862-66, 1868. Title varies: **Mauritius almanac and civil service register** (1864-1868). Ed. M.C.M. de Joux, Secretary to the Council. Includes civil and military list and commercial directory.

1691
Mauritius. **Mauritius almanac and colonial register.** Port Louis, 1869-1939/41. Annual.

Title varies: **Mauritius almanac** (1889-1919); **Mauritius almanac and commercial handbook** (1920-1939/41). One of the most substantial works of its kind (most issues running to 350/500pp.) containing historical, administrative and statistical information in addition to a civil list and an institutional and commercial directory. Civil list omitted after 1888 because of separately published *Civil service list*. Early issues contain texts of new laws, and cumulating "Index to laws of Mauritius". Numerous special articles in individual issues.

1692
Mauriceguide 1969-70 [etc.]: a commercial, industrial and tourist French-English directory of Mauritius, Madagascar and Réunion, and Seychelles. Port Louis, Standard Printing Establishment, 1969- . Annual. Issue for 1975/76 noted in *ALEA* 1980.

Ed. C.A. Moutou. Sub-title varies.

See also 1662.

Colonial reports

1693
G.B. Colonial Office. **[Annual reports]: Mauritius, 1845-1967.** London, 1846-1970.

As **Reports: the past and present state of HM colonial possessions, 1845-1885, Report on the Blue Book for Mauritius [etc], 1886-88, Annual reports for Mauritius and Rodrigues, 1889-1908, Annual report for Mauritius, 1909-19,** (all as Command papers); **Colonial Office annual report, 1920-67** (not issued 1939-45). 1964-65 issued by Commonwealth Office, 1966-67, issued by Foreign and Commonwealth Office. *For fuller details see Appendix.*

1694
G.B. Colonial Office. **[Annual reports]: Rodrigues Island, 1879-1967.** London, etc., 1881-1967.

As **Reports: the past and present state of HM colonial possessions, 1879-1885** (not pub. 1882), **Report on the Blue Book of Mauritius, Seychelles and Rodrigues, 1886-1888** (all as Command papers). Subsequently pub. with annual report on Mauritius (*see* 1693). From 1949-66 **Annual report on Rodrigues** was pub. in Mauritius (not issued 1955-58). Issue for 1959 includes information for 1958. *For fuller details see Appendix.*

STATISTICS

1695
Mauritius. Central Statistical Office. **Yearbook of statistics**. Rose Hill, 1946-1959. Annual.

continued by:

Quarterly digest of statistics. Rose Hill, 1961-1966.

continued by:

Bi-annual digest of statistics. Rose Hill, 1966-1982.

First issue covers 1938 to 1951.

continued by:

Annual digest of statistics. Rose Hill, 1984- .

Abridged version pub. as **Statistical summary** (1979- Annual).

1696
Statistik des Auslandes: Länderberichte: Mauritius. Wiesbaden, Statistisches Bundesamt, 1987- . Irreg.

Issue for 1987.

BIOGRAPHICAL SOURCES

1697
Dictionary of Mauritius biography/Dictionnaire de biographie mauricienne. Port Louis, Société de l'histoire de l'Île Maurice, 1941- . Fasc. 1- . (Fasc. 45, 1990).

Eds. A. Toussaint (1941-1948), L.N. Regnard (1952-1972), J.R. D'Unienville (1975-). Issued in fascs. with articles in English and French. Each fasc. contains an individual alphabetical sequence. 'Mutatanda et Addenda' issued as Supplements 1 to 7 in fascs. 12, 16, 20, 28, 32, 36, 40. Index to fascs. 1-40 (totalling 1223pp.) with c.1,800 names, issued 1984. "The *Dictionary* is to include notices of all who, identified with Mauritius whether by birth, adoption or temporary connection, played a part worth recording in [its] history" (introduction to Fasc. 1). All entries are signed and contain bibliographies. A major work of patient scholarship.

1698
Mauritius who's and what's: bio-data of personalities, official structures, private sector structures, company profiles. Port Louis, Mauriceguide, 1976. xvii, 249pp.

Ed. C.A. Moutou.

See also 665.

ATLASES & GAZETTEERS

Atlases

1699
Atlas for Mauritius. London, Macmillan Education, 1971. 33pp.

Maps 1-12, Mauritius; 13-17, Seychelles, Réunion, Madagascar; 18-19, rest of Africa; 20-32, rest of the world.

Gazetteers

1700 (*also entered at* 1721).
U.S.Board on Geographic Names. **Indian Ocean: official standard names, approved by the U.S.B.G.N.** Washington, DC, 1957. (Gazetteer, 32). 53pp.

Covers Mauritius and Seychelles (also Maldives, Cocos, Christmas Island), all in a single sequence. Includes a total of 4,000 names.

1701
Mauritius. Ministry of Education. **The place names of Mauritius.** Port Louis, H.F. Kelly, 1961. 22pp.

Comp. P.D. Hollingworth.

RÉUNION

HANDBOOKS

1702
Gérard, G. **Guide illustré de l'Île de la Réunion.** Néroe, J. Owen, [1970]. 413pp.

- - 2nd ed. **Guide historique de l'Île de la Réunion.** Néroe, 1978. 437pp.

1703
Encyclopédie de la Réunion. St. Denis, Livres-Réunion, 1980-1984. 10 vols.

Ed. R. Chaudenson. Vols. 1 to 8 each have a theme, e.g. vol. 4 'La vie économique'. Vol. 9 contains coloured slides. Vol. 10 is a supplement.

See also 1648.

YEARBOOKS

1704
Almanach de l'Île Bourbon. [?St. Denis], 1848-?

Title varies: **Annuaire de l'Île de la Réunion** (1852- ?)

See also 1662, 1691.

STATISTICS

1705
France. Institut national de la statistique et des études économiques, Service régional de la Réunion. **Annuaire statistique de la Réunion, 1952/55 [-1969/72].** Ste. Clothilde, 1956-1973. Annual (irreg.)

continued by:

Réunion. Service départmentale de statistique. **Mémento statistique.** St. Denis, 1974-1980. Annual.

continued by:

France. Institut national de la statistique et des études économiques, Service régional de la Réunion. **Panorama de l'économie de la Réunion.** Ste. Clothilde, 1981- . Annual.

Issued as supplement to **L'économie de la Réunion** (*see* 1706).

1706
France. Institut national de la statistique et des études économiques, Service régional de la Réunion. **Bulletin de statistiques mensuelles.** Ste. Clothilde, 1964- . Monthly.

Title varies: **L'économie de la Réunion: séries statistiques mensuelles** (1977-1979); **L'économie de la Réunion: revue d'information économique et sociale** (1982- 6 p.a.).

BIOGRAPHICAL SOURCES

1707
Ricquebourg, L.J.C. **Dictionnaire généalogique des familles de l'Île Bourbon (La Réunion) 1665-1890.** Rosny sur Seine, author, 1983. 3 vols. 2881pp.

ATLASES & GAZETTEERS

Atlases

1708
Petit atlas de Bourbon. n.p., [1962]. 27pp.

1709
Atlas des départments français d'outre-mer. I: La Réunion. Paris, Centre d'Études de géographie tropicale du Centre national de recherche scientifique & Institut géographique national, 1975. viii, 118 pp. text. 37 plates col. maps. 58 x 48cm.

Published with the co-operation of the Université de La Réunion. Thematic maps cover topography, geology, climate, vegetation, history, population, land use, industry, and communications. Base map at scale of 1:150,000 with transparent overlay showing topography and administrative divisions. Text includes statistics, illustrations, black and white reproductions of older maps and photographs. Town plans included in the text, e.g. Le Port (1:10,000). Review, *GJ*, 144, 1978, 376-377.

1710
Atlas linguistique et ethnographique de la Réunion. Paris, Éditions du Centre national de recherche scientifique, 1984-1989. (Atlas linguistique de France par régions).

Comp. M. Carayol & R. Chaudenson. Vol. 1, 1984, maps 1 to 307; vol. 2, 1989, maps 308-613.

Gazetteers

See 1643.

SEYCHELLES

HANDBOOKS

1711
G.B. War Office. General Staff. **Military report and general information concerning the Colony of Seychelles.** London, 1904. (A. 938). vi, 40pp. map in pocket.

Includes map of Mahé at 1:70,824.

1712
Hawtrey, S.H.C. **Handbook of Seychelles, compiled from official and reliable sources.** Mahé, Government Press, 1928. xxviii, 55pp.

For "the tourist and the merchant" (preface). Includes historical and geographical background, civil list, basic statistics, and a list of some 150 "representative planters and landowners".

1713
Seychelles. Central Statistical Office. **Seychelles handbook.** Mahé, 1976. iv, 159pp.

Covers topography, population, towns, trade, communications, and includes extensive statistical information.

YEARBOOKS

1714
Almanach des Îles Seychelles pour l'année bissextile, 1840. Mahé, L'Institut littéraire des Séchelles, 1840. 45pp.

Includes notes on the geography of the islands, texts of major laws, civil list, and miscellaneous information such as lists of boats built since 1810 and major shipwrecks.

1715
G.B. Colonial Office. **[Annual reports]: Seychelles, 1850-1968.** London, 1851-1970.

As **Reports: the past and present state of HM colonial possessions, 1850-**

1886 (not pub. 1851-54, 1857, 1862, 1864, 1867-69, 1872-73, 1875), from 1887 to 1898 pub. with annual report on Mauritius (*see* 1693), **Annual report for Seychelles,** 1898-1919 (all as Command papers); **Colonial Office annual report,** 1920-68 (not pub. 1938-1945). From 1949-1950 pub. biennially. 1963 & 1964 issued by the Commonwealth Office. 1965 & 1966-1967 & 1968 issued by Foreign and Commonwealth Office. *For fuller details see Appendix.*

See also 1662, 1691.

STATISTICS

1716
Seychelles. Chief Statistician/Statistics Division. **Quarterly statistical bulletin.** Victoria, 1975-1982.

1717
Seychelles. Chief Statistician/Statistics Division. **Statistical abstract.** Victoria, 1977- . Annual.

1718
Statistik des Auslandes: Länderberichte: Seschellen. Wiesbaden, Statistisches Bundesamt, 1984- . Irreg.

Issues for 1984, 1986, 1989.

ATLASES & GAZETTEERS

Atlases

1719
Atlas for Seychelles. London, Macmillan Education for Ministry of Education & Culture, Seychelles, 1977. 33pp.

1720
Petit atlas des îles Sechelles. St. Denis, Éditions du Centre de recherche India-Océanique, 1986. 57pp.

Ed. B. Rémy & M. Serviable.

Gazetteers

1721 (*also entered at* 1700)
U.S. Board on Geographic Names. **Indian Ocean: official standard names approved by the U.S.B.G.N.** Washington, DC, 1957. (Gazetteer, 32). 53pp.

Includes Mauritius and Seychelles (with Maldives, Cocos and Christmas Island) all in a single sequence of 4,000 names.

LUSOPHONE SOUTHERN AFRICA

ANGOLA

HANDBOOKS

1722

G.B. War Office. General Staff. **Military report on Angola (Portuguese South-West Africa)**. London, 1908. (A. 1273). viii, 73pp. illus. map in pocket.

Comp. Capt. C.C.M. Maynard. Standard War Office military report with map at 1:3M.

1723

G.B. Foreign Office. Historical Section. **Angola (including Cabinda)**. London, 1920. (F.O. Handbook, 120). 94pp.
Also published in F.O. **Peace handbooks**, vol. 19. London, 1920.

1724

Brandão de Mello, A. **Angola: monographie historique, géographique et économique de la colonie**. Lisbon, Delegação a Exposição Colonial Internacional de Paris, 1931. 146pp. illus.

A general encyclopaedic account.

1725

Gersdorff, R. von. **Angola: Portugiesisch-Guinea, São Tomé und Principe, Kap Verde-Inseln, Spanisch-Guinea**. Bonn, Schroeder for Deutsche Afrika-Gesellschaft, 1960. (Die Länder Afrikas, 23). 165pp.

Principally Angola: other Portuguese territories have only 18pp. between them.

1726

Gonzaga, N. **Angola: pequena monografia**. Lisbon, Agência-Geral do Ultramar, 1965. 286pp. illus.

One of a series of standard handbooks on Portuguese territories.

1727

Area handbook for Angola, comp. A.B. Herrick, *et al*. Washington, DC, U.S.

Department of Defense, 1967. xii, 439pp.

- - 2nd ed. **Angola: a country study,** comp. I. Kaplan, *et al.* Washington, DC, 1979. xxiii, 286pp.

1728
Martin, P.M. **Historical dictionary of Angola.** Metuchen, NJ, Scarecrow Press, 1980. (African historical dictionaries, 26). 196pp.

Includes 71pp. bibliography. Review, *Africana journal,* 9, 1980, 359.

- - 2nd ed. comp. S.H. Broadhead. Metuchen, NJ, 1992. (African historical dictionaries, 52). xlv, 296pp. illus.

See also 1739.

YEARBOOKS

1729
Anuário de Angola. Luanda, 1923- ? (Gregory)

1730
Anuário de Angola: indice econômica, 1938/39. Luanda, 1938- ? (NUC)

1731
Anuário comercial e industrial de Angola, 1950/54 [etc.]. Luanda, Editorial Ultramar, 1955- . Annual.

See also 655, 1366, 1368, 1415.

STATISTICS

1732
Angola. Direcção dos Serviços de Estatística [etc.]. **Boletim trimestral de estatística.** Luanda, 1933-1934, 1942-1943. Quarterly.

continued by:

Boletim mensal de estatística. Luanda, 1945-1973. Monthly.

1733
Angola. Direcção dos Serviços de Estatística [etc.]. **Anuário estatístico/Annuaire statistique.** Luanda, 1933-1973. Annual.

Text in Portuguese and French. Summary version published as **Angola: informações estatísticas** (1970- . Irreg.)

1734
Statistik des Auslandes: Länderberichte: Angola. Wiesbaden, Statistisches Bundesamt, 1984- . Irreg.

Issues for 1984, 1988, 1989, 1991.

DIRECTORIES OF ORGANIZATIONS

See 1482.

ATLASES & GAZETTEERS

Atlases

1735
Angola (1,246,700 kms^2) e os seus 15 distritos. Lisbon, 1966. 16pp.

Includes 15 black and white maps, one for each administrative district.

1736
Angola. Ministério da Educação e Cultura & Esselte Map Service, Stockholm. **Atlas geografico: República Popular de Angola.** Luanda, 1982- .

Vol. 1, 1982. 49pp. 33 x 45cm. Thematic maps, mostly at 1:6M. 21 maps cover Angola, 17 the rest of Africa and the world.

See also 753.

Gazetteers

1737
U.S. Board on Geographic Names. **Angola. Official standard names approved by the U.S.B.G.N.** Washington, DC, 1956. (Gazetteer, 20). iii, 234pp.

19,200 names from maps at 1:1,500,000.

- - **Gazetteer supplement: Africa and South-West Asia**, Washington, DC, 1972. (pp. 3-8, Angola).

- - 2nd ed. **Gazetteer of Angola**. Washington, DC, 1986. 549pp.

25,500 names taken from maps at 1:1,500,000.

1738
Milheiros, M. **Indice histórico-corográfico de Angola**. Luanda, Instituto de Investigação Científica de Angola, 1972. 291pp.

Historical gazetteer, citing references to legislation under which administrative divisions were created. Some lengthy entries, e.g. "Luanda", 3pp.

1739
Parreira, A. **Dicionário glossográfico e toponímico da documentação sobre Angola séculos XV-XVII**. Lisbon, Editorial Estampa, 1990. (Imprensa Universitária, 79). 250pp.

A general glossary and a glossary of place-names with references to their occurrence in the literature.

MOZAMBIQUE

HANDBOOKS

1740

Nyassa Co. **Handbook of the Nyassa Company, Companhia do Nyassa: District of Cabo Delgado, Province of Mozambique.** London, Spottiswode, 1898. 60pp. map.

Includes summary of various recent reports on the Company's territory, covering topography, climate, population, resources, minerals, trade and communications.

1741

G.B. War Office. General Staff. **Military report on Portuguese East Africa.** London, 1905. (A. 1026). ix, 118pp. maps in pocket.

Comp. Capt. H.D. Farquharson. General account followed by treatment of each individual administration.

1742

G.B. Admiralty. Naval Intelligence Division. Geographical Section. **A handbook of Portuguese Nyasaland.** London, 1917. (I.D. 1161). 250pp. (Reprinted, London, HMSO, 1920; New York, Negro Universities Press, 1969).

Covers territory of Cabo Delgado administered by Companhia do Nyassa. Includes topography, history, communications, peoples and the economy; pp. 104-228 give details of 40 itineraries.

1743

G.B. Admiralty. Naval Intelligence Division. **A manual of Portuguese East Africa.** London, HMSO, 1920. 552pp. Separate portfolio of 10 maps.

Detailed coverage of topography, history, administration, peoples and the economy.

1744

G.B. Foreign Office. Historical Section. **Mozambique.** London, 1920. (F.O. Handbooks, 121). 109pp.
Also pub. in F.O. **Peace handbooks,** vol. 19. London, 1920.

1745
Oliveira Boleo, J. de. **Moçambique**. Lisbon, Agência-Geral do Ultramar, 1951. (Monografias dos territórios do Ultramar). 562pp. illus. maps.

Sections for geography, flora and fauna, ethnology, history, administration, economics and social life. Brief summaries of each chapter in English and French.

1746
Gersdorff, R. von. **Moçambique**. Bonn, Schroeder for Deutsche Afrika-Gesellschaft, 1958. (Die Länder Afrikas, 14). 136pp.

1747
Oliveira Boleo, J de. **Moçambique: pequena monografia**. Lisbon, Agência-Geral do Ultramar, 1961. 166pp. illus.

- - 2nd ed. Lisbon, 1967. 204pp.

Also published in French as **Mozambique: petite monographie**. Standard handbook format covering topography, history, natural resources, administration, etc. Basically a summary version of his 1951 work (*see* 1746). 2nd ed. has chronological list of "grands-capitains, gouverneurs, etc." 1505-1964.

1748
Area handbook for Mozambique, comp. A.B. Herrick, *et al.* Washington, DC, U.S. Department of Defense, 1969. xiv, 351pp. maps.

- - 2nd ed. comp. I. Kaplan, *et al.* Washington, DC, 1977. xx, 240pp. maps.

- - 3rd ed. **Mozambique: a country study**, comp. H.D. Nelson, *et al.* Washington, DC, 1984. 342pp. illus. maps.

1st ed. remains the most detailed, and useful for information on the country at the end of the colonial period.

1749
Azevedo, M. **Historical dictionary of Mozambique**. Metuchen, NJ, Scarecrow Press, 1991. (African historical dictionaries, 47). xxx, 250pp. maps.

See also 524, 525, 1361, 1368, 1415, 1437.

YEARBOOKS

1750
Anuário de Moçambique, 1894. Lourenço Marques, 1895.

Comp. J. da Graça Correia e Lanca. (Costa, M. *Bibliografia geral de Moçambique*, Lisbon, 1946, records this as a separate work; Gregory and NUC suggest it is the first issue of **Anuário de Lourenço Marques** below).

1751
Delagoa directory. Lourenço Marques, A.W. Bayly, 1899-1952. Annual. 52 issues.

Title varies: **Lourenço Marques directory** (?1943-1947); **Mozambique directory** (1948-1952). 51st ed. 1950/51, xxii, 902pp. Extremely detailed survey for Mozambique as a whole, followed by sections for Lourenço Marques and each district: civil and military lists, commercial directory, statistics, historical, social and topographic information.

1752
Anuário de Lourenço Marques. Lourenço Marques, A.W. Bayly, 1914-1978/79 (?) Annual. 53 vols.

Title varies: **Anuário da Colonia de Moçambique** (1948-1950/51); **Anuário da Provincia de Moçambique** (1951/52-1970/71); **Anuário do Estado Moçambique** (1972/73); **Anuário de Moçambique** (1973/74-1978/79?). 53rd ed. 1978/79. Detailed commercial and administrative directory, which also includes considerable historical and topographical data. Portuguese language companion to the Delagoa directory *above*. (Sources disagree regarding the separate identities and dates of publication of the Mozambique directories. Details for items 1751 and 1752 largely follow Darch. Costa, M. *Bibliografia geral de Moçambique*, Lisbon, 1946 lists 1750 (not in Darch) as a separate item, while Gregory and NUC suggest it as the first issue of 1751. S.J. Gowan, *Portuguese-speaking Africa, 1900-1979: vol. 2, Mozambique*, Braamfontein, 1982, appears to conflate 1751 and 1752 into a single publication. Costa also records an **Anuário de Moçambique** comp. A. de Sousa Ribeiro with three issues in 1908, 1917 and 1940).

1753
Guia econômico de Moçambique: edição oficial, 1951/52 [etc.]. Lisbon, Tipografia Astoria, 1951- . Annual.

Includes commercial directory and statistics.

See also 541, 662, 1431, 1444, 1446, 1465.

STATISTICS

Bibliography

1754
Darch, C. 'Notas sobre fontes estatísticas oficias referentes à economia colonial moçambicana: uma crítica geral', *Estudos Moçambicanos* 4, 1983-85, 103-125.

Bulletins & yearbooks

1755
Mozambique. Direcção dos Serviços de Estatística [etc.]. **Boletim econômico e estatístico.** Lourenço Marques, 1925-1975. Monthly (irreg.)

Title varies: **Boletim mensal de estatística** (1932-38); **Boletim trimestral de estatística** (1938-1947); not published 1947-1960; **Boletim mensal estatístico** (1960-67); **Boletim mensal da Direcção Provincial dos Serviços de Estatistica Geral** (1967-1975). (for further details *see* Darch).

1756
Mozambique. Direcção dos Serviços de Estatística [etc.]. **Anuário estatístico/Annuaire statistique 1926/28 [etc.].** Lourenço Marques, 1929-1976. Annual.

Last issue covers statistics of 1973.

1757
Mozambique. Direcção Nacional de Estatística. **Informação estatística, 1975-1984.** Maputo, 1985. 96pp.

The first major compilation of statistics to be published after independence.

1758
Mozambique. Direcçâo Nacional de Estatística. **Moçambique: informação estatística 1980/81.** Maputo, 1982- . Annual.

1759
Statistik des Auslandes: Länderberichte: Mosambik. Wiesbaden, Statistisches Bundesamt, 1985- . Irreg.

Mozambique

Issues for 1985, 1987, 1989.

DIRECTORIES OF ORGANIZATIONS

See 1482.

BIOGRAPHICAL SOURCES

1760
Pinto, F. da S. **Roteiro histórico-biografico da cidade de Lourenço Marques.** [Lourenço Marques, Moçambique Editore], 1965. (Colectanea biografica). 206pp.

See also 665, 1511.

ATLASES & GAZETTEERS

Atlases

1761
Atlas de Moçambique. Lourenço Marques, Empresa Moderna, 1960. viii, 44pp. 28 x 38cm. (Reprinted 1962, with minor corrections).

Compiled by the Direcção dos Serviços de Agrimensura. 10 topographical maps at 1:1M on folding sheets; 21 thematic maps at 1:6M covering physical features, climate, demography, industry and communications. Includes gazetteer.

1762
Mozambique. Ministério da Educação e Cultura. **Atlas géografico.** [Maputo], 1980-1983. 2 vols. col. maps.

Prepared by Esselte, Stockholm, basically for school use. Coloured maps. Vol. 1 covers Mozambique (pp. 8-29, 46) and Africa; vol. 2, the world.

Gazetteers

1763
Mozambique. Direcção dos Serviços Geográficos e Cadastrais. **Primera relação de nomes geográficos da provincia de Moçambique.** Lourenço Marques,

Imprensa Nacional, 1962. 209pp.

Gives district locations for each name but no geographical co-ordinates.

1764
U.S. Board on Geographic Names. **Mozambique: official standard names approved by the U.S.B.G.N.** Washington, DC, 1969. (Gazetteer, 109). iv, 505pp.

Includes 32,500 names from maps at 1:250,000.

- - **Gazetteer supplement: Africa and South-West Asia**, Washington, DC, 1972. (pp. 121-123, Mozambique).

1765
Gonçalves, M.L. **Indice topononímico de Moçambique.** 2nd ed. Lisbon, Junta de Investigações do Ultramar, Centro de Botânico, 1971. 128pp.

1766
Cabral, A.C.P. **Dicionário des noms geográficos de Moçambique sua origen.** Lourenço Marques, [Empresa Moderna], 1975. 180pp.

Lists official forms with references from earlier variants, and explanations of origins and meanings.

See also 1673.

APPENDIX

ANNUAL REPORTS ON THE BRITISH POSSESSIONS IN AFRICA

compiled by I.C. McIlwaine

The following is a list of reports on the individual colonies and other possessions issued in series from 1846 until the year of independence. From 1846 the series of **Reports for the year ... with a view to exhibit the past and present state of H.M.'s colonial possessions** was issued annually as a Command paper. As the number of colonies increased it ultimately became three papers in any one session, sometimes assigned one command number with three sections, sometimes assigned separate numbers. These reports were the printed version of the report sent back to London from the various colonies accompanying the annual 'Blue Book'. From 1871 until 1886 they were entitled **Papers relating to H.M.'s colonial possessions.**

A new series, assigning the same number to all reports issued in any one year commenced in 1887, entitled **Colonial reports - annual** (though for a few years, some carry the title **Report on the Blue Book**). This series was issued as a command paper until 1920 and from that date was published in the non-parliamentary category. After 1920 volumes cease to be included in bound collections of parliamentary papers in libraries (whence they can be easily retrieved from the command number), and become one of a numbered Colonial Office series. The series ceased at the outbreak of the Second World War and was resumed in 1946 with the initiation of the series **Annual report on the colonies.**

In the nineteenth century the reports were brief summaries of events and statistical information. They later became much more comprehensive and a fairly standard pattern of contents was established, consisting of a general review of the year's developments, brief factual and statistical paragraphs on socioeconomic aspects, geography, history, and the administration and various bibliographies. Appendices have texts of special documents and statistical tables. The reports were published annually (or in a few cases biennially), until the time of independence. In the nineteenth century, before achieving colonial status, some reports were issued by the Foreign Office and in the case of the Sudan, this was always the case. In the 1960s, as the number of colonial possessions decreased and departmental responsibilities were altered, the reports were issued by the Commonwealth Office, in a few cases by the Commonwealth Relations Office, and by the Foreign and Commonwealth Office. The changes of issuing body are all noted in the listing. Also included are a few nineteenth and early twentieth century reports on areas which subsequently became colonies.

The reports on the Mandated Territories (Tanganyika, Togoland and British Cameroons) were submitted initially to the League of Nations, then, after their conversion into Trust Territiories to the Trusteeship Council and later to the General Assembly of the United Nations, and followed a rather different pattern of contents, concentrating on social and economic advances. They were issued in the series **Colonial**, which has a separate numbering from the **Colonial reports** series.

Until December 1961 reports on the three High Commission Territories (Basutoland, Bechuanaland Protectorate and Swaziland) were submitted to the Office of Commonwealth Relations (later the Commonwealth Office) by the High Commissioner who was also High Commissioner for South Africa. After the Republic of South Africa withdrew from the Commonwealth, the office in South Africa was changed to that of Ambassador responsible as High Commissioner of the Territories to the Colonial Office. The annual reports were published by the Colonial Office until independence. They contain short summaries of the principal events of the past year and a handbook, together with statistical information.

This list attempts to provide a complete guide to the user, so as to assist in the retrieval of any report from a library collection. The title changes are noted in bold, together with the year(s) covered, while the date of the appropriate parliamentary session (for the parliamentary papers) or of publication (for non-parliamentary papers) follows in normal style. Once the papers become non-parliamentary, inclusive years are given and where a report covers a twelve month period that does not coincide with the calendar year, the dates are connected by an oblique stroke to indicate coverage, while inclusive years of publication are denoted by a hyphen.

The arrangement reflects that of the main work and is outlined below. A list of territories covered by individual reports is appended, indicating under which modern country name they may be found.

North-East Africa: Somalia, Sudan
East Africa: East Africa, Kenya, Tanzania, Uganda
Central Africa: Malawi, Zambia
West Africa: Gambia, Ghana, Nigeria, Sierra Leone, St. Helena; Cameroon, Togo
Southern Africa: South Africa; Botswana, Lesotho, Swaziland; Mauritius, Seychelles

NORTH-EAST AFRICA

SOMALIA

G.B. Colonial Office. **[Annual reports]: Somaliland, 1904-1959.**

As **Annual report on Somaliland 1904/05**; 1906 (Cd.2684-14)
      1905/06; 1906 (Cd.2684-54)
      1906/07; 1908 (Cd.3729-6)
      1907/08; 1908 (Cd.3729-50)
      1908/09; 1909 (Cd.4448-32)
      1909/10; 1910 (Cd.4964-23)
      1910/11; 1911 (Cd.5467-26)
      1911/12; 1912-13 (Cd.6007-36)
      1912/13; 1914 (Cd.7050-2)
      1913/14; 1914-16 (Cd.7622-28)
      1914/15; 1914-16 (Cd.7622-58)
      1915/16; 1916 (Cd.8172-28)
      1916/17; 1917-18 (Cd.8434-31)
      1917/18; 1919 (Cmd.1-25)
      1918/19; 1920 (Cmd.508-5)
      1919/20; 1920 (Cmd.508-34)
      1920-1937; 1922-1939
As **Annual report on the Somaliland Protectorate for 1948**; 1949
      1949; 1950
      1950 & 1951-1958 & 1959; 1952-1960

SUDAN

G.B. Foreign Office. **[Annual reports]: Sudan, 1899-1952.**

The annual reports are preceded by an earlier **Report on the Soudan by Lt. Col. Stewart**; 1883 (C.3670)

Despatch ... enclosing a report on the Soudan by Sir William Garston; 1899 (C.9332)
As **Report by H.M.'s Agent and Consul-General on the finances, administration and condition of Egypt and the Soudan in 1899**; 1900 (Cd.95)
      1900; 1901 (Cd.441)
      1901; 1902 (Cd.1012)
      1902; 1903 (Cd.1529)
      1903; 1904 (Cd.1951)
      1904; 1905 (Cd.2409)

1905; 1906 (Cd.2817)
1906; 1907 (Cd.3394)
1907; 1908 (Cd.3966)
1908; 1909 (Cd.4580)
1909; 1910 (Cd.5121)
1910; 1911 (Cd. 5633)
1911; 1912-13 (Cd.6149)
1912; 1913 (Cd.6682)
1913; 1914 (Cd.7358)
1914/19; 1920 (Cmd.957)

Report by H.M.'s High Commissioner on the finances, administration and condition of Egypt and the Soudan for the year 1920; 1921 (Cmd.1487)
Report on the finances, administration and condition of the Sudan in 1921; 1923 (Cmd.1837)

1922; 1923 (Cmd.1950)
1923; 1924-25 (Cmd.2281)
1924; 1924-25 (Cmd.2544)
1925; 1926 (Cmd.1742)
1926; 1927 (Cmd.2991)
1927; 1928-29 (Cmd.3284)

Report on the finance, administration and condition of the Sudan in 1928; 1929-30 (Cmd.3403)

1929; 1930-31 (Cmd.3697)
1930; 1930-31 (Cmd.3935)
1931; 1931-32 (Cmd.4159)
1932; 1932-33 (Cmd.4387)
1933; 1933-34 (Cmd.4668)
1934; 1935-36 (Cmd 5019)
1935; 1935-36 (Cmd.5281)
1936; 1937-38 (Cmd.5575)
1937; 1938-39 (Cmd.5895)
1938; 1939-40 (Cmd.6139)

As **Report on the administration of the Sudan for 1939/41**; 1950-51 (Cmd.8097)

1942/44; 1950-51 (Cmd. 8098)
1945; 1947-48 (Cmd 7316)
1946; 1948-49 (Cmd.7581)
1947; 1948-49 (Cmd.7835)
1948; 1950-51 (Cmd. 8181)
1949; 1951-52 (Cmd.8434)
1950/51; 1955-56 (Cmd. 9798)
1951/52; 1955-56 (Cmd.9841)

EAST AFRICA

G.B. Colonial Office. **[Annual reports]: East Africa High Commission, 1948-68.**

As **Annual report on the East Africa High Commission, 1948-1952**; 1949-1953 [All pub. in the *Colonial* series]
      1953; 1954
      1954; [1955?] not pub. HMSO
      1955; [1956?] not pub. HMSO
      1956; 1957 pub. Nairobi, govt print.
      1957-1960; 1957-61
As **Annual report on the East African Common Services Organization for 1961-1966**; [1962]-?1967, pub. Nairobi
As **East African Common Services Organization annual report 1967**, pub. by Information Div. of the Secretary General's Office for the East African Common Services Organization, 1968?
As **East African Community. Annual report, 1968**, pub. by Information Div. of E.A. Community, [1969?]

KENYA

G.B. Colonial Office. **[Annual reports]: Kenya, 1891-1962**
1891/94-1903/04 issued by the Foreign Office.

As **Report by Commissioner Johnston of the first three years' administration, 1894** (C.7504)
As **Report of Sir A. Hardinge on the condition and progress of the East African Protectorate from its establishment to the 20th July 1897, with map.** [Africa no. 7 (1897]; 1898 (C.8683)
      1897/98; 1899 (C.9125)
      [Not pub. 1898/99]
As **Report by HM Commissioner on the East African Protectorate, [1899/1900-1900/01]**; 1901 (Cd.769)
      [1901/02-1902/03]; 1903 (Cd.1626)
As **Report for 1903/04;**1905 (Cd.2331)
[Henceforward issued by the Colonial Office]
      1904/05; 1906 (Cd.2684-21)
      1905/06; 1907 (Cd.3285-6)
      1906/07; 1908 (Cd.3729-21)
      1907/08; 1909 (Cd.4448-1)
      1908/09; 1910 (Cd.4964-9)
      1909/10; 1911 (Cd.5467-5)

1910/11; 1912-13 (Cd.6007-5)
1911/12; 1912-13 (Cd.6007-51)
1912/13; 1914 (Cd.7050-32)
1913/14; 1914-16 (Cd.7622-31)
1914/15; 1916 (Cd.8172-7)
1915/16; 1917-18 (Cd.8434-8)
1916/17; 1919 (Cmd.1-1)
1917/18; 1919 (Cmd.1-36)
1918/19; 1921

As **Report on the East African Protectorate, now known as Kenya Colony and Protectorate 1919/20**; 1921

As **Report for the Colony and Protectorate of Kenya 1920/21**; 1922

1921 (Apr-Dec.); 1923
1922-1938; 1924-1939
1946-1961; 1948-1963

TANZANIA

G.B. Colonial Office. **[Annual reports]: Tanganyika, 1918-60.**

As **Report to the Council of the League of Nations on the administration of Tanganyika Territory from the conclusion of the armistice to the end of 1920**; 1921 (Cmd.1428)

1921; 1922 (Cmd.1732)

All subsequent reports pub. in the *Colonial* series.

1922-1923; 1923-1924

As **Report on administration of Tanganyika under mandate 1924**; 1925

As **Report by HBM Government to the League of Nations on the administration of Tanganyika 1925**; 1926

1926-1938; 1927-1939

As **Report by HM Government to the Trusteeship Council of the UN on the administration of Tanganyika 1947**; 1948

As **Report by HM Government in the United Kingdom ... to the General Assembly of the UN on the administration of Tanganyika for the year 1948**; 1949

1949-1960; 1950-1961

G.B. Colonial Office. **[Annual reports]: Zanzibar, 1913-1960.**

The annual reports were preceded by four reports issued by the Foreign Office. **Reports on Zanzibar Protectorate 1893/94**; 1894 (C.6955)

As **Report on the revenue and administration of Zanzibar in 1894**; 1895

(C.7706)
As **Report by Vice Consul O'Sullivan on Island of Pemba, 1896/97**; 1898
(C.8701)
and by one report issued by the Colonial Office **Despatch from H.M.'s Agent
and Consul general furnishing a report on the administration, finance and
general condition of the Zanzibar Protectorate**; 1909 (Cd.4816)

As **Annual report on Zanzibar 1913**; 1914-16 (Cd.7622-14)
       1914; 1914-16 (Cd.7622-34)
       1915; 1916 (Cd.8172-12)
       1916; 1917-18 (Cd.8434-12)
       1917; 1918 (Cd.8973-22)
       1918; 1919 (Cmd.1-23)
       1919; 1920 (Cmd.508-35)
       1920-1938; 1921-1939
       1946-1948; 1948-1949
       1949 & 1950-1959 & 1960; 1952-1963

UGANDA

G.B. Colonial Office. **[Annual reports]: Uganda, 1901-1967.**
1901-1903/04 issued by the Foreign Office.

The annual reports are preceded by a **Preliminary report by H.M.'s Special
Commissioner on the Protectorate of Uganda [its climate, people, resources
and present condition].** 1900 (Cd.256); **Maps illus. of preliminary report.**
1900 (Cd.361)

As **Report ... with map.** 1901 (Cd.671)
       1902/03; 1904 (Cd.1839). lxii.799
       1903/04; 1905 (Cd.2250) lvi.275
Henceforward issued by the Colonial Office
As **Uganda report 1904/05**; 1906 (Cd.2684-13)
As **Uganda Protectorate report 1905/06**; 1907 (Cd.3285-12)
       1906/07; 1908 (Cd.3729-22)
As **Uganda report 1907/08**; 1909 (Cd.4448-9)
       1908/09; 1910 (Cd.4964-10)
       1909/10; 1911 (Cd.5467-6)
       1910/11; 1912-13 (Cd.6007-8)
       1911/12; 1912-13 (Cd.6007-43)
       1912/13; 1914 (Cd.7050-28)
       1913/14; 1914-16 (Cd.7622-22)
       1914/15; 1914-16 (Cd.7622-64)

1915/16; 1917-18 (Cd.8434-1)
1916/17; 1918 (Cd.8973-3)
1917/18; 1919 (Cmd.1-16)
1918/19; 1920 (Cmd.508-37)
1919/20; 1921
1920 (Apr-Dec); 1922
1921-1938; 1923-1939
1946-1961; 1948 -1963
As **Uganda, 1962/63**; Entebbe, govt. print., 1964
1964; 1965
1967; 1970 (Prepared by Min. of Information, Broadcasting & Tourism)

CENTRAL AFRICA

MALAWI

G.B. Colonial Office. **[Annual reports]: Nyasaland, 1891-1962.**
1894-1902/03 issued by the Foreign Office.

As **Report by Commissioner Johnston on the first three years administration of the Eastern portion of British Central Africa, dated 31st March 1894.** [Africa no. 6, (1894)]; 1894 (C.7504)
As **Report by Commissioner Sir Henry Johnston KCB on the trade and general condition of British Central Africa Protectorate, 1st April 1895 to 31st March 1896** (with a map). [Africa, no. 5 (1896)]; 1896 (C.8254)
As **Report by Consul and Acting Commissioner Sharpe on the trade and general conditions of the British Central Africa Protectorate for 1st April 1896 to 31st March 1897**; [Africa, no. 5 (1897)]; 1897 (C.8438)
As **Annual report on the British Central Africa Protectorate 1897/98**; 1899 (C.9048)
As **Report on the trade and general conditions of the British Central African Protectorate for the year 1902-03 by Major F.B. Pearce, Acting Commissioner**; 1904 (Cd.1772)
Henceforward issued by the Colonial Office.
1903/04; 1905 (Cd.2242)
As **British Central Africa Protectorate report for 1904/05**; 1906 (Cd.2684-18)
1905/06; 1906 (Cd.2684-45)
1906/07; 1908 (Cd.3729-1)
As **Nyasaland Protectorate report for 1907/08**; 1908 (Cd.3729-38)
1908/09; 1909 (Cd.4448-28)
As **Annual report on Nyasaland for 1909/10**; 1910 (Cd.4964-29)
1910/11; 1911 (Cd.5467-28)

1911/12; 1912-13 (Cd.6007-32)
1912/13; 1914 (Cd.7050-13)
1913/14; 1914-16 (Cd.7622-23)
1914/15; 1916 (Cd.8172-9)
1915/16; 1917-18 (Cd.8434-6)
1916/17; 1918 (Cd.8973-4)
1917/18; 1919 (Cmd. 1-19)
1918/19; 1920 (Cmd.508-24)
1919/20; 1921
1920-1925; 1921-1926
1927-1938; 1928-1939
1946-1961; 1948-1962
Subsequently published by the **Commonwealth Relations Office**
1962; 1964

ZAMBIA

G.B. Colonial Office. **[Annual reports]: Northern Rhodesia, 1924/25-1962.**
As Annual report on Northern Rhodesia, 1924/25; 1926
    1925/26; 1927
    1926-1938; 1928-40
    1946-1961; 1948-1963
    1961 & 1962; 1964

WEST AFRICA

GAMBIA

G.B. Colonial Office. **[Annual reports]: Gambia, 1848-1964/65.**

As **Reports: the past and present state of H.M.'s colonial possessions, 1848;**
1849 (1126)
    1849; 1850 (1232)
    1850; 1851 (1421)
    1851; 1852 (1539)
    1852; 1852-53 (1693)
    1853; 1854-55 (1919)
    1854; 1856 (2050)
    1855; 1857 (2198)
    1856; 1857-58 (2403)
    1857; 1859 session II (2567)
    1858; 1860 (2711)
    1859; 1861 (2841)

 1860; 1862 (2955)
 1861; 1863 (3165)
 1862; 1864 (3304)
 1863; 1865 (3432)
 1864; 1866 (3719)
 1865; 1867 (3812)
 1866; 1867-68 (3995)
 1867; 1868-69 (4090)
 1868; 1870 (C.149)
 1869; 1871 (C.415)
 1870; 1872 (C.617)
 1871; 1873 (C.709-II)
 1872; 1874 (C.882)
 1873; 1875 (C.1183)
 1875; 1876 (C.1622)
 1876; 1877 (C.1869)
 1877; 1878/79 (C.2444)
 1878; 1880 (C.2598)
 1879; 1881 (C.2829)
 1880; 1881 (C.3094)
 1881; 1883 (C.3642)
 1882; 1884 (C.4015)
 1883; 1884/85 (C.4404)
 1884; 1886 (C.4842)
 1885; 1887 (C.5071)
As **Report on the Blue Book of the Gambia for 1886**; 1888 (C.5249)
 1887; 1888 (C.5249-34)
 1888; 1889 (C.5620-19)
 1889; 1890 (C.5897-29)
As **Annual report on the Gambia 1890**; 1892 (C.6563-12)
 1891; 1892 (C.6563-25)
 1892; 1893-94 (C.6857-30)
 1893; 1894 (C.7319-4)
 1894; 1895 (C.7847-4)
 1895; 1896 (C.7944-17)
 1896; 1897 (C.8279-19)
 1897; 1898 (C.8650-27)
 1898; 1899 (C.9046-32)
 1899; 1900 (Cd.354-6)
 1900; 1901 (Cd.431-17)
 1901; 1902 (Cd.788-25)
 1902; 1903 (Cd.1388-15)
 1903; 1905 (Cd.2238)

1904; 1905 (Cd.2238-29)
1905; 1906 (Cd.2684-27)
1906; 1908 (Cd.3729)
1907; 1908 (Cd.3729-40)
1908; 1909 (Cd.4448-18)
1909; 1910 (Cd.4964-15)
1910; 1911 (Cd.5467-15)
1911; 1912-13 (Cd.6007-18)
1912; 1914 (Cd.7050-8)
1913; 1914 (Cd.7050-46)
1914; 1914-16 (Cd.7622-52)
1915; 1916 (Cd.8172-16)
1916; 1917-18 (Cd.8434-23)
1917; 1919 (Cmd.1-2)
1918; 1920 (Cmd.508-17)
1919; 1920 (Cmd.508-36)
1920-1938; 1922-1939
1946-1949; 1948-1951
1950 & 1951-1962 & 1963; 1953-1964

Report for 1964/65. Bathurst, Govt. of Gambia, 1966. [Format identical - covers up to and including year of independence - 18/2/65]

GHANA

G.B. Colonial Office. **[Annual reports]: Gold Coast, 1846-1954.**

As **Reports: the past and present state of H.M.'s colonial possessions 1846;** 1847 (869)

1847; 1847-48 (1005)
1848; 1849 (1126)
1849; 1850 (1232)
1850; 1851 (1421)
1851; 1852 (1539)
1852; 1852-53 (1693)
1853; 1854-55 (1919)
1854; 1856 (2050)
1855; 1857 session I (2198)
1856; 1857-58 (2403)
1857; 1859 session II (2567) no full report
1858; 1860 (2711)
1859; 1861 (2841)
1860; 1862 (2955)
1861; 1863 (3165) no full report

1867; 1868-69 (4090)
1868; 1870 (C.149)
1869; 1871 (C.415)
1870; 1872 (C.617)
1871; 1873 (C.709-II)
1875; 1876 (C.1622)
1876; 1877 (C.1869)
1877; 1878 (C.2149)
1878; 1878-79 (C.2444)
1879; 1881 (C.2829)
1881; 1883 (C.3642)
1882; 1884 (C.4015)
1884; 1887 (C.5071)
1885; 1887 (C.5071) (+ Lagos)
1886; 1887 (C.5071) (+ Reports on districts)
As **Report on the Blue Book for the Gold Coast 1888**; 1890 (C.5897-4)
As **Annual report on the Gold Coast for 1892**; 1893-94 (C.6857-38)[states, on
p. 3, no report issued since 1886]
1893; 1895 (C.7629-19)
1894; 1896 (C.7944-10)
1895; 1897 (C.8279-13)
1896; 1898 (C.8650-18)
1897; 1899 (C.9046-17)
1898; 1899 (C.9498-5)
1899; 1900 (Cd.354-12)
1900; 1902 (Cd.788-14)
1901; 1902 (Cd.788-45)
1902; 1904 (Cd.1768-2)
1903; 1905 (Cd.2238-3)
1904; 1906 (Cd.2684-11)
1905; 1906 (Cd.2684-24)
1906; 1907 (Cd.3285-12)
1907; 1908 (Cd.3729-37)
1908; 1909 (Cd.4448-22)
1909; 1910 (Cd.4964-28)
1910; 1911 (Cd.5467-24)
1911; 1912-13 (Cd.6007-25)
1912; 1914 (Cd.7050-11)
1913; 1914 (Cd.7050-47)
1914; 1914-16 (Cd.7622-50)
1915; 1916 (Cd.8172-20)
1916; 1917-18 (Cd.8434-35)
1917; 1919 (Cmd.1-21)

1918; 1920 (Cmd.508-13)
1919; 1921 (Cmd.1103-9)
1920; 1922
1921; 1923
1922/23-1938/39; 1924-1939
1946-1954; 1948-1956

G.B. Colonial Office. **[Annual reports]: Gold Coast (Northern Territories)**
1901-1925/26.
As **Annual report on the Gold Coast (Northern Territories) 1901**; 1902
(Cd.788-27)
1903; 1905 (Cd.2238-6)
1904; 1906 (Cd.2684-3)
1905; 1906 (Cd.2684-39)
1906; 1907 (Cd.3285-17)
1907; 1908 (Cd.3729-30)
1908; 1909 (Cd.4448-11)
1909; 1910 (Cd.4964-13)
1910; 1911 (Cd.5467-19)
1911; 1912-13 (Cd.6007-22)
1912; 1914 (Cd.7050-6)
1913; 1914 (Cd.7050-48)
1914; 1914-16 (Cd. 7633-54)
1915; 1917-18 (Cd.8434-4)
1916; 1918 (Cd.8973-5)
1917; 1918 (Cd.8973-19)
1918; 1919 (Cmd.1-34)
1919-1921; 1920-1922
1922/23-1925/26; 1924-1927
Subsequently continued in **[Annual reports]: Gold Coast** (above)

G.B. Colonial Office. **[Annual reports]: Ashanti, 1905-1925/26.**

As **Annual report on Ashanti 1905**; 1906 (Cd.2684-29)
1906; 1907 (Cd.3285-10)
1907; 1908 (Cd.3729-28)
1908; 1909 (Cd.4448-12)
1909; 1910 (Cd.4964-14)
1910; 1911 (Cd.5467-16)
1911; 1912-13 (Cd.6007-19)
1912; 1914 (Cd.7050-12)

1913; 1914-16 (Cd.7622-3)
1914; 1914-16 (Cd.7622-55)
1915; 1916 (Cd.8172-19)
1916; 1917-18 (Cd.8434-36)
1917; 1918 (Cd.8973-11)
1918; 1919 (Cmd.1-35)
1919; 1921 (Cmd.1103-1)
1920; 1922
1921; 1922
1922/23-1925/26; 1923-1927

Subsequently continued in [**Annual reports**]: **Gold Coast** (*see above*)

NIGERIA

G.B. Foreign Office. [**Annual reports**]: **Niger Coast Protectorate, 1891-99.**

As **Report on the administration of the Niger Coast Protectorate, 1891/94;** 1895 (C.7596)
1894/95; 1895 (C.7916)
As **Annual report for Niger Coast Protectorate, 1896/97;** 1898 (C.8775)
1897/98; 1899 (C.9124)
1898/99; 1900 (Cd.3-12)

Subsequently pub. as **Annual report on Southern Nigeria** (*see below*)

G.B. Colonial Office. [**Annual reports**]: **Northern Nigeria, 1900/01-1913.**

As **Report on Northern Nigeria for the period from 1st Jan. 1900 to 31st March 1901;** 1902 (Cd.788-16)
1901; 1903 (Cd.1388-1)
1902; 1904 (Cd.1768-14)
1903; 1905 (Cd.2238-14)
1904; 1906 (Cd.2684-22)
1905/06; 1907 (Cd.3285-3)
1906/07; 1908 (Cd.3729-15)
1907/08; 1909 (Cd.4448-3)
1908/09; 1910 (Cd.4964-7)
1909; 1911 (Cd.5467-10)
1910/11; 1912-13 (Cd.6007-4)
1911; 1912-13 (Cd.6007-38)
1912; 1914 (Cd.7050-26)
1913; 1914-16 (Cd.7622-12)

G.B. Colonial Office. [Annual reports]: Southern Nigeria, 1899/1900-1913.

As **Report on Southern Nigeria for 1899/1900**; 1901 (Cd.431-7)
       1900; 1902 (Cd.788-23)
       1901; 1903 (Cd.1388-5)
       1902; 1904 (Cd.1768-10)
       1903; 1905 (Cd.2238-10)
       1904; 1906 (Cd.2684-5)
       1905; 1906 (Cd.2684-58)
       1906; 1908 (Cd.3729-18)
       1907; 1908 (Cd.3729-47)
       1908; 1910 (Cd.4964-4)
       1909; 1911 (Cd. 5467-1)
       1910; 1911 (Cd.5467-31)
       1911; 1912-13 (Cd.6007-38)
       1912; 1914 (Cd.7050-23)
       1913; 1914-16 (Cd.7622-16)

G.B. Colonial Office. [Annual reports]: Southern Nigeria (Lagos), 1862-1905.
As **Reports...: the present and past state of H.M.'s colonial possessions**
       1862; 1864 (3304) no full report
       1863; 1865 (3423)
       1864; 1866 (3719)
       1865; 1867 (3812) no full report
       1866; 1867-68 (3995) no full report
       1867; 1868-69 (4090)
       1868; 1870 (C.149)
       1869; 1871 (C.415)
       1871; 1873 (C.709-I)
       1872; 1874 (C.882)
       1873; 1874 (C.1102)
       1874; 1875 (C.1335)
       1875; 1876 (C.1622)
       1876; 1877 (C.1869)
       1877; 1878 (C.2149)
       1878; 1878-79 (C.2444)
       1879; 1881 (C.2829)
       1880; 1882 (C.3218)
       1881; 1883 (C.3642)
       1882; 1883 (C.3794)
       1885; 1887 (C.5071) (includes Gold Coast)
       1885; 1887 (C.5239) (Lagos only) [Lagos was only erected into a

separate colony on 1/1/86 - the previous year its Blue Book was supplied to 2/4/1886 to the Gold Coast Colony of which, till 1885, it formed a part. The failure of the Gold Coast to render a separate Blue Book for 1885 necessitated the present compilation - *see Lagos 1885 report*]

1886; 1887 (C.5239)

As **Report on the Blue Book of the Gold Coast for 1886**; 1888 (C.5249)

1887; 1889 (C.5620-26)

1888; 1890 (C.5897-10)

As **Annual Report on Lagos for 1889**; 1892 (C.6563-15)

1890; 1892 (C.6563-16)

1891; 1893-94 (C.6857-8)

1892; 1893-94 (C.6857-45)

1893; 1895 (C.7629-15)

1894; 1896 (C.7944-2)

1895; 1897 (C.8279-9)

1896; 1898 (C.8650-17)

1897; 1899 (C.9046)

1898; 1900 (Cd.3-7)

1899; 1901 (Cd.431-13)

1900/01; 1902 (Cd.788-18)

1902; 1904 (Cd.1768-5)

1903; 1905 (Cd.2238-4)

1904; 1906 (Cd.2684-16)

1905; 1906 (Cd.2684-53)

G.B. Colonial Office. **[Annual reports]: Nigeria, 1914-57.**

As **Report on Nigeria for 1914**; 1916 (Cd.8172-4)

1915; 1917-18 (Cd.8434-7)

1916; 1917-18 (Cd.8434-33)

1917; 1919 (Cmd.1-31)

1918; 1920 (Cmd.508-14)

1919; 1921 (Cmd.1103-7)

Report by Sir F.D. Lugard on the amalgamation of Northern and Southern Nigeria, and administration 1912-19; 1919 (Cmd. 468) As **Annual report on Nigeria for 1920-38**; 1921-39

1946-55; 1948-58

As **Annual report for Federal Nigeria, 1957**; 1961

SIERRA LEONE

G.B. Colonial Office. [**Annual reports**]: **Sierra Leone, 1846-1958.**

As **Reports: the past and present state of H.M.'s colonial possessions for
1846**; 1847 (869)
    1847; 1847-48 (1005)
    1848; 1849 (1126)
    1850; 1851 (1421)
    1851; 1852 (1539)
    1852; 1852-53 (1693)
    1853; 1854-55 (1919)
    1854; 1856 (2050)
    1855; 1857 session I (2198)
    1856; 1857-58 (2403)
    1857; 1859 session II (2567)
    1858; 1860 (2711) no full report
    1859; 1861 (2841) no full report
    1860; 1862 (2955)
    1861; 1863 (3165)
    1862; 1864 (3304) no full report
    1863; 1865 (3423)
    1864; 1866 (3719) no full report
    1866; 1867-68 (3995) no full report
    1867; 1868-69 (4090)
    1868; 1870 (C.149)
    1869; 1871 (C.415) no full report
    1870; 1872 (C.617)
    1871; 1873 (C.709-II)
    1872; 1874 (C.882) no full report
    1873; 1874 (C.1102)
    1875; 1875 (C.1335) no full report
    1876; 1878-79 (C.2444)
    1880; 1881 (C.3094)
    1881/82; 1884 (C.4015)
As **Report on the Blue Book for Sierra Leone for 1887**; 1889 (C.5620)
    1888; 1890 (C.5897-5)
    1889; 1890-91 (C.6221-4)
As **Annual report on Sierra Leone for 1890**; 1890-91 (C.6269-14)**1891**; 1893-94
(C.6857-14)
    1892; 1893-94 (C.6857-46)
    1893; 1895 (C.7629-12)
    1894; 1896 (C.7944-12)

1895; 1896 (C.7944-22)
1896; 1898 (C.8650-6)
1897; 1899 (C.9046-2)
1898; 1899 (C.9498-7)
1899; 1900 (Cd.354-5)
1900; 1901 (Cd.431-16)
1901; 1902 (Cd.788-31)
1902; 1903 (Cd.1388-13)
1903; 1905 (Cd.2238-1)
1904; 1906 (Cd.2684-6)
1905; 1906 (Cd.2684-57)
1906; 1907 (Cd.3285-18)
1907; 1908 (Cd.3729-52)
1908; 1909 (Cd.4448-20)
1909; 1910 (Cd.4964-22)
1910; 1911 (Cd.5467-30)
1911; 1912-13 (Cd.6007-24)
1912; 1914 (Cd.7050)
1913; 1914 (Cd.7050-49)
1914; 1914-16 (Cd.7622-42)
1915; 1916 (Cd.8172-14)
1916; 1917-18 (Cd.8434-26)
1917; 1919 (Cmd.1-13)
1918; 1920 (Cmd.508-16)
1919; 1921 (Cmd.1103-8)
1920-1938; 1921-1939
1946-1958; 1948-1960 (Corrigendum to **1956** issue pub. 1958)

St HELENA

As G.B. Colonial Office. **[Annual reports]: St Helena, 1845-1973.**

As **Reports: the past and present state of H.M.'s colonial possessions** for
1845; 1846 (728)
    1846; 1847 (869)
    1847; 1847-48 (1005)
    1848; 1849 (1126)
    1849; 1850 (1232)
    1850; 1851 (1421)
    1851; 1852 (1539)
    1853; 1854-55 (1919)
    1854; 1856 (2050)
    1855; 1857 session I (2198)

1856; 1857-58 (2403)
1857; 1859 session II (2567)
1858; 1860 (2711)
1859; 1861 (2841)
1860; 1862 (2955)
1861; 1863 (3165) no full report
1862; 1864 (3304)
1863; 1865 (3423) no full report
1864; 1866 (3719) no full report
1865; 1867 (3812) no full report
1866; 1867-68 (3995) no full report
1867; 1868-69 (4090) no full report
1868; 1870 (C.149) no full report
1869; 1871 (C.415)
1870; 1872 (C.617)
1871; 1873 (C.709-I)
1872; 1874 (C.882)
1873; 1874 (C.1102)
1875; 1876 (C.1622)
1876; 1877 (C.1825)
1877; 1878 (C.2149)
1878; 1878-79 (C.2444)
1879; 1880 (C.2730)
1880; 1881 (C.3094)
1881; 1882 (C.3218)
1882; 1883 (C.3794)

Report on the agricultural resources of the island, 1883; (C.4015) 1884

As **Report on St. Helena for 1884**; 1884-85 (C.4583)

1885; 1886 (C.4842)
1886; 1887 (C.5239)

As **Report on the Blue Book for St Helena [1887]**; 1888 (C.5249-15)

1888; 1889 (C.5620-16)
1889; 1890-91 (C.6221-7)

As **Annual report on St Helena 1890**; 1892 (C.6563-10)

1891; 1893-94 (C.6857-13)
1892; 1893-94 (C.6857-49)
1893; 1895 (C.7629-8)
1894; 1896 (C.7944-6)
1895; 1897 (C.8279)
1896; 1898 (C.8650-11)
1897; 1899 (C.9046-8)
1898; 1899 (C.9046-33)
1899; 1901 (Cd.431-1)

1900; 1901 (Cd.431-15)
1901; 1902 (Cd.788-41)
1902; 1903 (Cd.1388-16)
1903; 1904 (Cd.1768-25)
1904; 1905 (Cd.2238-25)
1905; 1906 (Cd.2684-32)
1906; 1907 (Cd.3285-13)
1907; 1908 (Cd.3729-24)
1908; 1909 (Cd.4448-6)
1909; 1910 (Cd. 4964-12)
1910; 1911 (Cd.5467-11)
1911; 1912-13 (Cd.6007-14)
1912; 1913 (Cd.6667-4)
1913; 1914 (Cd.7050-40)
1914; 1914-16 (Cd. 7622-38)
1915; 1916 (Cd.8172-22)
1916; 1917-18 (Cd.8434-20)
1917; 1918 (Cd.8973-23)
1918; 1919 (Cmd.1-33)
1919; 1920 (Cmd.508-22)
1920-1938; 1921-1939
1947-1949; 1949-1950
1950 & 1951-1962 & 1963; 1952-1965
Subsequently published by the **Commonwealth Office**
1964 & 1965; 1967
Subsequently published by the **Foreign and Commonwealth Office**
1966 & 1967; 1969
1968 & 1969; 1971
1970/73; 1976

CAMEROON

G.B. Colonial Office. **[Annual reports]: Cameroons, c.1917/21-1958.**

As **Report on the British sphere of the Cameroons** [1st annual report in response to the Secretary of State's despatch 19th August **1920**]; 1922 (Cmd. 1647) [Covers from c.1917 to April 1922]
As **Reports on the British sphere for 1922, with a covering despatch from the acting governor of Nigeria.** 1923.
As **Report on British Mandated sphere of the Cameroons 1923**; 1924
[This, and all subsequent reports pub. in the *Colonial* series]
As **Report on administration under mandate of British Cameroons 1924**;

1925
As **Report on the administration of the British Cameroons 1925-1928**; 1926-1929
As **Report on the Cameroons under British Mandate, 1929-1938**; 1930-1939
As **Report of H.M.'s Government in the UK...** to the Trusteeship Council of the UN on the administration of the Cameroons under UK Trusteeship for 1947; 1948
As **Report by H.M.'s Government in the UK...** to the General Assembly of the UN on the administration of the Cameroons under UK Trusteeship for **1948-1953**; 1949-1954
As **Report on the Cameroons under UK administration 1954-1959**; 1955-61

TOGO

G.B. Colonial Office. **[Annual reports]: Togoland, 1920-1955.**

As **Report to the Council of the League of Nations on the British Mandated sphere of Togoland for 1920/21**, with a covering despatch from the Governor of the Gold Coast; 1922 (Cmd.1698)
      1922; 1923
[This, and all subsequent reports pub. in the *Colonial* series]
As **Report on the administration under mandate of Togoland 1923**; 1924
As **Report of administration under mandate 1924-1938**; 1925-1939
As **Report by H.M.'s Government in the United Kingdom ...** to the Trusteeship Council of the UN on the administration of Togoland for 1947; 1948
As **Report by H.M.'s Government in the United Kingdom ...** to the General Assembly of the UN on the administration of Togoland for the year 1948; 1949
      1949-1955; 1950-1956

SOUTHERN AFRICA

SOUTH AFRICA

G.B. Colonial Office. **[Annual reports]: Cape of Good Hope, 1846-1882.**

As **Reports: the past and present state of H.M.'s colonial possessions, 1846**; 1847 (869)
      1848; 1850 (1232)
      1853; 1856 (2050) no full report

1854; 1857 session I (2198)
1855; 1857 session I (2198)
1857; 1859 session II (2567) no full report
1858; 1860 (2711) no full report
1859; 1861 (2841) no full report
1860; 1862 (2955) no full report
1861; 1863 (3165)
1862; 1864 (3304)
1863; 1865 (3423)
1864; 1866 (3719) no full report
1865; 1867 (3812)
1866; 1867-68 (3995)
1867; 1868-69 (4090) no full report
1868; 1870 (C.149)
1869; 1871 (C.415) no report received
1870; 1872 (C.617)
1871; 1873 (C.709-1)
1872; 1874 (C.882)
1873; 1875 (C.1183)
1874; 1875 (C.1336)
1875; 1876 (C.1662-1)
1879; 1880 (C.2730)
1882; 1883 (C.3794)

G.B. Colonial Office. **[Annual reports:] Natal, 1853-92.**

As **Reports: the past and present state of H.M.'s colonial possessions for
1853**; 1854-55 (1919)

1854; 1856 (2050)
1855; 1857 session I (2198)
1856; 1857-58 (2403) no full report
1857; 1859 session II (2567)
1858; 1860 (2711)
1859; 1861 (2841) no full report
1860; 1862 (2955)
1861; 1863 (3165)
1862; 1864 (3304)
1863; 1865 (3423) no full report
1864; 1966 (3719) no full report
1865; 1867 (3812) no full report
1866; 1867-68 (3995)
1867; 1868-69 (4090)

1868; 1870 (C.149)
1869; 1871 (C.415)
1870; 1872 (C.617)
1871; 1873 (C.709-I)
1880; 1881 (C.3094)
As **Report on the Blue Book for Natal for 1887**; 1888 (C.5249-7)
    1888; 1889 (C.5620-18)
    1889; 1890 (C.5897-34)
As **Annual report for Natal 1891/92**; 1893-94 (C.6857-11)

G.B. Colonial Office. [Annual reports]: **Griqualand West, 1873-75.**

As **Reports: the past and present state of HM colonial possessions, 1873;**
1875 (C.1183)
    1874; 1875 (C.1183)
    1875; 1877 (C.1825)

G.B. Colonial Office. [**Annual reports**]: **Transvaal, 1878.**

As **Papers relating to colonial possessions 1878**; 1880 (c.2598)

G.B. Colonial Office. [**Annual reports**]: **Zululand, 1889-1896.**

As **Report on the Blue Book for Zululand, 1889**; 1890 (C.5897-19) As **Annual
report on Zululand for 1890**; 1890-91 (C.6269)
    1891; 1893-94 (C.6857-6)
    1892; 1893-94 (C.6857-41)
    1893; 1894 (C.7319-13)
    1894; 1895 (C.7629-20)
    1895; 1896 (C.7944-21)
    1896; 1897 (C.8279-18)

BOTSWANA

G.B. Colonial Office. [**Annual reports**]: **Bechuanaland, 1887/88-1965.**

As **Report of the acting Administrator** for the year ended 30 Sept. **1888**; 1889
(C.5620-2)
Report of administrator for **1889**; 1890 (C.5897-27)

Annual report on British Bechuanaland, 1889/90; 1890-91 (C.6269-2)
Report on Bechuanaland Protectorate, 1890/92; 1892 (C.6829-11)
   1892/93; 1893-94 (C.6857-50)
   1893/94; 1895 (C.7629-13)
   1894/95; 1896 (C.7944-15)
   1896/97; 1898 (C.8650-24)
   1902/03 & 1903/04; 1905 (Cd.2238-17)
   1904/05; 1906 (Cd.2684-25)
   1905/06; 1907 (Cd.3285-4)
   1906/07; 1908 (Cd.3729-2)
   1907/08; 1909 (Cd.4448-2)
   1908/09; 1909 (Cd.4448-23)
   1909/10; 1910 (Cd.4964-26)
   1910/11; 1911 (Cd.5467-32)
   1911/12; 1912-13 (Cd.6007-28)
   1912/13; 1914 (Cd.7050-14)
   1913/14; 1914-16 (Cd.7622-6)
   1914/15; 1914-16 (Cd.7622-48)
   1915/16; 1916 (Cd.8172-24)
   1916/17; 1917-18 (Cd.8434-37)
   1917/18; 1919 (Cmd.1-10)
   1918/19; 1919 (Cmd.1-38)
   1919/20; 1921 (Cmd.1103)
   1920/21-1927/28; 1921-1928
   1928-1938; 1928-1939
   1946; 1948
Subsequently published by the **Commonwealth Relations Office 1947-1960;**
1949-1963
   1961 & 1962; 1964
Subsequently published by the **Colonial Office**
   1963; 1965
   1964; 1965
Subsequently published by the **Commonwealth Office**
   1965; 1966

LESOTHO

G.B. Colonial Office. **[Annual reports]: Basutoland, 1883-1964.**

As **Report of the Resident Commissioner** [from 1883] to 30/6/**1886;** 1886
(C.4907)
Report of the Resident Commissioner to 10th June **1887;** 1887 (C.5238)
   1887/88; 1888 (C.5249-28)

Report of the Resident Commissioner for the year ended 30 June **1888/89**; 1890 (C.5897)

      1889/90; 1890-91 (C.6221-3)

Annual report on Basutoland for 1890/91; 1892 (C.6563-4)

      1891/92; 1893-94 (C.6857-12)

      1892/93; 1893-94 (C.6857-39)

      1893/94; 1895 (C.7629-6)

      1894/95; 1896 (C.7944-4)

      1895/96; 1897 (C.8279-10)

      1896/97; 1898 (C.8650-22)

      1897/98; 1899 (C.9046-23)

      1898/99; 1900 (Cd.3-11)

      1899/1900; 1901 (Cd.431-5)

      1900/01; 1902 (Cd.788-13)

      1901/02; 1903 (Cd.1388-4)

      1902/03; 1904 (Cd.1768-13)

      1903/04, with returns of the census, 1904; 1905 (Cd.2238-21)

      1904/05; 1906 (Cd.2684-26)

      1905/06; 1907 (Cd.3285)

      1906/07; 1908 (Cd.3729-20)

      1907/08; 1909 (Cd.4448-4)

      1908/09; 1910 (Cd.4964-8)

      1909/10; 1911 (Cd.5467-13)

      1910/11; 1912-13 (Cd.6007-10)

      1911/12; 1912-13 (Cd.6007-29)

      1912/13; 1914 (Cd.7050-10)

      1913/14; 1914-16 (Cd.7622-4)

      1914/15; 1914-16 (Cd.7622-49)

      1915/16; 1916 (Cd.8172-37)

      1916/17; 1917-18 (Cd.8434-34)

      1917/18; 1919 (Cmd.1-20)

      1918/19; 1919 (Cmd.1-39)

      1919/20; 1920 (Cmd.508-28)

      1920/21-1923/24; 1921-1924

      1924-1934; 1925-1935

      1934/35; 1935

      1935-1938; 1936-1939

      1946; 1948

Subsequently published by **Commonwealth Relations Office**

      1947-1960; 1949-1962

Subsequently published by the **Colonial Office, 1961 & 1962**; 1964.

      1963; 1965.

      1964; 1965 [pub. by Govt. of Basutoland].

SWAZILAND

G.B. Colonial Office. **[Annual reports]: Swaziland, 1906/07-1966**.

As **Annual report on Swaziland for 1906-07**; 1908 (Cd.3729-23)
      1907/08; 1909 (Cd.4448-5)
      1908/09; 1910 (Cd.4964-1)
      1909/10; 1910 (Cd.4964-35)
      1910/11; 1911 (Cd.5467-33)
      1911/12; 1912-13 (Cd.6007-40)
      1912/13; 1914 (Cd.7050-18)
      1913/14; 1914-16 (Cd.7622-21)
      1914/15; 1914-16 (Cd.7622-57)
      1915/16; 1916 (Cd.8172-27)
      1916/17; 1917-18 (Cd.8434-32)
      1917/18; 1919 (Cmd.1-6)
      1918/19; 1920 (Cmd.508-4)
      1919/20; 1920 (Cmd.508-39)
      1920/21; 1922
      1921-1938; 1922-1939
      1946; 1948
Subsequently published by the **Commonwealth Relations Office**
      1947-1962; 1949-1964
Subsequently published by the **Colonial Office**
      1963; 1965
Subsequently published by the **Commonwealth Office**
      1964; 1966
      1965; 1967
Subsequently published by the **Foreign and Commonwealth Office**
      1966; 1969

MAURITIUS

G.B. Colonial Office. **[Annual reports]: Mauritius, 1845-1967**.

As **Reports: the past and present state of H.M.'s colonial possessions**
      1845; 1846 (728)
      1846; 1847 (869)
      1847; 1847-48 (1005)
      1848; 1849 (1126)
      1849; 1850 (1232)
      1850; 1851 (1421)
      1851; 1852 (1539)

1852; 1852-53 (1693)
1853; 1854-55 (1919)
1854; 1856 (2050)
1855; 1857 (2198)
1856; 1857-58 (2403)
1857; 1859 session II (2567)
1858; 1860 (2711)
1859; 1861 (2841)
1860; 1862 (2955)
1861; 1863 (3165)
1862; 1864 (3304)
1863; 1865 (3432)
1864; 1866 (3719)
1865; 1867 (3812)
1866; 1867-68 (3995)
1867: 1868-69 (4090)
1868; 1870 (C.151)
1869; 1871 (C.407)
1870; 1872 (C.583)
1871; 1873 (C.709-I)
1872; 1874 (C.882)
1873; 1875 (C.1183)
1874; 1875 (C.1336)
1875; 1877 (C.1825)
1876; 1877 (C.1869)
1877; 1878-79 (C.2273)
1878; 1880 (C.2598)
1879; 1881 (C.2829)
1880; 1882 (C.3218)
1881; 1883 (C.3642)
1882; 1884 (C.4015)
1883; 1884-85 (C.4404)
1884; 1886 (C.4904)
1885; 1887 (C.5071)

As **Report on the Blue Book of Mauritius, Seychelles and Rodrigues, 1886**; 1888 (C.5249)

    1887; 1888 (C.5249-39)
    1888; 1890 (C.5897-18)

As **Annual report on Mauritius 1889**; 1890-91 (C.6269-1)

    1890; 1892 (C.6563-11)

As **Annual report on Mauritius, Seychelles and Rodrigues, with report on the Island of Aldabra 1889 and 1890**; 1892 (C.6563-24)

As **Annual report on Mauritius 1891**; 1893-94 (C.6857-7)

1892; 1893-94 (C.6857-2)
1893; 1895 (C.7629-3)
1894; 1896 (C.7944-8)
1895; 1897 (C.8279-7)
1896; 1898 (C.8650-13)
As **Annual report on Mauritius and Rodrigues 1897**; 1899. (C.9046-18)
1898; 1900 (Cd.3-2)
1899; 1900 (Cd.354-8)
1900; 1902 (Cd.788-5)
1901; 1903 (Cd.1388-8)
1902; 1904 (Cd.1768-17)
1903; 1905 (Cd.2238-7)
1904; 1906 (Cd.2684-19)
1905; 1906 (Cd.2684-52)
1906; 1908 (Cd.3729-11)
1907; 1908 (Cd.3729-45)
1908; 1909 (Cd.4448-33)
1909; 1911 (Cd.4567-2)
1910; 1912-13 (Cd. 6007)
1911; 1912-13 (Cd.6007-44)
1912; 1914 (Cd.7050-29)
1913; 1914-16 (Cd.7622-17)
1914; 1916 (Cd.8172-1)
1915; 1917-18 (Cd.8434-3)
1916; 1918 (Cd.8973-10)
1917; 1919 (Cmd.1-8)
1918; 1920 (Cmd.508-19)
1919; 1921 (Cmd.1103-5)
1920-1938; 1922-1939
1946-1960; 1948-1962
1961/62; 1964
1963; 1965
Subsequently published by the **Commonwealth Office**
1964; 1966
1965; 1967
Subsequently published by the **Foreign and Commonwealth Office**
1966; 1968
1967; 1970

Rodrigues

G.B. Colonial Office. **[Annual reports]: Rodrigues Island, 1879-1967.**

As **Reports: the past and present state of H.M.'s colonial possessions for 1879**; 1881 (C.2829) [within **Mauritius**]

    1880; 1882 (C.3218)

    1881; 1883 (C.3794)

    1883; 1886 (C.4842)

    1884; 1886 (C.4904)

    1885; 1887 (C.5071)

As **Report on the Blue Book of Mauritius, Seychelles and Mauritius for 1886**; 1888 (C.5249)

    1887; 1888 (C.5249-39)

    1888; 1890 (C.5897-18)

As **Annual report on Mauritius, Seychelles and Rodrigues with report on the Island of Aldabra 1889 and 1890**; 1892 (C.6563-24)

As **Annual report on Rodrigues 1891**; 1893-94 (C.6857-7)

    1892; 1893-94 (C.6857-48)

    1893; 1895 (C.7629-2)

    1894/95; 1897 (C.8279-7)

    1896; 1898 (C.8650-21)

As **Annual report on Mauritius and Rodrigues 1897**; 1899 (C.9046-18)

    1898; 1900 (Cd.3-2)

Subsequent years listed under **Mauritius**

From 1949/66 an annual report on Rodrigues was published in Mauritius: Colony of Mauritius. **Annual report on Rodrigues for the year 1949**. Port Louis, Govt. print., 1950.

    1950-1954; 1951-1957

    1959; 1960 [includes info. for 1958]

    1960-1966; 1961-1968

SEYCHELLES

G.B. Colonial Office. **[Annual reports]: Seychelles, 1850-1968.**

As **Reports: the past and present state of H.M.'s colonial possessions for 1850**; 1851 (1421)

    1855; 1857 session I (2198)

    1856; 1857-58 (2403)

    1858; 1860 (2711) [within **Mauritius**]

    1859; 1861 (2841) [within **Mauritius**]

    1860; 1862 (2955) [within **Mauritius**]

    1861; 1863 (3165) [within **Mauritius**]

    1863; 1865 (3423) [within **Mauritius**]

    1865; 1867 (3812)

1866; 1867-68 (3995)
1870; 1872 (C.583)
1871; 1873 (C.709-I)
1874; 1875 (C.1336)
1876; 1877 (C.1869)
1877; 1878-79 (C.2273)
1878; 1880 (C.2598)
1879; 1881 (C.2829)
1880; 1882 (C.3218)
1881; 1883 (C.3642)
1882; 1884 (C.4015)
1883; 1886 (C.4842)
1884; 1886 (C.4904)
1885; 1887 (C.5071)

As **Report on the Blue Book of Mauritius, Seychelles and Rodrigues for 1886**; 1888 (C.5249)

1887; 1888 (C.5249-39)
1888; 1890 (C.5897-18)

As **Annual reports on Seychelles and Rodrigues with a report on the Island of Aldabra for 1889 and 1890**; 1892 (C.6563-24)

As **Annual report on Mauritius (Seychelles) for 1891**; 1892 (C.6829-1)

As **Annual report on Seychelles for 1894**; 1896 (C.7944-3)

1895; 1897 (C.8279-6)
1896; 1898 (C.8650-12)
1897; 1899 (C.9046-20)
1898; 1900 (Cd.3-8)
1899; 1900 (Cd.354-7)
1900; 1902 (Cd.788-3)
1901; 1902 (Cd.788-34)
1902; 1904 (Cd.1768)
1903; 1905 (Cd.2238-8)
1904; 1906 (Cd.2684-2)
1905; 1906 (Cd.2684-25)
1906; 1907 (Cd.3285-7)
1907; 1908 (Cd.3729-31)
1908; 1909 (Cd.4448-15)
1909; 1910 (Cd.4964-17)
1910; 1911 (Cd.5467-29)
1911; 1912-13 (Cd.6007-21)
1912; 1914 (Cd. 7050-1)
1913; 1914 (Cd.7050-42)
1914; 1914-16 (Cd.7622-37)
1915; 1916 (Cd.8172-23)

1916; 1917-18 (Cd.8434-16)
1917; 1918 (Cd.8973-13)
1918; 1919 (Cmd.1-28)
1919; 1921 (Cmd.1103-4)
1920-1937; 1922-1939
1946-1948; 1948-1949
1949 & 1950-1961 & 1962; 1951-1963
Subsequently published by the **Commonwealth Office**
1963 & 1964; 1966
Subsequently published by the **Foreign and Commonwealth Office**
1965 & 1966; 1968
1967 & 1968; 1970

Index to individual reports showing country headings under which they are listed above

Nigeria
Northern Nigeria *see* Nigeria
Northern Rhodesia *see* Zambia
Nyasaland *see* Malawi
Nyasaland Protectorate *see* Malawi
Pemba *see* Tanzania
Rodrigues *see* Mauritius
St Helena
Seychelles
Sierra Leone
Somaliland *see* Somalia
Somaliland Protectorate *see* Somalia
Soudan *see* Sudan
Southern Nigeria *see* Nigeria
Southern Nigeria (Lagos) *see* Nigeria
Sudan
Swaziland
Tanganyika *see* Tanzania
Togoland *see* Togo
Transvaal *see* South Africa
Uganda
Zanzibar *see* Tanzania
Zanzibar Protectorate *see* Tanzania
Zululand *see* South Africa

INDEX

This includes entries for **authors** (personal and corporate) with short titles of their works; also **title** entries not only for works without an author, but in many cases where it is thought likely that a title may be more memorable than an author, as is often the case with reference material. Since the great majority of the works listed are either broad-ranging in their subject coverage by their very nature (especially encyclopedias, handbooks and yearbooks) or are already largely defined by the category in which they are placed under each country (statistical sources, directories of organizations, biographical sources, atlases and gazetteers) an attempt to provide detailed **Subject** entries would be both impossible and unhelpful. Entries have been made for each broad topographic region country or smaller administrative division used as a main heading in the text, and for alternative names of countries; also for specialized topics such as art, ethnography, language, literature, etc. where there is a *specific* reference source devoted to these. It should be noted that there are no entries for broad topics such as "history", "politics", "economics" since several hundred titles could be cited for each of these, but that there are for example entries for the more specific "political parties: directories".

All references are to **item numbers**, not pages.

A & A directory and who's who (Liberia) 1096
The AED African financial directory 223
AEF *see* Afrique équatoriale française
AOF *see* Afrique occidentale française
Abbreviations in Africa 197
Abbreviations in the African press 198
Abrahams, R.G. 527
Abshire, D.M. & Samuels, M.A. *Portuguese Africa* 48
Abyssinia *see* ETHIOPIA
Académie royale des sciences d'outre-mer. *Atlas générale de la République du Zaire* 892
Atlas générale du Congo 834
Biographie belge d'outre-mer 833
Adami, G. 425
Adamu, S.O. *The Nigerian statistical system* 1031
Adébárá, D. 910
Adefidiya, A. 1036

Adey, D. *Companion to South African literature* 1410
Adighibe, J. 1096
Adloff, R. 799
Admiralty. Naval Intelligence Division *see* G.B. Admiralty. Naval Intelligence Division
Adressbuch für Deutsch-Ostafrika 139
Adressbuch für Deutsch-Süd-westafrikanischesgebiet 1580
Advertising & press annual of Africa 106
Afrari, M. 31
Africa (Stanford's compendium) 1, 5
L'Africa 8
Africa: a handbook to the continent 9
Africa: a reference volume 116
'Africa: human rights directory and bibliography' 224
Africa: maps and statistics 333
Africa 1968 etc. 113
Africa annual 109